THIRD EDITION

Case Approach to Counseling and Psychotherapy

About the Author

Gerald Corey is professor and coordinator of the Human Services Program at California State University at Fullerton and a licensed psychologist. He received his doctorate in counseling from the University of Southern California. He is a Diplomate in Counseling Psychology, American Board of Professional Psychology; is registered as a National Health Service Provider in Psychology; and is a National Certified Counselor. He is a Fellow of the American Psychological Association (Counseling Psychology). His memberships include the American Association for Counseling and Development and the American Psychological Association. In addition to coordinating an undergraduate program in human services, each semester Jerry teaches both undergraduate and graduate courses in group counseling, teaches theories and techniques of counseling, conducts experiential groups and training groups, and teaches courses on the counseling profession and on professional ethics. He often presents workshops for professional organizations and at various universities. Along with his wife, Marianne Schneider Corey, and other colleagues, he offers weeklong residential personal-growth groups and residential training and supervision workshops each summer in Idyllwild, California.

The recent books that Jerry has authored or co-authored (all published by Brooks/Cole Publishing Company) are:

- *Theory and Practice of Counseling and Psychotherapy,* Fourth Edition (and *Manual*) (1991)
- *I Never Knew I Had a Choice,* Fourth Edition (1990)
- *Theory and Practice of Group Counseling,* Third Edition (and *Manual*) (1990)
- *Becoming a Helper* (1989)
- *Group Techniques,* Revised Edition (1988)
- *Issues and Ethics in the Helping Professions,* Third Edition (1988)
- *Groups: Process and Practice,* Third Edition (1987)

THIRD EDITION

Case Approach to Counseling and Psychotherapy

Gerald Corey

California State University at Fullerton
Diplomate in Counseling Psychology,
American Board of Professional Psychology

Brooks/Cole Publishing Company
Pacific Grove, California

Brooks/Cole Publishing Company
A Division of Wadsworth, Inc.

Printed in the United States of America

10 9 8 7 6 5

Library of Congress Cataloging-in-Publication Data
Corey, Gerald.
Case approach to counseling and psychotherapy / Gerald Corey.
p. cm.
Includes bibliographical references.
ISBN 0-534-13782-2
1. Psychotherapy—Case studies. 2. Counseling—Case studies. 3. Case method. I. Title.
RC465.C67 1990
616.89'14—dc20 90-36724
CIP

Sponsoring Editor: *Claire Verduin*
Editorial Assistant: *Gay C. Bond*
Production Editor: *Fiorella Ljunggren*
Manuscript Editor: *William Waller*
Permissions Editor: *Carline Haga*
Interior and Cover Design: *Sharon L. Kinghan*
Cover Illustration: *David Aguero*
Interior Illustration: *Cloyce Wall*
Photo Editor: *Ruth Minerva*
Typesetting: *Execustaff*
Cover Printing: *Phoenix Color Corporation*
Printing and Binding: *Arcata Graphics/Fairfield*

To my mother, Josephine Corey,
and in memory of my father, Dr. Joseph Corey

About the Contributors

Dr. James Robert Bitter is a professor of counseling and the chairman of the Counseling Department at California State University at Fullerton. He has a considerable range of experience in applying Adlerian principles to counseling children and families. His scholarly activities include publications, in the areas of family mapping and family constellation, created memories and early recollections, and family reconstruction.

Dr. William Blau has a private practice, teaches graduate students, and is a program director at Patton State Hospital in Patton, California. Although his theoretical orientation is psychoanalytic, he often uses techniques from such diverse approaches as cognitive therapy, applied psychophysiology, and transpersonal psychology. His specialty areas include clinical biofeedback and therapy for psychotic clients.

Dr. David J. Cain is founder and editor of the *Person-Centered Review* and founder and coordinator of the Association for the Development of the Person-Centered Approach. For more than 15 years he has been a client-centered therapist, teacher, supervisor, consultant, and frequent speaker and workshop presenter. He is in private practice in Carlsbad, California.

Dr. John M. Dusay is a psychiatrist in private practice in San Francisco and an associate clinical professor at the University of California, San Francisco. He was a protégé of Eric Berne and is a founding member and past president of the International Transactional Analysis Association. He has written and lectured extensively on transactional analysis.

Dr. Albert Ellis is the founder and director of the Institute for Rational-Emotive Therapy in New York. Considered the grandfather of the cognitive-behavioral approaches, he continues to work hard at developing RET. Ellis has written about 600 journal articles and has authored or co-authored more than 50 books.

Dr. Rainette Eden Fantz is one of the founders of the Gestalt Institute of Cleveland. She is chairwoman of the institute's Intensive Postgraduate Training Program and is engaged in the private practice of psychotherapy. She also teaches, works with groups, and conducts special-interest workshops. She is on the editorial board of the Gestalt Institute Press.

Dr. William Glasser is the president and founder of the Institute for Reality Therapy in Canoga Park, California. He presents many workshops each year, both in the United States and abroad. His practical approach continues to be popular among a variety of practitioners. He has written a number of books on reality therapy and control therapy.

Dr. Arnold A. Lazarus is a Distinguished Professor in the Graduate School of Applied and Professional Psychology at Rutgers University. He has written numerous books and professional papers. He developed the multimodal approach to behavior therapy, which calls for technical eclecticism but remains firmly grounded in social-learning theory.

Dr. Donald Polkinghorne is a professor of counseling at California State University at Fullerton. He is vice president of the Association for Humanistic Psychology and is a consulting editor of the *Journal of Phenomenological Psychology.* Among his many publications are writings on phenomenological research methods and existential psychotherapy and social values.

Preface

Case Approach to Counseling and Psychotherapy reflects my increasing emphasis on the use of demonstrations and the case-approach method to bridge the gap between the theory and practice of counseling. Students in the courses I teach have found that a demonstration in class often clears up their misconceptions about how a therapy actually works. This book is an attempt to stimulate some of the unique learning that can occur through seeing a therapeutic approach in action. It also gives students a chance to work with cases from the vantage point of nine therapy approaches: psychoanalytic, Adlerian, existential, person-centered, Gestalt, transactional analysis, behavior, rational-emotive and other cognitive-behavioral approaches, and reality.

The format of this book provides an opportunity to see how each of the various therapeutic approaches is applied to a single client, Ruth, who is followed throughout the text. A new feature of this third edition is an introduction to Ruth's case by an outside consultant in each of the nine theoretical perspectives. I decided to ask for this consultation so that readers could benefit from the broad perspective of a practitioner who specializes in a given approach. In certain cases I was able to get the founder of a theory to describe what his approach to working with Ruth would be. For example, Albert Ellis describes his analysis of Ruth and demonstrates his style in providing rational-emotive therapy. William Glasser offers an assessment of her in the context of control theory and illustrates his interventions using reality therapy. Arnold Lazarus, the founder of multimodal therapy, provides an overview of how he would assess Ruth's current functioning with his BASIC ID framework. For the other chapters highly competent practitioners assess and treat Ruth from their particular theoretical orientation.

The nine theory chapters use a common format, allowing for comparisons among approaches. This format includes the expert's commentary, followed by my way of working with Ruth from that particular perspective. I discuss the theory's basic assumptions, an initial assessment of Ruth, the goals of therapy, and the therapeutic procedures to be used. The therapeutic process is concretely illustrated by client/therapist dialogues, which are fleshed out with process commentaries explaining the rationale for my interventions. ''Questions for Reflection'' help readers apply the material to their personal lives and offer guidelines for continuing to work with Ruth within each of the theoretical orientations. A second case is then presented as a further illustration of how the concepts and techniques of each approach can be applied, and students are again asked to deal with the case within a specific theoretical framework.

Following these nine theory chapters, Chapter Eleven is devoted to bringing the approaches together and helping students develop their own therapeutic style. I demonstrate how I would counsel Ruth in an eclectic fashion by drawing on all nine approaches. New to this revised chapter is a discussion of working with Ruth within the framework of family therapy and from a multicultural perspective. After readers have been exposed to nine individual counseling approaches to Ruth, they have a chance to see how it would be to include her family as a part of the treatment process. Then, guidelines are provided for working with Ruth if she came from different cultural backgrounds.

The final chapter contains 20 supplementary cases for further practice, some that are identified with a particular theory and others that let students make a choice about how to intervene. This edition contains several new cases, some of which illustrate issues involved in counseling clients in the context of cultural diversity.

Ideally, *Case Approach to Counseling and Psychotherapy* will be used as part of an integrated learning package that I have written for courses in counseling theory and practice. By letting students experience counseling in action, this casebook is an excellent supplement to the theoretical approach of the core textbook, *Theory and Practice of Counseling and Psychotherapy* (Fourth Edition, 1991), which gives an overview of the key concepts and techniques of the nine models of contemporary therapy. The accompanying *Manual for Theory and Practice of Counseling and Psychotherapy* offers many experiential activities and exercises designed to help students apply the theories to themselves and connect theory with practice. The present book assumes that the sudent has been exposed to the major theories. Unless students have had a course in counseling theory or have at least read a textbook covering the range of standard theories, they will have trouble in working with the cases in this book, for it is not designed as a substitute for a text surveying the counseling theories.

Acknowledgments

A number of teachers and clinicians have reviewed the manuscript for this edition, and I have used their responses to refine the present material. I am most appreciative of the diversity of their reactions and of their many specific and helpful comments, which helped bring more reality to the cases and improve the effectiveness of their presentation. The reviewers are Cheryl Bartholomew of George Mason University; William Blau of Patton State Hospital in California; James Robert Bitter of California State University at Fullerton; David J. Cain, editor of the *Person-Centered Review*; James F. Carroll of Tacoma Community College; William Cottrell of Lamar University; Don Dinkmeyer of the Communication and Motivation Training Institute in Coral Springs; John M. Dusay of the University of California, San Francisco; Albert Ellis, president of the Institute for Rational-Emotive Therapy; Richard Ellis of New York University; Rainette Eden Fantz of the Gestalt Institute of Cleveland; William Glasser, president of the Institute of Reality Therapy; Robert Goulding, co-director of the Western Institute for Group and Family Therapy; Carlos M. Grillo of Harvard Medical School; Melvin T. Henderson of Metro State University; James T. Herbert of Pennsylvania State University; Ruth Hitchcock of Wichita State University; James L. Jarrett of the University of California at Berkeley; Alan E. Kazdin of Yale University; Arnold A. Lazarus of Rutgers University; Michael Nystul of New Mexico State University; Beverly Palmer of California State University at Dominguez Hills; Donald Polkinghorne of California State University at Fullerton; Robert E. Wubbolding of Xavier University; and Joseph Zinker of the Cleveland Institute of Gestalt Therapy. The student reviewers include Katie Dutro and Becky Mueller.

Other practitioners and professors have offered helpful commentaries on selected cases or provided prerevision reviews. They include Patrick Callanan, in private practice in Santa Ana, California; Michael Dougherty of Western Carolina University; and Jerome Wright of California State University at Fullerton. Mary Moline of Loma Linda University provided assistance on the inclusion of the family-therapy approach. Special recognition goes to Jorja Manos Prover of California State University at Fullerton, who reviewed the cases and met with me to discuss their revision. She helped bring a wider and richer range of cases to this third edition and contributed a valuable cross-cultural perspective to many of them.

My gratitude for their efforts goes to the staff of Brooks/Cole Publishing Company, particularly Claire Verduin and Fiorella Ljunggren, who have given much time and attention to this revised edition. I wish to express my special appreciation to Bill Waller, the manuscript editor, whose editorial skills contribute in many important ways to the readability of my books. Debbie DeBue deserves thanks for her patience in retyping much of the manuscript as well as providing other clerical assistance.

I am especially grateful to Marianne Schneider Corey, my wife and colleague, for her support and her contributions to this revision. Drawing on her clinical experience as a marriage and family therapist, she painstakingly went over each case, challenging me to pay attention to subtle yet important nuances.

Finally, I want to acknowledge the special clients with whom I have worked in groups and workshops, as well as the students in my human-services and counseling courses at California State University at Fullerton. Over the years, contact with these people has taught me more than I ever learned taking courses and reading textbooks. Indeed, through these encounters I have developed many of the themes explored in this book. The struggles and life themes of these people appear in disguised form in the cases presented in the book.

Gerald Corey

Contents

CHAPTER ONE

Introduction and Overview

STRUCTURE OF THE BOOK

Even after reading about a theory of therapy and discussing it in class, students sometimes still have unclear notions about its applications. I began experimenting with asking students to volunteer for a class demonstration in which they served as "clients." Seeing concepts in action has given them a clearer picture of how therapists from various approaches work. This book illustrates nine therapies in action and gives you experience in working with different cases. It also shows you how to selectively borrow concepts and techniques from *all* of the major therapeutic approaches. Additionally, it encourages you to integrate techniques that are appropriate to your client population into a style that is an expression of who you are as a person. From my perspective, effective counseling involves the personality of the therapist even more than the technical skills that he or she employs. In order to apply techniques appropriately, it is essential to consider your personal style and theoretical orientation in relation to each client's unique life situation.

Before this large task of developing a personalized approach can be accomplished, however, it is necessary to know the basics of each of the theories and to have some experience with these therapies. This book aims to provide a balance between describing the way therapists with a given orientation might proceed with a client *and* challenging you to try your hand at showing how you would proceed with the same client.

In this initial chapter I describe methods of conceptualizing a case, and I provide background material on the central figure in this book, Ruth. Her intake form and autobiography can be referred to frequently as you work with her in the nine theory chapters. Ruth is not an actual client. I have created her by combining many of the common themes that I observe in my work with clients. Thus, in her case as in all of the other cases in this book, the clients have a basis in fact, but details have given them a new identity. In this way, I believe, the clients represent some of those you may meet.

Ruth appears in each of the chapters on individual theories (Chapters Two–Ten). These chapters begin with an outside consultant's commentary on her case. Each consultant is a representative of the particular theoretical orientation under discussion. The consultant was given Ruth's background information and also read my perspective on her for each of the theories. Then this representative wrote a section describing the following:

- the core concepts and goals of the particular therapeutic approach
- the themes in Ruth's life that might serve as a focus for therapy
- an assessment of her dynamics, with emphasis on her current life situation
- the techniques and procedures that would probably be used in counseling her

You will notice that the first three chapters dealing with Ruth have more detailed sections written by practitioners who represent the psychoanalytic, Adlerian, and existential approaches. This was done intentionally as a way to provide you with richer background information on Ruth. Having seen these three perspectives, each dealing with the same data on the same case, you will have a good framework for working with Ruth from the other theoretical orientations.

After this section by the practitioner, I look at the approach's basic assumptions, make an initial assessment of Ruth, and examine the theory's therapeutic goals and procedures. The therapeutic process is made concrete with samples of dialogues between Ruth and her therapist, along with process commentaries to provide an explanation of the direction that therapy is taking.

You are asked to become an active learner by evaluating the manner in which the consultants and I work with Ruth from each of the nine theoretical perspectives. You are asked to show how you would proceed with her counseling, using the particular approach being considered in the chapter. To guide you in thinking of ways to work with her, I provide questions. I strongly suggest that besides reflecting on these questions by yourself, you arrange to work with fellow students in small discussion groups and explore various approaches. You will learn even more from these cases if you are willing to exchange viewpoints on them.

Following Ruth's case, in Chapters Two–Ten, there is another case for additional practice. This second case shows you how the same therapy approach can be applied to a client with different life themes and issues. It also allows me to describe techniques from each therapy besides those employed with Ruth. As with the case of Ruth, you are invited to become an active participant and show how you would continue working with each of these cases if the client were referred to you. You will learn the nine therapy systems best if you think and work within the general framework of each theory. You will also be able to determine what aspects of that approach you would most like to draw from as you begin putting together your own synthesis, your personal counseling style.

You can further enhance your learning by participating in a variety of role-playing exercises in which you ''become'' the client under discussion and also by participating in group discussions based on the cases. Rather than merely reading about these cases, you can use them to stimulate reflection on ways in which you have felt like the given client. Thus, as you read about Ruth, Moe, Marion, and others, it will help if you think about the degree to which you see yourself in these people. In experiential practice sessions you can draw on your own concerns in becoming the client, and you can also gain some valuable practice in becoming the counselor. Think of as many ways as possible to use these cases as a method of stimulating introspection and providing lively class discussion.

In the final chapter I provide 20 additional cases. Nine of these cases correspond to the approaches discussed in this book, and 11 give you an opportunity to combine various approaches. If you have the time and the interest, you can refer to these cases as you study each chapter. Of course, using Chapter Twelve as a review of all the theories is another option. The more practice you can get with different clients, the better sense you will have of each theory. I have decided to provide more cases than can realistically be discussed in class, so that you can select those that you find most meaningful. After each of the cases I raise a number of questions to serve as catalysts for your thinking. I suggest that you focus on those questions that seem to best put the cases into perspective for you.

In Chapter Eleven I encourage you to consider the advantages of eventually developing your own counseling theory and style. Such an *eclectic perspective* of counseling entails selecting concepts and methods from various sources and theories. It does not necessarily refer to developing a new theory; rather, it emphasizes a systematic integration of underlying principles and techniques of the various therapy systems. Those who call themselves eclectic range from practitioners who haphazardly pick and choose to those who seriously look for ways to validate their own personal perspective. I am not endorsing a sloppy eclecticism of grabbing at any technique that appears to work. Instead, I encourage you to strive to build a unified system that fits you and is appropriate for the particular setting in which you practice. It is also essential to be willing to challenge your basic assumptions, test your hypotheses as you practice, and revise your theory as you confirm or disconfirm your clinical hunches.

Although it may be unrealistic to expect you to complete the formulation of your personal perspective while reading this book, my hope is that you will begin this process. Toward this end I suggest that you develop your own reading program, emphasizing those theories that you find the most valuable in understanding and working with a diverse range of clients. At the end of each of the theory chapters you will find reading suggestions. The ''Recommended Supplementary Readings'' are a few selected works that you might find most useful if you want to learn more about each theory. The next section, ''Suggested Readings,'' lists 11 textbooks on counseling theory, and cites the specific appropriate chapter or chapters for the theory under discussion. If you feel a need to review some of these theories, any of these references could be of value. This book is not intended to be a substitute for a theory textbook, so you will want to read selected chapters from such a text if you need a refresher.

To get a general overview of the structure of this book and the best way to use it, I strongly recommend that you (1) read the Preface, (2) glance at the main headings of all the chapters, and (3) at least skim Chapter Eleven, so that you can begin to see how the nine theories can be used together in working with a single case (Ruth).

OVERVIEW OF THE THERAPEUTIC PERSPECTIVES

In the nine chapters to follow, as mentioned, the case of Ruth will be analyzed and discussed from various therapeutic perspectives. For each of these perspectives we will consider its basic assumptions, its view of how to assess clients, its goals for therapy, and its therapeutic procedures. This section presents the essence of the various approaches. As a way of laying the foundation for developing an eclectic, integrative approach, we will look for common denominators among the nine perspectives and also differences among them.

Basic Assumptions

When therapists make initial contact with a client, this theoretical perspective determines what they look for and what they see. It largely determines the focus and course of therapy, and it influences their choice of therapeutic procedures and strategies. As you are developing your counseling stance, it would be good to pay attention to your own basic assumptions as well as their effect on how you view clients and work with them. Developing a counseling stance is more involved than merely accepting the tenets of a particular theory or combination of theories. Your theoretical approach is an expression of your unique life experiences.

How do theoretical assumptions influence practice? Your view about the assessment of clients, the goals that you think are important in therapy, the techniques and strategies that you employ to reach these goals, the way in which you divide responsibility in the client/therapist relationship, and your view of your role and functions as a counselor are largely determined by your theoretical orientation.

Attempting to practice counseling without at least a general theoretical perspective is somewhat like flying a plane without a map and without instruments. But a counseling theory is not a rigid structure that prescribes the specific steps of what to do in therapeutic work. Instead, a theoretical orientation is a set of general guidelines that you can use to make sense of what you are doing.

One way to approach the basic assumptions underlying the major theoretical orientations is to consider three categories under which most of the contemporary systems fall. These are (1) the *psychodynamic approaches,* which stress insight in therapy (psychoanalytic and Adlerian therapy); (2) the *experiential and relationship-oriented approaches,* which tend to stress feelings and subjective experiencing (existential, person-centered, and Gestalt therapy); and (3) the *cognitive and behavioral approaches,* which stress the role of thinking and doing and tend to be action oriented (transactional analysis, behavior therapy, the rational-emotive and other cognitive-behavioral approaches, and reality therapy). Actually, Adlerian therapy, which I classify as a psychodynamic approach, could be placed in the cognitive-behavioral camp as well, for in some respects it foreshadowed the current interest in the cognitive therapies. Although I have separated the theories into three general camps, in reality many common denominators will become evident as you study the theories, so this categorization is somewhat arbitrary. There are overlapping concepts and themes that make it difficult to neatly compartmentalize these theoretical orientations. What follows is a thumbnail sketch of the basic assumptions underlying each of these nine therapeutic systems.

Psychoanalytic therapy. The psychoanalytic approach views people as being significantly influenced by unconscious motivation, conflicts between impulses and prohibitions, defense mechanisms, and early childhood experiences. Because the dynamics of behavior are buried in the unconscious, treatment consists of a lengthy process of analyzing inner conflicts that are rooted in the past. Therapy is largely a process of restructuring the personality; therefore, clients must be willing to commit themselves to an intensive, long-term process.

Adlerian therapy. According to the Adlerian approach, people are primarily social beings, influenced and motivated by societal forces. Human nature is viewed as creative, active, and decisional. The approach focuses on the unity of the person and on understanding the individual's subjective perspective. Adler holds that inherent feelings of inferiority immediately initiate a striving for superiority. He asserts that we acquire inferiority feelings, which stem from childhood, and that we then develop a style of life aimed at compensating for such feelings and becoming the master of our fate. This style of life consists of our views about ourselves and the world and of distinctive behaviors that we adopt in the pursuit of our life goals. We can shape our own future by actively and courageously taking risks and making decisions in the face of unknown consequences. Clients are not viewed as being "sick" and needing to be "cured"; rather, they are seen as discouraged and needing encouragement to correct mistaken self-perceptions. Counseling is not simply a matter of an expert therapist making prescriptions for change. It is a collaborative effort, with the client and the therapist actively working on mutually accepted goals.

Existential therapy. The existential perspective holds that we define ourselves by our choices. Although outside factors restrict the range of our choices, we are ultimately the authors of our lives. We are thrust into a meaningless world, yet we are challenged to accept our aloneness and create a meaningful existence. Existential practitioners contend that clients often lead a "restricted existence," seeing few if any alternatives to limited ways of dealing with life situations and tendencies to feel trapped or helpless. The therapist's job is to confront these clients with their restricted life and to help them become aware of their own part in creating this condition. As an outgrowth of the therapeutic venture, clients are able to recognize outmoded patterns of living, and they begin to accept responsibility for changing their future.

Person-centered therapy. The person-centered approach rests on the assumption that we have the capacity to understand our problems and that we have the resources within us to effectively resolve them. Seeing people in this light means that therapists focus on the constructive side of human nature and on what is *right* with people. Person-centered therapy places emphasis on feelings about the self. Clients can move forward toward growth and wholeness by looking within rather than focusing on outside influences, including that of the therapist. They are able to change in the absence of a high degree of structure and direction from the therapist. What they need from the therapist is understanding, genuineness, support, acceptance, caring, and positive regard.

Gestalt therapy. The Gestalt approach is based on the assumption that people must find their own way in life and accept personal responsibility if they hope to achieve maturity. The therapist's task is to provide a climate in which clients can fully experience their here-and-now awareness and can recognize how they are preventing themselves from living in the present. Clients carry on their own therapy as much as possible by doing experiments aimed at change and finding their own meanings. They are encouraged to experience their conflicts directly instead of merely talking about them. In this way they gradually expand their own level of awareness and integrate the fragmented and unknown aspects of themselves.

Transactional analysis. TA acknowledges that we were influenced by the expectations and demands (injunctions) of significant others. Our early decisions were made when we were children and were highly dependent on others. We were not passively "scripted," however, for we did cooperate in making these early decisions. Thus, we can recognize how certain early decisions may be archaic or nonfunctional, and we can make new decisions that are more appropriate. Therapists play an active and directive role and function much like teachers and resource people in therapy. Clients are viewed as equal partners in the therapeutic endeavor. They carry out contracts that specify what they will change.

Behavior therapy. Although behavior therapy assumes that people are basically shaped by learning and sociocultural conditioning, this approach focuses on the client's ability to eliminate maladaptive behavior and acquire constructive behavior. Behavior therapy is a systematic approach that begins with a comprehensive assessment of the individual to determine the present level of functioning as a prelude to setting therapeutic goals. After clear and specific behavioral goals are established by the client, the therapist typically suggests strategies that are most appropriate for meeting these stated goals. It is assumed that clients will progress only if they are willing to practice new behaviors in real-life situations. A basic part of therapy is continual evaluation to determine how well the procedures and techniques are working for the client.

Rational-emotive therapy and other cognitive-behavioral approaches. From the perspective of RET our problems are caused by our perception of life situations and our thoughts, not by the situations themselves, not by others, and not by past events. Thus, it is our responsibility to recognize and change distorted thinking that leads to emotional and behavior disorders. RET also holds that people tend to incorporate these irrational beliefs from external sources and then continue to indoctrinate themselves with this faulty thinking. To overcome irrational thinking, therapists use active and directive therapy procedures, including teaching, suggestion, and assigning of homework. Therapists have the job of persuading clients to do what is necessary to make long-lasting and substantive change.

Other cognitive-behavioral therapies share some of the assumptions of RET. A basic assumption of many of these approaches is that people are prone to learning erroneous, self-defeating thoughts, but that they are capable of unlearning, or correcting, them. They perpetuate their difficulties through their self-talk. By pinpointing their cognitive errors and by correcting them, individuals can create a more self-fulfilling life for themselves. Cognitive restructuring plays a central role in these therapies. People are assumed to be able to make changes by learning to listen to their self-talk, by learning a new internal dialogue, and by learning coping skills needed for behavioral changes.

Reality therapy. From the perspective of reality therapy, counselors have the task of challenging clients to look at their current behavior to help them assess how much what they are doing is getting them what they want. A basic assumption is that if clients examine their wants and needs, they will be in a better position to determine whether what they are doing is working effectively for them. Total behavior includes doing, thinking, feeling, and physiology. It is easier to change what clients are doing or thinking than it is to change their emotional and physiological reactions. Therefore, the best focus of therapy is behavior. Clients can gain effective control of their lives if they are willing to accept responsibility for their actions.

Ethical and clinical issues emerging from basic assumptions. The contemporary theories of therapeutic practice are grounded on assumptions that are part of Western culture. Many of these assumptions are not appropriate when they are applied to non-Western cultures. The basic assumptions of the nine orientations described above emphasize values such as choice, the uniqueness of the individual, self-assertion, and the strengthening of the ego. Therapeutic outcomes that are emphasized in these systems include improving assertive coping (by changing the environment, changing one's coping behavior, and learning to manage stress). By contrast, non-Western orientations focus on interdependence, play down individuality, and emphasize the losing of oneself in the totality of the cosmos. Counseling from an Asian perspective, for example, reflects the life values associated with a focus on inner experience and acceptance of one's environment.

Whereas the Western therapeutic approaches are oriented toward change, non-Western approaches focus more on the social framework than on the development of the individual. Applying the Western world model of therapy to the Chinese culture does have certain limitations. Likewise, this model has its limitations when it is applied to many minority groups such as Asian Americans, Hispanics, Native Americans, and Blacks. Seeking professional help is not customary for many minority groups, and they will typically turn first to informal systems (family, friends, community).

The point is that counselors need to be aware of the basic assumptions underlying their theoretical orientations. In considering counseling in a pluralistic society, there is an ethical imperative to avoid forcing all clients to fit into a mold that is not appropriate for their cultural background. Therefore, we need to learn how our assumptions influence practice.

Perspectives on Assessment

Some approaches stress the importance of conducting a comprehensive assessment of the client as the initial step in the therapeutic process. The rationale is that specific counseling goals cannot be formulated or appropriate strategies designed until a thorough picture of the client's past and present functioning is completed. In this section various views of the role of assessment in therapy are described. Some ways of conceptualizing an individual case are also presented, with emphasis given to the types of information that it is helpful to gather during the initial stages of therapy.

Psychoanalytic therapy. Psychoanalysts assume that normal personality development is based on dealing effectively with successive psychosexual and psychosocial stages of development. Faulty personality development is the result of inadequately resolving a specific developmental conflict. Therapists are interested in the client's early history as a way of understanding how past situations have contributed to a dysfunction. Projective personality testing—techniques such as the Rorschach test or the thematic apperception test, which are designed to tap a client's unconscious processes—may be used to identify themes running through the client's life. This approach emphasizes the importance of comprehensive assessment techniques as a basis for understanding personality dynamics and the origin of emotional disorders. However, some analysts shy away from gathering information. They think that it will unfold during the process of analytic therapy.

Adlerian therapy. Assessment is a basic part of Adlerian therapy. During the initial session the focus is on creating a relationship based on trust and cooperation. Soon after this cooperative relationship is established, the therapist conducts a comprehensive interview to gather specific information, including an assessment of the client's family constellation, birth order, parental relationship and family values, and early recollections. Clients are often asked to complete a detailed lifestyle questionnaire. (You will see a detailed example of a lifestyle questionnaire in Chapter Three.)

Attention is devoted to how the family structure has influenced the client's development. Childhood experiences are connected to the shaping of one's unique style of life, which includes one's views of self, others, and the world. Therapists identify major patterns that appear in the questionnaire and thus get a picture of the client's basic personality. This process helps clarify "basic mistakes" (faulty perceptions and assumptions about life) and assets (strengths and resources) that the client has developed and has carried through into present functioning. This assessment provides a direction for the course of therapy.

Existential therapy. Existentially oriented counselors maintain that the way to understand the client is by grasping the essence of the person's subjective world. The primary purpose of existential clinical assessment is to understand the assumptions that clients use in structuring their existence. The focus of this assessment is on how clients experience their world. This approach is different from that of the American Psychiatric Association's *Diagnostic and Statistical Manual of Mental Disorders,* Third Edition, Revised (DSM-III-R). The focus is not on understanding the individual from an external perspective but, instead, on grasping the essence of the client's inner world.

Person-centered therapy. In much the same spirit as existential counselors, person-centered therapists maintain that assessment and diagnosis are detrimental, because they are external ways of understanding the client. The reasons for this objection to objective assessment procedures, leading to a diagnosis, are that (1) the best vantage point for understanding another person is through his or her subjective world; (2) the practitioner can become preoccupied with the client's history and thus neglect present attitudes and behavior; and (3) therapists can develop a judgmental attitude, with the responsibility being shifted too much in the direction of telling clients what they ought to do. Focusing on gathering information about a client can lead to an intellectualized conception *about* the client. The client is assumed to be the one who knows the dynamics of his or her behavior, and for change to occur, the client must experience a perceptual change, not simply receive data. Thus, therapists listen actively, attempt to be present, and allow clients to identify the themes that they choose to explore.

Gestalt therapy. Like the two previous approaches Gestalt therapy does not gather information about clients as a prerequisite to counseling. It does not use diagnostic labels, because it sees them as an escape from full participation in the client/therapist relationship. Assessment and diagnostic procedures can foster talking about a client's life, whereas the focus of Gestalt therapy is gaining awareness by *direct experiencing.* The premise is that the salient points in a person's developmental history will surface as the client pays attention to where he or she is stuck in the present. Themes that run through a person's life will become evident during the therapeutic process itself.

Transactional analysis. A rather detailed life-script questionnaire may be used to collect significant information about parental messages that the client accepted, early decisions that were made based on such messages, and other relevant data that tie into the client's life script. Once clients have reviewed some of their decisions that are influencing the course of their life, they are able to select specific goals for therapy. This assessment process culminates with clients' developing a therapeutic contract that spells out what they will change.

Behavior therapy. The behavioral approach begins with a comprehensive assessment of the client's present functioning, with questions directed to past learning that is related to current behavior patterns. It includes an objective appraisal of specific behaviors and the stimuli that are maintaining them. Some of the reasons for conducting a thorough assessment at the outset of therapy are that (1) it identifies behavioral deficiencies as well as assets, (2) it provides an objective means of appraising both a client's specific symptoms and the factors that have led up to the client's malfunctioning, (3) it facilitates the selection of the most suitable therapeutic techniques, (4) it specifies a new learning and shaping schedule, (5) it is useful in predicting the course and the outcome of a particular clinical disorder, and (6) it provides a framework for research into the effectiveness of the procedures employed.

Multimodal therapy, developed by Arnold Lazarus, is an example of a broad-based, systematic, and comprehensive approach to behavior therapy. It calls for technical eclecticism, but it remains firmly grounded on social-learning theory. In the multimodal orientation a comprehensive assessment process attends to each area of a client's BASIC ID (behavior, affect, sensation, imagery, cognition, interpersonal relationships, and drugs and biological factors). Interactive problems throughout each of these seven areas are identified, and appropriate techniques are selected to deal with each difficulty.

Rational-emotive therapy and other cognitive-behavioral approaches. The assessment used in RET is based on getting a sense of the client's patterns of thinking. Attention is paid to various beliefs that the client has developed in relation to certain events. Therapists are concerned not merely with gathering data about past events; rather, they are alert to evidences of faulty thinking and irrational beliefs that the client has incorporated. Once rigid, unrealistic, absolutist ideas have been identified, the therapeutic process consists of actively undermining these self-defeating beliefs and substituting constructive ones.

Reality therapy. Assessment of clients is typically not a formal process; psychological testing and diagnoses are not generally a part of this approach. However, through the use of skillful questioning reality therapists help clients make an assessment of their present behavior. There is little interest in the causes of an individual's current problems or in gathering information about the client's past experiences. Instead, the focus is on getting clients to take a critical look at what they are doing now and then to determine the degree to which their present behavior is effective. This informal assessment directs clients to pay attention to their pattern of wants, needs, perceptions, successes, personal strengths, and assets. Clients also focus on what they are doing and thinking, as a way to evaluate whether their lives are moving in the direction they want.

The place of diagnosis and assessment in counseling and case management. Assessment consists of evaluating the relevant factors in a client's life to identify themes for further exploration in therapy. Diagnosis consists of identifying some specific category of psychological problem. Based on a pattern of symptoms, it is possible to formulate a tentative diagnosis. Diagnosis is frequently a part of the assessment process. The main purpose of a diagnostic approach is to allow therapists to plan treatments tailored to the needs of the individual. It should be noted that there are several types of diagnosis. *Medical diagnosis* is the process of examining physical symptoms, inferring causes of physical disorders or diseases, providing a category that fits the pattern of a disease, and prescribing an appropriate treatment. *Psychological diagnosis* entails identifying an emotional or behavioral problem and making a statement about the current status of a client. It includes the identification of the possible causes of the individual's emotional, psychological, and behavioral difficulties. It also entails suggesting the appropriate therapeutic techniques to deal effectively with the identified problem and estimating the chances for a successful resolution. *Differential diagnosis* consists of distinguishing one form of psychiatric disorder from another by determining which of two (or more) diseases or disorders with similar symptoms the person is suffering from. The latest edition of the *Diagnostic and Statistical Manual of Mental Disorders* (DSM-III-R) is the standard reference for the nomenclature of psychopathology. (The DSM-IV is in press and will be replacing the existing manual.)

A practitioner's view of diagnosis will depend on his or her theoretical orientation, as we have seen. For instance, psychoanalytically oriented therapists tend to favor diagnosis. Assessment is one way of understanding how past situations have contributed to an individual's dysfunction. Practitioners with a behavioral orientation also favor diagnosis, for they emphasize observation and other objective means of appraising both a client's specific symptoms and the factors that have led up to the client's malfunctioning. Such an assessment process allows them to employ techniques that are appropriate for a particular disorder and to evaluate the effectiveness of a treatment program. On the other side of the diagnostic issue are person-centered practitioners, who maintain that diagnosis is not essential for counseling because it tends to pull clients away from an internal and subjective way of experiencing themselves and fosters an external conception about them.

Regardless of your theoretical orientation it is likely that you will be expected to work within the framework of DSM-III-R if you are involved in community-agency counseling. Even if you are in private practice, you will have to provide a diagnosis on the client's insurance form if you accept insurance for mental-health services. Because you will need to think in the framework of assessing and diagnosing clients, it is essential that you become familiar with the diagnostic categories and the structure of the DSM-III-R.

My own perspective on assessment. I see assessment and diagnosis, broadly construed, as a legitimate part of therapy. The assessment process does not necessarily have to be completed during the intake interview, nor does it have to be a fixed judgment that the therapist makes about the client. It is a continuing process that focuses on understanding the client. Ideally, assessment is a collaborative effort by the client and the therapist that is a part of their interaction. Both should be involved in discovering the nature of the client's presenting problem, a process that begins with the initial sessions and continues until therapy ends. The questions that are helpful for a therapist to consider during this early assessment phase are:

- What are my immediate and overall reactions to the client?
- What is going on in this client's life at this time?
- What are the client's main assets and liabilities?
- What are the client's resources for change?
- Is this a crisis situation, or is it a long-standing problem?
- What does the client primarily want from therapy, and how can it best be achieved?
- What should be the focus of the sessions?
- What major factors are contributing to the client's current problems, and what can be done to alleviate them?
- What significant past events appear to be related to the client's present level of functioning?
- What specific family dynamics might be relevant to the client's present struggles and interpersonal relationships?
- What support systems can the client tap in making changes? Who are the significant people in the client's life?
- What are the prospects for meaningful change, and how will we know when that change has occurred?

As a result of questions such as these, therapists will develop tentative hypotheses, and they can share them with their clients as therapy proceeds. This process of assessment does not have to result in classifying the client under some clinical category. Instead, counselors can describe behavior as they observe it and encourage clients to think about its meaning. In this way assessment becomes a process of thinking about issues *with* the client, rather than a mechanical procedure conducted by an expert therapist. From this perspective assessment and diagnostic thinking are vital to the therapeutic procedures that are selected, and such a process helps practitioners conceptualize a case.

Even if practitioners are required to diagnose someone for administrative or insurance reasons, they are not bound rigidly to that view of their client. The diagnostic category is merely a framework for viewing and understanding a pattern of symptoms and for making treatment plans. It is not necessary to restrict clients to a label or to treat them in stereotypical ways. It is essential that practitioners be aware of the dangers of labeling and adopt a tentative stance toward diagnosis. As therapy progresses, additional data are bound to emerge, which may call for a modification of an original diagnosis.

General guidelines for assessment. The intake interview typically centers on making the assessment described earlier and prescribing an appropriate course of treatment. As we have seen, depending on the practitioner's orientation, this assessment may take various forms. For example, Adlerians look for ways in which the family structure has affected the client's development, whereas a psychoanalytic practitioner is interested in intrapsychic conflicts. This section will present a fairly comprehensive scheme for conceptualizing an individual case. After looking at several intake forms and case summary forms, I have pulled together some guidelines that might be helpful in thinking about ways of getting significant information and about where to proceed with a client after making an initial assessment. Below are ten areas that are a basic part of conceptualizing an individual case:

1. *Identifying data.* Get details such as name, age, sex, appearance, ethnic background, socioeconomic status, marital status, religious identification, and referral source (who referred the client, and for what purpose?).

2. *Presenting problem(s).* What is the chief complaint? This area includes a brief description, in the client's own words, of immediate problems for which he or she is seeking therapy. The presenting situation includes a description of the problems, how long they have existed, and what has been done to cope with them.

3. *Current living circumstances.* Information to collect here includes marital status and history, family data, recent moves, financial status, legal problems, basic conflicts in one's lifestyle, support systems, and problems in personal relationships.

4. *Psychological analysis and assessment.* What is the client's general psychological state? For example, how does the client view his or her situation, needs, and problems? What is the client's level of maturity? Is there evidence of detrimental influences in the client's life? What are the client's dominant emotions? Is the client excited, anxious, ashamed, angry? This phase of assessment entails describing the client's ego functioning, including self-concept, self-esteem, memory, orientation, fantasies, ability to tolerate frustration, insight, and motivation to change. The focus is on the client's view of self, including perceived strengths and weaknesses, the client's ideal self, and how the client believes that others view him or her. What is the client's level of security? What is the client's ability to see and cope with reality, capacity for decision making, degree of self-control and self-direction, and the ability to deal with life changes and transitions? Standardized psychological tests of intelligence, personality, aptitudes, and interests may be used. Another assessment procedure is the *mental-status examination,* which is a structured interview leading to information about the client's psychological level of functioning. The mental-status examination focuses on areas such as appearance, behavior, feeling, perception, and thinking. For example, under the *behavior* category the counselor making the assessment will note specific dimensions of behavior, including posture, facial expressions, general body movements, quality of speech, and behavior in the interview situation. Under the *thinking* category it is important to assess factors such as the client's intellectual functioning, orientation, insight, judgment, memory, thought processes, and any disturbances in thinking.

5. *Psychosocial developmental history.* The focus here is on the developmental and etiological factors relating to the client's present difficulties. Five types can be considered here: (1) precipitating factors—for example, maturational or situational stress, school entry, divorce, or death of a parent;

(2) predisposing factors—for example, parent/child relationships and other family patterns, personality structure, and hereditary or constitutional factors; (3) contributory factors—for example, a current or past illness or the problems of family members; (4) perpetuating factors—for example, secondary gains such as the sympathy that a sufferer from migraine headaches elicits; and (5) sociocultural factors—that is, customs, traditions, family patterns, and cultural values. From a developmental perspective the following questions could be asked: How well has the client mastered earlier developmental tasks? What are some evidences of conflicts and problems originating in childhood? What were some critical turning points in the individual's life? What were some major crises, and how were they handled? What key choices were made, and how are these past decisions related to present functioning? How did the client's relationships within the family influence development? What was it like for the client to be in the family? What are family relationships like now? How are the client's cultural experiences related to his or her personality? This section might conclude with a summary of developmental history, which could include birth and early development, toilet training, patterns of discipline, developmental delays, educational experiences, sexual development, social development, and the influence of religious, cultural and ethical orientations.

6. *Health and medical history.* What is the client's medical history? What was the date of the client's last consultation with a physician, and what were the results? Is there any noticeable evidence of recent physical trauma or neglect (for example, battering, welt marks, bruises, needle marks, sloppy clothing, sallow complexion)? What is the client's overall state of health? This section should include an assessment of the client's mental health. Has the client been in previous treatment for the present problem? Has there been a prior hospitalization? Has the client been taking medications? What were the outcomes of previous treatments? Is there any history of emotional illness in the family? It is important to be alert to signs that may indicate an organic basis for a client's problem (such as headaches, sudden changes in personal habits or in personality, and other physical symptoms).

7. *Adjustment to work.* What does the client do or expect to do? How satisfied is the client with work? What is the meaning of work to the person? Does he or she have future plans? What are the benefits and drawbacks of work? What is the client's work history? Has the person had long-term employment or a history of employment problems? What is the balance between work and leisure? What is the quality of the client's leisure time? Work is used in the broad sense, whether or not the person receives pay for it. For instance, it would be important to inquire about a woman's satisfaction with her work as a housewife and mother, even if she is not formally employed.

8. *Lethality.* Is the client a danger to self or others? Is he or she thinking about suicide or about hurting someone or something? Does the client have a specific plan either for committing suicide or for harming another

person? Have there been prior attempts at self-destruction or violent behavior toward others?

9. *Present human relationships.* This area includes a survey of information pertaining to marriage, siblings, parents, children, friends, work, school and social life. Included are the level of sexual functioning, family beliefs and values, and satisfaction derived from relationships. What are the client's main problems and conflicts with others? How does he or she deal with conflict? What support does the client get from others?

10. *Summary and case formulation.* Provide a summary of the client's psychodynamics, major defenses, and ego strengths, and make an assessment. What are the major recommendations? What is the suggested focus for therapeutic intervention? (This formulation might specify the frequency and duration of treatment, the preferred therapeutic orientation, and the mode of treatment.)

After the initial assessment of the client is completed, a decision is made whether to refer the client for alternative or additional treatment. If the client is accepted by the therapist, the two can discuss the results. This information can be used in exploring the client's difficulties in thinking, feeling, and behaving and in setting treatment goals. Assessment can be linked directly to the therapeutic process, forming a basis for developing methods of evaluation of how well the counselor's procedures are working toward the client's goals.

Because most mental-health agencies require interns and professionals alike to do intake interviews, familiarity with these assessment procedures is essential.

Therapeutic Goals and Procedures

After the initial comprehensive assessment of a client, *therapeutic goals* need to be established. These goals will vary, depending in part on the practitioner's theoretical orientation. For example, psychoanalytic therapy is primarily an insight approach that aims at regressing clients to very early levels of psychological development so that they can acquire the self-understanding necessary for major character restructuring. It deals extensively with the past, with unconscious dynamics, with transference, and with techniques aimed at changing attitudes and feelings. At the other extreme is reality therapy, which focuses on evaluating current behavior in the hope that the client will develop a realistic plan leading to more effective ways of behaving. Reality therapy is not concerned with exploring the past, with unconscious motivation, with the transference clients might develop, or with attitudes and feelings. It asks the key question "What is the client doing now, and what does the client want to be doing differently?" It assumes that the best way to change is by focusing on what one is doing and thinking. If these dimensions change, it is likely that the client's feelings and physiological reactions will also change.

Therapeutic goals are diverse and include restructuring personality, finding meaning in life, creating an I/thou relationship between the client and the counselor, eliminating irrational beliefs, teaching clients how to rewrite their life script, helping them look within themselves to find answers, substituting effective behaviors for maladaptive ones, and correcting mistaken beliefs and assumptions. Given this wide range, it is obvious that the perspectives of the client and the therapist on goals will surely have an impact on the course of therapy and on the therapeutic interventions chosen.

Despite this diversity of goals all therapies share some common denominators. They aim at increasing the individual's autonomy—that is, at intervening to encourage the client to make changes that will lead to self-reliance. To some degree they also have the goal of identifying what the client wants and then modifying the client's thoughts, feelings, and behaviors.

Each theoretical orientation focuses on a particular dimension of human experience as a route to changing other facets of personality. For example, both Adlerian and rational-emotive therapists emphasize the client's cognitions under the assumption that if they are successful in modifying beliefs and thought processes, behavioral changes will follow and feelings will eventually be modified.

Selecting *therapeutic techniques,* then, depends on whether a counselor's goals are oriented toward changing thoughts, feelings, or behaviors. Psychoanalytic therapists, for example, are primarily concerned that their clients acquire *insights* into the nature and causes of their personality problems. They employ techniques such as free association, analysis of dreams, interpretation of resistance, and analysis of transference as tools to uncover the unconscious and lead to the desired insight. Gestalt therapists are interested in helping clients fully experience what they are *feeling* moment to moment; they use a wide range of exercises and experiments designed to intensify this experiencing of feelings. Rational-emotive therapists are mainly concerned that clients identify and demolish irrational *thinking,* and they have a variety of cognitive (as well as behavioral and emotive) techniques. Behavior therapists are interested in helping clients decrease or eliminate unwanted *behaviors* and increase adaptive ones. Thus, they employ many procedures aimed at teaching clients new behaviors. Whatever techniques you employ, it is essential to keep the needs of your client in mind. Some clients relate best to cognitive techniques, others to techniques designed to change behavior, and others to techniques aimed at eliciting emotional material. The same client, depending on the stage of his or her therapy, can profit from participating in all of these different techniques.

As a therapist you would do well to think of ways to take techniques from all of the approaches so that you are able to work with a client on *all levels* of development. Take the case of Ruth, with whom you will become very familiar in this book. At the outset your interventions may be directed toward getting her to identify and express feelings that she has kept bottled up for much of her life. If you listen to her and provide a place where she can experience what she is *feeling,* she is likely to be able to give more expression to emotions that she has distorted and denied. As her therapy progresses, you may well direct interventions toward getting her to think about early decisions that still have an influence in her life. At this time in her therapy you are likely to shift the focus from exploration of feelings to exploration of her attitudes, her *thinking processes,* her values, and her basic beliefs. Still later your focus may be more on helping her develop *action programs* in which she can experiment with new ways of *behaving,* both during the sessions and outside of them. It is not a matter of working with one aspect of Ruth's experiencing while forgetting about the other facets of her being; rather, it is a case of selecting a focus for a particular phase of her therapy. The challenge that you will face as you encounter Ruth (and the other "clients" in this book) is how to utilize an *eclectic approach* as you draw on a variety of techniques to effectively help clients work through their struggles. In working within a multicultural framework, it is especially important for counselors to use techniques in a flexible manner. Clients should not be forced into a strict mold. Rather, techniques are most effective when they are tailored to what the individual client needs, which means therapists will have to modify their strategies. Some clients will resist getting involved in techniques that are aimed at bringing up and expressing intense emotions. Highly confrontive techniques may close down some clients. In such cases it may be best to focus more on cognitive or behavioral techniques or to modify emotive techniques that are appropriate for the client. On the other hand, some clients need to be confronted if they are to move. Confrontation at its best is an act of caring. It is designed to challenge clients to examine what they are thinking, feeling, and doing. Relying strictly on supportive techniques with certain clients will not provide the impetus they need to take the steps necessary to change. Techniques work best when they are designed to help clients explore thoughts, feelings, and actions that are within the client's cultural environment. Again, the value of bringing the client into the counseling process as an informed partner cannot be overemphasized.

The rest of this section summarizes the goals of therapy from the various theoretical perspectives and some of the techniques commonly used by each of the nine therapeutic approaches. Also addressed are these questions: When are clients ready to terminate therapy? How are the outcomes of therapy evaluated?

Psychoanalytic therapy. The main goal is to resolve intrapsychic conflicts, toward the end of reconstructing one's basic personality. Analytic therapy is not limited to problem solving and learning new behaviors; there is a deeper probing into the past in order to develop one's level of self-understanding.

From the psychoanalytic perspective all techniques are designed to help the client gain insight and bring repressed material to the surface so that it can be dealt with consciously. Major techniques include gathering of life-history data, dream analysis, free association, and interpretation and analysis of resistance and transference. Such procedures are aimed at increasing awareness, gaining intellectual insight, and beginning a working-through process that will lead to the reorganization of personality.

When are clients ready to leave therapy? How are the outcomes of therapy evaluated? Psychoanalytic clients are ready to terminate their sessions when they and the therapist agree that they have clarified and accepted their emotional problems, have understood the historical roots of their difficulties, and can integrate their awareness of past problems with present relationships. Successful analytic therapy answers the "why" questions that clients pose.

Adlerian therapy. Therapists help clients develop social interest, provide encouragement to discouraged individuals, and facilitate insight into clients' mistaken ideas (notions) and their personal assets. Adlerian practitioners are not bound by any set of prescribed techniques. They may use a variety of methods that are suited to the unique needs of their clients. A few of these therapeutic procedures are attending, encouragement, confrontation, paradoxical intention, interpretation of the family constellation and early recollections, suggestions, homework assignments, and summarizing.

Because Adlerians stress a democratic approach, termination is typically discussed and decided on by the client and therapist. The stress on goal alignment gives both of them a frame of reference to assess the outcomes of therapy.

Existential therapy. The principal goal is to challenge clients to recognize and accept the freedom they have to become the authors of their lives. Therapists confront them on ways in which they are avoiding their freedom and the responsibility that accompanies it.

The existential approach places primary emphasis on understanding the client's current experience, *not* on using therapy techniques. Thus, counselors are not bound by any prescribed techniques, so they can borrow strategies from other schools of therapy. Interventions are used in the service of broadening the ways in which clients live in their world.

Issues of both termination and evaluation are typically the result of an open exchange between the client and therapist. Since the client generally makes the choice to enter therapy, it seems fitting that it be his or her choice and responsibility to decide when to leave therapy. If clients continue to rely on the therapist for this answer, they are not yet ready to terminate. However, therapists are given the latitude to express their reactions and views about the client's readiness for termination. The choices that clients are making and the changes in their perceptions of themselves in their world are the basis for an evaluation of therapeutic outcomes.

Person-centered therapy. The person-centered approach seeks to provide a climate of understanding and acceptance through the client/therapist relationship that will enable clients to nondefensively come to terms with aspects of themselves that they have denied or disowned. Other goals are enabling clients to move toward greater openness, an increased trust in themselves, a willingness to be a process rather than a finished product, and greater spontaneity.

Because this approach places primary emphasis on the client/therapist relationship, it specifies few techniques. Techniques are secondary to the therapist's attitudes. Procedures that are minimized include directive intervention, interpretation, questioning, probing for information, advice giving, collecting history, and diagnosis. Person-centered therapists maximize active listening, reflection, and clarification. Current formulations of the theory stress full and active participation of the therapist as a person in the therapeutic relationship.

In keeping with the spirit of person-centered therapy, it is the client who largely determines when to stop coming for therapy. Likewise, the therapist assumes that clients can be trusted to determine the degree to which therapy has been successful for them. As clients increasingly assume an inner locus of control, they are in the best position to assess the personal meaning of their therapeutic venture.

Gestalt therapy. The goal of the Gestalt approach is to challenge clients to move from environmental support to self-support and to assist them in gaining awareness of moment-to-moment experiencing. Clients are encouraged to directly experience, in the present, their struggles with "unfinished business" from their past. This process allows them to integrate fragmented parts of their personality.

A wide range of techniques is designed to intensify experiencing and to resolve emotional conflicts. Gestalt therapy stresses confrontation of discrepancies and of ways in which clients are avoiding responsibility for their feelings. The client engages in role playing by performing all of the various parts and polarities, thus gaining greater awareness of inner conflicts. Techniques commonly used are dialogue with conflicting parts of oneself, exaggeration, focusing on body messages, staying with particular feelings, reexperiencing past unfinished situations in the here and now, and working with dreams. Clients interpret their own dreams.

Clients are ready to terminate therapy when they become increasingly aware of what they are feeling, thinking, sensing, and doing in the present moment. When they have recognized and worked through their unfinished business, they are ready to continue therapy on their own. As with the other experiential therapies (existential and person-centered) the evaluation of therapeutic outcomes is rooted in the client's subjective experience and perceptions about the changes that have occurred.

Transactional analysis. Therapists strive to help clients become script-free, game-free, autonomous people capable of choosing intimate relationships. They assist clients in examining the basis on which early decisions were made and in making more appropriate decisions based on new evidence.

A life-script questionnaire is useful in identifying injunctions, games, life positions, and early decisions. Contracts are an essential part of TA, specifying the topics to be explored in therapy. Other procedures include questioning, teaching, family modeling, role playing, and analysis of games and life scripts.

Because TA is a contractual form of therapy, clients are ready to end the sessions when their contract has been completed. In assessing the outcomes of TA therapy, both the client and therapist would look to specific cognitive, behavioral, and affective changes that were specified as a part of the therapeutic contract.

Behavior therapy. The main goal is to eliminate clients' maladaptive behavior patterns and replace them with more constructive ones. Therapists identify thought patterns that lead to behavioral problems and then teach new ways of thinking that are designed to change the clients' ways of acting.

The main behavioral techniques are systematic desensitization, relaxation methods, reinforcement, modeling, assertion training, self-management programs, behavioral rehearsal, coaching, and various multimodal techniques. Assessment and diagnosis are done at the outset to determine a treatment plan. "What," "how," and "when" questions are used (but not "why" questions).

Generally, the client makes the decision to terminate therapy. This approach has the advantage of specifying clear and concrete behavioral goals that can be monitored and measured. Because therapy begins with an assessment of baseline data, the degree of progress can be evaluated by comparing the client's behavior on a given dimension at any point in the therapy with the baseline data. Moreover, assessment and treatment occur simultaneously. The client is frequently challenged to answer the question "Is what is going on in these sessions helping you make the changes you desire?"

Rational-emotive therapy and other cognitive-behavioral approaches. The goal is to eliminate clients' self-defeating outlook on life and assist them in acquiring a more tolerant and rational view of life. Clients are taught how they incorporated irrational beliefs, how they are maintaining this faulty thinking, what they can do to undermine such thinking, and how they can teach themselves new ways of thinking that will lead to changes in their ways of behaving and feeling.

Typically, RET practitioners use a variety of cognitive, affective, and behavioral techniques. Procedures are designed to get the client to critically examine present beliefs and behavior. *Cognitive* methods include disputing irrational beliefs, carrying out cognitive homework, and changing one's language and thinking patterns. *Emotive* techniques include role playing, RET imagery, and shame-attacking exercises. A wide range of active and practical *behavioral* procedures is used to get clients to be specific and committed to doing the hard work required by therapy.

Clients are ready to terminate when they give up their *must*urbatory thinking. When they no longer badger themselves with "*shoulds,*" "*oughts,*" and "*musts,*" and when they replace their irrational and self-destructive beliefs with rational and constructive ones, they do not need formal therapy. Therapeutic outcomes can be evaluated by looking at the specific cognitive, affective, and behavioral changes demonstrated by the client.

Reality therapy. The overall goal of reality therapy is to help individuals find more effective ways of meeting their needs for belonging, power, freedom, and fun. The approach challenges clients to make an assessment of their current behavior to determine if what they are doing and thinking is getting them what they want from life. As clients become aware of the ineffective behaviors they are using to control the world, they are then more open to learning alternative ways of behaving.

Reality therapy is an active, directive, and didactic therapy. The therapist assists clients in making plans to change specific behaviors that they determine are not working for them. Skillful questioning and a variety of behavioral methods are often used to encourage clients to evaluate what they are doing. If they decide that their present behavior is not effective, they develop a specific plan for change and make a commitment to follow through.

When clients are more effectively fulfilling their wants and needs and when they have gained (or regained) control of their world, they are ready to leave counseling. This approach has the advantage of being anchored in a specific plan for change. This plan is not nebulous, but specific, which allows objective evaluation of outcomes.

My perspective on the integration of goals and techniques. I attempt to integrate goals from most of the major theories by paying attention to changes that clients want to make in how they typically think, feel, and behave. My early interventions are aimed at helping clients identify specific ways in which they want to be different. Once they have formulated concrete goals, we can then utilize a variety of techniques that foster modification of thinking processes, feelings, and ways of behaving.

In the counseling of culturally diverse client populations it is important to consider the degree to which the general goals and methods employed are congruent with the cultural background and values of clients. It is essential that both the therapist and the client recognize their differences in goal orientation. For example, it can be a therapeutic mistake to strongly encourage some clients to learn to be assertive with their parents and tell them exactly what they are thinking and feeling. An Asian-American client might hold to the value that it is rude to confront parents and that it is inappropriate to bring out conflicts. The therapist who would push such a client to be independent and to deal with conflicts within the family would probably alienate this client. Interdependence, thinking about what is best for the social group, and striving for harmony may be the dominant values operating in this person's life. It becomes critical that therapists listen to their clients and enter their perceptual world. The process of therapy is best guided by the particular goals and values of each client, not by what the therapist thinks is best. Questions that therapists can frequently ask of their clients are "Why are you seeking counseling from me?" "What is it that you would like to explore?" "What is it about yourself or your life situation that you most want to change?" By staying focused on what their clients want, therapists can greatly reduce the dangers of imposing their goals.

Having considered a survey of nine therapy perspectives from the vantage point of their basic assumptions, views of assessment, goals of therapy, and therapeutic procedures, we are now ready to consider a specific case. As you study Ruth's case, look for ways in which you can apply what you have just read in gaining a fuller understanding of her.

THE CASE OF RUTH

The themes in Ruth's life are characteristic of many of the clients I have worked with individually and, especially, in groups. In essence, I took typical struggles from a number of clients and based a clinical picture on them. Pulled together, these common themes form Ruth. Her intake form, reproduced here, and autobiography will provide you with much of the information you need to understand and work with her. Each of the theory chapters will provide you with extra information, especially the commentary of the consultant who is an expert in the given theoretical orientation. As you read the next nine chapters, I suggest that you refer back to this information about Ruth to refresh you on some of the details and themes in her life.

Ruth's Autobiography

As a part of the intake process the counselor asked Ruth to bring the autobiography that she had written for her counseling class. Although most therapists do not make it a practice to ask their clients to write an

CLIENT'S INTAKE FORM

AGE	SEX	RACE	MARITAL STATUS
			Married
39	Female	Caucasian	SOCIOECONOMIC STATUS
			Middle class

APPEARANCE

Dresses meticulously, is overweight, fidgets constantly with her clothes, avoids eye contact, speaks rapidly.

LIVING SITUATION

Recently graduated from college as an elementary-education major, lives with husband (John, 45) and her children (Rob, 19, Jennifer, 18, Susan, 17, and Adam, 16).

PRESENTING PROBLEM

Client reports general dissatisfaction. She says her life is rather uneventful and predictable, and she feels some panic over reaching the age of 39, wondering where the years have gone. For two years she has been troubled with a range of psychosomatic complaints, including sleep disturbances, anxiety, dizziness, heart palpitations, and headaches. At times she has to push herself to leave the house. Client complains that she cries easily over trivial matters, often feels depressed, and has a weight problem.

HISTORY OF PRESENTING PROBLEM

Client made her major career as a housewife and mother until her children became adolescents. She then entered college part time and obtained a bachelor's degree. She has recently begun work toward a credential in elementary education. Through her contacts with others at the university she became aware of how she has limited herself, how she has fostered her family's dependence on her, and how frightened she is of branching out from her roles as mother and wife.

Ruth completed a course in introduction to counseling that encouraged her to look at the direction of her own life. As a part of the course she participated in self-awareness groups, had a few individual counseling sessions, and wrote several papers dealing with the turning points in her own life. One of the requirements was to write an extensive autobiography that was based on an application of the principles of the counseling course to her own personal development. This course and her experiences with fellow students in it acted as a catalyst in getting her to take an honest look at her life. Ruth is not clear at this point who she is, apart from being a mother, wife, and student. She realizes that she does not have a good sense of what she wants for herself and that she typically lived up to what others in her life wanted for her. She has decided to seek individual therapy for the following reasons:

HISTORY OF PRESENTING PROBLEM (CONT'D)

*A physician whom she consulted could find no organic or medical basis for her physical symptoms and recommended personal therapy. In her words, her major symptoms are these: "I sometimes feel very panicky, especially at night when I am trying to sleep. Sometimes I'll wake up and find it difficult to breathe, my heart will be pounding, and I'll break out in a cold sweat. I toss and turn trying to relax, and instead I feel tense and worry a lot about many little things. It's hard for me to turn off these thoughts. Then during the day I'm so tired I can hardly function and I find that lately I cry very easily if even minor things go wrong."

*She is aware that she has lived a very structured and disciplined life, that she has functioned largely by taking care of the home and the needs of her four children and her husband, and that to some degree she is no longer content with this. Yet she reports that she doesn't know what "more than this" is. Although she would like to get more involved professionally, the thought of doing it does frighten her. She worries about her right to think and act selfishly, she fears not succeeding in the professional world, and she most of all worries about how becoming more professionally involved might threaten her family.

*Her children range in age from 16 to 19, and all of them are now finding more of their satisfactions outside of the family and the home and are spending increasing time with their friends. Ruth sees these changes and is concerned about "losing" them. She is having particular problems with her daughter Jennifer, and she is at a loss how to deal with Jennifer's rebellion. In general, Ruth feels very much unappreciated by her children.

*In thinking about her future, she is not really sure who or what she wants to become. She would like to develop a sense of herself apart from the expectations of others. She finds herself wondering what she "should" want and what she "should" be doing. Ruth does not find her relationship with her husband, John, at all satisfactory. He appears to be resisting her attempts to make changes and prefers that she remain as she was. But she is anxious over the prospects of challenging this relationship, fearing that if she does, she might end up alone.

*Lately, Ruth is experiencing more concern over aging and losing her "looks." All of these factors combined have provided the motivation for her to take the necessary steps to initiate individual therapy. Perhaps the greatest catalyst that triggered her to come for therapy is the increase of her physical symptoms and her anxiety.

PSYCHOSOCIAL HISTORY

Client was the oldest of four children. Her father is a fundamentalist minister, and her mother, a housewife. She describes her father as distant, authoritarian, and rigid; her relationship with him was one of unquestioning, fearful adherence to his rules and standards. She remembers her mother as being critical, and she thought that she could never do enough to please her. At other times her mother was supportive. The family demonstrated little affection. In many ways Ruth took on the role of caring for her younger brother and sisters, largely in the hope of winning the approval of the parents. When she attempted to have any kind of fun, she encountered her father's disapproval and outright scorn. To a large extent this pattern of taking care of others has extended throughout her life.

One critical incident took place when Ruth was 6 years old. She reported: "My father caught me 'playing doctor' with an 8-year-old boy. He lectured me and refused to speak to me for weeks. I felt extremely guilty and ashamed." It appears that Ruth carried feelings of guilt into her adolescence and that she repressed her own emerging sexuality.

In her social relationships Ruth had difficulty in making and keeping friends. She felt socially isolated from her peers because they viewed her as "weird." Although she wanted the approval of others, she was not willing to compromise her morals for fear of consequences.

She was not allowed to date until she completed high school; at the age of 19 she married the first person she had dated. She used her mother as a role model by becoming a homemaker.

autobiography, I think that doing so can be a beneficial experience for the client, as a way of reviewing significant life experiences, as well as a useful tool to give the therapist insight into the client's self-perception. Ruth wrote:

Something I've become aware of recently is that I've pretty much lived for others so far. I've been the superwoman who gives and gives until there is little left to give. I give to my husband, John. I've been the "good wife" and the "good mother" that he expects me to be. I do realize that I need John, and I'm afraid he might leave me if I change too much. I've given my all to seeing that my kids grow up decently, but even though I'm trying my best, I often worry that I haven't done enough.

When I look at my life now, I must admit that I don't like what I see. I don't like who I am, and I certainly don't feel very proud of my body. I'm very overweight, and despite my good intentions to lose weight I just can't seem to get rid of the pounds. I've always enjoyed eating and often eat too much. My family nagged me as a child, but the more they wanted me to stop, the more I seemed to eat, sometimes to the point of making myself sick. I make resolutions to start an exercise program and stick to a diet, but I've yet to find a way to follow through with my plans.

One of the things I do look forward to is becoming a teacher in an elementary school. I really think this would make my life more meaningful. Right now I worry a lot about what will become of me when my kids leave and there is just John and myself in that house. I know I should at least get out there and get that job as a substitute teacher in a private school that I've wanted (and have an offer for), yet I drag my feet on that one, too.

One big thing that troubles me a lot is the feeling of panic I get more and more of the time. I don't remember ever feeling that bad. Often during the day, when I'm trying to do well at school, I feel dizzy, almost like fainting, and have a hard time breathing. Sometimes I'll be sitting in class and get hot flashes, and then I sweat profusely, which is really embarrassing to me. At times my hands start to tremble, and I'm afraid that others will notice this and think I'm weird. And sometimes when I'm sitting in class or even doing shopping, my heart is racing so fast that I worry I'll die of a heart attack. Then there are times when I wake up at night with my heart beating very fast, in a cold sweat, and sometimes shaking. I feel a terrible sense of doom, but I don't know what over. I get so scared over these feelings, which just seem to creep up on me at the times I least expect them. It makes me think that that maybe if I don't get better control of myself, I might go crazy. I know that I worry about death—about my dying—a lot. Maybe I still fear going to hell. As a kid I was motivated by fear of fire and brimstone. Nine years ago I finally broke away from my strong fundamentalist church, because I could see that it was not me. Somehow, taking that philosophy class in the community college years ago got me to thinking about the values I was taught. It was the gospel, and who was I to question? So, when I was 30, I made the break from the fundamentalist religion that I had so closely lived by. I'm now attending a less dogmatic church, yet I still feel pangs of guilt that I am not living by the religion my parents brought me up with. They haven't formally disowned me, but in many ways I think they have. I know I'll never win their approval as long as I stay away from the religion that's so dear to them. But I find it more and more difficult to live by something I don't believe in. The big problem for me is that I so often feel lost and confused, wanting some kind of anchor in my life. I know what I don't believe, but I still have little to replace those values that I once lived by. I sometimes wonder if I really discarded those values, because I so often hear the voices of my parents inside my head!

As a part of my college program I took a course that was an introduction to counseling, and that opened my eyes to a lot of things. One of our guest speakers was a licensed clinical psychologist, who talked about the value of counseling for people even though they are not seriously disturbed. I began to consider that maybe I could benefit from getting some counseling. Up until that time I had always thought you had to be a psycho before going to a psychotherapist. I see that I could work on a lot of things that I've neatly tucked away in my life. Yet even though I think I've almost made the decision to seek therapy, there is still this nagging fear within me, and I keep asking myself questions. What if I find out things about me that I don't like? What will I do if I discover there's nothing inside of me? What if I lose John while I'm getting myself together? I so much want those magical answers. All my life I've had clear answers to every question. Then nine years ago, when I became a questioner to some extent, I lost those neat answers. What if I open Pandora's box and too much comes out and I get even more overwhelmed than I already am?

What I most want from therapy is that the therapist will tell me what I have to do and push me to do it, so that I can begin to live before it's too late. The trouble is that I think I could settle for my nice and comfortable life that I have now, even though a great part of it is driving me nuts. Sure, it's boring and stale, but I don't have to make any decisions either. Then again it's uncomfortable to be where I am. But new decisions are so scary for me to make. I'm scared I'll make the wrong decisions and that in doing so I'll ruin not only my life but John's life and the future of my kids. I feel I owe it to them to stay in this marriage. I guess I'm trapped and don't see a way out. And that would be the last straw if my father ever found out that I was seeing a counselor! He'd tell me I was foolish—that all the answers to life are found in the Bible. Sometimes I wonder if I should turn my life over to God and let Him take over. I so much wish He *would* take over! I don't know what lies ahead. I'm afraid and excited at the same time.

Diagnostic Impressions of Ruth

About the time that I was beginning the revision of this book, I had a telephone call from Michael Nystul, a professor at New Mexico State University, who informed me that he was using *Case Approach to Counseling and Psychotherapy* for one of his summer classes. He asked: "Dr. Corey, what diagnosis would you give Ruth? My students are discussing her case, and they were interested in getting your opinion about her diagnostic category."

"Well, Dr. Nystul," I replied, "I generally don't think in diagnostic terms, so I would be hard pressed to give Ruth a diagnosis."

"But if you *had* to give her a diagnosis, what would it be?"

We then exchanged our views on a possible diagnosis for Ruth. Since there were several possible diagnoses that seemed to fit in her case, I began thinking about the process a practitioner goes through in attempting to identify the most appropriate diagnostic category for a client. I then asked several of my colleagues at the university who were familiar with Ruth's case to suggest a diagnosis. Interestingly, I got a variety of interpretations, all with a good supporting rationale. I also asked some of those who were reviewing this manuscript to give me their impressions of the most appropriate diagnostic category for Ruth. As you might suspect, there were a variety of diagnostic impressions.

Before you continue reading, I suggest that you consider what your diagnosis would be for Ruth. Examine some of the various diagnostic classifications in the DSM-III-R, and identify what you would consider to be her primary diagnosis and her secondary diagnosis as well. Justify the diagnoses you select on the basis of the information presented above. Keep in mind this matter of formulating a tentative diagnosis as you read through the following nine chapters. In reading about the various approaches to counseling Ruth, you may find new evidence or emerging patterns of behavior that warrant modifying your original diagnosis. A provisional diagnosis is given in the Appendix. I encourage you to resist the temptation of looking at this diagnosis until after you have formulated your own diagnosis of Ruth.

RECOMMENDED SUPPLEMENTARY READINGS

Case Studies in Psychotherapy (1989), edited by D. Wedding and R. J. Corsini (Itasca, IL: F. E. Peacock), consists of brief verbatim accounts of a variety of theoretical approaches to case histories. It stresses application of techniques advocated by different schools of therapy.

Diagnostic and Statistical Manual of Mental Disorders (3rd. ed. rev., 1987), by the American Psychiatric Association, is the official system of classifying psychological disorders. It is the resource to consult for identifying patterns of emotional and behavioral disturbance. It gives specifc criteria for the classifications and shows the differences among the various disorders.

DSM-III Case Book (1981), by R. L. Spitzer, A. E. Skodol, M. Gibbon, and J. Williams (Washington, DC: American Psychiatric Association), is a collection of case vignettes that grew out of the authors' experiences. The cases are designed as a learning companion to the DSM-III-R above. Most of the cases are brief descriptions of actual clients, and the discussions focus on ways of making an assessment and formulating a diagnosis.

AACD Ethical Standards Casebook (4th. ed., 1990), by B. Herlihy & L. Golden, contains a variety of useful cases that are geared to the 1988 *Ethical Standards of the American Association for Counseling and Development.* The examples illustrate and clarify the meaning and intent of the standards. The Appendix contains the divisional codes of ethics for a number of groups and the ethical standards of the National Board for Certified Counselors. Also described are the specific steps to be followed in reporting and processing allegations of unethical behavior by members. (This book can be purchased from the AACD, 5999 Stevenson Avenue, Alexandria, VA 22304; telephone: (703) 823-9800.)

''Emotions in Psychotherapy'' (1989), by L. S. Greenberg and J. D. Safran (*American Psychologist,* vol. 44, pp. 19–29), examines the role that emotion plays in therapeutic change. The authors contend that no single therapeutic perspective has been able to encompass within its own theoretical framework the role of emotion in psychotherapy.

"Theoretical Orientations and Work Settings of Clinical and Counseling Psychologists: A Current Perspective" (1989), by A. Zook and J. M. Walton (*Professional Psychology: Research and Practice,* vol. 20, pp. 23–31), provides useful information about trends in theoretical orientations of psychologists.

"Counseling Theory: Understanding the Trend toward Eclecticism from a Developmental Perspective" (1985), by M. M. Brabeck and E. R. Welfel (*Journal of Counseling and Development,* vol. 63, pp. 343–348), examines the current trend toward eclecticism from a developmental perspective. Surveys of practitioners' identification with eclecticism are discussed, as are suggestions for teachers and researchers.

"Models of Helping and Coping" (1982), by P. Brickman, V. C. Rabinowitz, J. Kanuza, D. Coates, E. Cohn, and L. Kidder (*American Psychologist,* vol. 37, pp. 368–384), offers a useful framework for clarifying the assumptions that guide one's therapeutic practice by drawing a distinction between attribution of responsibility for a problem and attribution of responsibility for a solution.

CHAPTER TWO

Case Approach to Psychoanalytic Therapy

INTRODUCTION

In this chapter and the eight to follow I assume the identity of a therapist with the particular orientation being considered. As much as possible I attempt to stay within the spirit of each specific approach, but I again want to emphasize that you will be seeing my interpretation and my own style. There are many differences in therapeutic style among practitioners who share the same theoretical orientation. Thus, there is no "one right way" of practicing psychoanalytic therapy or any of the other systems. I encourage you to do your best in assuming each of the separate theoretical perspectives as you follow the case of Ruth through the nine theory chapters and take up the other case example in each chapter. Doing this will help you decide which concepts and techniques you want to incorporate into your own therapeutic style.

In each of these nine chapters I am Ruth's therapist. I have read her intake form and her autobiography before meeting her for the first time. In these chapters I give an overview of the particular theory by describing the following: the basic assumptions underlying practice, my initial assessment of Ruth, the goals that will guide our work, and the therapeutic procedures and techniques that are likely to be employed in attaining our goals. A section on the therapeutic process shows samples of our work together. It is illustrated with dialogues between Ruth and me, along with an ongoing process commentary that explains my rationale for the interventions that I make and the general direction of her therapy.

Before I demonstrate my way of working with Ruth from each of the perspectives, there is a section written by an expert in each of the theoretical orientations. It is a good practice for counselors to consult with other practitioners at times, for doing so provides them with ideas of other ways to proceed with a client. In working with Ruth, I am using this model of consultation.

Background data on Ruth's case were sent to a well-known representative of each approach, who was asked: "How would you assess Ruth's case? What themes would you probably focus on? What procedures would you be likely to use? How would you expect the therapeutic process to unfold? The contributions of these consultants are used to introduce each therapeutic approach.

A PSYCHOANALYTIC THERAPIST'S PERSPECTIVE ON RUTH by William Blau, Ph.D.

William Blau has a private practice, teaches graduate students, and is a program director at Patton State Hospital in Patton, California. Although his theoretical orientation is psychoanalytic, he often uses techniques from such diverse approaches as cognitive therapy, applied psychophysiology, and transpersonal psychology. His specialty areas include clinical biofeedback and therapy for psychotic clients. He and his wife, Cathey Graham Blau, LCSW, work together in teaching stress management and providing couples therapy. His outside interests include astronomy, speculative fiction, and ecology.

Assessment of Ruth

Psychoanalytic perspective and overview of case material. As a psychoanalytically oriented therapist I suspect that Ruth's background descriptions of her parents, her siblings, and herself are less than objective. Moreover, I predict that the areas of inaccuracy will turn out to be clues to the core of her personality problems. I anticipate finding that her symptoms (anxiety attacks, overeating, fear of accomplishment, panic over being 39, fear of abandonment, and so forth) can be interpreted as outward manifestations of unconscious conflicts that have their origins in childhood experiences and defensive reactions to these experiences that were necessary to her as a child. I suspect, given her intelligence and motivation, that her current exacerbation of symptoms is related to her recognition of discrepancies between what makes sense to her logically and what seems to drive her emotions and behavior. I hypothesize that Ruth is experiencing a split (a struggle between opposing dimensions of herself). This conflict is between the part of her that wants to change and the other part of her that clings to old patterns that were once necessary and have helped her maintain mental stability all her life. Although some of her defenses seem maladaptive from my perspective, I believe I cannot give her the most effective help unless I can fully understand *why* her patterns of defense seem necessary to her *now* and why, once, they were necessary to her psychological survival.

In contrast to some therapeutic practitioners, I am very interested in why Ruth thinks, feels, and behaves as she does. I have no interest in excusing her behavior or condemning others, but I believe that her problems can be most fully helped by answering the "why" as well as the "what" questions regarding her life. I believe that this fundamental interest in the "whys" of an individual client's experience and behavior is a critical distinction between analytic therapy and other approaches.

Unraveling the dynamics of her history and filling in the story of her life with newly emerging memories will be an ongoing part of Ruth's treatment; hence, this aspect of assessment is never complete, although it becomes less important in the final phases of treatment.

Assessing Ruth's suitability for analytic therapy. Before establishing a contract to do analytic therapy with Ruth, I would need to ascertain if she was a good candidate for the treatment and if she had the perseverance and resources to make this approach the treatment of choice. Assessment of her need for analytic therapy would include determining whether she wants and needs to understand the unconscious roots of her neurosis. If simply teaching her about the pathological nature of some of her behavior would lead to significant change, she would probably not need analytic therapy. Didactic approaches would suffice. I suspect, however, that Ruth does not consciously know why she reacts in symptomatic ways, and I suspect that she is repeatedly frustrated when she has been given good advice by others (or by herself) but still finds the old patterns persisting.

As a psychoanalytic therapist I believe that the economics of treatment, both in terms of financial arrangements and also in the investment of time and energy in therapy, cannot be separated from the process of therapy or expectations for a successful outcome. I would assess the degree of commitment Ruth brings to the initial sessions and would establish not only her ability to pay for a lengthy course of treatment but also the relationship of her method of payment to the dynamics of treatment. Her case history indicates that she works as a housewife and student and fears abandonment. Would the therapy be financed by her husband, either directly or through insurance? Would her university be providing the treatment as a health benefit, and, if so, would her eligibility end once she obtained her teaching credential? These issues are important not only to ensure continuation of treatment but also to understand the role of the fee in the dynamics of the therapy. If, for example, Ruth's husband is financing the therapy, how will that affect her struggles for independence?

Ruth's case history does include a number of factors suggesting that she could be a good candidate for analytic treatment. Her autobiography shows her to be a woman for whom understanding the meaning of her life is important and for whom achieving individuation is a meaningful goal. Her autobiography also shows that she has the ability to look at herself from a somewhat objective perspective. Her need for symptom alleviation is sufficient to provide strong motivation for change, yet her symptoms are not currently incapacitating.

Ruth fantasizes that the therapist will tell her what to do with her life and take the place of her father and the God of her childhood religion. In contracting with her for treatment, I would let her know that fulfillment of this fantasy is not provided by analytic psychotherapy; however, this would by no means end the issue. Despite the formal contract I anticipate that she will continue to demand that the therapist take charge of her life. This aspect of transference will be of ongoing significance in treatment. On the whole, Ruth is the sort of client for whom analytically oriented psychotherapy might be indicated.

Diagnosis. DSM-III-R diagnosis of Ruth is of limited value. It is necessary in that physical causes for Ruth's symptoms must be ruled out. Analytic therapy is more clearly indicated for some disorders than for others, and some disorders require extensive modification of technique. But traditional diagnosis is limited in that the individual's ability to form a therapeutic alliance, which is the key issue in assessment for analytic treatment, is largely independent of diagnosis.

From a diagnostic standpoint (once it has been determined that Ruth is not suicidal or homicidal) the most important issues would be to determine the role of organic factors in her symptomatology and to determine if she should be referred for medication. At age 39 Ruth could be experiencing premenopausal symptoms, and feminist sensitivity to the misuse of this diagnosis should not blind the nonmedical practitioner to the fact that hormonal changes may elicit or exacerbate psychological symptoms. Ruth's reported unhappiness with her life could be her way of expressing symptoms of a major depression that could be helped by medication in addition to psychotherapy. Her panic attacks could result from a neurological problem.

If we rule out the possibilities just mentioned, Ruth presents a blending of neurotic symptoms and existential concerns. Her symptoms seem to be at a critical stage and could flower into an eating disorder; counterphobic impulsive behavior; any of the anxiety disorders; agoraphobia; a psychosomatic, conversion disorder; or depression. Her difficulties in establishing a sense of self suggest that her individuation is an important goal of treatment. I do not anticipate overtly psychotic symptoms, and Ruth's basic reality testing appears sufficiently stable that she can be expected to undergo some degree of regression in the course of treatment without danger of precipitating a psychotic break.

Key Issues and Themes in Working with Ruth

Intrapsychic conflicts and repression of childhood experiences. As a psychoanalytically oriented psychotherapist I accept the role of detective in ferreting out the secrets of the past that are locked away in Ruth's unconscious. Although I am guided by theory to suspicious content areas, Ruth's psyche and the secrets therein are uniquely hers, and it is ultimately she who will know the truth of her life through her own courage and perceptions.

I suspect that the psychosexual aspects of her relationships with her parents (and possibly her siblings) remain key conflict areas for her, even now. In the classical Freudian model of healthy development, she would have experienced early libidinal attraction to her father, which she would eventually have replaced with normal heterosexual interests in male peers; likewise, her feelings of rivalry with her mother for her father's affection would have been replaced with identification with her mother. In the ideal model, moreover, Ruth would have experienced rebellion against parental constraints, particularly during the developmental period associated with toilet training and also in adolescence.

In reality Ruth appears to have superficially avoided normal rebellion and to have repressed her sexuality except for adopting a wifely role with the first man she dated. Although she followed the format of using her mother as role model and having children by an acceptable husband, she apparently abdicated in the struggles of sexuality, rebellion, and identification, leaving these conflicts unresolved. Her conscious recollections of her parents are of a rigid, fundamentalist father and a "critical" mother. I would be interested in knowing what these parents were really like, as perceived by Ruth in childhood. How did her father handle his feelings for his children? Did his aloofness mask strongly suppressed incestuous feelings that she intuitively sensed? Were these ever acted out?

A Freudian view of the father's harsh reactions to Ruth's "playing doctor" would emphasize the Oedipus/Electra aspects of this father/daughter encounter. Her father's refusal to speak to her for weeks after this incident suggests jealousy rather than simply moral rejection of childhood sexual activity. This suspicion is supported by the parentally imposed isolation of the children that delayed dating until after high school. Ruth's attempts to win her father's approval by supplanting the role of mother (by caring for her younger siblings) is also consistent with these Oedipus/Electra dynamics. Ruth internalized her father's overtly negative attitude to sexuality.

If these hypotheses are correct, a theme in therapy will be Ruth's reexperiencing of the sensual aspects of her attachment to her father and his response to her. As she is able to first "own" these feelings and memories and then to relinquish the fantasy of fulfillment with her father, she can become open to an adult relationship in which her sexuality is appreciated rather than scorned or distorted.

Although there is no direct evidence of sexual abuse in the case material, the family dynamics are such that there is the possibility of actual incestual acts by the father, the memories of which have been repressed by Ruth. Even more likely is the pattern wherein the father's incestuous feelings were not overtly acted out but were so intense that he developed defenses of reaction formation and projection, labeling her sexuality (rather than his) as reprehensible. The jealous response of Ruth's mother is consistent with either of the above patterns of paternal behavior, but the mother's response is more pathological (and more pathogenic) if actual abuse occurred.

Oedipus/Electra feelings by both parent and child are considered part of normal development. However, intense conflicts and guilt regarding these feelings or experiences are very common in clients seeking counseling or psychotherapy, and all too often, actual molestation is eventually determined to have occurred.

Regardless of the details of the actual memories and buried feelings unearthed in the therapy, the analytic therapist is alert for indications of psychological traumas in the client's early life, psychic wounds that may be associated with a family *secret* that the client has needed to protect from exposure through suppression, denial, and repression. The probability of a secret being at the heart of Ruth's neurosis is increased by the indication in the case material that she was socially isolated and that her lack of relationships outside the family was enforced by the parents, at least in terms of dating. The entire family may have lived with their unspoken secrets in relative isolation. Although incestuous themes in one form or another are the most common secrets unearthed, other "unthinkable" secrets may be at the center of the repression—namely, the hidden mental illness, homosexuality, or alcoholism of a family member.

To what extent is Ruth bringing themes from her family of origin to her present family? She defines her husband only by what he is not (her father) and by his potential to reject her (as her father had rejected her). Does she know the man she married at all, or is he merely a stand-in for the real man in her life? Is her husband's apparent rejection of her attempts at personal growth a facet of his personality, or is he being set up? Her reaction to her daughter Jennifer may very likely be related to her own failure to rebel. Acceptance and nurturance by Ruth of the suppressed child-rebel aspect of herself may well improve her relationship with her daughter.

Symptoms and Psychodynamics

A psychoanalytic approach views psychological symptoms as active processes that give clues to client's underlying psychodynamics. Some acute symptoms are valuable in that they alert the client that something is wrong. Other symptoms, particularly when chronic, may be extremely resistant to intervention and may severely impair or even threaten the life of the client.

Ruth's symptoms (assuming that organic factors are absent or minimal) suggest compatibility with psychoanalytically oriented therapy. I would use analytic theory to help understand the role of anxiety in her life and the methods she uses to control her anxiety.

I view Ruth's current existential anxiety as related to these issues: Her early training by her parents clearly made individuation (in the object-relations sense) a very scary proposition for her; hence, any attempt toward individuation is anxiety-provoking for her. She is, therefore, terrified not only of acting impulsively but also of acting independently. She hopes to make her own choices in life but also hopes that her therapist will make her decisions for her.

Ruth's symptom of overeating probably gratifies her need for affection, but a psychoanalytic approach to this symptom would also explore its developmental origin. Oral gratification is the primary focus of libidinal energy in the earliest stage of development. Symptoms associated with this stage can appear if the client suffered deprivation during this period *or* if the period was relatively gratifying. If the symptom relates to early deprivation, the adult is fixated on getting the satisfaction never adequately obtained during the childhood stage. I am inclined to suspect that Ruth's overeating is regressive, and that she experienced her most satisfactory developmental stage in infancy when she may have been accepted by her mother and when her libidinal needs could be satisfied at her mother's breast without being labeled as "sexual" by her father. This hypothesis is supported by her having a relatively intact adult personality and a reasonable amount of ego strength. She is able to seek therapy for her needs to individuate without having had to exhibit the extreme problems in social living (suicide attempts, inability to maintain any relationship, and failure to tolerate the stresses of mothering) that are diagnostic of the borderline syndrome. Significant deprivation during the "pre-oedipal" stages of early childhood, particularly the oral stage, is associated, in analytic thinking, with psychosis, sociopathic character formation, and borderline/narcissistic personality disorders. Ruth's current mental status suggests problems at the later stages of development in which Oedipus/Electra dynamics are prominent. This distinction is relevant to her treatment in that the treatment of pre-oedipal conditions requires more deviation from traditional technique than does the treatment of neurotic states, which have their origins primarily in the later developmental stages.

Ruth's weight problem also has psychodynamic meaning. Being overweight may lead to her feeling sexually unattractive and, therefore, less likely to be faced with sexual arousal. To the degree that her morality is based on compliance with authority rather than on personal choice, she would be tempted by anyone demanding sex from an authoritative position. Moreover, her overweight may be directly related to Oedipus/Electra themes. She may be in some sense saving her sexuality for her father or for a fantasy hero who will break the spell cast by her father. If her overweight has been more severe since she began experiencing the "empty-nest" syndrome, her obesity may represent a symbolic pregnancy.

Ruth's increasing difficulty in leaving home suggests a fear of meeting others who might threaten the stability of her marriage. This symptom is consistent with the dynamics of her overweight.

The exacerbation of physical symptoms and anxiety is cited in the background information as being the catalyst for Ruth's seeking therapy at this time. A psychoanalytic approach to these symptoms would explore the "secondary gain" associated with each symptom. A symptom is expected to include elements of both sides of an intrapsychic conflict. For instance, a headache might serve to keep her sexually distant from her husband while also providing a pretext for avoiding social contacts that might threaten the marriage.

Analytic therapy provides a means for treating Ruth's symptoms, but only in the context of broader treatment of her psychological problems. Some psychosomatic, phobic, and eating disorders can be treated directly, and at lesser expense, by nonanalytic therapies. When the client wants understanding as well as symptom relief or when the "secondary gain" of the symptom leads to either failure of the direct approach or to the substitution of a new symptom for the old one, analytic therapy is indicated. Ruth gives evidence of multiple symptoms and of a desire to examine her life. Hence, consideration of analytic therapy rather than a symptom-focused behavioral approach is reasonable.

Treatment Techniques

Psychoanalytically oriented psychotherapy versus psychoanalysis. The treatment approach I propose for Ruth is psychoanalytically oriented psychotherapy rather than psychoanalysis. This choice does not indicate a theoretical disagreement with the methods of classic analysis; psychoanalytic psychotherapy is a form of analytic treatment that has advantages and disadvantages compared with classical psychoanalysis. In classical analysis the analyst adopts a "blank-screen" approach in which expressions of the real analyst/client relationship are minimized in order to promote development of the client's transference relationship with the analyst. Transference leads the client to react to the analyst as if he or she were a significant person from the client's past life.

Psychoanalytic therapy does not require the blank-screen approach, is less frustrating to the patient, allows the therapist more flexibility in technique, is less costly, may be shorter in duration, and provides "support" for the patient's least maladaptive defenses. Hence, it is often the treatment of choice. The drawbacks of analytic psychotherapy as compared with psychoanalysis are directly related to the advantages. The variations in technique lead to a lowering of expectations, as many aspects of the client's personality will remain unanalyzed due to elimination of the blank screen and the consequent intrusion of aspects of the "real" relationship between therapist and client into the analysis of their "as-if" transference relationship. If, for example, Ruth is in analysis with me, free-associating from the couch, and she states her belief that I disapprove of some feeling or behavior of hers, I can be reasonably sure that she is reacting to me as if I were some other figure in her life. In contrast, if she makes the same assertion in face-to-face psychotherapy, my actual nonverbal behavior (or prior self-disclosure of any sort) may have given her valid clues to my actual (conscious or unconscious) disapproval of her feeling or behavior. I can never know the exact degree to which her response is a transference response as opposed to a response to my "real" behavior in our "real" relationship. In psychoanalytically oriented psychotherapy with Ruth I must keep in mind that every aspect of our interaction will have a mix of "real" and "as-if" components. To the degree that I participate in the "real" relationship by providing support, by giving advice, or by sharing an opinion or personal experience, I am limiting my ability to maintain an analytic stance to the material she presents.

Although significant therapeutic work is possible using this model, I must be very sensitive to the meanings that Ruth will attribute to my "real" interactions with her. If I disapprove of a particular act or intention of hers, for example, I can reasonably expect her to assume that I approve of all her reported acts or intentions to which I have *not* expressed disapproval. Thus, although I am free to use the "real" as well as the "as-if" relationship in making therapeutic interventions, I am not free to vacillate in my therapeutic stance without risk of doing harm.

The therapeutic contract. I will form as clear a therapeutic contract as possible with Ruth, explaining the goals, costs, and risks of the treatment as well as briefly describing the methods and theory of psychotherapy. My expectations regarding payment will be made explicit, including the analytic rule that fees are charged for canceled sessions. This contractual clarity regarding fees has therapeutic implications in that Ruth's obligation to me for my services is specified at the outset of treatment. Thereafter, she can feel free of any additional requirement to meet my needs, and I can interpret any concerns that she does express about my needs in terms of the "as-if" relationship. As indicated in the assessment section above, the method by which she pays for the sessions is significant. Ideally, she should pay enough to be motivated to make good use of each hour, but she should not be placed under a financial strain that will create a hardship or precipitate a premature termination of treatment.

A treatment schedule of two or three sessions per week, each session lasting 50 minutes, is typical for psychoanalytically oriented therapy. Any planned vacations in the next six months or so, by either Ruth or me, should be noted, and therapy should not commence shortly before a vacation.

Other aspects of the contract include confidentiality (and its limitations), the degree to which I am available for emergencies or other between-session contacts, and an admonition to generally avoid making major life decisions during the course of treatment. The latter "rule" for clients in analysis is relevant to Ruth. She indicates that she wants a therapist to make decisions for her, and I have some concern about the possibility of her leaping to decisions while experiencing regression in the course of treatment.

Free association. Free association is a primary technique in psychoanalysis and is the "basic rule" given to clients. In my therapy with Ruth I will emphasize the technique of free association at certain times, such as when she comments that she doesn't know what to talk about. However, we will have verbal interaction in addition to her free associations, even in the early phases of therapy. She will often be instructed to express her associations to her dreams, to elements of her current life, and to memories of her past life, particularly new memories of childhood events that emerge in the course of treatment.

Dreams, symptoms, jokes, and slips. Dreams are considered the "royal road" to the unconscious, and I will encourage Ruth to report her dreams and to associate to them. As an analytically oriented therapist I will conceptualize each of her dreams as having two levels of meaning, the manifest content and the latent meaning. Analytic theory postulates that each dream is a coded message from Ruth's unconscious, a message that can be interpreted so as to understand the unconscious wish that initiated the dream and the nature of the repression that forced the wish to be experienced only in disguised form. Hypotheses about the latent meaning of dream symbols can be derived from theory, but the actual interpretation of Ruth's dream elements will be based on her own unique associations to her dream symbols.

In addition to dreams, the hidden meanings inherent in Ruth's symptoms are subject to analysis. Her presenting symptoms, manifestations of resistance, memories, and spontaneous errors (slips of the tongue) are clues to her underlying dynamics. The wordplay involved in slips of the tongue is meaningful, as may be any intentional joke or pun made or recalled by Ruth in a session.

Interpretations of resistance and content. My initial interpretations will be of resistance, and I will follow the rule of interpreting the resistance that Ruth presents relative to a content area before actually interpreting the content. I recognize that every accurate interpretation is an assault on her defenses, and I know that she will react to the interpretation as a threat to her present adjustment. Hence, in choosing the timing of a particular interpretation, I will be guided by her readiness to accept it as well as by my sense of its accuracy. I also follow the general rule that more inferential interpretations should be made in the later stages of therapy after a therapeutic alliance and trust have been established. Early interpretations should be minimally inferential, often only noting a correspondence. For example, commenting to Ruth that she wrote less in her autobiography about her mother than she did about her father is much less inferential than interpreting her overeating as a defense against sexuality.

Many interpretations, particularly in the later stages of therapy will relate to her transference reactions and will be geared to helping her work through childhood-based conflicts in the context of her therapeutic relationship with me.

Transference and countertransference. Ruth's experience in therapy will be both gratifying and frustrating. It will be gratifying in that we will spend each hour focusing on her life. Her needs, hopes, disappointments, dreams, fantasies, and everything else of importance to her are accepted as meaningful, and she need not share center stage with anyone else. It is her hour, and I listen to everything without criticizing her or demanding that she see anything my way or do anything to please me. My sustained, active attention to and interest in her are different from any other interpersonal interaction. Other people in her life insist on wanting things from her, or they want to criticize her, or, at the very least, they expect her to be as interested in them as they are in her.

But the sessions are also frustrating. She wants help, and all I seem to do is listen and occasionally ask a question or comment on what she has said. Do I like her? Or am I only pretending to be interested because that's what I am paid for? When, she wonders, will the therapy start helping? When will she find out how to resolve her issues about her marriage and her boring life?

Given this mixture of gratification and frustration, it is not surprising that she begins to see *me* as a source of both of those emotions. Moreover, it is not surprising that she will "transfer" onto me attributes of others in her life who have been sources of gratification and frustration to her. Hence, she begins to react to me as if I were her father, mother, or other significant figure.

The permissiveness of the sessions will also allow Ruth to regress—to feel dependent and childlike, and to express her thoughts and feelings with little censorship. I take almost all the responsibility for maintaining limits; she need only talk. Her regression is fostered to the degree that I maintain the classic analytic stance, and it is ameliorated to the degree that I interact with Ruth in terms of our "real" relationship—for example, by expressing empathy.

Ruth's past haunts her present life and interpersonal relationships, and, to an even greater degree, it haunts her relationship with me. But the distortions projected onto me exist in a controlled interpersonal setting and, therefore, are amenable to interpretation and resolution. The therapeutic session provides a structure in which the nature of her conflicts can be exposed and understood, not only in the sense of intellectual insight but also in the analysis of their actual impact on Ruth's perceptions and feelings about me and the therapeutic relationship.

The therapeutic relationship provides gratification and frustration for the therapist as well as for the client. My therapeutic task includes monitoring not only the content of the sessions but also my feelings that grow out of this relationship. There are aspects of Ruth that I will like and others that I will dislike. I will find her dependency both appealing and irritating. I will enjoy the positive attributes she projects onto me, and I will experience some hurt when she projects negative attributes onto me. Nevertheless, I must minimize indulgence in these reactions and concentrate instead on ensuring that my participation consistently promotes her self-understanding and individuation. Although she is free to demand anything and everything from me, I must deny myself almost all the rewards of a "real" relationship with her.

Understanding the theory of therapeutic techniques helps me keep my perspective, as does recollection of my own therapy. The therapy I have received is useful to me in understanding the psychotherapeutic experience from the client's point of view, and it helps me understand some of my conflicts that could impair my effectiveness as a therapist. Nevertheless, my adherence to the ideal role will be imperfect. To some extent I will inadvertently let my feelings and conflicts distort my perceptions of Ruth. My distortions will include my projecting onto her attributes of significant figures in my own life; I will experience countertransference. Although I can minimize countertransference, it can never be eliminated. Therefore, to minimize the negative impact of my countertransference on Ruth's treatment, I will monitor my feelings, positive and negative, about her, and I will periodically discuss my treatment of her, including these feelings, with a trusted colleague. Voluntary consultation about my feelings and interventions is, in my opinion, an effective method for assessing and minimizing deleterious effects of countertransference. If I find myself uncomfortable discussing a particular aspect of Ruth's treatment, I suspect countertransference is at work. Consultations must be conducted so as to protect her confidentiality; this usually includes her releasing of the information by her and my altering information about her identity during the consultation.

My scrutiny of my countertransference reactions to Ruth may be of value in helping me understand her; often my unconscious reactions to a patient give clues to that patient's dynamics and to the reactions that others have to the patient. Countertransference can be used in the service of the therapy if it can be understood and controlled. My monitoring of my countertransference feelings serves as a major source of clinical information about the client. If I were to find my countertransference to be having a significant negative effect on Ruth's treatment, I would, after consultation, enter therapy myself and either refer her to a colleague or continue to treat her under supervision.

Some aspects of countertransference may be partially inseparable from the conscious motivation of the therapist to engage in the arduous work of psychotherapy. As I work actively with Ruth to break the spell cast on her in her past, I apply my understanding of the nature of the spell and of the "magic" needed to break it. As I engage in this struggle, I run the countertransference risk of becoming invested in the hero role, thereby fostering her dependence and prolonging her regression. But to some extent I have opted for this role by choosing the profession of psychotherapist. Thus, by participating in Ruth's life as the hero she has dreamed of, I am fulfilling my own not-so-unconscious needs. But if I am to stay a hero in the sense of being a good therapist, I must renounce the role of hero to Ruth at precisely the moment in therapy in which I have released her from the past's constricting spell.

JERRY COREY'S WORK WITH RUTH FROM A PSYCHOANALYTIC PERSPECTIVE

Basic Assumptions

As I work with Ruth within a psychoanalytic framework, I am guided by both the *psychosexual perspective* of Sigmund Freud and the *psychosocial perspective* of Erik Erikson. My work with her is also influenced to some extent by contemporary psychoanalytic trends, which are often classified in terms of ego psychology and object-relations theory. I am moving beyond Freud to illustrate that contemporary psychoanalysis is an ever-evolving system rather than a closed and static model.

The psychosexual theory, as seen in traditional Freudian psychoanalysis, places emphasis on the internal conflicts of an individual during the first six years of life. This theory assumes that certain sexual and aggressive impulses are repressed during these formative years, because if they were to become conscious, they would produce extreme anxiety. Although these memories and experiences are buried in the unconscious, they exert a powerful influence on the individual's personality and behavior later in life.

The psychosocial theory, developed primarily by Erikson, emphasizes sociocultural influences on the development of personality. It assumes that there is a continuity in human development. At the various stages of life we face the challenge of establishing an equilibrium between ourselves and our social world. At each crisis or turning point, in the life cycle we can either successfully resolve our conflicts or fail to resolve them. Failure to resolve a conflict at a given stage results in fixation, or the experience of being stuck. It is difficult to master the psychosocial tasks of adulthood if we are psychologically stuck with unresolved conflicts from an earlier period of development. Although such a failure does not necessarily doom us to remain forever the victim of fixations, our lives are, to a large extent, the result of the choices we make at these stages.

The more recent work in the *psychoanalytic approach* is represented by the writings of Margaret Mahler, Heinz Kohut, and Otto Kernberg, among others. Contemporary psychoanalytic practice emphasizes the origins and transformations of the self, the differentiation between the self and others, the integration of the self with others, and the influence of critical factors in early development on later development. Predictable developmental sequences are noted in which the early experiences of the self shift in relation to an expanding awareness of others. Once self/other patterns are established, they influence later interpersonal relationships. Human development can best be thought of as the evolution of the way in which individuals differentiate self from others. One's current behavior in this work is largely a repetition of the internal patterning during one of the earlier stages of development.

In viewing Ruth's case I make the assumption that her early development is of critical importance and that her current personality problems are rooted in repressed childhood conflicts. Borrowing from Kohut's thinking, I surmise that she was psychologically wounded during childhood and that her defensive structure is an attempt to avoid being wounded again. I expect to find an interweaving of old hurts with new wounds. Thus, I pay attention to the consistency between her emotional wounding as a child and those situations that result in pain for her today. Much of our therapeutic work is aimed at repairing the original wounding.

The work of repairing early wounds takes time. Therefore, I expect to see Ruth at least a couple of times a week for a minimum of three years. One of the reasons that therapy will take so long is that it entails a reliving of early childhood memories and events and that, for it to be effective, the client must do some basic reorientation. I am interested in a characterological, or structural, change in Ruth, not in mere problem solving or in removal of symptoms. I see therapy as an uncovering process that delves into repressed experiences. I assume that for many years a person such as Ruth has been storing away conflicts, intense feelings, and other impulses. Even though she may not be conscious of it, these repressed feelings influence her current behavior. It would also be important to pay attention to the social and cultural factors influencing her present struggles.

I make many of these assumptions before meeting a client. The psychoanalytic perspective on the developmental process provides me with a conceptual framework that helps me make sense of an individual's current functioning. Although I do not force my client to fit this theoretical mold, I do make certain general assumptions about the normal sequence of human development.

Assessment of Ruth

The following assessment is based on a few initial sessions with Ruth, her intake form, and her autobiography. Her relationships with her parents are critically important from a therapeutic standpoint. She describes her father as "distant, authoritarian, and rigid." My hunch is that this view of her father colors how she perceives all men today, that her fear of displeasing her husband is connected to her fear of bringing her father displeasure, and that what she is now striving to get from her husband is related to what she wanted from her father. I expect that she will view me and react to me in many of the same ways she responded to her father. Through this transference relationship with me she will be able to recognize connecting patterns between her childhood behavior and her current struggles. For example, she is fearful of displeasing her husand, John, for fear he might leave. If he did, there would be a repetition of the pattern of her father's psychological abandonment of her after she had not lived up to his expectations. She does not stand up to John or ask for what she needs out of fear that he will become disgruntled and abandon her. She is defending herself against being wounded by him in some of the same ways that she was by her father.

From a psychosexual perspective I am interested in Ruth's early childhood experiences in which she developed her personal sexuality. Her father's response when he caught her in an act of sexual experimentation needs to be considered as we work with her present attitudes and feelings about sex. As a child and adolescent she felt guilty and ashamed over her sexual feelings. She internalized many of her father's strict views of sexuality. Because her father manifested a negative attitude toward her increased sexual awareness, she learned that her sexual feelings were evil, that her body and sexual pleasure were both "dirty," and that her curiosity about sexual matters was unacceptable. Her sexual feelings became anxiety provoking and were thus rigidly controlled. The denial of sexuality that was established at this age has been carried over into her adult life and gives rise to severe conflicts, guilt, remorse, and self-condemnation. Like Dr. Blau, I have a hunch that her weight problem is partially associated with her denial of sexuality. She does not allow herself to experience sexual attraction to men, nor does she allow herself to enjoy a sexual relationship with her husband. If she is not physically and sexually attractive either to herself or to others, she will not have to deal with anxiety.

Viewing Ruth from a psychosocial perspective will shed considerable light on the nature of her present psychological problems. As an infant she never really developed a basic trust in the world. She learned that she could not count on others to provide her with a sense of being wanted and loved. Throughout her early childhood she did not receive affection, a deprivation that now makes it difficult for her to feel that she is worthy of affection. The task of early childhood is developing *autonomy,* which is necessary if one is to gain a measure of self-control and any ability to cope with the world. In Ruth's case she grew up fast, was never allowed to be a child, and was expected to take care of her younger brother and sisters. Although she seemed to be "mature" even as a child, in actuality she never became autonomous.

Ruth will not feel truly independent until she feels properly attached and dependent. This notion means that to be independent, one must be able to depend on others. Ruth, however, never felt a genuine sense of attachment to her father, whom she perceived as distant, or to her mother, whom she viewed as somewhat rejecting. For Ruth to have developed genuine independence, she would have needed others in her life whom she could count on for emotional support. But this support was absent from her background. During the school-age period she felt inferior in social relationships, was confused about her sex-role identity, and was unwilling to face new challenges. During adolescence she did not experience an identity crisis, because she did not ask basic questions of life. Rather than questioning the values that had been taught to her, she compliantly accepted them. In part, she has followed the design established by her parents when she was an adolescent. She was not challenged to make choices for herself or to struggle to find meaning in life. In her adulthood she managed to break away from her fundamentalist religion, yet she could not free herself of her guilt over this act. She is still striving for her father's approval, and she is still operating without a clearly defined set of values to replace the ones she discarded. A major theme of her life is her concern over how to fill the void that she fears will result when her children leave home.

Psychoanalytic theory provides a useful perspective for understanding the ways in which Ruth is trying to control the anxiety in her life. As one of her primary ego defenses she readily accepted her parents' rigid morality, because it served the function of controlling her impulses. Further, there is a fundamental split within her between the "good girl" and the "bad girl." Either she keeps in control of herself and others by doing things for them, or she gets out of control when she enjoys herself, as she did when she was "playing doctor." She feels in control when she takes care of her children, and she does not know what she will do once they leave home. Coupled with this empty-nest syndrome is her ambivalence about leaving the security of the home by choosing a career. This change brings about anxiety because she is struggling with her ability to direct her own life as opposed to defining herself strictly as a servant of others. This anxiety will be a focal point of therapy.

Goals of Therapy

The goal of our analytically oriented work will be to gradually uncover unconscious material. In this way Ruth will be able to use messages from the unconscious to direct her own life instead of being driven by her defensive controls. Therapy is aimed at the promotion of integration and ego development. The various parts of her self that she has denied will become more connected. The ideal type of identity is an autonomous self, which is characterized by self-esteem and self-confidence, capable of intimacy with others.

Therapeutic Procedures

I suspect that a major part of our work will entail dealing with resistance, at least at the start of therapy. In spite of the fact that Ruth has come to therapy voluntarily, any number of barriers will make her progress slow at times.

She has learned to protect herself against anxiety by building up defenses over the years, and she will not quickly surrender them. As we have seen, some of her primary defenses are repression and denial. The chances are that she will have some ambivalence about becoming aware of her unconscious motivations and needs. Merely gaining insight into the nature of her unconscious conflicts does not mean that her therapy is over, for the difficult part will be the exploration and working through of these conflicts.

I mentioned earlier that therapy would be a long process. One of the reasons is that much of our time will be devoted to exploring Ruth's reactions to me. I expect that I will become a significant figure in her life, for I assume that she will develop strong feelings toward me, both positive and negative. She will probably relate to me in some of the same ways that she related to her father. Working therapeutically with this transference involves two steps. One is to foster this development of transference; the second consists of working through patterns that she established with significant others in her past as these feelings emerge toward me in the therapy relationship. This second step is the core of the therapy process. *Working through* refers to repeating interpretations of her behavior and overcoming her resistance, thus allowing her to resolve her neurotic patterns. Although I do not use a blank-screen model, keeping myself mysterious and hidden, in this type of intensive therapy the client is bound to expect me to fulfill some of her unmet needs. She will probably experience again some of the same feelings she had during her childhood. How she views me and reacts to me will constitute much of the therapy work, for this transference material is rich with meaning and can tell her much about herself.

In addition to working with her resistances and with any transference that develops in our relationship, I will probably use a variety of other techniques to get at Ruth's unconscious dynamics. Dream analysis is an important procedure for uncovering unconscious material and giving her insight into some areas of unresolved problems. She will be asked to recall her dreams, to report them in the sessions, and then to learn how to free-associate to key elements in them. Free association, a major procedure in our therapy, involves asking her to clear her mind of thoughts and preoccupations and to say whatever pops into her head without censoring, regardless of how silly or trivial it may be. This procedure typically leads to some recollection of past experiences and, at times, to a release of bottled-up feelings. Another major technique at my disposal is interpretation, or pointing out and explaining to Ruth the meanings of behavior manifested by her dreams, her free-association material, her resistances, and the nature of our relationship. Timed properly, these interpretations (or teachings) can help her assimilate new learning and uncover unconscious material more rapidly. This, in turn, will help her understand and deal with her life situation more effectively.

The Therapeutic Process

The crux of my therapeutic work with Ruth consists of bringing her past into the present, which is done mainly through exploring the transference relationship. My aim is to do more than merely facilitate recall of past events and insight on her part; instead, I hope that she will see patterns and a continuity in her life from her childhood to the present. When she realizes how her past is still operating, character change is possible, and new options open up for her.

Elements of the process

Exploring Ruth's transference. After Ruth has been in therapy for some time, she grows more disenchanted with me because she does not see me as giving enough. For instance, she becomes irritated because I am not willing to share anything about my marriage or my relationships with my children. She says that I give her very analytical responses, when she is simply trying to get to know something about me personally. She complains that she is the one doing all the giving and that she is beginning to resent it. Here is a brief sample of a session in which we talk about these feelings:

RUTH: I want you to be more of a real person to me. It feels uncomfortable for you to know so much about me, when I know so little about you.

JERRY: Yes, it's certainly the case that I know a lot more about your life than you know about mine and that you're more vulnerable than I am.

RUTH: Well, you seem so removed and distant from me. You're hard to reach. This is not easy for me to say . . . uhm . . . I suppose I want to know what you really think of me. You don't tell me, and I'm often left wondering what you're feeling. I work hard at getting your approval, but I'm not sure I have it. I get the feeling that you think I'm bad.

JERRY: Has anyone else made you feel like this?

RUTH: Well, ah . . . you know that I always felt this way around my father. No matter what I did to get his approval, I was never really successful. And that's sometimes the way I feel toward you.

I am consciously not disclosing much about my reactions to Ruth at this point because she is finally bringing out feelings about me that she has avoided for so long. I encourage her to express more about the ways in which she sees me as ungiving and unreachable and as not being what she wants. It is through this process of exploring some of her persistent reactions to me, I hope, that she will see more of the connection between her unfulfilled needs from the past and how she is viewing me in this present relationship. At this stage in her therapy she is experiencing some very basic feelings of wanting to be special and wanting proof of it. By working over a long period with her transference reactions, she will eventually gain insight into how she has given her father all the power to affirm her as a person and how she has not learned to give herself the approval she so much wants from him. I am not willing to reassure her, because I want to foster the expression of transference.

Working with Ruth's internalized mother. At another period in Ruth's therapy we spend many sessions exploring her relationship to her mother. We focus on how she felt toward her mother as a child and how she feels toward her now. As a child Ruth attempted to become to her father what her mother was, but she never managed to replace her mother in her father's eyes. She tried by becoming "mother" to her younger brother and sisters and by working as hard as she could for recognition. But this was to no avail, for she did not get the recognition that she wanted from either her father or her mother. Much later in her sessions we explore the parallels between her giving to her brother and sisters and the way in which she has devoted much of her adult life to giving to her own children, only to feel a lack of appreciation and recognition for her efforts at being a good mother.

Process commentary

I am not working with Ruth from the perspective of classical psychoanalysis. Rather, I am drawing from psychosocial theory and from concepts in the newer psychoanalytic thinking, especially from Kohut's work. I direct much of our therapy to the exploration of Ruth's old issues, her early wounding, and her fears of new wounds. The bruises to her self that she experiences in the here and now trigger memories of her old hurts. Especially in her relationship with me, she is sensitive to rejection and any signs of my disapproval. Therefore, much of our therapeutic effort is aimed at dealing with the ways in which she is now striving for recognition as well as the ways in which she attempted to get recognition as a child. In short, she has a damaged self, and she is susceptible to and fearful of further bruising. We discuss her attachments, how she tried to win affection, and the many ways in which she is trying to protect herself from suffering further emotional wounds to a fragile ego.

As Ruth's therapy progresses, she is able to let more material rise to consciousness. We focus on the conflicts between her id (the impulsive and "spoiled-brat" side of her personality, which craves indulgence in physical gratification immediately), and her superego (her conscience and all the morals and standards that she has incorporated into her self-system). It is obvious that Ruth has an extremely strong superego, one that is based on some unrealistically high standards of perfection and that punishes with guilt. Through her therapy, I hope, she will learn to relax the boundaries of her superego so that she will not be controlled by its demands for perfection.

Much of Ruth's work involves going back to early events in her life—recalling them and the feelings associated with them—in the hope that she can be free from the restrictions of her past. She comes to realize that her past is an important part of her and that some old wounds will take a long time to heal.

One of the major ways in which Ruth gains insight into her patterns is by learning to understand her dreams. We regularly focus on their meanings, and she free-associates to some symbols. She has a very difficult time giving up control and simply allowing herself to say freely whatever comes to mind in these sessions. She worries about "saying the appropriate thing," and of course this is material we examine in the sessions. Dream work is one of the major tools to tap her unconscious processes.

Ruth also discovers from the way she responds to me some key connections between how she related to significant people in her life. She looks to me in some of the same ways that she looked to her father for approval and for love. I encourage her recollection of feelings associated with these past events, so that she can work through barriers that are preventing her from functioning as a mature adult.

Questions for Reflection

As you continue working with the nine therapeutic approaches described in this book, you will have many opportunities to apply the basic assumptions and key concepts of each theory to your own life. Some of the questions below will assist you in becoming more involved in a personal way. The rest of the questions are designed to give you some guidance in beginning to work with Ruth. They are intended to help you clarify your reactions to how the consultant and I worked with her from each of the therapeutic perspectives. Select the questions for reflection that most interest you:

1. Dr. Blau emphasizes the importance of understanding the "whys" of a client's experience and behavior. What advantages and disadvantages do you see in this focus?
2. Dr. Blau suggests that the psychosexual aspects of Ruth's relationships with her parents, and possibly her siblings, still represent key conflict areas in her present behavior. In what ways may her early experiences be having a significant impact on her life today? How might you explore these dynamics with her?
3. Do you share the emphasis of this approach on the importance of Ruth's father in her life? How might you go about exploring with her the ways in which conflicts with her father are related to some of her present conflicts?
4. Reflecting on your own childhood, what do you consider to be some significant events that still have an impact on your life today? (How did you get approval or disapproval? How much trust did you feel

toward significant people in your life? What attitudes did you develop toward sex? How were your dependency needs met?)

5. Do you think that your relationships with your mother or father influence your life today, especially the ways in which you relate to significant women and men? What might you not have received from either parent that you are now seeking from other people?
6. What is one of the most significant themes (from the analytic perspective) that you would focus on in your sessions with Ruth?
7. How might you respond to Ruth if she challenged you over your aloofness and your unwillingness to give of yourself personally? Might you become defensive if she compared you to her father and accused you of being just like him? If you were more revealing, how do you expect that your therapy would be any different with her?
8. In what ways would you encourage Ruth to go back and relive her childhood? How important is delving into the client's early childhood in leading to personality change?
9. What defenses do you see in Ruth? How do you imagine you would work to lessen these defenses?
10. Dr. Blau discusses the importance of both the therapist's "real" relationship and the "as if" relationship with Ruth. How might you differentiate between her transference reactions and her "real" reactions to you?

MOE: A PASSIVE/AGGRESSIVE CLIENT WHO WANTS TO ESCAPE WITH ALCOHOL

Moe has been in therapy with me for a year. Besides describing his character and what he is doing in therapy, I will give a running commentary explaining why I am proceeding as I am and clarifying what is occurring between us.

Some Background Data

Moe, who is 37 years old, originally became involved in analytically oriented therapy with me on the recommendation of his physician. It was clear to the physician that he had a major drinking problem, which was a manifestation of more deeply rooted personality problems. Initially, he resisted seeing himself as a "problem drinker," let alone a confirmed alcoholic. After an intake session I gave him a tentative general diagnosis of *substance use disorder,* with a more specific diagnosis of *alcohol abuse* and *alcohol dependence.* As an adjunct to his treatment in individual therapy with me he agreed to join Alcoholics Anonymous, which he now continues in by his choice. In AA he has learned that his drinking controls him and that he is an alcoholic.

So far in therapy we have done a lot of reviewing of Moe's early childhood years, which were rather traumatic. His mother died when he was 10, and his father sent him to a private boarding school in another state, for he was sure that he could not manage to bring up Moe by himself. He felt abandoned by both his parents: by his mother, who died and left him, and by his father just when he most needed love, companionship, and support.

Moe has had three marriages, each of which ended when his wife left. Typically, each woman grew tired of his continual drinking binges and all that went with his alcoholism: getting fired from job after job, not being a father to his children, being abusive both verbally and physically to her, and being extremely dependent on her. Moe decided that he did not have what it took to keep a wife, and he grew increasingly bitter toward women. They *all* left him when he was most in need of them. Clearly, one of his conflicts is his dependency on women and his hostility toward them.

In his work life Moe feels a great deal of anger toward a former boss who fired him from his executive position in a business firm. He has complained that, when "I was broke, financially and personally, my boss took my job away from me instead of giving me the support I needed." In Moe's eyes important men always let him down. His father sent him away, and his boss sent him away; what few male friends he did have broke contact with him, mainly because they felt put off by his drinking.

Moe has many ambivalent feelings toward me, which we have been working on in our sessions. He feels a liking and respect for me, and he says he needs me. He also feels hostility, fears letting himself "become dependent" on me, and in many ways is constantly defying me and testing me to see if I will be like other men in his life. We are now working on his *resistance* and his feelings toward me.

Highlights of Moe's Therapy

My goals in working with Moe. Thinking within the analytic framework, I see psychotherapy as a process that should foster major character changes in Moe. This reconstruction will be accomplished by assisting him to become aware of his unconscious needs and motives. Examples of some of his unconscious dynamics are his dependency on strong women to take care of him and his conflicts with his bosses, whom he views as authority figures. My focus will be on using therapeutic methods designed to open the doors to his unconscious processes. I work on the assumption that it is necessary to recall and relive early childhood memories and experiences. These experiences will be reconstructed, discussed, interpreted, and analyzed with the aim of significantly changing his personality. Although I do not want to direct the entire focus of therapy toward his drinking, it will be imperative that we deal with his alcoholism. There will be a focus on the unconscious motivations and dynamics associated with his drinking as well as with some of his other passive/aggressive and highly dependent character traits. As Moe and I continue our sessions, I identify and diagnose him as a passive/aggressive client who is using alcohol as one of his major defenses and escape mechanisms.

To unlock Moe's unconscious, I focus on past experiences, such as the impact of his mother's death on him, his being sent away to a private boarding school, and other occasions when he felt a sense of abandonment and rejection. I pay special attention to linking these traumatic situations and feelings from the past with present situations. Working with some of his reactions toward me and his expectations of me, I help him gradually acquire self-understanding.

Moe begins to learn about his ego defenses. Moe is gradually developing some insights into the typical defenses he uses to deal with anxiety. He is acquiring this understanding through talking about subjects that he typically avoids and through my interpretations. I am attempting to teach him the meaning of certain patterns of behavior by pointing out significant connections between dreams and his everyday behavior, by working with his resistances, and by exploring early events with him. For example, Moe will need to recognize that he typically numbs his feelings of sadness. By denial and avoidance he attempts to deaden himself to the hurt and abandonment he felt first as a child, when his mother died, and later as an adult, when his wives divorced him. He does this most strikingly by drinking. Moe is beginning to understand that *denial* is a way in which he has continued to deceive himself and thus ward off anxiety. In particular, his alcoholism is a fact that he has denied; he has kept himself from looking at his inability to handle alcohol by placing blame on others and looking to external events for his personal failures. If reality is too painful for him to accept, he typically ignores it.

Working with Moe's alcoholism. Moe is a chemically dependent person. It would be a mistake to treat only his symptoms while ignoring the chemical dependency itself. Theoretically, I view the dynamics of his alcoholism as a fixation at an infantile level (oral stage). He is still unconsciously striving to be loved and taken care of in a way that is more appropriate to an infant. Part of my role with Moe will be to assist him in developing insight into the connection between many of his personality problems and his addiction to alcohol. As is true for most alcoholics, he feels socially isolated, unable to love others or receive love from them; he feels chronic guilt; he experiences depression and self-pity frequently; and he feels frightened in interpersonal relationships. Alcohol, a depressant drug, probably promotes or deepens the depression that Moe experiences. Sexual dysfunctions are common among alcoholics, as are broken marriages. Eventually, Moe will have to be confronted in a caring and concerned manner with his alcoholism. He is continuing his drinking even though he is in treatment. At this point he is using excuses, rationalization, denial, and minimizations. If I am well versed in the alcoholic's confused system of beliefs, all of these defenses can be effectively dealt with and eventually turned around and used as information leading to insight on Moe's part. Yet timing is critical. At this point he is not likely to "hear" interpretations pertaining to his alcoholism, so we begin with the exploration of issues that are less threatening for him to consider. Eventually, however, his problem of chemical dependency will need to be thoroughly dealt with in therapy. It is a good sign that Moe has agreed to attend AA meetings. I think it would be a helpful adjunct to his therapy with me if he continued attending these meetings. There is no reason why we cannot work on the problem of his chemical dependency and his underlying personality problems at the same time.

Procedures and Techniques Used with Moe

Keep in mind that the techniques I employ with Moe are part of the framework of psychoanalytically oriented therapy (rather than psychoanalysis). The techniques of free association, dream analysis, interpretation and analysis of resistance, and interpretation of the transference relationship are all routes to bringing out unconscious dynamics. The assumption is that the main way for Moe to change is to acquire insight and to work through places in his life where he got stuck. This is a relatively slow process that demands both patience and commitment.

Free association. A basic tool for uncovering repressed material is free association, which consists of expressing whatever comes to mind, regardless of how painful, illogical, or irrelevant it may seem. At times I might begin a session with a free-association exercise that goes something as follows:

JERRY: Moe, I'd like you to close your eyes and try to clear your mind for a time. Let yourself say aloud whatever comes to your mind. Try not to make any sense out of what you're saying; just report any reactions, thoughts, and feelings you're experiencing. Simply flow with your words with as little censorship as possible.

The purpose of this exercise is to encourage Moe to become more spontaneous and to uncover unconscious processes. During this time I pay attention to patterns in his associations, especially noting areas where he tends to block or censor. In one session, for example, it is evident that he is censoring any information pertaining to the times he physically abused his wife in each of his marriages. This blocking is important to interpret and analyze. I am interested in identifying the patterns and themes that become apparent through his therapy sessions. I simply listen carefully to what he is saying, how he is saying it, and what he is not saying. I may use this free-association technique with a particular word, especially when he makes a significant "slip." For example, in one session Moe inadvertently refers to his "Mother" when he is talking about one of his former wives. Using this as a clue, I ask him to free-associate to the word *mother.* His associations are "Never there . . . strong . . . doesn't care . . . all alone . . . [a long pause] lonely . . . dead and gone" [another pause, and he begins sobbing].

Following up on Moe's slip leads him to uncover some painful feelings toward his mother, which provide therapeutic material. This example shows that the free-association process may lead to a recall of past experiences that release intense feelings, which can then be explored in depth. In a later session we come back to explore the implications of Moe's slip in referring to his ex-wife as "Mother." This leads to a series of discussions of his dependency on and resentment of women.

Working with Moe's dreams. I am extremely interested in Moe's dreams, for I see them as a rich avenue to tapping his unconscious wishes, fears, conflicts, needs, desires, and impulses. At times, he is reluctant to report his dreams, saying that he has "forgotten" them or that he has not been dreaming lately. Sometimes he does bring in a dream, and my task is to work with him to uncover its disguised meaning by studying the symbols involved. Again, when it is appropriate, I attempt to teach him about himself and his current conflicts through interpreting the meanings of his dreams. The following excerpts represent the manner in which we work.

Moe reports a dream in which several large women are chasing him with clubs. He is frightened that they will catch him and beat him to a pulp. They get closer to him, he trips . . . Then he wakes up in a panic.

I ask Moe to free-associate with every element in the dream, even though every aspect is not necessarily symbolic. His associations to this dream are as follows:

MOE: I'm afraid of those big clubs. They have thorns on them, and if I get hit, that could be it for me! Where can I run to and hide? I'm afraid I can't run fast enough, that I'll get caught and they'll hurt me. These women seem to hate me, and they want to do me in! I feel so helpless and scared. This is the way I felt so often when I was a child. I felt that I'd get hurt, and nobody would be around to protect me. I'm afraid I'll make a mistake, that I'll trip up, and that my mother will punish me by beating me. I tried to do my best, but I was always afraid I'd do the wrong thing and get hit. I remember wishing that my father would protect me, but he just looked the other way.

From these associations Moe begins to understand the meaning of his dream: "The women are my mother and other strong and oppressive women in my life who have the power and desire to hurt me. Nobody will protect me from the wrath of women!"

His dream contains interesting symbolism, which he avoids and which I choose not to interpret at this stage of his therapy. It seems to me that clear oedipal themes are being expressed unconsciously in his dream. Yet I need to be careful of introducing an interpretation or material that he does not seem ready to consider as being part of him. Even though I don't share with him my interpretation of the oedipal content of his dream, I do keep this in the background, and it provides me with more clues to some of his struggles. Moreover, it should be emphasized that I do not rely on one dream to uncover meaningful connections between his past and his present struggles. A dream is an additional resource for learning about his psychodynamics. Taken in conjunction with other material, it can provide clues to solving a puzzle.

I should add that dream analysis is not a simple matter, and the therapist needs to know a great deal about the client's life to accurately interpret a given dream. It takes years of clinical experience and study to explore dreams from a psychoanalytic perspective.

Working with Moe's resistance. Resistance is Moe's way of avoiding opening the doors to unconscious material. Thus, a basic technique in analytic therapy is interpreting these avoidance patterns so that the client can begin to work through these barriers. Moe understands that his resistances are something to be understood and worked with in therapy, for they are ways of learning about some painful reality in his past.

Some manifestations of Moe's resistance that I have observed are:

- not remembering many of his dreams
- avoiding exploring sexual and aggressive themes in his dreams
- "forgetting" to show up for some appointments
- being late to some sessions
- talking about superficial topics
- his failure to pay some of his bills on time
- his insistence at times that I tell him what to talk about in the session
- his typical style of looking outside of himself for reasons to justify any failures on his part
- attending a session drunk

I see avoidance behavior, in whatever form it may take, as part of Moe's defenses against the anxiety that is aroused in him when he gets close to unconscious content. How do I deal with his resistances? First of all, they are not just something to be overcome. Both he and I need to recognize that his resistances are valuable indications of his defenses against anxiety, and they need to be understood and worked with. Generally, I call attention to the more readily observable resistances and work with these behaviors first. I take care not to criticize him, for that would be likely to increase his resistance. Also, I do not make dogmatic pronouncements, telling him what a certain pattern of behavior means; instead, I ask him to think for himself about some of these patterns and what they may indicate.

Working with our relationship. As I mentioned earlier, Moe's reactions to me represent a rich resource for understanding conflicts that stem from relationships to significant people in his past. At times he treats me in many ways as a father figure—sometimes, the father he feels he had and, at other times, the father he wishes he had as a child.

Moe goes through a period of several months expecting me to "kick him out" of therapy. He feels that because he has not been a cooperative and ideal patient, I will abandon him by refusing to see him in therapy any longer. Of course, there is a connection between what he experienced with his father and what he fears he will experience with me. We work in depth on these feelings that I will not be there when he needs me, sorting out what this means to him. We also explore some of his expectations and needs of me. In a very hostile way he continues asserting that I would not have the slightest interest in being with him if I were not being paid for the relationship. He feels resentment that he has to pay high fees to be listened to and cared about. We explore the reality of this situation as well as some of his own narcissism relating to his expectation that he be cared about unconditionally on his terms. He continues thinking that I am not providing enough direction and that merely letting him struggle will not get him anywhere. I agree that I provide little structure, telling him that this is part of my therapy approach. Instead, I deal with his reactions toward being in a situation in which I will not meet his demands and in which he has to decide what to bring up in his sessions.

We are devoting much of our time in current sessions to exploring Moe's dependency on me, which is primarily manifested by his wanting me to make important decisions for him. He looks to me for advice on how to proceed in life; when such advice is not forthcoming, he typically reacts with some hostile remark. He also has loving feelings for me, which are frightening to him. He is learning that he denies these positive feelings at times, so that he can remain angry.

Most of Moe's resistances that emerge from the sessions are an unconscious attempt to set me up to dislike him and ultimately to reject him. This follows the pattern of his significant relationships in the past. Related to his resistive behavior is the importance of maintaining my own objectivity. I must not get caught up in my own feelings and counterdefensive reactions toward him. If I get entangled in countertransference (my own defensive reactions that are a manifestation of my unconscious conflicts), I miss opportunities to help him work through places where he is now stuck. By remaining objective and not overreacting personally to his behavior, I am able to foster his transference toward me so that we can analyze and interpret it. His reactions to me provide rich clues to the ways in which he was emotionally wounded as a child and to how much of his current behavior is unconsciously aimed at defending him against being wounded again.

Paradoxically, the very thing that Moe wants to avoid—being rejected and abandoned—he is unconsciously repeating. The difficult and time-consuming part of our therapy consists of his gradually becoming aware of ways in which he is replicating earlier interpersonal relationships. Once he gains insight into how he is bringing his past into present relationships in a self-defeating way, we will have to work through these barriers to his growth. In an early session, for example, Moe disclosed to me his appreciation for how much I had done for him and how much I meant to him. After expressing his affection and respect for me he seemed very embarrassed and then made some indirect and sarcastic remarks. The next session he showed up 30 minutes late and drunk. The following week we dealt at length with his having appeared for his appointment drunk. He expressed his fear that I had judged him and had decided that he was a worthless person with no hope of getting better. Instead, I confronted him with what he had done and then explored with him the meaning of his behavior. I did not judge him as a worthless person, and I did not abandon him, even though on some levels he was setting me up to do so, as he had set up other significant people to criticize and eventually leave him.

By staying focused on the unconscious meanings of Moe's behavior and by not reacting to him in negative ways that he is used to from past experiences, I am teaching him that there can be a new ending to certain life dramas. Thus, in this transference situation we have the basis for him to learn new lessons about interpersonal relationships. He is acquiring the ability to perceive people differently than he perceived his parents.

I see Moe as a very dependent person, one who is looking for me to "feed" him. In his childhood he was deprived of the love and guidance he so much needed. Now in this relationship with me he is hoping that I will meet some of his infantile needs by protecting him, reassuring him, telling him that he is a special patient, approving of him, recognizing any progress he makes in therapy, and in many ways replacing the father that he never had. Rather than merely meeting his dependency needs, I am more interested in his coming to understand how he is repeating in his relationship with me some of his ineffective attempts to be recognized as a child. If I cater to his wants, I merely support his passivity and his helplessness.

The core of much of our work in therapy consists of Moe's becoming aware of those feelings that he had toward men such as his father and his boss that he is now projecting onto (or attributing to) me. Because these transference feelings are so essential for him to both understand and to work *through* in his relationship with me, I want to foster a climate in which they can be recognized, brought out into the open, discussed, and analyzed. The goal is that he will eventually no longer need to make men such as myself into father figures and thus keep himself as a "little boy." I hope that he can work through the transference relationship with me successfully, giving a *new ending* to our relationship and escaping the self-destructive ending he has had with other significant people in his life.

In order to create a therapeutic climate that will better enable Moe to both recognize the nature of his intense feelings toward me and to work through (resolve) these feelings, I do not engage in much self-disclosure. By keeping many of my reactions from him, I keep myself an ambiguous figure. Because of this ambiguity his manner of perceiving and responding to me will be largely a matter of his projections, which we work with in therapy.

If I am to be therapeutic for Moe, I must be aware of any of my own unresolved conflicts that can easily surface in my relationship with him. For example, I need to be aware of my reactions towards dependency on me. If I have an unconscious need to keep him dependent on me, it can seriously impede therapeutic progress. If I am unaware of my feelings toward him when he responds to me in passive/aggressive ways, I can become ensnarled in my own countertransference feelings. If I have a need to be appreciated by him and instead he refuses to cooperate with me, my own unconscious reactions toward him will prove counterproductive. Thus, it is essential that I be aware of my own needs, motivations, and unresolved personal issues from my past and of how these factors are likely to intrude in our work together. Many psychoanalytically oriented therapists become aware of these countertransference issues by being a client themselves.

It is clear that the task of personality restructuring in Moe's case will take several years of intensive work, for gaining insight into the origins of his present conflicts is not sufficient. He will need to see patterns in his present behavior and, over time, learn about the connections between his past and present. It is also necessary that he integrate these insights into a fuller awareness of how he is bringing his unresolved conflicts into his relationships with people in his life today.

Follow-Up: You Continue as Moe's Therapist

When I ask you to imagine that I am referring a client to you for further therapy, my hope is that you will function as much as possible within the conceptual framework of the model under discussion in each chapter. Also, you will learn best if you think of other directions to move with the client and if you use techniques other than the ones I have described. Assume that you can go beyond the point I left off with the particular client, which in most of these cases is just a beginning. Build on my work and what you know about the client, as well as *your reactions* to him or her, and modify the approach I have initiated in any way that seems appropriate to you.

In Moe's case I hope that you will let yourself *think psychoanalytically,* so that you can begin to get some sense of how you might approach him from an analytic perspective and draw on its techniques. Attempting to "get the feel" of the psychoanalytic approach by staying as much as possible within its spirit will help you determine what aspects of it you might incorporate into your own style of counseling.

Some questions for you to consider as you evaluate my work with Moe and decide on the direction you might proceed with him are:

1. What clues in Moe's behavior patterns would you look for as you formulated a tentative diagnosis in his case? If you worked in an agency that expected you to diagnose a client during the intake session, would assessment present any difficulties for you? If so, what? Would you be inclined to share your diagnostic impressions with your client? Why or why not?
2. How would you answer Moe if he asked: "Have you ever had a drinking problem? If you haven't, I don't see how you can understand what it's like for me to crave a drink, especially when I get down. If you haven't been there yourself, you won't be able to help me." How do you think you'd react to this confrontation? In the case of alcoholism, do you think that a therapist who has never personally experienced substance abuse could establish an effective therapeutic relationship with a client such as Moe?
3. What ethical issues are involved if you accept Moe without having the background and training to deal competently with his alcoholism? Do you see any ethical considerations in working with him if you do not like him or find yourself reacting negatively to him? When might you consider a referral?
4. What are some of your reactions to Moe? Would you like to work with him as a client? Why or why not?
5. What are your reactions to the way in which I worked with Moe? How might you have used techniques differently? What themes might you have paid more attention to than I did? What different kinds of interpretations from me might you have made about the material that he produced?
6. To what extent do you feel a sense of empathy with Moe's struggles? Do you have a personal perspective that would enable you to identify with him to the extent that you could understand his world? If you didn't think that you could identify with him, what would you be likely to do?
7. How might you deal with Moe's feelings toward you, especially if they were hostile? How do you imagine that you would react if Moe were to treat you as his father? or as his mother? or as an all-wise authority figure?
8. How might you deal with the various manifestations of Moe's resistance? Can you see yourself as becoming defensive? Can you think of ways in which you could deal with his resistance therapeutically?
9. What countertransference issues could come up for you in your relationship with Moe? Might you foster his dependency on you out of your needs? Might he remind you of certain traits in yourself that

you would like to deny? Are you aware of any unresolved problems of your own that could interfere with a *therapeutic* relationship?
10. How would you proceed with Moe? Discuss some areas that you would explore with him, as well as the techniques that you might use.

RECOMMENDED SUPPLEMENTARY READINGS

The Fifty-Minute Hour (1954), by R. Linder (New York: Bantam Books), is a collection of true psychoanalytic tales. This book is considered a classic that presents a descriptive illustration of psychoanalysis in action.

One Little Boy (1964), by D. Baruch (New York: Dell [Delta]), is a fascinating account of one boy's feelings and problems. Using play therapy, it reveals how his personal conflicts originated in family dynamics. The book gives the reader a sense of appreciation for the struggles most children experience during early childhood in relationship with their parents.

Childhood and Society (2nd. ed., 1963), by E. Erikson (New York: Norton), uses a modified and extended version of psychoanalytic thought. The author describes a psychosocial theory of development, delineating eight stages and their critical tasks.

Psychoanalysis: The Impossible Profession (1982), by J. Malcolm (New York: Random House [Vintage]), is a popular book that captures some of the analytic process in an interesting and accurate way. It is highly recommended as a nontechnical illustration of how the psychoanalytic process unfolds.

August (1983), by J. Rossner (New York: Warner Books), is a best-selling novel. It provides examples of client/therapist dialogue, helping bring to life many of the concepts and techniques of psychoanalysis.

SUGGESTED READINGS

Belkin, G. S. (1988). *Introduction to counseling* (3rd ed.). Dubuque, IA: William C. Brown. (Chapter 7)

Belkin, G. S. (1987). *Contemporary psychotherapies.* Pacific Grove, CA: Brooks/Cole. (Chapters 1 & 3)

Burke, J. F. (1989). *Contemporary approaches to psychotherapy and counseling.* Pacific Grove, CA: Brooks/Cole. (Chapter 6)

Corey, G. (1991). *Theory and practice of counseling and psychotherapy* (4th ed.). Pacific Grove, CA: Brooks/Cole. (Chapter 4)

Corsini, R., & Wedding, D. (Eds.). (1989). *Current psychotherapies* (4th ed.). Itasca, IL: F. E. Peacock. (Chapter 2)

Gilliland, B., James, R., Roberts, G., & Bowman, J. (1984). *Theories and strategies in counseling and psychotherapy.* Englewood Cliffs, NJ: Prentice-Hall. (Chapter 2)

Hansen, J., Stevic, R., & Warner, R. (1986). *Counseling: Theory and process* (4th ed.). Boston: Allyn & Bacon. (Chapters 2 & 3)

Ivey, A. E., Ivey, M. B., & Simek-Downing, L. (1987). *Counseling and psychotherapy: Integrating skills, theory, and practice* (2nd ed.). Englewood Cliffs, NJ: Prentice-Hall. (Chapter 8)

Patterson, C. H. (1986). *Theories of counseling and psychotherapy* (4th ed.). New York: Harper & Row. (Chapters 9 & 10)
Prochaska, J. O. (1984). *Systems of psychotherapy: A transtheoretical analysis* (2nd ed.). Pacific Grove, CA: Brooks/Cole. (Chapter 2)
Wedding, D., & Corsini, R. J. (Eds.). (1989). *Case studies in psychotherapy.* Itasca, IL: F. E. Peacock. (Chapter 1)

CHAPTER THREE

Case Approach to Adlerian Therapy

AN ADLERIAN THERAPIST'S PERSPECTIVE ON RUTH
by James Robert Bitter, Ed.D.

Jim Bitter is a professor of counseling and chairman of the Counseling Department at California State University, Fullerton. He has a considerable range of experience in applying Adlerian principles to counseling children and families. His scholarly activities include publications in the areas of family mapping and family constellation, created memories and early recollections, and family reconstruction. He has been associated with the Avanta Network, which is Virginia Satir's group of trainers.

I consulted with Dr. Bitter on the case of Ruth and asked for his help in conducting a thorough initial interview and a summary of impressions based on this initial interview. He also provided a lifestyle assessment, including a summary of the family constellation, a record of early recollections, and an interpretation of Ruth's pattern of basic convictions.

The lifestyle information was collected and interpreted by two therapists using a technique called multiple therapy. The client is initially interviewed by one therapist, who then presents the data to a second therapist. The client experiences social interest in the very structure of therapy. The model of two therapists cooperating in a single effort is often therapeutic in and of itself.

As I mentioned in the first chapter, this section is longer than those of other contributors because of my desire to provide you with a detailed and comprehensive assessment of Ruth's early background and her current functioning so that you can use this material as you work with her case in this book. This section begins with a general diagnosis and an initial interview using the *Individual Psychology Client Workbook,* which was developed by Robert L. Powers and Jane Griffith.*

**The Individual Psychology Client Workbook.* Robert L. Powers and Jane Griffith. © 1986 by The Americas Institute of Adlerian Studies, Ltd., 600 North McClurg Court, Suite 2502A, Chicago, IL 60611-3027.

GENERAL DIAGNOSIS: INITIAL INTERVIEW

The Life Situation (Items 1–20)

1. Date: February 20, 1989
2. Present Age: 39
3. Date of Birth: January 15, 1950
4. Name, address, home phone, maiden name; full name of spouse:
   Name: Ruth Walton; Maiden name: Dowell; Spouse's name: John
   All other information deleted.
5. Occupation, position, address, work phone; occupation of spouse:
   Homemaker, mother, student seeking certification as elementary schoolteacher; spouse is a sales manager.
6. Preferred phone and mailing address (home or work):
   Information deleted.
7. Marital status (age of spouse, how long married, anniversary, previous marriages of both spouses; or, current love relationship, how long, level of relationship):
   Married to John, age 45; wedding was on June 17, 1968; no previous marriages for either spouse.
8. Children (names, ages, sex; deceased children and other pregnancies; adoptions, difficulties of conception; from other marriages):
   Rob, age 19 (male); Jennifer, age 18 (female); Susan, age 17 (female); and Adam, age 16 (male); no other children or pregnancies.
9. Level of education; military service; religion:
   Attending college, seeking B.A. plus teacher certification; no military service; childhood religion: fundamentalist Christian.
10. Parents (intact marriage, divorced, or separated; remarriages of parents; if parents deceased, date and cause; CL's age at time of any family disruption; parents' current life situation and state of health; other adults present in pre-adolescent household):
    Parents are still married. Marriage seems to work for them. It seems stiff and formal to client, but they stand by each other. Their general state of health is satisfactory.
11. Siblings (list by first names from oldest to youngest, placing CL, deceased siblings, and mother's other known pregnancies in their ordinal positions; using CL's age as a baseline, note the difference in years between CL and siblings; in parallel column note step-siblings and CL's age when they entered the family; note present whereabouts and occupations of all siblings):

Ruth, age 39	Living with husband in California
Jill (–4), age 35	Architect in Chicago
Amy (–6), age 33	Social worker and homemaker in California
Steve (–9), age 30	Clerk in shipping office; still lives at home with mom and dad

12. **When you were a child, if anything could have been different, what would you have wanted it to be?**
Client wishes she wouldn't have had to work so hard at everything just to achieve at an acceptable level; she wishes things had come as easy for her as they seemed to come for Jill. And mostly, she wishes her father and mother had been proud of her.

13. **Are you currently under a physician's care? What for? (Note type of problem; if the "presenting problem" which brought CL in to see you is a physical symptom, see item 21; note signs):**
Yes. General physician. For sleep disturbance, anxiety, dizziness, heart palpitations, and headaches.

14. **Are you taking medication? (purpose, name, dosage, how long, effects and side effects):**
None.

15. **Date of last physical examination:**
August 11, 1988.

16. **Name, address, and specialty of physician(s) being consulted, if any:**
Information deleted.

17. **General health (energy level; appetite; sleep; exercise; level of sexual activity; use of alcohol and drugs, including "recreational drugs"; tobacco; caffeine; note physical signs):**
Energy varies, but mostly low; appetite is constant; she eats a lot of food and has a problem with weight; sleep is often interrupted—she wakes up, finds it difficult to breathe, her heart is pounding, and she sweats; gets little exercise, sometimes does not leave house for days; sexual activity is seldom and often not desired; no alcohol, drugs, tobacco; caffeine from soft drinks. Client looks tired and is 20+ pounds overweight.

18. **Previous counseling or therapy (when, reason, type, with whom, how long, outcome):**
Participated in a self-awareness group at the college and had a few individual sessions with a college counselor she does not remember. The experience was mostly stimulating and motivated her to seek more. She sees therapy as a way to extend her current knowledge of self.

19. **Referral source:** Course instructor: (name deleted)

20. **Emergency contact (name, address, phone, relationship):**
Husband: John (all other information deleted)

The Presenting Problem (Items 21–28)

21. **What brought you in to see us? If a physical symptom, describe location, sensations, intensity, frequency.**
Client reports general dissatisfaction. She says her life is rather uneventful and predictable, and she feels some panic over reaching the age of 39, wondering

where the years have gone. For two years she has been troubled by a range of psychosomatic complaints, including sleep disturbances, anxiety, dizziness, heart palpitations, and headaches. At times she has to push herself to leave the house. Client complains that she cries easily over trivial matters, often feels depressed, and has a weight problem.

22. **When did it start? What else was going on in your life at that time?**
About two years ago. Nothing particular was happening when these general symptoms started. Her kids were teenagers and gone much of the time, and she found herself getting older but "not better."

23. **Have you noticed a pattern?**
Only that she is not very active, eats a lot, and feels that she is not doing what she should be doing with her life.

24. **What happens as a consequence of having this problem? Who is most affected by it?**
Client says she guesses that she is. Family is mostly kind and understanding. She seems to be the only one who is unhappy with her life at the moment.

25. **What have you done about it until now?**
Sought a physician's help. Physician recommended therapy.

26. **How do you explain this situation to yourself?**
Client made a major career as a housewife and mother until her children became adolescents. She then entered college part time and obtained a bachelor's degree. Through her contacts with others at the university she has become aware of how she has limited herself, how she has fostered her family's dependence on her, and how frightened she is of branching out from her roles as mother and wife.

27. **How would your life be different if you did not have this problem?**
She would be happy at home and at work. She would have a job as an elementary schoolteacher and would work with a third-grade class. She would have energy for her children's activities and those of her husband, and she would see her family more often.

28. **What do you expect will come out of our work together?**
She is seeking therapy for the following reasons: (a) to handle the anxiety and depression she feels; (b) to explore what else might be added to her life beyond the structured existence she feels she lives as a wife and mother; although she would like to get more involved professionally, the thought of doing it does frighten her; she worries that she might be selfish in pursuing her goals, that she might not succeed, and that she might threaten her family; (c) she needs help at home handling Jennifer's rebellion, and she is worried about losing all of the children; (d) she is also concerned about who she is (an identity for herself) and what she should be doing with her life—she's 39, is getting older, and is losing her looks.

NOTE: If the presenting problem reveals an acute difficulty requiring immediate counseling, defer the remainder of the Initial Interview Inquiry (The Life Tasks) until a subsequent session.

The Life Tasks (Items 29–34)

Love

29. *Situation.* Tell me about your love relationships. (If CL lacks relationships of emotional or sexual closeness, ask: How do you account for this?)

    Key prompting questions: What makes a man a "masculine" man to you? What makes a woman a "feminine" woman? How do you compare yourself to your list of associations for your own sex? Do you experience difficulty in expressing love and affection for others? Difficulty in receiving such expressions from others? What does your partner complain about in you? What do you complain about in your partner? Describe your first encounter with your partner. What was there about him or her that impressed you at that time?

    "I have had only one relationship. John and I started going out after I graduated from high school. We got married, and we've been together ever since. John says he had been interested in me for a long time before we went out. He had seen me in church. We met formally at a church social. He stayed with me for a whole day. We talked, and he listened to everything I said. He was very attentive. When he walked me home, he asked if we could go to a movie. I said yes, and my parents didn't object. John was strong minded, knew what he wanted, and had goals and dreams. I liked his dreams, especially since they included me. He was always calm and never seemed to get angry. He's still very patient, the way I think men should be. He's the only man I ever dated, but he was good for me.

    "I think being feminine means that you are caring and nurturing and give a great deal of yourself to others. You have to be able to balance family, which is your responsibility, and community. There is always a lot to do. I think being feminine also means that you're attractive to men. I do really well at the first part, but I doubt that I'm attractive to men, especially with the weight I've put on.

    "John hardly ever complains. He would probably like to have sexual relations more often, but I have never enjoyed sex that much. It's OK, I mean, but I don't get in the mood as often as John. If I have any complaint, it's that I would like to make more decisions in the family and even for myself, but I would probably botch it up."

30. *Goals.* What do you want to improve or change in this area of your life?

    "I would like to feel more feminine and appreciated and loved. I would like to feel comfortable doing things for myself without feeling as if I'm letting John down or, worse, losing him."

Work

31. *Situation.* Tell me about your work. (If CL has no occupation or is currently unemployed, ask: How do you account for this? Explore interests and ambitions in this area.)

    Key prompting questions: What has been most satisfying to you in the jobs you have held? Least satisfying? What other work have you done? Why have you left those jobs? Are you aware of anything about the way you work that causes trouble for you (e.g., procrastination)? Do you feel appreciated at work? How do you evaluate your relationships with others at these levels: superiors, peers, and subordinates? Members of the opposite sex?

"I have worked all my life in the home: first my father's home and now my own home. I have taken care of children and a home since I was a young teenager. I have occasionally done some volunteer work, but very little really. There's so much to do with the children and John. What I like most about being a homemaker, or housewife, is when people like what I do for them. Sometimes, though, it feels as if the kids don't even notice. They just expect everything. John notices more. I notice all the things that never get done. Especially now that I'm in school. I guess school is my work for the moment. It's still hard, but I like it more than I liked high school. I'm learning a lot, but it takes a lot of time and energy, and I'm way behind at home."

32. *Goals.* What do you want to improve or change in this area of your life?

"I want very much to finish my certification as a teacher and to teach in an elementary school, third grade. I want to help students who have a hard time."

Friendship and community

33. *Situation.* Tell me about your friends and your life in the community. (If CL reports few or no connections with others, ask: How do you account for this?)

Key prompting questions: From where do you draw your friends? How many close friends do you have? How often are you together? What do you do? Do you have friends of the other sex? How do your friendships end? How much do you feel you are able to confide in your friends? What sort of impression do you think you make on people the first time they meet you? Does this impression change over time? If I were to call one of your close friends and ask, "What do you value in (CL)?" what would he or she say? What kind of connections do you have in your community?

"I have developed some good friends recently at school. I feel that school is really a turning point for me, both for work and for having people I can talk to. My classes have helped me meet people who really seem to like me and whom I feel comfortable talking to.

"Most of my friends are women, and I don't have very many. I maybe have one or two long-term friends, but I have shared more with college friends than I have with my long-term friends. I guess people like it that I listen real well. I'm interested in what people have to say. I'm not a leader by any stretch of the imagination, but I like to be a part of things.

"I think when people first meet me, they think I'm not much; but after they get to know me, they know that I'm dependable and that I care about people. I think I make a good friend, but this is new for me.

"I also know people who work around John, but we don't socialize with them much, and I don't know what they think of me. I'm not nearly as community oriented as my mother was."

34. *Goals.* What do you want to improve or change in this area of your life?
"I would like to see the friendships I have started at school really grow and develop. I would like to have some of them as fellow teachers and get to work in the same school. That would be great, to have a friend just down the hall."

Date: February 20, 1989

Summary of Impressions Derived from the Initial Interview

The second therapist (ST) dictates the *Summary of Impressions Derived from the Initial Interview* to the first therapist (FT) in the presence of CL at the conclusion of the review and interpretation of the *Initial Interview.*
[In the following Summary, Ruth is referred to in the third person to allow her to stand back from her experience and see her difficulties through a narrative that puts her life in context and shows its dynamic movement.]

Ruth has presented herself for therapy at a turning point in her life. She has spent many years doing what she began preparing to do early in life. Ruth, the oldest of four children, was drafted into caring for her brother and two sisters at a young age. She used her mother as a role model of a "good homemaker" and continued her work when she married her husband, John. John and Ruth have four children, who are now adolescents. When her children became teenagers, she decided to seek work where she would continue to feel needed. Returning to school, she completed a bachelor's degree and is seeking a teacher's certificate. College and her fellow students opened a whole new world to Ruth. She began to see many new possibilities for herself, including a place in the world as a professional teacher and as a person with many more friends than she has been used to having. She is feeling both excited by the new possibilities and worried about losing the people and world she has known all her life.

Ruth feels pulled by both worlds. In one world (school) the opportunities seem limitless and exciting and full of opportunity, if new and somewhat overwhelming and risky. In the other world (home) her life is safe, known, familiar, and predictable, and she knows exactly what she needs to do in order to succeed. She wants both worlds to fit together, but she is not always sure how to make that happen. She also wants to perform *perfectly* in both worlds. Even though part of her knows that the demand for perfection at both home and school is impossible, she has not let herself off the hook. Mostly, she wants everyone involved to be happy with her: she wants John to be happy; she wants her children to be happy; she wants her instructors to be happy; she wants her new friends to be happy; and, last and least, she wants herself to be happy. When she cannot figure out how to make it all happen, she often finds herself becoming worried, anxious, and depressed. When she doesn't have time to become worried, anxious, or depressed, she settles for dizziness, headaches, heart palpitations, sleeplessness, and other physical disturbances, which act as a message to her family and herself that she needs some rest and needs some care.

Ruth has put everyone else in life first. She comes from a family in which at least one other child achieved success easily, and she found it hard to please her mother and father. She could not guess what would make them happy, and she feared their disapproval and rejection. The family atmosphere was strict and controlled, and she found her place by caring for children and others in the way that she believed women are supposed to do. It is hard for her to put herself first at this point in life without fearing that she will lose everything.

She has a well-defined set of goals for therapy. They include dealing with the physical and emotional symptoms that express the conflict and demands she feels in her life; finding a balance between seeking what she wants and maintaining what she has; getting help with at least one daughter, whose rebellion acts as a constant reminder of "what can happen if Mom is not ever-present and vigilant"; and, mostly, discovering what she can make of herself and her life with the opportunities opening up and time running out. She is, after all, 39 years of age, and "losing it" . . . fast!

SPECIAL DIAGNOSIS: LIFESTYLE ASSESSMENT

CL's present age: 39 Date: February 27, 1989

Family Constellation, Part I: Parents, Other Adults, Milieu

1. Father's name: Patrick Occupation: Minister
   Age at CL's birth: 25 Age, if living: 64 Or, at death:
   Yr & cause of death: CL's age at death:
2. What kind of a man was your father when you were a child, up to age 10 or 11, in the pre-school and grammar school years? Consider activities, personality, health, level of education, and values (i.e., what was important to father):
   He was devoted to his work. He was stern, and he was the authority figure in the community. He was respected and righteous. He was also cool and detached. With Ruth, he was often distant, strict, and ungiving.
3. How did he relate to you and the other children?
   "He was rather aloof from all of us and insisted on respect."
   Favorite child: Jill—he liked her accomplishments.
   Discipline and how you felt about it:
   He would yell at children. He would withdraw from a misbehaving child totally and not talk to the child for weeks on end. Client felt scared and, at times, disowned.
   Expectations regarding your behavior and achievement:
   He wanted his children to be God-fearing and grow up to be righteous adults who did what was right.
4. How do you see yourself now as like father? Unlike father?
   "Both of us have high standards; both of us are critical. I'm much closer to my children than he was to us. I'm a good wife and mother."
5. Tell me briefly about father's background and family of origin.
   Client doesn't know what nationality her dad was, but he was the oldest of four boys, and he came from a religious family. It was assumed early in his life that he would be a minister, and he prepared for it all his life. His family was poor but always got by, and they were always proud.

6. Mother's name: Edith Occupation: Homemaker
Age at CL's birth: 20 Age, if living: 59 Or, at death:
Yr & cause of death: CL's age at death:

7. What kind of a woman was your mother when you were a child, up to age 10 or 11, in the pre-school and grammar school years? Consider activities, personality, health, level of education, and values (i.e., what was important to mother):

Ruth's mother was a hard worker; she rarely complained out loud. She was very proper, always did the right thing, and was quite dignified. She was proud of her role as a minister's wife. She was self-sacrificing. She would go without so that her husband or the kids could have the things they needed. She would even give up things for herself so that people in the church could have food or clothing or shelter.

It was very important to mother that the children maintain a good image in the church and the community. As unselfish as she could be, she was emotionally ungiving, very serious, not very happy (or so it appeared), and very strict with children.

8. How did she relate to you and the other children?

She was devoted to seeing that the children grew up right, but she was not personally involved in their lives unless they got in trouble.

Favorite child: Steve—he could do no wrong in her eyes.

Discipline and how you felt about it:

Scoldings or withdrawal. Not much more.

Expectations regarding your behavior and achievement:

She did not want any of the children to bring shame on the family, and she wanted all of them to be hard workers.

9. How do you see yourself now as like mother? Unlike mother?

Both are hard workers: "I guess we both sacrifice a lot for others, too." Client sees herself as more emotional and more emotionally giving.

10. Tell me briefly about mother's background and family of origin.

Ruth's mother was Scotch-Irish. She was also poor when she was little. She was the youngest of three girls, and she was the only one to marry. "She always told us how lucky we were to have a Christian life."

11. Parents' relationship. Tell me about how your parents got along with each other when you were a child. (Were they affectionate? Was one of them "the boss"? If they argued, what about? Who seemed to initiate the trouble, and what was the outcome? Did you take sides, openly or covertly? How did you feel about the trouble? Did you feel sorry for one of them?)

They had a stiff and formal relationship. Very little affection was demonstrated, and they rarely laughed. They did not argue; mother stood behind whatever father said or did. Ruth mostly took her own side. She wanted to make them happy, but it was not an easy task.

12. Other significant adults. Tell me about any other adults who were important to you when you were a child. (If not already clear: Describe

the character and role of any other adults living in the pre-adolescent household. Describe other adults who impressed you as a child, either positively or negatively.)

Her grandmother on her father's side took an interest in her. She seemed to understand her, and she would often talk to Ruth and give her good advice. She was the one who first approved of John.

13. Family milieu. If not already clear, inquire into: socio-economic, ethnic, religious, and cultural characteristics of the family and into the family's standards and values.

"We were a middle-class family, I guess." Client reports that their life centered on the church. They were fundamentalist Christians, and their family values included doing right, working hard, and reflecting well on the family. What stands out most is how scared Ruth was of her father and yet how much she wanted him to like her and think well of her: "That's what happens in a God-fearing family."

Date: February 27, 1989

Family Constellation, Part II: The Situation of the Child

Sibling array

Using the following page, array the siblings' names from oldest to youngest, across the page from left to right. Include CL, and any siblings deceased or separated from the family and living in institutions or elsewhere. Also note mother's other known pregnancies terminated by abortion, miscarriage, or still-birth, entering them in the appropriate ordinal positions. Using CL's age as baseline, note the difference in years, plus or minus, between each of them and CL. Include stepsiblings, and note CL's age at any time they entered the family. Use the following items to guide the discussion with CL, placing appropriate information in the boxes on the following page.

14. What kind of children were you? Describe each of the children, beginning with yourself, with respect to personality, health, and activities.
15. Note any subgroupings among the children: who played with whom; who fought and argued with whom; who looked after and took care of whom; who taught and guided whom.
16. Note how each of the children distinguished him- or herself from the others; for example, by taking the place of the one who was:

academic	the problem child
athletic	religious
artistic	socially successful
entrepreneurial	handicapped
the good child	sickly

17. If any of the children was handicapped or sickly, note the child's and family's attitudes toward the difficulty.

18. Which sibling were you most like? Least like? In what ways?
19. To what extent did each of the children accept, reject, or modify the family's standards and values?
20. Childhood chronology. If not already clear, note any changes in the course of CL's childhood and adolescent development experienced by CL as major events or turning points (e.g., divorce, a move to another community), and CL's age at those times.

Sibling Array

Ruth (39)	Jill (−4)	Amy (−6)	Steve (−9)
Responsible, hard-working, organized, dedicated, capable, trustworthy, self-critical, undemanding, scared, unable to please either parent. I was lonely; I felt useful and needed; I wanted approval from my folks; I was a good girl, and I took care of my sisters and brother.	Bright, pretty, accomplished, conforming, well-behaved. Got along with Dad; got along fairly well with Mom. Jill was the most like me; she was good and was successful at life. Things came more easily to her. She won honors at school.	Immature, demanding, the family "troublemaker"; admiring of me, hard-working, independent. In trouble with Dad, and tried to please Mom, without success. Amy was the most different from me; she seemed irresponsible by comparison.	Pampered, overprotected, in trouble with Dad but protected by Mom. Got Mom's affection. Sensitive, argumentative with me, not too accomplished. Steve was also different from me; in Mom he found a shelter from life.

Family Constellation: The Situation of the Child (continued)

21. What were your favorite stories, TV shows, fictitious or historical characters? What was there about them that you liked?
    Cinderella. "I liked it that she gets the prince in the end."
22. Did you daydream? What about?
    No. Ruth wasn't allowed to daydream and doesn't remember doing it much.
23. Do you remember any night dreams? Describe. How did you feel when you woke up?
    "I had dreams about being chased, and I would wake up scared. Or I had dreams about doing stupid things, and I would wake up with my heart pounding. Once in a while, I would dream about flying and being up above everyone. I loved to fly in my dreams."
24. Did you have any particular fears as a child? How did others respond?
    Being alone, not being liked, doing something wrong, being yelled at by her father or disappointing her mother. Fear was not addressed in her family.

25. **Was food and eating an issue in the household? In what way?**
Ruth was told to eat everything on her plate, and she couldn't leave the table until she did. Same for the other children.

26. **What were you good at? What did you most enjoy?**
Taking care of sisters and brothers, reading, taking care of the house.

27. **Was there anything you did not enjoy? Anything that was particularly hard for you?**
School was a challenge. She always had to work hard at school. She didn't do particularly well at math or the sciences.

28. **Did you experience difficulty in your mental or emotional development? How was this addressed in the family? In school? How did you feel about it?**
Nothing stronger than childhood fears and worries. No one paid much attention.

29. **Think back to your early years, up to age 6 or 7. What did you want to be when you grew up? What was there about that that appealed to you? How and when did this change?**
"I wanted to become a minister and have people look up to me."

Family Constellation: The Situation of the Child (conclusion)

30. **Describe how you got along in the world of the neighborhood. How would you characterize your role among the children (e.g., leader, follower, jester, outsider, etc.)? Did you have friends of the other sex?**
Client didn't play much. Children from church were sometimes invited to the house, but mostly siblings worked or played with one another, if at all. She didn't have any real friends of either sex. Just her brother and sisters.

31. **Describe how you got along in the world of the school. Was your role in this setting different from your role in the neighborhood? If so, in what ways, and how do you account for it? Did you have friends of the other sex? How did you get along with teachers? What were your favorite and least favorite subjects, and what was there about them that you liked or disliked?**
Ruth was expected to do well in school. It was hard for her. She had to work at it all the time. Even when she worked hard, she sometimes didn't do very well. Math and sciences were the hardest for her. English and history were best subjects. She liked to read, and that helped. She would get so nervous when she was doing math or science that she couldn't concentrate. The teachers generally liked her (with one or two exceptions), but they always felt that she was not living up to her potential, and that's what they told her parents. She didn't socialize with other kids much. She was quiet and kept to herself. Other kids thought she was "weird."

32. **Describe your bodily development in childhood, and how you felt about it. How did it compare with that of your peers? Consider height, weight,**

strength, speed, coordination, vision, hearing, anomalies. Did you have any special difficulties (e.g., bed wetting)?

"I developed like everyone else, I guess. I wasn't much different from other girls. But I didn't get to talk with kids my age very much, and my mother wouldn't tell me anything." No special difficulties.

33. **Desribe your sexual development, and your sexual experience and initiation. How did you learn about sex? How did you feel about the bodily changes that took place at puberty? (Females: How old were you at the menarche? Describe what happened. Did you understand what was happening? How did you feel about it?) Describe your experience as a sexual person during adolescence and young adulthood, and your evaluation of yourself at that time.**

    When client was 6 years old, she reports: "My father caught me 'playing doctor' with an 8-year-old boy. He lectured me and refused to speak to me for weeks. I felt guilty and ashamed." Ruth reached adolescence with minimal information from her mother, father, or peers. She remembers being scared at 12 when menarche occurred. "I didn't know what was happening. My mother gave me the things I needed and a booklet to read." She was not allowed to date until she completed high school; at the age of 19 she married the first person she dated. "I was lucky to find a good man. All I knew was my mother's version of how to be a homemaker."

Date: February 27, 1989

Summary of the Family Constellation

ST dictates the *Summary of the Family Constellation* to FT in the presence of CL at the conclusion of the review and interpretations of the family material.

Ruth is the oldest of four children, raised in a family where hard work and perfection were the expected standard; unfortunately, as she learned early in life, hard work was no guarantee that perfection could be achieved. Even after a huge effort, the slightest mistake could lead to a rebuke or a rejection that was deeply felt, leaving her lonely, cautious, and scared.

Her father set a masculine guiding line that was characterized by a harsh, strict, stern, and angry persona; his every stance was authoritarian, critical, and religiously perfectionistic. Indeed, her father was such a dominant authority in her life that it was easy for her to confuse God-fearing with father-fearing. Like a female version of Cain in the Bible, she was locked in a struggle for approval in which she would never be good enough and her sister Jill could do no wrong. The struggle to please her father gradually settled into strategies for avoiding his displeasure, and fear became the operative motivator in her life.

Ruth's mother set a feminine guiding line that was characterized by a serious devotion to principle, righteousness, duty, and her husband. Her behavior suggested that life was filled with hard work and sacrifice, a burden that women should suffer quietly, with dignity, and without complaint. Although she provided for the children's physical and spiritual needs, she did little to provide relief from the harsh stance that her husband took in the world.

Only Ruth's grandmother provided her with a different role model for womanhood. She demonstrated that it was possible for women to be interested in, involved with, and caring of young children.

The family atmosphere was characterized by formality and stiffness, a rigid consistency and discipline in which frivolity and, indeed, happiness were out of place. The family values included hard work, perfectionism, and a belief that appearances were extremely important. No crack in the architecture could be tolerated.

Under her father's regime it was impossible for Ruth to match the privilege and talent that was extended to Jill, her younger sister by four years. Jill was born to be accomplished, approved of, and rewarded; the combination of Ruth's mistakes and Jill's favored position rendered mythical the notion that hard work was its own reward—or even that it would ultimately pay off. Ruth formed an alliance with Amy, an equally disfavored and hard-working sibling: they were the children who would struggle through a hard life together. Amy looked up to Ruth, but she was not about to suffer her father's tyranny quietly or respectfully. Her rebellion became the only sure way she had to establish her independence.

In her father's kingdom the subservient queen birthed a prince, who stole her heart. Because no mere boy could hope to compete with the stature of the king, Steve entered into and accepted the protection of the queen. He became both spoiled and helpless in her care. In this way he avoided the family demands for hard work and perfectionism while putting the most powerful of family members in his service.

Like Cinderella, Ruth hoped that hard work, a pleasing personality, and patience would one day be rewarded with a prince who would discover her true beauty behind the ashes of a hard life. She lived in fear and captivity but longed to be free to fly. When the first prince came along, Ruth slipped on the slipper and moved out. Leaving with a prince is not the same as flying free, however, and she is still searching for a way to get off the ground.

In a world where men are powerful and women serve, her hope of becoming a minister, strong and powerful like her father, seems an unrealistic fantasy. To teach in an elementary school, however, offers her a position of significance in the lives of young people entrusted to her care and her own special world not too far from the safety of the castle of the "good" prince. Even a good prince can become displeased: Ruth's approval rating has always been and is now only as good as her last accomplished deed and as fleeting as her next discovered error. Entry into a new and different world must be balanced with the needs and demands of the old; she senses that it would not do for her to risk what is known and familiar in pursuit of what is unknown, risky, and possibly, reserved only for men or the women favored by them.

Date: February 27, 1989

Record of the Early Recollections

Ask for CL's Early Childhood Recollections (ERs). After recording the account of the recollection, narrow its range to the moment most vividly recalled, as if in a snapshot capturing a moment in the action, and ask how CL felt at that moment.

Prompting questions: How far back can you remember? What is the first incident or moment you remember in your life? Tell me about it. How old were you at the time? What is the most vivid moment in the action of the story? How did you feel about that moment?

Note that the first ER to be recorded is to be the first incident of memory. ERs recorded after the first need not be in chronological order. After recording the first ER, ask, ''What is the next thing you are able to recall from before age 9 or 10?'' Or, ''What comes up next from your childhood before age 9 or 10?''

1. Age: 3
   I remember my father yelling at me and then putting me in another room, because I was crying. I don't remember why I was crying, but I know I was scared, and after he shouted, I was petrified.
   Most vivid moment: father yelling.
   Feeling: scared, petrified.
2. Age: 4½
   I was in church, talking with a boy. My mother gave me dirty looks, and my father, who was conducting the service, gave me a stern lecture when we got home.
   Most vivid moment: the looks parents gave me.
   Feeling: scared and confused.
3. Age: 6
   An 8-year-old neighbor boy and I had our clothes off and were "playing doctor" when my father caught us in my bedroom. He sent the boy home and then told me in a cold and solemn voice that what I had done was very wrong. He did not speak to me for weeks, and I remember feeling very dirty and guilty.
   Most vivid moment: being caught by my father.
   Feeling: scared, "bad," and guilty.
4. Age: 7
   I remember my second-grade teacher saying that I was not doing well in school and that I was going to get a bad report card. I tried so hard to do well because I didn't want to bring home bad grades. This teacher didn't like me very much, and I couldn't understand what I had done wrong. I thought I was trying my best. I was scared.
   Most vivid moment: the teacher telling me I was getting a bad report card.
   Feeling: scared.
5. Age: 8
   I was in a church play, and I worked for months at memorizing my lines. I thought I had them down perfectly. My parents came to the play, and for a time I was doing fine, and I was hoping they would like my performance. Then toward the end I forgot to come in when I was supposed to, and the director had to cue me. My mistake was apparent to my father, who later commented that I had spoiled a rather good performance by my lack of attention. I remember feeling sad and disappointed, because I had so hoped that they would be pleased. And I don't recall my mother saying anything about the play.
   Most vivid moment: father commenting on my mistake.
   Feeling: embarrassed.

After recording eight ERs, ask CL if there is any other recollection that is important to him or her that has not been recorded in the Life-Style Inquiry to this point. If another ER is forthcoming, record it here:

Age: ______
Nothing reported.
Most vivid moment:
Feeling:

Date: February 27, 1989

ER Summary: The Pattern of Basic Convictions

ST dictates the summary of *The Pattern of Basic Convictions* to FT in the presence of CL at the conclusion of the review and interpretations of the ERs.
"I live in a man's world that is often harsh, uncaring, and frightening. Helplessness and emotion will not be tolerated in this world and will lead to being separated from it. In a man's world women must not speak, not even to other men. The rebuke of authority is both immediate and frightening. Men and their world are never available to women. A women is wrong to want to know about men or explore them. Dabbling in a man's world can lead to banishment and total exile.

"Only achievement counts in the real world. No amount of hard work can make up for a lack of performance. No amount of pleasing can win over someone who is against you. Significant people always find out about mistakes: the most important people always seem to be present when a lack of attention leads to an error that ruins even a good effort. To err in the real world is embarrassingly human; to forgive is against policy."

Date: February 27, 1989

ER Summary: The Interfering Ideas

This summary is also dictated in the presence of CL, immediately after the presentation of *The Pattern of Basic Convictions*.

The power and importance of men are exaggerated, as is her fear of their disapproval.
Pleasing seems to her the best route to safety in a man's world, but it leaves her unsure of her own identity and in constant fear of rejection.
The inevitability of mistakes and failure is exaggerated and feared: the slightest human errors are to be avoided; 100% is passing; 99% is the start of creeping failure.
Doing the right thing, being "good," is required just to survive; doing the wrong thing signals impending doom: caution is always warranted in an unpredictable world.
Murphy's Law governs: what can go wrong will go wrong.
Hard work is always demanded but will not necessarily produce the desired results or achievements sought.

JERRY COREY'S WORK WITH RUTH FROM AN ADLERIAN PERSPECTIVE

With the detailed information about Ruth derived from the initial interview and the lifestyle assessment provided by Jim Bitter, I will proceed with counseling Ruth from an Adlerian orientation.

Basic Assumptions

As an Adlerian therapist I view my work with Ruth as teaching her better ways of meeting the challenges of *life tasks.* One assumption that will guide my interventions with her is that although she has been influenced by her past, she is not necessarily molded by it. This premise of self-determination leaves little room for a client to take the role of a passive victim. I assume that Ruth has the capacity to influence and create events. What is crucial is not what she was born with but what she is making of her natural endowment.

Ruth's childhood experiences are of therapeutic interest to me. They are the foundation and early context for the social factors that contributed to her psychological development. True to the Adlerian spirit, I function as a therapist on the belief that it is not her childhood experiences in themselves that are crucial; rather, it is her *attitude* toward these events. Since these early influences may have led to the development of a *faulty style of life,* I will want to explore with her what it was like at home as she was growing up. Our focus will be on understanding and assessing the structure of her family life, known as the family constellation, and her earliest recollections (both of which were reported in detail in the previous section by Dr. Bitter).

Because I operate from a phenomenological stance (dealing with the client's subjective perception of reality), I will want to find out how she views the major events and turning points of her life. I assume that she has created a unique style of life that helps to explain the patterns of her behavior. My attention will be on how she has developed her distinctive behaviors in the pursuit of her life goals.

Assessment of Ruth

Adlerian therapists typically use the lifestyle questionnaire in making an initial assessment of the client and in formulating the goals and directions for therapy. This questionnaire gathers information about the client's childhood experiences, especially as they relate to family influences, birth order, relationships of each of the other family members, early memories, and other relevant material that will provide clues about the social forces influencing the client's personality formation. (In his assessment Dr. Bitter drew heavily from the framework of Adlerian lifestyle assessment as presented by Powers and Griffith in their 1987 book *Understanding Life Style: The Psycho-Clarity Process*.)

When this material on family background has been summarized and interpreted, it provides a rich avenue for understanding Ruth and highlights specific themes that we might pay special attention to during the course of her therapy. From summaries of her family constellation, early development, and early recollections it is possible to develop a list of her "basic mistakes," the mistaken notions by which she lives. I also summarize her major assets, so that we can build on them in therapy. Ruth and I review these lifestyle summaries, and I help her to understand some themes that appear to be running through her life.

1. *Summary of Ruth's family constellation and early development.* In a family that demanded perfection, Ruth came in second to her younger sister Jill. Ruth's four-year head start in life could not overcome the ease and skill with which Jill seemed to achieve her goals. Ruth formed an alliance with Amy, who also had to struggle to meet "minimal standards" of perfection, but Ruth retained her stature as the oldest child by constantly trying to please. (Her youngest sibling, her brother, Steve, found his place by feigning helplessness under the protection of his mother. In this manner he defused his parents' demands for hard work and accomplishment and got people in his service. In the end he received the most with the least amount of effort.) The atmosphere in this family was strict, formal, and controlled. Embarrassment was to be avoided at all costs. The family values stressed hard work and religious devotion. Ruth learned early, however, that hard work and proper behavior were not enough to please her parents. Mistakes were treated as disasters and were met with harsh criticism and personal rejection, the two experiences that Ruth fears the most to this day.

2. *Summary of early recollections.* Men are loud, terrifying, and unsympathetic. Socializing with them can lead to disapproval and rebuke. Exploring them and trying to understand them is even worse; it is wrong, forbidden, sinful, and will lead to rejection. Life is harsh and critical. No amount of hard work will overcome mistakes and failure. Being inadequate or, at least, being "discovered" to be inadequate is to be feared. Mistakes can ruin everything. Once disappointed, significant people in one's life are impossible to please.

3. *Summary of basic mistakes.* Ruth's pattern and profile show a number of mistaken and self-defeating perceptions, some of which are:

- It is impossible to please men, but she feels that she must keep trying anyway.
- She should work harder and harder until she achieves perfection.
- Taking a chance with men can lead to rejection, which is harsh and awful and should be avoided at all costs.

- She must be "good" at all times. If she is not, she will be caught, punished, and rejected.
- She must always know and do the right thing, or she will ruin everything.
- She must be cautious and pay attention at all times; nothing ventured, nothing lost.
- She exaggerates the importance of self-control.

4. *Summary of assets.* Personal assets are strengths that can be a foundation for growth and encouragement in therapy. Some of the positive directions and strengths in Ruth's case are:

- She is beginning to question values that she uncritically accepted.
- She is beginning to see that there are too many people to please in life, and it might be important to include herself on the list.
- She is capable, bright, and hard working, knows right from wrong, and is willing to face her fears and struggles in life.
- She is courageous.
- She can plan: she knows the importance of "looking before she leaps."
- She is kind, considerate, pleasant, and cares about others.

Goals of Therapy

There are four major goals of an Adlerian approach to therapy with Ruth, which correspond to the four phases of the therapeutic process. These goals are (1) to establish and maintain a good working relationship between Ruth and me as equals, (2) to provide a therapeutic climate in which she can come to understand her basic beliefs and feelings about herself and discover how she acquired these faulty beliefs, (3) to help her reach insight into her mistaken goals and self-defeating behaviors through a process of confrontation and interpretation, and (4) to assist her in developing alternative ways of thinking, feeling, and behaving by encouraging her to translate her insights into action.

Therapeutic Procedures

The four phases of Adlerian therapy that Ruth will experience are as follows. First, I emphasize establishing an empathic relationship with her. It is important that our relationship be based on cooperation and mutual respect. Therapeutic cooperation requires that our goals be aligned, so we develop a clear contract that specifies what she wants from therapy, spells out our responsibilities, and guides the course of the therapeutic venture.

In the second phase I explore Ruth's dynamics by seeing how her lifestyle is affecting her current functioning in all the tasks of life. We spend several sessions summarizing, reviewing, integrating, and interpreting the material derived from her lifestyle questionnaire.

This process leads to the third phase, insight. Through my Adlerian spectacles I view insight as only a step toward change, which can best be defined as translating self-understanding into constructive action. Ruth can play a "Yes, but . . ." game if all she acquires is intellectual insights. Through well-timed interpretations, which I suggest as therapeutic hunches, she can examine her beliefs and behavior and discover the purpose her behavior serves.

Phase four is reorientation. One of the aims of Ruth's therapy is to challenge her to take risks and make changes. Throughout the entire process *encouragement* is of the utmost importance. My assumption is that with encouragement Ruth will begin to experience her own inner resources and the power to choose for herself and to direct her own life. By now she will ideally have challenged her self-limiting assumptions and will be ready to put plans into action. Even though she may regress to old patterns at times, I will ask her to "catch herself" in this process and then continue to experiment with and practice new behavior. Throughout her therapy I will use a variety of techniques aimed primarily at challenging her cognitions (beliefs and thinking processes). Adlerians contend that first comes thinking, then feeling, and then behaving. So if we want to change behavior and feelings, the best way is to focus on Ruth's mistaken perceptions and faulty beliefs about life and herself. Drawing on a variety of techniques, some borrowed from other modalities, I will use confrontation, questioning, encouragement, assigning of homework, interpretation, giving of appropriate advice, and any other methods that can help her begin to change her vision of herself and her ability to behave in different ways.

The Therapeutic Process

In many ways the process of Adlerian therapy can be understood by recalling some basic ideas from contemporary psychoanalytic therapy. There is a link between these two approaches, especially on the issue of looking at how early patterns are related to our present personality functioning.

Elements of the process

Uncovering a mistaken belief. Ruth and I have been working together for some time, and she is beginning to see striking parallels between the role she assumed as an adolescent, by becoming the caretaker of her sisters and brother, and her contemporary role as "supermother" to her own children. She has discovered that for all of her life she has been laboring under the assumption that if she gave of herself unselfishly, she would be rewarded by being acknowledged and feeling a sense of personal fulfillment. As a child she wanted to be loved, accepted, and taken care of emotionally by her father, and she worked very hard at being the "good girl." As a married woman she has outdone herself in being the perfect wife and the devoted mother to their children. In this way she hopes to relate to her husband so he will love and accept her. Still, she has never really felt appreciated or emotionally nurtured by him, and now she is realizing that she has built her life on a personal mythology: if people loved her, she would be worthwhile and would find happiness through her personal sacrifices.

Helping Ruth reach her goals. At this time in Ruth's therapy we are exploring some other options open to her. Lately we have been talking a lot about her goals and about her vision of herself in the years to come.

RUTH: I'm hoping to finish my degree and get a teaching credential, but I keep telling myself that I don't have a right to do this for myself. It seems so selfish. School is very demanding of my time and energies, and it means that I have that much less to give at home. If only I could throw myself more fully into my studies and at the same time feel good about that choice!

JERRY: And what stops you from doing what you say you want to do?

RUTH: I guess it's my guilt! I keep feeling I shouldn't be at school and should be at home. John keeps telling me how much he and the kids miss me. If only I could stop feeling that I should be the dedicated mother and wife! But then I wouldn't be sure of my place in the family, either, and everything would be up in the air.

JERRY: It's probably not guilt that keeps you from what you want. My guess is that guilt is one of your ways of being "good." After all, a really rotten person would "desert" her family and not even have the common decency to feel bad. At least, you're kind enough to feel bad about it.

RUTH [smiling and giving a little chuckle]: This is not a laughing matter.

JERRY: You say that John keeps telling you how much he and the kids miss you. It's really very nice to be missed; but you interpret his meaning to be "Ruth, you should stay home. You're displeasing everyone."

RUTH: That's true. That's what I think he believes.

JERRY: Well, it's an old, but mistaken, notion you have. You could check it out. You could ask John what *he* means when he says he misses you. Maybe all he means is that he loves you [pause], and believes that the kids love you too. You could ask.

RUTH: Asking John how he really feels about my school and career and what I'm doing is extremely hard. [pause] He could tell me that he hates my school and career goals and that they're threatening our relationship.

JERRY: Oh, it could be *much* worse than that. If John said all of that, he would be giving you a very clear, direct message that you could address just as clearly. But what if John said "Being without you while you're in school is extremely hard, a real sacrifice for me and for the kids, but we're willing to suffer that hardship for you." Now, this would really hurt, wouldn't it? Have you been good enough to accept such a gift from your family? Are you worth their sacrifices for you?

RUTH [pausing and then beginning slowly]: Yes. Yes, I am. You're right. I need to know what everyone is really thinking and stop guessing. I need to face this with John. I really do believe that he loves me.

I am hoping that Ruth, by confronting a mistaken notion, will find the courage to check a lifelong idea against a current reality. She will be scared to be sure. Without some fear there is no need for courage. A week passes, and Ruth returns.

RUTH: Guess what? John and I talked. A long, wonderful talk. We both cried. He was afraid that I wouldn't need him anymore. Afraid of losing *me*! Can you believe it? But he didn't want me to stop school. "Not for anything in the world," he said.

JERRY: Ruth, that's wonderful. I'm very happy for you. What a treat to have a real risk work out so well for you.

RUTH: When John talked about the kids wanting their mother home, I started to feel guilty all over again. But a couple of hours later, I remembered what you had said about "guilt" being what a "good" person does. I still felt guilty, but I also felt a little silly feeling the guilt.

JERRY [laughing]: Good! At this point in your life, guilt is a habit. Like any habit, it takes time to change it. For now you're catching yourself after the fact, after the guilt. Soon you'll catch yourself in the middle of it and just stop. And someday you'll know you don't need guilt to be a good person, and you'll skip it altogether. So stick to it, but give yourself time.

RUTH: The thing is, I miss time with my kids as much as they miss me. When I'm studying, I can't help wondering what they're doing and what I'm missing by not being with them.

JERRY: Maybe we can spend some time looking at how you could build guaranteed "husband time" and "children time" into each week. Time that is special. Time that is not violated by school any more than "school time" can be interrupted by family.

From here we proceed to look at a week of Ruth's time and how she might balance personal needs with the needs of others. Planning special time for her family maintains (Ruth's) sense of belonging and her real need for social interest without short-circuiting the gift of time her family is giving her for school. It also provides her with a structure by which she can devote her full attention to the tasks or people at hand: quality time in both cases.

Process commentary

My major aim in our sessions is to both encourage and challenge Ruth to consider alternative attitudes, beliefs, goals, and behaviors. By seeing the link between her mistaken beliefs and her current feelings and behaviors, she is able to consider options and change. She takes some big risks in approaching her husband. Given her history with and interpretation of men, she risks a harsh, rejecting rebuke. What she gains, however, is an increased sense of her worth and value to this important man in her life. She also gains in courage and confidence.

At times I use a technique called "spitting in the client's soup." My response to Ruth's expression of guilt is an example of this technique. I suggest that guilt is a way for her to be noble, to be good. Later, she reports feeling guilty but also *feeling silly* about feeling guilty. Her report is the way I know that the technique was successful. As the name of the technique suggests, the client may continue to eat the soup (feel guilty), but he or she will feel uncomfortable, as if someone had spit in it.

Once Ruth has made some new decisions and modified her goals, I teach her ways in which to challenge her own thinking. At those times when she is very critical of herself, I provide encouragement. Partly because of my faith in her and my encouragement, she comes closer to experiencing her inner strength. She becomes more honest about what she is doing, and she augments her power to choose for herself instead of merely following the values she uncritically accepted as a child.

A most important ingredient of the final stages of Ruth's therapy is commitment. She is finally persuaded that if she hopes to change, she will have to be willing to set specific tasks for herself and then take concrete action in dealing with her problems. Although she attempts to live up to what she believes is the role of the "good person," she eventually develops increased tolerance of learning by trial and error, and with this she becomes better at "catching herself" at repeating ineffective behavior.

Questions for Reflection

1. As you review the lifestyle-assessment form used to gather background information on Ruth, what associations do you have with your own early childhood experiences? If you were considering getting into therapy as a client, what do you imagine it would be like for you to complete the lifestyle questionnaire? Do you have any personal reactions to the information on Ruth?
2. Look at the initial interview form and the lifestyle-assessment form used by Dr. Bitter in his assessment of Ruth. Answer these questions as they apply to you. Do you see any patterns emerging?
3. As you think about your own family constellation, what most stands out for you? (As a child, how did you view your mother? father? How did they view and treat you? What was your parents' relationship to each other? What was their relationship to the other children? What was your position in your family? How did you get along with your

siblings?) After reflecting on your early experiences in your family, attempt to come to some conclusions about the ways in which these experiences are operating in your life today.

4. What are three of your earliest recollections? Can you speculate on how these memories might have an impact on the person you are now and how they could be related to your future strivings?
5. List what you consider to be the major "basic mistakes" in your life. Do you have any ideas about how you developed these mistaken perceptions about yourself and about life? How do you think that they are influencing the ways in which you think, feel, and act today?
6. Compare and contrast the Adlerian and the psychoanalytic ways of working with Ruth. What are some of the major differences? Do you see any ways to combine Adlerian and psychoanalytic concepts and techniques?
7. From what you learned about Ruth through the lifestyle questionnaire, what aspects of her life might you want to give the primary focus? What themes running through her life lend themselves especially well to Adlerian therapy?
8. One of the goals of Adlerian therapy is to increase the client's social interest. Can you think of ways in which you could work with Ruth to help her attain these goals? (How might you help her develop new friendships or make her social involvements more meaningful?)
9. Ruth describes herself as coming from a middle-class family. They were fundamentalist Christians, and the family values involved doing right, working hard, and living in a way that would reflect well on the family. Considering this background, how well do Adlerian concepts and therapeutic procedures fit for Ruth? How would the Adlerian approach fit for her if she were an Asian American? Hispanic? Black? Native American?
10. What major cultural themes do you see in Ruth's case? How would you address these themes, using an Adlerian framework?

JULIE: "IT'S MY FATHER'S FAULT THAT I CAN'T TRUST MEN"

Some Background Data

Julie is interested in exploring her relationships with men. She says that she cannot trust me because I am a man and that she cannot trust men because her father was an alcoholic and was therefore untrustworthy. She recalls that he was never around when she needed him and that she would not have felt free to go to him with her problems in any case, because he was loud and gruff. She tells me of the guilt that she felt over her father's drinking because of her sense that in some way she was causing him to drink. Julie, who is now 35 and unmarried, is leery of men, convinced that they will somehow let her down if she gives them the chance. She has decided in advance that she will not be a fool again, that she will not let herself need or trust men.

Although Julie seems pretty clear about not wanting to risk trusting men, she realizes that this notion is self-defeating and would like to challenge her views. Though she wants to change the way in which she perceives and feels about men, somehow she seems to have an investment in her belief about their basic untrustworthiness. She is not very willing to look at her part in keeping this assumption about men alive. Rather, she would prefer to pin the blame on her father. It was he who taught her this lesson, and now it is difficult for her to change, or so she reports.

My Way of Working with Julie as an Adlerian Therapist

I would be inclined to begin my counseling of Julie with a question: "If trusting men is so hard for you, why did you choose me?" She might reply that she has heard that I was "a good counselor." I would note that there are many good counselors and that many of them are women. She might say that she wanted to work with a male counselor to learn how to trust men. I would ask her if she knew why she was so angry and upset with men. If she mentioned her father, I would say: "He is just one man. Do you know why you react in this way to most men—even today?" If it was appropriate to her response, I might suggest: "Could it be that your beliefs against men keep you from having to test your ability to be a true friend?" Or "Could it be that you want to give your father a constant reminder that he has wrecked your life? Could you be getting your revenge for an unhappy childhood?"

Even if it is true that her father was untrustworthy and treated her unkindly, my assessment is that it is a "basic mistake" for her to have generalized what she believes to be true of her father to all men. My hope is that our relationship, based on respect and cooperation, will be a catalyst for her in challenging her assumptions about men.

As part of the assessment process I will be interested in exploring her early memories, especially those pertaining to her father and mother, the guiding lines for male and female relationships. We will also explore what it was like for her as a child in her family, what interpretation she gave to events, and what meaning she gave to herself, others, and the world. Some additional questions that I might pose are:

- What do you think you get from staying angry at your father and insisting that he is the cause of your fear of men?
- What do you imagine it would be like for you if you were to act as if men were trustworthy? And what do you suppose really prevents you from doing that?

- What would happen or what would you be doing differently if you trusted men?
- If you could forgive your father, what do you imagine that would be like for you? for him? for your dealings with other men?
- If you keep the same attitudes until you die, how will that be for you?
- How would you like to be in five years?
- If you really want to change, what can you do to begin the process? What are you willing to do?

I have already indicated that my relationship with Julie is the major vehicle with which to work in the sessions. A male counselor who emphasizes listening, mutual respect, honesty, partnership, and encouragement will give her a chance to examine her mistaken notions and try on new behaviors. A lifestyle assessment will help her see the broad pattern of her life and will reveal the convictions that are leading her to safeguard herself against all male relationships. She is an adult child of a person who has had a serious problem with alcohol. She will not be alone in her tendency to generalize from this childhood experience, but she can be helped to take charge of her own life and her current relationships with men.

Julie needs to take some action if she expects to change her views toward men. Thus, we work together to determine what she can do outside of the sessions. Here is one possibility, with the follow-up that would occur within the therapy session:

Julie can write an uncensored letter to her father, explicitly airing all of her grievances. It is critical that she express her anger—that she tell him all the things she has been saying to me and other things that she has felt but kept to herself. I encourage her *not* to mail the letter, as this is only an exercise for her to symbolically work through some of her issues toward her father. At the following session we can discuss what it was like for her to write this letter and what she learned from it.

After she reports on the letter, I might ask her to use an empty chair, symbolically placing her father in it, and telling him what she would still like to say to him. As she says what is on her mind, I will ask her to switch chairs and respond as her father would respond before continuing with her comments to him. She can respond in her father's behalf in several ways. One way is to act as her father typically did; another idea is to respond as she wished her father would someday respond; another way is for her to talk to a mythical representative of all men, especially those men with whom she wants to be close but will not.

By playing both parts Julie may increase her understanding of herself, her father, or even men in general. The empty chair, when used to make a relationship explicit, often has the effect of increasing the client's social interest in fellow human beings.

The letter writing and the empty chair are avenues for Julie to examine her convictions, beliefs, and feelings. She can benefit by focusing on what she brings to her relationships and what she can learn about the humanity of others.

A major part of my work with Julie is directed at confronting her with the ways in which she is refusing to take responsibility for the things in herself that she does not like and at encouraging her to decide on some course of action to begin the process of modifying those things. A very important phase of therapy is the reorientation stage, the action-oriented process of putting one's insights to work. As an Adlerian therapist I am concerned that Julie do more than merely understand the dynamics of her behavior. My goal is that she eventually see new and more functional alternatives. This reorientation phase of her therapy consists of her considering alternative attitudes, beliefs, goals, and behaviors. She is expected to make new decisions. I encourage her to "catch herself" in the process of repeating old patterns. When she meets a man and then immediately assumes that he cannot be trusted, for example, it helps if she is able to observe what she is doing. She can then ask herself if she wants to persist in clinging to old assumptions or if she is willing to let go of them and form impressions without bias.

This phase of counseling is a time for Julie to commit to the specific ways in which she would like to be different. Encouragement during the time that she is trying new behavior and working on new goals is most useful. This encouragement can take the form of having faith in her, of support, of recognizing the changes she makes, and of continuing to be psychologically available for her during our sessions.

Follow-Up: You Continue as Julie's Therapist

1. What are some of your impressions and reactions to my work with Julie? Knowing what you know about these sessions and Julie, what might you *most* want to follow up with if you could see her for at least a couple of months?
2. How much do you imagine that your approach with Julie would be affected by your life experiences and views? How much would you want to share of yourself with her? In what ways do you think you could use yourself as a person in your work with her?
3. How might you deal with her apparent unwillingness to accept personal responsibility and her blaming of her father for her inability to trust men now?
4. What are some additional Adlerian techniques you might use with Julie?
5. Outline some of the steps in Adlerian counseling that you would expect to take for a series of sessions with Julie, showing why you are adopting that particular course of action. Specifically, how would you (a) establish a good therapeutic relationship with her? (b) conduct an assessment of her individual dynamics, including family constellation

and early recollections? (c) help her gain insight into her dynamics? (d) assist her in considering an alternative set of attitudes, beliefs, goals, and behaviors?

RECOMMENDED SUPPLEMENTARY READINGS

The Individual Psychology of Alfred Adler (1956), by H. L. Ansbacher and R. R. Ansbacher (New York: Basic Books), is the classic text, organizing and annotating all of Adler's basic writings on the theory and practice of Individual Psychology. Many Adlerians consider this book to be the fundamental source for their work.

Superiority and Social Interest: A Collection of Later Writings (3rd rev. ed., 1979), by A. Adler (New York: Norton), is an excellent source for readers who want to review some of Adler's writings. The introduction, written by H. L. Ansbacher and R. R. Ansbacher, is a clear statement on the increasing recognition of Adler's position in the development of counseling. Part 6 contains a comprehensive and interesting biographical essay of Adler. Part 3 deals with case interpretations and treatment.

An Adlerian Lexicon (1985), by R. L. Powers and J. Griffith (Chicago: AIAS), is an outstanding quick reference, which lists over 50 terms that are fundamental to Adlerian basic assumptions and theory. Each term is cross-referenced to quotations and literature that provide a conceptual context for the definition.

Individual Psychology Client Workbook (1986), by R. L. Powers and J. Griffith (Chicago: AIAS), is a guide for the initial Adlerian interview and lifestyle assessment. The workbook is a supplemental Adlerian approach to the authors' *Understanding Lifestyle: The Psycho-Clarity Process* (see below) and can be ordered from AIAS Ltd., 600 North McClurg Court, Suite 2502A, Chicago, IL 60611; telephone: (312) 337-5066.

Understanding Life Style: The Psycho-Clarity Process (1987), by R. L. Powers and J. Griffith (Chicago: AIAS), is a thorough presentation of Adlerian theory in relation to lifestyle assessment and its therapeutic uses. The authors do an excellent job of relating process to skill development. This book is fast becoming the reference for Adlerian therapeutic practice.

Adlerian Counseling and Psychotherapy (2nd ed., 1987), by D. Dinkmeyer, D. Dinkmeyer, Jr., and L. Sperry (Columbus, OH: Charles E. Merrill), gives an excellent basic presentation of the theoretical foundations of Adlerian counseling. The specific focus is on stages of the counseling process, Adlerian techniques, applying Adlerian methods to a variety of populations, and working with individuals, groups, and families.

Individual Psychology: Theory and Practice (1982), by G. M. Manaster and R. Corsini (Itasca, IL: F. E. Peacock), is a highly readable overview of Adlerian psychology. There is a clear summary of basic Adlerian concepts, with emphasis on application of these principles to practice. An accurate, interesting, and clear book.

SUGGESTED READINGS

Belkin, G. S. (1988). *Introduction to counseling* (3rd ed.). Dubuque, IA: William C. Brown. (Chapter 7)

Belkin, G. (1987). *Contemporary psychotherapies* (2nd ed.). Pacific Grove, CA: Brooks/Cole. (Chapter 2)

Burke, J. F. (1989). *Contemporary approaches to psychotherapy and counseling.* Pacific Grove, CA: Brooks/Cole. (Chapter 7)

Corey, G. (1991). *Theory and practice of counseling and psychotherapy* (4th ed.). Pacific Grove, CA: Brooks/Cole. (Chapter 5)

Corsini, R., & Wedding, D. (Eds.). (1989). *Current psychotherapies* (4th ed.). Itasca, IL: F. E. Peacock. (Chapter 3)

Gilliland, B., James, R., Roberts, G., & Bowman, J. (1984). *Theories and strategies in counseling and psychotherapy.* Englewood Cliffs, NJ: Prentice-Hall. (Chapter 3)

Hansen, J., Stevic, R., & Warner, R. (1986). *Counseling: Theory and process* (4th ed.). Boston: Allyn & Bacon. (Chapter 4)

Prochaska, J. O. (1984). *Systems of psychotherapy: A transtheoretical analysis* (2nd ed.). Pacific Grove, CA: Brooks/Cole. (Chapter 6)

Wedding, D., & Corsini, R. J. (Eds.). (1989). *Case studies in psychotherapy.* Itasca, IL: F. E. Peacock. (Chapter 2)

CHAPTER FOUR

Case Approach to Existential Therapy

AN EXISTENTIAL THERAPIST'S PERSPECTIVE ON RUTH by Donald Polkinghorne, Ph.D.

Donald Polkinghorne is a professor of counseling at California State University, Fullerton. A few of his professional activities include serving as vice president of the Association for Humanistic Psychology, consulting editor of the *Journal of Phenomenological Psychology,* and a member of the editorial boards of the *Journal of Humanistic Psychology* and *The Humanistic Psychologist.* Among his many publications are writings on phenomenological research methods and existential psychotherapy and social values.

Introductory Comments

Counselors who approach psychotherapy from an existential perspective view it as a process for helping clients sort out and clarify the ways in which they construct meaning. The working model for existential sessions is a tutorial relationship. The counselor coaches clients in uncovering and reflecting on the assumptions that form their experience of themselves, others, and the world. The counseling relationship is an unfolding and dynamic process that moves through the following phases: (1) understanding one's present modes of existence, (2) modifying and expanding these modes into a renewed direction for one's life, and (3) assessing and developing one's skills as a means to carry out this new life agenda.

My reactions to Ruth outlined in this essay are necessarily presumptive and rudimentary. They are based on the descriptions provided in her intake form, autobiography, and transcript. In actually working with Ruth I would expect these initial responses to become more focused on the unique and distinctive themes that emerge as she learns to reflect on the structure of her experience. In addition, because the existential approach emphasizes the central role of clients in their own therapy, I would expect her to correct, expand, and deepen my impressions.

Assessment of Ruth

The purpose of an existential clinical assessment is to formulate descriptions of the assumptions that clients use in constructing their experience. These descriptions indicate how clients, from their perspective, understand the various dimensions of their existence. The existential approach to assessment differs from, but is not antagonistic to, the diagnostic approach of the DSM-III-R. Whereas the focus of an existential assessment is on clients' experience of their world, the DSM-III-R categories are based on how clients' symptoms appear to the clinical observer. Existential assessment shares with other clinical approaches a concern for identifying possible organic factors that initiated and are maintaining the client's problems. In Ruth's case a physical examination could find no organic or medical basis for her symptoms.

As a means for assessing how clients are experiencing their world, the existential therapist examines how they structure their relationships in four basic dimensions of human existence: (1) the natural world, with its physical and biological dimensions; (2) the public world, with its social dimensions of human relationships and interactions;(3) the private world, with its psychological dimension of intimate and personal experience of one's own self, including those relationships with others; and (4) the ideal world, which includes the values one holds.

The natural world. One's structured relationship to the natural world includes attention to bodily awareness of the whole range of physical sensations, both internal and external. Included in a client's particular natural world is body image, the ability to stave off illness, physical fitness or weakness, and attitude toward food, sex, and procreation. Ruth has difficulties in managing her natural existence. She is "not very proud" of her body, is overweight, and is unable to control her eating. She experiences her body as aging and no longer attractive. She is alienated from her body with its headaches, heart palpitations, sleep disturbances, and dizziness. She is "sexually dead." Because human existence is always anchored in an actual physical presence in the material world, the natural dimension is the most fundamental. Assisting Ruth in reflecting on her assumptions about her body and whether she chooses to continue to accept these assumptions would be one of my important tasks.

The public world. The second dimension of human existence included in an existential assessment is the world of public relations to others and society. This public dimension includes people's relationships to their race, their social class or other reference group; their country, language, and cultural history; their family and work environments; and their general attitude toward authority and the law. The public dimension of existence is often maintained by polarized assumptions about relations with others.

These polarities include dualistic versus submission, acceptance versus rejection, and love versus hate. Ruth appears to relate to her public world through these dualistic constructs. She is submissive to her children and experiences herself as a victim of her devotion to them. The only alternative approach she is able to consider is one of dominance, in which she would "think and act selfishly." The possibilities she experiences for relating with her father are also polarized: either gaining his love through submission and complete obedience to his ideas or being dominant and following only her own ideas, thereby earning his disapproval and rejection. As part of my work with Ruth I would help her expand her repertoire for experiencing and understanding her public world. I would encourage her to abandon the limited, either/or polarities that she presently assumes and open herself to the many possibilities that lie on the continuum between submission and domination.

The private world. The third dimension of Ruth's experiences to be assessed is her relationship to her core self. This dimension encompasses everything that is felt to be a part of her private self. She has constricted her approach to her own self and, thus, experiences an inner void and deprivation. Without a solid experience of a self to rely on, she feels adrift, without purpose and direction. I would work with her toward opening up access to her inner self. She will need these inner resources to discover her own life direction and to feel alive and vigorous. The core self extends beyond the "who I am" to include others; thus, a part of who I am incorporates the "who we are." These others become integral to a person's own identity. People who have not taken in others as part of their own self feel isolated and cut off from others. They limit their experience of others to the public dimension and relate only through social roles and scripts. When Ruth describes her relations with her husband and children, they appear as public relations confined to the public dimension of social expectations and defined roles. My counseling work with her would explore the structures she has built that are denying her access to these experiences of her inner self. Once she begins to accept an intimate and secure relationship with herself, including its paradoxes and strengths and weaknesses, she can start to clarify how others can be integrated into her inner world and become a part of her own identity. By opening up her self to include others, she will transform these relationships from social duties to love and union.

The ideal world. The final dimension in the existential assessment is focused on the ideals and values that inform clients' notions of right and wrong or good and bad. This dimension includes people's beliefs about what is worth doing with their existence and is the source of their ethical and spiritual sensitivities; it is the dimension that gives meaning and direction to their lives. This ideal dimension is part of the core of one's being and is to be distinguished from the social codes and rules of the public world. Ruth is out of touch with her realm of personal values. As a result she is adrift without direction for her life. The authority for the religious beliefs adopted in her childhood was not transferred from her father to her inner self. Instead, these childhood beliefs have served to block access to experiences of her own intrinsic ethical and spiritual sensibilities. Because she did not develop her own sense of values when she discarded her childhood beliefs, she was left without access to any ground for life direction. Not having contact with her own ethical inclinations, she has been left with only two discernible options: to readapt the ideals of the religion of her father and her childhood or to adopt a narcissistic value system in which she would attend only to her own needs. Neither option conforms to her own core value system, which is not yet available to her direct awareness. Its presence is merely indicated by her discomfort with the two perceived alternatives. I would work with her to gain access to and make explicit this covered-over system of beliefs. In clarifying her own position we would explore what it is she holds to be worth living for and would be willing to die for. I would be careful to help her distinguish the public values to which she has acquiesced from the values that are expressions of her own selfhood. After she became aware of her own deeply centered ideals, I would work with her to reflect on and reconfirm these beliefs and to choose from among them priorities and directions for her life. The purpose of these explorations is to support her in determining her own aspirations and purposes. With these clarifications she will come to develop her own motivating beliefs, and these can be the source from which she gathers the courage to act and thereby create a more fulfilling existence.

In actuality these four dimensions of human existence are interrelated. In working with clients it is not possible to isolate them and focus exclusively on one sphere. Nevertheless, in the course of the initial phase of therapy there is a natural progression through the order in which I have described them. In working with Ruth I would probably ask her to begin with an exploration of her psychosomatic complaints, including reflections on the way she has structured her relationship with her body. These are aspects of the natural, or physical, dimension of her existence. Usually, the dimension that next becomes available for reflection is the client's public world. The assumptions about one's own identity, the private world, are often more difficult for a person to bring into awareness for clarification. Before being able to make one's intrinsic values and ethical sensitivities explicit, clients need to be at ease with their private world.

Ruth's personal assessment of her problem is that she needs to find a set of values and directions for her life. She implores the counselor to provide her with a new set of values. In counseling with her I would advise her that the capacity to determine a set of personal values develops out of clarifications of the first three dimensions of her existence. I would suggest that until she has gained a sense of confidence in the natural, public, and private worlds of her life, she will probably continue to look for life directions in the public world, hoping to find out what she should do from some external authority. When she feels at home with and accepting of her self, she will come to trust her ability to cope with the responsibility of making her own moral judgments and of determining the future directions for her life.

Key Themes and Issues

Existential counselors construct the counseling process around two major themes, anxiety and authenticity. *Existential anxiety* differs from what is commonly meant by the term *anxiety.* The common meaning of anxiety refers to worry about some life circumstance and accompanying psychological symptoms such as restlessness, muscle tension, shortness of breath, irritability, difficulty concentrating, and the like. Existential anxiety refers to a symptomless, deep feeling of unease that accompanies the awareness that one's existence is limited and frail and that one is ultimately responsible for the purpose and direction of one's own existence.

Authenticity is a descriptive term that refers to the kind of existence people have when they accept responsibility for chosing the constructs and assumptions that direct their actions. The authentic mode of existing is contrasted to the inauthentic mode, in which people lack awareness of personal responsibility for their lives and passively assume that their existence is under the control of external forces.

Authenticity and existential anxiety are interlinked, in that the more a person comes to accept the obligation of self-direction, the more directly he or she experiences the anxiety of personal responsibility. A major challenge for existential counselors is to assist clients in accepting the charge to guide their own lives in spite of the increasing feeling of existential anxiety that accompanies this acceptance.

Anxiety. The existential tradition holds that life is given to each person in an unfinished condition. We are the caretakers of our life substance and are responsible for creatively forging and shaping it into a morally worthy and aesthetically meaningful existence. We are not, however, given criteria, or guidelines, laying out what the good and meaningful are. Each of us is required to decide what a personally worthy existence is. Thus, in addition to being responsible for what we become, we must decide what we want to become.

The life task must be accomplished within the limited time we are alive. Although we expect and hope to have the normal "three score and ten" or more years, we are aware of the possibility that this time can be shortened unpredictably by accident, illness, or violence. Thus, within the uncertain duration of our being we are obligated to fashion an existence of personally meaningful ethical and aesthetic robustness.

Existential anxiety is our bodily response to the recognition that we are accountable for fashioning a worthy existence in a limited time without the surety of some authority telling us what worthiness is. Existential anxiety has a different feel from ordinary anxiety. In ordinary anxiety we experience a pressure, or disquiet, whose source is the fear of rejection or sanctions that will come from not fulfilling the demands and expectations of others. In existential anxiety the source of the feelings is one's own self. In existential counseling the experience of existential anxiety is understood as a positive sign. It means the client has begun to acknowledge the obligation to take charge of his or her own existence and has moved beyond the mere passive acceptance of social definitions of "who I am."

Because recognition of the existential obligation to mold our lives is accompanied by the discomfort of existential anxiety and because the burden of this personal responsibility is heavy, we have a natural disposition to refuse to acknowledge it. In our everyday living we seek tranquillity and refuge from our self-task by placing the responsibility for what we are becoming on society or others. We develop various strategies to cover over the feelings of existential anxiety; however, these strategies often break down during those times when we are faced with the exigencies of living. At these times people feel that their lives are adrift and that they are not being true to the inherent possibility of a meaningful and full life. This feeling of "not being who I could be" is termed *existential guilt* and is distinguished from the anxiety of responsibility. It is the emotion that is felt when a person has not fulfilled the existential obligation to fashion a worthy existence. Existential guilt disrupts the serenity of a passive acceptance of being what others have defined. It is understood as a call from within to take control of one's own existence. It is often existential guilt that leads people to seek therapy. Ruth comes for counseling after two years of confusion, depression, neurotic anxiety, inability to sleep, and a range of psychosomatic complaints. As an existential counselor in her case I interpret these symptoms as manifestations of existential guilt.

Earlier in her life Ruth evaded the necessity of making her own judgments about what would be a worthy life for her by passively accepting a publicly given set of beliefs, social roles, and scripts as appropriate definitions of what and who she should be. These publicly supported values provided a tightly woven, protective diversion from her responsibility to judge for *herself* what would be a worthwhile life for her. This protective garment started to unravel when she began, as part of her counseling, to examine her life. The process of unraveling continued through the pull of the inevitable crises of personal existence: the esteem she had received from her children was disrupted by their adolescence, and her role of mother was coming to an end as the children prepared to leave home. She experienced her physical attractiveness waning, and her 39th birthday brought her to that stage of life when we are all faced with an awareness of our vulnerability and the possibility of our death. When her protective garment was torn apart, she had nothing with which to replace it. Without the cover provided by her success in meeting the expectations of the public dimension, she was confronted with the emptiness that lay underneath it. She felt deflated and depressed.

Ruth suggests that one escape from her neurotic anxiety would be to learn to "settle for my nice and comfortable life I have now." She does not, however, actually accept that such a choice would provide comfort and relief from her symptoms. She also suggests that if the counselor provided a new and correct belief system for her, it would alleviate the panic and fear she experiences in making decisions. As an existential counselor I do not believe that either of these choices would eliminate her anxious symptoms of existential guilt. The artificial relief she would receive from one of these choices would be only a temporary postponement of her anxiousness until the time when her fundamental lack of reflective awareness and personal responsibility was exposed again. I would help her understand that her anxiety is a reminder that she cannot continue to avoid the obligation to decide what a worthy life would be for her and to begin to form her life in that direction. I would also emphasize that her existential anxiety is a positive reminder to her that she has within her the vitality and power to carry out her life project. I would reassure her of her capacity to take charge of her existence with all its complexity and challenges. She need not retreat into a disengagement from her self or accept life as it is with no choice in the matter. I would use her experience of existential guilt as the instigator for reflection on her inner strength and her ability to explore and clarify the self that is the core of her existence.

Authenticity. Although Ruth comes to counseling preoccupied with the sense of being lost, confused, and stuck, she is primarily interested in finding the right direction so that she can start proceeding that way. She asks to be told what to do. The existential approach understands that she cannot stop feeling lost or confused and "get on her way" until she has decided where she wants to go. It is only when she gains clarity about her goals that the motivation to proceed will be activated. No artificial goals will do, not even those prescribed by a counselor. At times Ruth has used her father's values as the criteria by which to judge the worth of her own life. To abandon the responsibility for determining one's values is to live inauthentically. It would be my role to ensure that Ruth reaches into herself to locate her own inclinations and purposes. I would need to assist her in becoming increasingly capable of following the directions that she has judged worthy for her. Existentialists understand that living authentically means being true to one's own evaluation of what is a valuable existence for oneself.

Authentic living is sometimes mistakenly assumed to consist merely of doing as one pleases, being able to choose freely and pursue the inclination of the moment and live spontaneously. Such a notion of living "selfishly," as Ruth defines it, is a caricature of authenticity. Authentic living consists of establishing one's own personal direction. It includes taking into account the realistic limitations of one's self, the givens of the situation, and one's own and others' values and rights. To live authentically is to make well-informed and reflective choices in accordance with the values that one recognizes as worth committing oneself to. This means developing a reflective rather than an impulsive "do-your-own-thing" attitude. In helping Ruth live authentically I would act on the assumption that within herself she does have a notion of what kind of life would be worthy for her. First, I would work with her to discover this as yet ill-formed idea. Next, I would encourage her to check on this notion in order to judge its ultimate rightness under the light of reflection. Out of this judgment would come a clarity of direction for her life grounded on her own assessment.

Existential Techniques

The existential method shares with other psychotherapeutic approaches the use of basic counseling skills such as attending to clients' descriptions of their experience rather than assuming to know what they have experienced, reflecting rather than distorting the client's meaning, and reassuring rather than confusing the client. The work of existential counselors is based on philosophical assumptions about the essential nature of human existence. This approach to counseling is not driven by techniques, nor can it be identified by the use of a specific set of techniques. Different existential counselors use different techniques that they have found personally helpful in enabling clients to move through the course of therapy.

This does not mean that existential counselors are eclectic in the sense of possessing a collection of techniques developed by the various theoretical schools of counseling for application depending on the clients' specific problem. Nor are they eclectic in the sense of being nontheoretical and guided by the pragmatic criterion of "doing whatever works to relieve the symptom." The various techniques that existential counselors use are chosen to serve the goals of existential therapy. From an existential perspective the use of a diversity of unintegrated techniques, procedures, and treatments based on different assumptions about human change and development presents clients with an incoherent and confused therapeutic experience, at times more harmful than helpful. What distinguishes existential therapy is its understanding that the human task is to mold one's life substance into a caring and worthy existence. Until clients take on this responsibility, their lives will lack integrity and meaning. This understanding serves to inform the techniques and work of an existential therapist. Existential counselors engage with clients in a mutual effort to achieve a greater clarity of the dimensions of their existence, to formulate a worthy purpose for their lives, and to act in light of this purpose.

Because existential counseling is theory-driven rather than technique-driven, I will use this section to describe the sequence of stages in which issues would be taken up during the course of existential counseling. It is the focus of the therapeutic work in each stage that determines what the counselor does in the sessions.

Existential therapy usually lasts from six months to a year. Counselors act more as tutors than as expert healers. Their basic task is to teach clients to uncover and reflect on their life structures. They maintain the focus of the counseling sessions on the clients' work of bringing to awareness the assumptions that compose their experience. They then join with clients to think through and reflect on these assumptions. The relationship with clients is based on a mutual quest for the clients' self-understanding. A relationship of honesty and trust is essential for freeing clients to expose their inner selves both to the therapist and to themselves.

The purpose of existential therapy is to help clients sort out and make sense of their particular way of being, reorder their experience, and find more centered ways to create a meaningful life. Because existential counseling requires a rigorous self-examination, clients can benefit only insofar as they commit themselves to explore the basic dimensions of their existence. If clients only want to rid themselves of specific symptoms or solve a particular problem without touching on the rest of their existence, they will not be well served by the existential approach. This method presupposes their full engagement and honest intention to face their lives more completely than they have so far been able to do on their own.

Existential psychotherapy often follows a course of development consisting of three phases. First, there is an examination of the client's assumptions about the world in all four of the dimensions described previously. In this phase the counselor encourages clients to recognize, define, and question the ways in which they structure their experience. Clients examine the notions they normally hold to be true without question—that is, those notions that construct their experience of the world, others, and themselves as real or unreal. This phase leads to a clearer understanding and acceptance of the inner self; it enables clients to feel at home and at one with themselves. Second, after clients have come to know themselves more fully, they are assisted in determining who they want to become. They review and evaluate the assumptions uncovered in the first phase. They are helped to discern what kind of life they consider worthy—that is, to determine what they hold to be ultimately valuable. This clarification of their personal values provides a basis for commitment and action. The third phase concentrates on helping clients recognize, define, and elaborate on their personal talents and plans in order to increase their capacity to actually move in the directions they have identified as worthy. This phase also attends to the difficulties the clients experience in creating the self they have decided to become. Because we are not all-powerful, we do not control all the consequences of our actions, and because we are not perfect, not all of what we decide to do is carried out. The forging of a life of value is not a smooth process without adversity. During this final phase clients are helped to come to terms with the challenge to become what they have determined to be. I will now discuss these three phases in more detail.

Self-exploration. In the first phase of work with clients existential counselors assist them in uncovering and clarifying their assumptions. The task is to enable clients to become aware of themselves as responsible, active creators of their own existence. Many clients initially present their problems in living as entirely the result of external causes. Ruth places the responsibility for her predicament on her parents and on John, her husband, who have told her who and what she should be. Although she hopes that she will discover ways of taking charge of her own destiny, she has no inkling of how to proceed in gaining such insight and mastery. She has spent considerable time struggling with her problems without much success. She has come to feel increasingly lost, lonely, and isolated.

As an existential therapist I would encourage Ruth not to take anything for granted but to clarify, explain, define, and explore as a means to learn to reflect. When she describes how others have contributed to her problems, I would remind her to consider things from her own perspective rather than speculating about other people's perspectives and would bring the discussion back to reflection on her assumptions. The point would be to make explicit what was implied by her descriptions. In order to assist her in making her implied assumptions explicit, I would use small interventions such as "What is your perception of that?" "How do you see that?" "What is that like for you?" "What is your experience of that?" "What does that evoke for you?" "What does that mean to you?" "How does that strike you?" "What do you make of that?" "How do you respond to that?" Or if Ruth were to say "Every birthday it's the same story; everybody expects me to organize the party," I would respond with something like "Do you mean you have the impression that you're being exploited?" This kind of question shifts the focus onto her inner experience and to her assumptive interpretations. I would not present myself as the authority on her assumptions but as a guide to support her own recognition and identification of them. If I did suggest what scheme lay behind an experience, I would do so tentatively and with an invitation for her to correct my interpretation. But these types of intervention would need to emerge from my genuine openness to understanding and comprehending her world view, not from a wish to implement a certain technique or play a clever game with her.

During this phase of uncovering assumptions I would work to have Ruth take responsibility for noticing and identifying her interpretive schemes by teaching her basic monitoring and reflective skills. I would tutor her in an existential attitude of constant alertness and openness to her own processes and coach her in how to conduct her own investigations into her assumptions about life. She would be taught to reconsider and think through her reactions rather than passively accepting the feelings that have been produced by her presumptions. I would remain alert for the implied assumptions and keep querying her about these and encouraging further exploration and clarification. If she began to realize how important her reconsideration of her assumptions and opinions was, she would sometimes catch herself in the middle of her sentence to reflect on the notion that led to the experience she was describing. Clients usually become fascinated with the examination of their own world and their views and come to see how every facet of their experience expresses their expectations and standpoints. The existential method assumes that clients are able to make sense of their experience for themselves and that reflection does not require superior levels of intelligence. I would support Ruth in her reflective efforts and hope she gained trust in her competence to recognize her schemes and to develop her own insights. I would work to stimulate in her a desire for self-investigation while letting her experiment with the skills required for its successful exercise.

As mentioned in the section on assessment, the course of uncovering assumptions optimally proceeds sequentially through the natural, public, private, and ideal dimensions of human existence. The purpose of this exploration is to enable clients to get a clear picture of their self-structures as they presently exist. In this phase existential counseling shares with many cognitive approaches an emphasis on the importance of examining personal assumptions. However, cognitive therapies often understand these assumptions to be either the negative result of unfortunate learning processes and in need of correction or as simply wrong and in need of rejection. In existential therapy the purpose of pursuing knowledge of one's assumptions is not simply to remove the symptoms that are the result of inappropriate beliefs but also to gain a deeper understanding of one's own interpretive schemes. Self-understanding is a necessary step on the way to self-direction.

Choice of life direction. When clients have achieved some depth of awareness of their present intentions and assumptions, the counselor helps them determine if these are the directions they consider worthy for guiding their future commitments and actions. The self-awareness gained in the first phase brings with it an acceptance of one's self, including both those aspects seen as worthy and those seen as unworthy. Clients come to understand that "they are who they are" and that changes can come only from what they already are. From the experience of being at home with themselves, clients can genuinely start to take stock of their lives rather than having to defend their past actions and can move toward determining what they deem to be worthy for them to become.

In the second phase of therapy clients are encouraged to examine further the source and authority of their present value system. Out of this exploration they can gain new insight into the purpose of their life. Those values that had been assumed because of public expectations ultimately lack power to provide personal meaning and motivation. Even if the content of one's values is not changed, they need to be converted from doctrines maintained for public acceptability to beliefs integral to one's self definition. Only values that emerge from the center of one's being can inspire one's life with vitality and power.

The original source of a person's values, ideals, and norms has little bearing on their ultimate worthiness. Ruth's childhood religious values need not be rejected out of hand because they were taught to her by her father. From the perspective of self-acceptance and awareness she could decide that acting on either all or part of this value system would give her life a form she would judge worthy.

In determining what kind of life they would value for themselves, clients can imagine themselves on their death bed, looking back over what they did with the life that they had been given. Using this perspective, they can sometimes more easily understand what they would consider to be a worthy life for them. Also, as described earlier, an examination of what it is that they would be willing to die for, if necessary, provides insight into what would be worth living for. In assisting clients to determine the values they want to live by, it is also important to help them think through the implications and consequences of the sort of life they are determining to live. Choices for the direction that one's life is to take affect the assumptions in the other dimensions of one's existence. Work in this second phase of therapy includes recognition of the implications that value choices have for one's relationships to nature and one's body, to the social world, and to one's private self. Clients often find that deciding on a worthy direction for one's life increases their existential anxiety. It is not easy to overcome habits of thought and response, thus, becoming aware of what one values is not a one-time act. There are cycles of retreat and renewal that must be recognized by both therapist and client.

Manifesting the worthy life. The determination of what has ultimate value is not an end in itself, it is only a prelude to actually living the value and engaging in the life process of creating a worthy existence. The goal is always to enable clients to find ways in which they can use their values in some concrete way. The third phase of existential counseling concerns the carrying out of a personally valued life. The beginning of this phase involves assisting clients to recognize their talents and to explore ways of developing them further and putting them to positive use. Once Ruth has identified what values she wants to live by, it is important to help her think through how she can implement these values in practice. In working with her I would assist her in bringing to light those strengths that were previously unsuspected or that were used in self-destructive, rather than constructive, ways. For example, her ability to care for her family might be an ability that she can draw on as a teacher. The search to identify her talents would need to focus on her inner experience of herself and her world. The emphasis would be on identifying the talents themselves, not on how she might have been misusing them. She says that she has "pretty much lived for others so far," and this has fostered her family's dependence on her. By looking at the basic root of this negative behavior and identifying the talent that it implies, she can see how it could be used in service of her values. She says that she "gives and gives" and that she has been told that this is wrong. We would explore her acceptance of the notion that she should not be a giving person. There is nothing inherently wrong in such activity, and although she may have misused this talent, her capacity to serve others may be one of her major assets. She could come to recognize that the polarities of total giving and total lack of giving are not the only possibilities. There is a continuum of possibilities between these poles, and she can apply her talent flexibly. Thus, instead of dismissing the talent, she could use it in ways appropriate to situations. In addition to helping her identify and make use of the talents that she already has, I would want to work with her on expanding her existing repertoire of talents. By identifying and cultivating new talents she will be better able to bring into being the life she has chosen as worthy.

We are never able, however, to actualize completely the goals we have set for ourselves. We are unable to lead a life that is entirely modeled according to our intentions and values. Life is much more encompassing than our individual wills. What we actually become is the result of the interaction between our intentions and skills and the actions of nature, social forces, and other people. Eventually even the most determined of us will have to acknowledge our failures and limitations to become what we have envisioned. We will have to have the compassion to forgive ourselves for the existential guilt we feel for not becoming what we have judged to be worthy. At the same time we need to exercise the courage to continue striving.

Whereas the focus of the first phase of existential counseling is on helping clients develop self-knowledge and the focus of the second phase is on assisting them to determine what would make their lives worthy, the third phase is concerned with working with clients in their efforts to realize the values they have chosen. On the one hand, it involves encouraging clients to continue to act out their values, even when the consequences are tempered and redirected by circumstances and social forces. On the other hand, it involves helping them cultivate an acceptance of themselves when they are unfaithful to their own values. The ultimate aim of existential counseling is to enable clients to engage themselves in resolute action that is based on the authentic purpose of creating a worthy existence out of their life substance.

JERRY COREY'S WORK WITH RUTH FROM AN EXISTENTIAL PERSPECTIVE

Basic Assumptions

The existential approach to counseling assumes that the relationship the therapist establishes with the client is of the utmost importance in determining how successful therapy will be. Therapy is not something that I do *to* the person (in this case, Ruth); I am not a technical expert who acts on a passive client. I view therapy as a dialogue in the deepest and most genuine sense, an honest exchange between Ruth and me. We will be partners traveling on a journey, and neither of us knows where it will end. At times we will not even have a clear idea of where we are heading. She and I may both be changed by the encounter, and I expect that she will touch off powerful associations, feelings, memories, and reactions within me. My hope is to understand her world from a subjective viewpoint and, at the same time, to let her know my personal reactions her in our relationship.

A fundamental aspect of this approach is respect for the client, which implies having faith in Ruth's capacity to recognize her role in creating her current life situation and to discover new ways of being. My job as her therapist is to help her understand how she is dealing with the basic issues in her life, such as responsibility, choice, and meaning. I hope that she will discover, through self-exploration in therapy and her willingness to take risks, that she can live without remaining committed to earlier assumptions about life that may no longer be valid or useful. Primarily through the therapeutic relationship that we create, she will find the resources to challenge some of the ways in which she is living a restricted existence, and she will be able to live more freely and responsibly.

Initial Assessment of Ruth

Ruth appears to be a good candidate for existential therapy. She is courageous enough to question the meaning of life and to challenge some of her comfortable, but dull, patterns. She is facing a number of developmental crises, such as wondering what life is about now that her children are getting ready to leave home. As she begins to expand her vision of the choices open to her, her anxiety is increasing. The process of raising questions has led to more questions, yet her answers are few. She is grappling with what she wants for herself, apart from her long-standing definition of herself as wife and mother. A major theme is posed by the question ''How well am I living life?'' One of Ruth's strengths is her willingness to ask such anxiety-producing questions. Another of her assets is that she has already made some choices and taken some significant steps. She did diverge from her fundamentalist religion, which she no longer found personally meaningful; she has returned to college; she is motivated to change her life; and she has sought out therapy as a way to help her find the paths she wants to travel.

Goals of Therapy

The purpose of existential therapy is not to ''cure'' people of disorders; rather it is to help them become aware of what they are doing and to prod them out of the stance of a victim. It is aimed at helping people like Ruth get out of their rigid roles and see more clearly the ways in which they have been leading a narrow and restricted existence. The basic purpose of her therapy is to provide her with the insights necessary to discover, establish, and use the freedom that she possesses. In many ways she is blocking her own freedom. My function is to help her recognize her part in creating her life situation, including the distress she feels. I assume that as she sees the ways in which her existence is limited, she will take steps toward her liberation. My hope is that she can create a more responsible and meaningful existence.

Therapeutic Procedures

As an existential therapist I do not rely on a well-developed set of techniques. Instead, I focus on certain themes that I consider to be part of the human condition, and I emphasize my ability to be fully present with my client by challenging her and by reacting to her. My role is to help Ruth clarify what it is that brought her to me, where she is right now, what it is she wants to change, and what she can do to make these changes happen. I will borrow techniques from several therapies as we explore her current thoughts, feelings, and behaviors within the current situations and events of her life. When we deal with her past, I will encourage her to relate her feelings and thoughts about past events to her present situation. To get some idea of the questions I might pursue with her, consider the following, any of which we might eventually explore in therapy sessions:

- "In what ways are you living as fully as you might? And how are you living a restricted existence?"
- "To what degree are you living by your own choices, as opposed to living a life outlined by others?"
- "What choices have you made so far, and how have these choices affected you?"
- "What are some of the choices you are faced with now? How do you deal with the anxiety that is a part of making choices for yourself and accepting personal freedom?"
- "What are some of the changes that you most want to make, and what is preventing you from making them?"

In essence, Ruth is about to engage in a process of opening doors to herself. The experience may be frightening, exciting, joyful, depressing, or all of these at times. As she wedges open the closed doors, she will also begin to loosen the deterministic shackles that have kept her psychologically bound. Gradually, as she becomes aware of what she has been and who she is now, she will be better able to decide what kind of future she wants to carve out for herself. Through her therapy she can explore alternatives for making her visions become real.

The Therapeutic Process

At this point in her therapy Ruth is coming to grips more directly than she has before with the midlife crisis that she is experiencing. She has been talking about values by which she lived in the past that now hold little meaning for her, about her feelings of emptiness, and about her fears of making "wrong" choices. Below are some excerpts from several of our sessions.

Elements of the process

Examining Ruth's marital problems. One of the areas that I will explore with Ruth is her relationship with John.

RUTH: At 39 I'm just now agonizing over who I am. Perhaps it's too late.

JERRY: Well, I don't know that there's a given time when we should ask such questions. I feel excited for you and respect you for asking these questions now.

RUTH: What I know is that my life has been very structured up to this point, and now all this questioning is unsettling to me and is making me anxious. I wonder if I want to give up my predictable life and face the unknown. Sometimes I feel more powerful, and there are moments when I believe I can change some things about my life. But I wonder if it's worth the risk!

JERRY: I'm very touched by what you're saying, and I remember some of my own struggles in facing uncertainty. When you say you're anxious, it would help me to understand you better if you could tell me some of the times or situations in which you feel this anxiety.

RUTH: Sometimes I feel anxious when I think about my relationship with John. I'm beginning to see many things I don't like, but I'm afraid to tell him about my dissatisfactions.

JERRY: Would you be willing to tell me some of the specific dissatisfactions you have with John?

Ruth then proceeds to talk about some of the difficulties she is experiencing with John. I also encourage her to share with me some of the impulses that frighten her. I am providing a safe atmosphere for her to express some new awarenesses without reacting judgmentally to her. I also give her some of my personal reactions to what she is telling me. Then I ask her if she talks very often with John in the way she is talking with me. I am receptive to her and wonder out loud whether he could also be open to her if she spoke this way with him. We end the session with my encouraging her to approach him and say some of the things to him that she has discussed in this session.

Helping Ruth find new values. In a later session Ruth initiates her struggles with religion.

RUTH: I left my religion years ago, but I haven't found anything to replace it. I'm hoping that you can help me find some new values. You have so much more experience, and you seem happy with who you are and what you believe in. On my own I'm afraid that I might make the wrong decisions, and then I'd really be messed up.

JERRY: If I were to give you answers, that wouldn't be fair to you. It would be a way of saying that I don't see you as capable of finding your own way. Maybe a way for you to begin is to ask some questions. I know, for me, one way of getting answers is to raise questions.

RUTH: I know that the religion I was brought up in told me very clearly what was right and wrong. I was taught that once married, always married—and you make the best of the situation. Well, I'm not so willing to accept that now.

JERRY: How is that so?

RUTH: Sometimes I'm afraid that if I stay in therapy, I'll change so much that I'll have little in common with John, and I may eventually break up our marriage.

JERRY: You know, I'm aware that you've somehow decided that your changes will cause the breakup of your marriage. Could it be that your changes might have a positive effect on your relationship?

RUTH: You're right, I haven't thought about it in that way. And I guess I've made the assumption that John won't like my changes. I more often worry that what I'm doing in therapy will eventually make me want to leave him, or he might want to leave me. Sometimes I have an impulse to walk away from my marriage, but I get scared thinking about who I would be without John in my life.

JERRY: Why not imagine that this did happen, and for a few minutes talk out loud about who you would be if John weren't a part of your life. Just let out whatever thoughts or images that come to your mind, and try not to worry about how they sound.

RUTH: All my life I've had others tell me who and what I should be, and John has picked up where my parents and church left off. I don't know what my life is about apart from being a wife and a mother. What would our kids think if John and I were to split up? How would it affect them? Would they hate me for what I'd done to the family? I know I'm tired of living the way I am, but I'm not sure what I want. And I'm scared to death of making any more changes for fear that it will lead to even more turmoil. John and the kids liked the "old me" just fine, and they seem upset by the things I've been saying lately.

JERRY: In all that you just said, you didn't allow yourself to really express how you might be different if they were not in your life. It's easier for you to tune in to how the people in your life might be affected by your changes than for you to allow yourself to imagine how you'd be different. It does seem difficult for you to fantasize being different. Why not give it another try? Keep the focus on how you want to be different, rather than the reactions your family would have to your changing.

Dealing with Ruth's anxiety. Ruth has trouble changing. There is immediate anxiety whenever she thinks of being different. She is beginning to see that she has choices, that she does not have to wait around until John gives her permission to change, and that others do not have to make her choices for her. Yet she is terrified by this realization, and for a long time it appears that she is immobilized in her therapy. She will not act on the choices available to her. So I go with her feelings of being stuck and explore her anxiety with her. Here is how she describes these feelings.

RUTH: I often wake up in the middle of the night with terrible feelings that the walls are closing in on me! I break out in cold sweats, I have trouble breathing, and I can feel my heart pounding. At times I worry that I'll die. I can't sleep, and I get up and pace around and feel horrible.

JERRY: Ruth, as unpleasant as these feelings are, I hope you learn to pay attention to these signals. They're warning you that all is not well in your life and that you're ready for change.

I know that Ruth sees anxiety as a negative thing, something she would like to get rid of once and for all. I see her anxiety as the possibility of a new starting point for her. Rather than simply getting rid of these symptoms, she can go deeply into their meaning. I see her anxiety as the result of her increased awareness of her freedom along with her growing sense of responsibility for deciding what kind of life she wants and then taking action to make these changes a reality.

Exploring the meaning of death. Eventually we get onto the topic of death and explore its meaning to Ruth.

RUTH: I've been thinking about what we talked about before—about what I want from life before I die. You know, for so many years I lived in dread of death because I thought I'd die a sinner and go to hell for eternity. I suppose that fear has kept me from looking at death. It has always seemed so morbid.

JERRY: It doesn't have to be morbid. As we talked about before, unless you can confront your own death, I don't think you'll be able to live life to its fullest. There are ways that you may be "dead" even though you're still physically alive.

RUTH: How do you mean that?

JERRY: Why don't you talk about areas of your life where you don't feel really alive. How often do you feel a sense of excitement about living?

RUTH: It would be easier for me to tell you of the times I feel half dead! I'm dead to having fun. Sexually I'm dead.

JERRY: Can you think of some other ways you might be dead?

I am trying to get Ruth to evaluate the quality of her life and to begin to experience her deadness. After some time she admits that she has allowed her spirit to die. Old values have died, and she has not planted new ones. She is gaining some dim awareness that there is more to living than breathing. It is important that she allow herself to recognize her deadness and feel it as a precondition for her rebirth. I operate under the assumption that by really experiencing and expressing the ways in which she feels dead, she can begin to focus on how she wants to be alive, if at all. Only then is there hope that she can learn new ways to live.

JERRY: Ruth, I wonder if you would let yourself imagine that you're dying, and even fantasize your funeral. What might each of the significant people in your life say about you at your funeral?

I ask her to close her eyes and say aloud all the things that John, her parents, her brothers and sisters, and her children might say. Then I ask her to make up her own eulogy. I pose a number of questions about her life and ask her in fantasy to think about her answers. "What have you done with life so far? Whom have you touched? What have you left behind? What dreams never came to fruition? How did you make a difference by having lived? What regrets do you have? What do you wish you had done differently? What opportunities have you passed up? What choices have you not made? What unfinished projects are left behind? And what would you do differently if you could live all over again?" Although I do not ask her all of these questions at once, I do challenge her to reflect on what she might begin to do today to lessen the chances of having too many regrets.

Process commentary

Ruth's experience in therapy accentuates the basic assumption that there are no absolute answers outside of herself. She learns that therapy is a process of opening up doors bit by bit, giving her more potential for choices. This process happens largely because of the relationship between us. She becomes well aware that she cannot evade responsibility for choosing for herself. She learns that she is constantly creating herself by the choices she is making, as well as by the choices she is failing to make. As her therapist I support her attempts at experimenting with new behaviors in our sessions. Our open discussions, in which we talk about how we are experiencing each other, are a new behavior for her. These sessions provide a safe situation for her to extend new dimensions of her being. At the same time, I teach her how she might use what she is learning in her everyday life. She risks getting angry at me, being direct with me, and telling me how I affect her. We work on ways in which she might continue this behavior with selected people in her environment.

One of my aims is to show Ruth the connection between the choices she is making or failing to make and the anxiety she is experiencing. I do this by asking her to observe herself in various situations throughout the week. In what situations does she "turn the other cheek" when she feels discounted? When does she put her own needs last and choose to be the giver to others? In what specific instances does she fail to be assertive? Through this self-observation process she gradually sees some specific ways in which her choices are directly contributing to her anxiety.

My goal in working with Ruth is not to eliminate her anxiety; rather, it is to help her understand what it means. From my perspective anxiety is a signal that all is not well, that a person is ready for some change in life. Ruth does learn that how she deals with her anxiety will have a lot to do with the type of new identity she creates. She sees that she can take Valium to dissipate the anxiety or she can listen to the message that her anxiety is conveying.

Perhaps the critical aspect of Ruth's therapy is her recognition that she has a choice to make: She can continue to cling to the known and the familiar, even deciding to settle for what she has in life and quitting therapy. She can also accept the fact that in life there are no guarantees, that in spite of this uncertainty and the accompanying anxiety she will still have to *act* by making choices and then living with the consequences. She chooses to commit herself to therapy.

Questions for Reflection

1. What are some critical choices that you have made? Can you think of any turning points in your life? How have some of your choices affected the life you now experience?
2. What does freedom mean to you? Do you believe that you are the author of your life? that you are now largely the result of your choices? How do you suppose that your personal view of freedom would influence the way you worked with Ruth?
3. Dr. Polkinghorne focuses on existential anxiety and authenticity. Apply his work with Ruth to themes in your own life. Can you recall any periods in your life when you experienced anxiety over the necessity of making choices? In looking at your own life, to what degree has your freedom led you to assume responsibility for your choices? In what ways have you experienced anxiety over the realization of your freedom and responsibility? In what ways are your answers to these questions relevant to the way you would approach Ruth?
4. What life experiences have you had that could help you identify with Ruth? Have you shared any of her struggles? Have you faced similar issues? How have you dealt with these personal struggles and issues? How are your answers to these questions related to your potential effectiveness as her therapist?
5. What are your general reactions to the ways in which Dr. Polkinghorne and I have worked with Ruth? What aspects of both of these styles of counseling might you carry out in somewhat the same manner? What

different themes might you focus on? What different techniques might you use?

6. Compare this approach to working with Ruth with the previous approaches, psychoanalytic therapy and Adlerian therapy. What major differences do you see?
7. How might you work with Ruth's fears associated with opening doors in her life? Part of her wants to remain as she is, and the other part yearns for a fresh life. How would you work with this conflict?
8. Using this approach, how would you deal with her fears related to dying? Do you see any connection between her anxieties and her view of death?
9. What are your thoughts and feelings about death and dying as they apply to you and to those you love? To what extent do you think that you have explored your own anxieties pertaining to death and loss? How would your answer to this question largely determine your effectiveness in counseling a person such as Ruth?
10. What are some of the other existential themes mentioned in this chapter that have personal relevance to your life? How do you react to the question "Can therapists inspire their clients to deal with their existential concerns if they have not been willing to do this in their own lives?"

WALT: "WHAT'S THERE TO LIVE FOR?"

Some Background Data

The question of meaning in life is especially critical to Walt, a 74-year-old retiree who has lived with his son and daughter-in-law in Wisconsin for four years since his wife, Rose Ann, died. Walt lived in Honolulu from his birth until shortly after Rose Ann lost a long battle with cancer. The couple were married for 50 years. As a Pacific Islander he has experienced a great deal of loneliness and dislocation since he moved away from his home. Although he admits that the people in his new community near Green Bay are friendly, it has just not been the same for him. Not only has a huge gap been created in his life with the loss of Rose Ann, but he also must contend with feelings of being cut off from his roots in Hawaii.

During the last few months of Rose Ann's life a number of people in the community helped Walt care for her at home. He says that he is surprised by how much he was able to do for her when she was so sick. However, he does feel guilty for having let her down in some ways. Shortly before she died, she wanted to talk with him about her impending death. However, he felt that he could not handle the reality of her death, and he kept hoping that somehow she would be cured or would live several more years. Even though she has been dead for four years, Walt still suffers from guilt and regret over not having talked with her more. He feels that there were so many things left unsaid between the two of them, and now he ruminates over what he wishes he had done differently. He reports that he sleeps terribly, and when he is awake he simply cannot find enough things to keep him busy and to distract him from his endless rumination. He says that he misses all the friends they had for so many years in Honolulu and that he fears making new friends because "they'll all die anyway." He often wishes that he had died instead of Rose Ann, for she would have been better able to cope with his death than he has managed to do.

During this last four-year period he spent some time in a mental-health facility because of prolonged periods of depression, disorientation, and suicidal tendencies. As a part of his recovery he participates in a day-treatment program. As an outpatient he is involved in individual therapy a couple of times each week, and this therapy has continued for several months.

Walt has discussed a number of current life issues with me, including the following:

- He feels depressed most of the time and often wishes that he could die so that he would not have to feel such loneliness, emptiness, and hopelessness. He says that he does not have much to look forward to in his life; there is only a past that is filled with mistakes and regrets.
- Walt was very dependent emotionally on Rose Ann, and when she died of cancer, a big part of him died. He continues to feel lost and like a child in so many ways. He does not feel close to anyone, and he is convinced that his presence in his son's home is a burden to all.
- He has never made the adjustment from Hawaii to Wisconsin, saying that he feels out of his element. He loved the sense of community that he and his wife enjoyed for almost 50 years. Although he has tried to make a new home, he says that he just cannot forget everything and start a new life now.
- Before he was forced to retire, Walt taught in a high school. As a teacher he felt good, because he had some measure of worth. He enjoyed working with young people, especially encouraging them to think about the direction of their lives. He was a fantastic teacher, well-liked by his students. After Rose Ann died, he went into a long and deep depression; coupled with his age, this resulted in the beginning of his retirement years.
- For Walt retirement is next to death. He feels "put out to pasture," simply passing time without getting in people's way. His major problem is this lack of purpose in life. He is searching for something to take the place of his wife, his home, and his job, yet he sees little chance that he will find a substitute that will bring any meaning to his life. The losses are simply too great.

My Way of Working with Walt as an Existential Therapist

My goal in working with Walt is to provide adequate support for him at a very difficult time in his life. What I see him as needing is an opportunity to talk about his regrets and what it feels like to be depressed; he needs to feel that he is being heard and cared for. At the same time, I must challenge him to begin to create his own meaning, even though most of his support systems are gone. To accomplish this goal, I encourage Walt to talk, recounting things about his past that he regrets and wishes had been different. I urge him to talk about the losses he feels with Rose Ann gone, with his island community far away, and with his teaching career over. Early in his therapy he needs to talk freely and to be listened to, and he needs to express his feelings of guilt, regret, sorrow, and separation.

Walt's weaknesses and strengths. Where do I proceed with Walt? I do not ignore his depression, for this is a symptom that carries a message. By beginning with his full recognition and acceptance of his hopelessness, I may be able to help him change. I am especially interested in how he derived meaning through his work. I want to know the ways in which the school contributed to his feeling that he had something to offer people. So we talk of all the things that he got from teaching adolescents and what he learned about life from them. In many ways Walt, who did not have much of an adolescence, tried to make up for this gap in his youth through his work with young people. He found them floundering and lost, in search of who they were. He derived a great deal of personal meaning from seeing his students get excited about literature and in seeing them relate the struggles of the characters they were reading about to their own search for meaning in life.

Although Walt does need this opportunity to relive times from his past, I see a danger that we could stop here. In that case our sessions would be little more than "talks" and remembrances of days gone by. I want more for Walt. This desire may be part of my own need to see him move in other directions. I may be fearful of getting lost in his depression with him. And if he does not find new hope and a will to continue to live, I could be threatened in many ways. For one thing, it might jar me into seeing that I could someday be faced with the same search for something to hope for. For another, if he does not move beyond his depression, I will look at myself as a therapist and wonder if I have given him enough. Would he find a meaning for living if I were more of a person to him or more skilled in helping him at this juncture in his life?

Our therapeutic relationship. Let me proceed by saying more about how I see Walt and what is being generated within me as I work with him. Because the existential therapist assumes that therapy is an I/thou encounter and that what happens between the two people is central to determining outcomes, I will focus on this relationship. Questions that I will explore are: How do I see Walt at this time in his life? Where does he want to go? What does he want from me? How can I be instrumental in his life?

In some ways Walt is telling me that he is a *victim*—that his choices have mostly been taken from him, that there is little he can do to change the situation he finds himself in, and that he is for the most part doomed to live out a sterile future. He continually tells me that there is nothing that either of us can do to bring back his wife; he feels almost as hopeless when it comes to getting some kind of work; and he sees no way of being able to return to Hawaii to live out his remaining years. Although I think that it is necessary for me to perceive his world as he does, I find it hard to accept his conclusions. I want to provide a supportive atmosphere, so that he can communicate to me what it is like for him to be in his world; yet at the same time I want to challenge his passive stance toward life. Although he cannot change some of the events of his life, he can change how he continues to look at his life situation. I surely would not tell Walt all the things that I mention below in any single session. But over the course of our time together these are some of the points I would make:

- "You're not a helpless victim. If I see you as a victim and accept the stance you present, I won't be able to help you move beyond being stuck in this place. I want you to at least challenge the assumption that there is little you can do to change. It's this very assumption that's limiting your potential for change."
- "How could you find some of what you had in Hawaii here in Wisconsin? Is there a way that you could hold onto your values and also find new values to give your life meaning?"
- "I see you leading a restricted existence. You've narrowed down the boundaries in which you can take action. I'll try to help you expand these boundaries and act in a greater range of ways."
- "You live in the past much of the time. In telling me all of your failures and dwelling on all of the missed opportunities, you *contribute* to your depression. You wanted to talk about how your life might have been different. Now it may be time to look at what you can do to make *today* different, so that tomorrow you won't look back in regret over one more lost day. Although I accept that your choices are somewhat limited, you do have possibilities for action that you're not recognizing."
- "I hope you can accept your past, even though it wasn't what you wanted, yet not be bound by it. Instead of looking back, you could look ahead and begin walking, however slowly, toward where you want to go."
- "Think about your death. You've fantasized about suicide and thought that death would put an end to a miserable life. What are some of the things you want to complete? What are some of the projects you'd like to finish before you die? What do you want to be able to say at the time of your death about how you've lived? What can you do today to begin working on these projects that have some meaning to you?"

In terms of Walt's themes of not finding meaning in life and thinking about death, especially his suicidal fantasies, I think it is important to confront him with questions such as "What are you living for? What stops you from killing yourself?" I would not want to take lightly Walt's mention of suicide. In light of the fact that he experiences a good deal of depression, it is critical to make an assessment of how likely he is to attempt to take his life. To make such an assessment, I want to find out how often he thinks about suicide and with what degree of detail. Is he preoccupied with suicidal impulses, or is such a fantasy rare? Does he have a detailed plan? Has he cut off social contacts? Has he made any prior attempts on his life? It is essential to carefully consider how seriously he is considering suicide before we take up other themes in his life. This may be his cry for help or a signal that in some way he wants me to offer him hope for a better existence. His prior hospitalization for his suicidal tendencies makes it even more imperative that we explore the degree of suicidal danger. I would arrange for a referral or hospitalization if Walt were acutely suicidal. Moreover, I'd let him know that I was legally obliged to take action if I determined that he was likely to take his life.

Let's briefly look at what I think Walt wants from me and some of the ways in which I can be instrumental as a person for him. As I indicated earlier, working with him challenges me to look at my own life. What would it be like to be in his place? How might I deal with life if I lost my wife and felt abandoned during my later years? What would become of me if I could not work? How might I handle feelings of meaninglessness in my life? I think that it can be useful for me to explore with Walt some of these questions in our sessions. I need to take the time to reflect on these questions, for the degree to which I can face and deal with them is the degree to which I will be a significant force in encouraging him to do the same thing in his life. How can I offer him any hope if I am not willing to struggle with my own potential for depression and hopelessness? If I avoid contemplating my eventual death and what I want to accomplish and experience before that time, how can I challenge him to look to his death for some lessons in learning how to live? One of the most powerful means of understanding him lies within me and my willingness to explore what is being touched off in me as a result of our relationship.

I think that what Walt wants from me is the potential for an interchange of ideas and feelings. He does not want mere reassurance, nor does he want me to cooperate with him in perpetuating his view that there is nothing left to live for and little he can do to actively change his situation. He needs my honest response, my support and caring, my gentle pushing, my insistence that he begin asking how he wants to be different, and my exchanges with him as another human being. I do not know where we will end up, even where we are going. I am not aiming for major personality reconstruction in his case, yet I am pushing for some significant steps that will lead to new action.

So much depends ultimately on Walt and what he is willing to choose and do for himself. I must not let myself be duped into thinking that I can create a will to live in him, that I can do his changing for him, or that I will have an answer for him. Where he ends up will largely be determined by *his* willingness to begin to move himself by taking the initial steps. The best I can offer to him is the inspiration to begin taking those steps. I hope that, through our relationship, he will see that he can move further than he previously allowed himself to imagine.

Follow-Up: You Continue as Walt's Therapist

In what directions would you, as an existential therapist, move with Walt?

1. What are some of your main reactions to my style of working with Walt? Do you have ideas on how to proceed differently or about issues that you would pursue further?
2. How do you see Walt? What are your reactions to him? Would you be willing to accept him as a client? Why or why not?
3. Walt brings out a number of key themes: his wife's death, his forced retirement, his having to leave his home in Hawaii and coming to live with his son's family, his feeling of alienation from the sense of community he once knew, and his personal struggles. Which of these themes (or other ones) would you be most likely to encourage Walt to explore with you? Why?
4. If you are of a different age, gender, and ethnicity from Walt, do you think you'd be able to enter into his subjective world? How would you respond to him if he were to say: "I don't see how you can really understand what I'm going through. You're much younger than I am, you haven't lost your wife or husband, you don't really know about the culture I grew up with, and you've never felt as crazy as I sometimes do. It's just that you're too different from me to know what I have to live with every day." To what extent would you have to be like Walt to identify with his world? If you felt he was right, what would you say or do?
5. In what ways do you think that you could be a positive force in Walt's life? What life experiences or personal characteristics of yours might be instrumental in establishing a *therapeutic* relationship with him? In what ways might your own needs, problems, values, and lack of life experiences actually get in the way of forming a relationship that would be of benefit to him?
6. In what ways does Walt's depression (and feeling of utter hopelessness) affect you personally? How are you likely to respond to him as a result? Might you tend to give him answers? or cheer him up? or agree that his life is hopeless? or reassure him that he *can* find a new meaning in life?
7. I spent time in Walt's sessions allowing him to talk about his past mistakes, regrets, and losses as well as his memories of what gave his

life meaning. For an older person such as Walt what potential value do you see in reminiscing? Or do you think that you might steer him away from such discussion about his past by encouraging him to talk about his life *now* or the future he hopes for?

8. The existential approach is based on the therapist's seeing the world through the perspective of the client. In Walt's view he is a victim with little chance of changing his destiny. He feels that he is doomed to a meaningless existence, and he has resigned himself to simply marking time. What are the implications if you accept and respond to him from his vantage point? Can you think of ways in which you are likely to reinforce his very perceptions that change is unlikely? How might you help him open up to other possibilities for a different future? Would you respond differently if his feelings resulted from his having a painful and incurable chronic illness?
9. How might you respond to Walt's talking about his suicidal fantasies? What would you feel (and probably do) if he told you that he was going to kill himself because he saw no real hope for his future? How do you think that your views and values relating to suicide would affect the way in which you worked with him? What are your legal and ethical responsibilities if you make the assessment that he is indeed at risk of taking his life?
10. What would you see as your main function as Walt's therapist? Would you want mainly to support him? confront him? guide him into specific activities? teach him skills? be his friend?

RECOMMENDED SUPPLEMENTARY READINGS

Existential Psychotherapy (1980), by I. D. Yalom (New York: Basic Books), is a superb treatment of the ultimate human concerns of death, freedom, isolation, and meaninglessness as these issues relate to therapy. This book has depth and clarity, and it is rich with clinical examples that illustrate existential themes. If you were to select just one book on existential therapy, this would be my recommendation as a comprehensive and interesting discussion of the topic.

The Art of the Psychotherapist (1987), by J. F. T. Bugental (New York: Norton), is an outstanding book that bridges the art and science of psychotherapy, making places for both. The author is an insightful and sensitive clinician who writes about the journey of the psychotherapist and the client. It contains a number of case studies and illustrates the therapeutic process through dialogue between client and therapist.

I Never Knew I Had a Choice (1990), by G. Corey and M. Corey (Pacific Grove, CA: Brooks/Cole), is written from an existential perspective and deals with existential themes. It contains many exercises and activities that both counselors and clients can use, especially as "homework assignments" between sessions. The topics covered include our struggle to achieve autonomy; the roles that work, love, sexuality, intimacy, and solitude play in our lives; the meaning of loneliness, death, and loss; and the ways in which we choose our values and philosophies of life. Each chapter is followed by numerous annotated suggestions for further reading.

Existential Counselling in Practice (1988) by E. van Deurzen-Smith (London: Sage), is highly recommended as an excellent overview of the basic assumptions, goals, and key concepts of the existential approach. The author clearly puts into perspective topics such as anxiety, authentic living, clarifying one's worldview, determining values, discovering meaning, and coming to terms with life. There are many rich clinical examples that make the concepts understandable. This book offers practitioners a framework for practicing counseling from an existential perspective.

Man's Search for Meaning (1975), by V. Frankl (New York: Pocket Books), describes the author's experiences in a concentration camp. Frankl shows how it is possible to find meaning in life through suffering. His thesis is that we all have a need to discover meaning.

Freedom and Destiny (1981), by R. May (New York: Norton), focuses on the paradoxes of freedom and destiny and develops implications of these concepts for the practice of psychotherapy. Key issues given attention include choice, freedom and anxiety, death and life's meaning, the renewal of life, and despair and joy.

SUGGESTED READINGS

Belkin, G. (1987). *Contemporary psychotherapies* (2nd ed.). Pacific Grove, CA: Brooks/Cole. (Chapter 13)

Belkin, G. S. (1988). *Introduction to counseling* (3rd ed.). Dubuque, IA: William C. Brown. (Chapter 8)

Burke, J. F. (1989). *Contemporary approaches to psychotherapy and counseling.* Pacific Grove, CA: Brooks/Cole. (Chapter 8)

Corey, G. (1991). *Theory and practice of counseling and psychotherapy* (4th ed.). Pacific Grove, CA: Brooks/Cole. (Chapter 6)

Corsini, R., & Wedding, D. (Eds.). (1989). *Current psychotherapies* (4th ed.). Itasca, IL: F. E. Peacock. (Chapter 10)

Ivey, A. E., Ivey M. B., & Simek-Downing, L. (1987). *Counseling and psychotherapy: Integrating skills, theory, and practice* (2nd ed.). Englewood Cliffs, NJ: Prentice-Hall. (Chapter 10)

Patterson, C. H. (1986). *Theories of counseling and psychotherapy* (4th ed.). New York: Harper & Row. (Chapter 15)

Prochaska, J. O. (1984). *Systems of psychotherapy: A transtheoretical analysis* (2nd ed.). Pacific Grove, CA: Brooks/Cole. (Chapter 3)

Wedding, D., & Corsini, R. J. (Eds.). (1989). *Case studies in psychotherapy.* Itasca, IL: F. E. Peacock. (Chapter 9)

CHAPTER FIVE

Case Approach to Person-Centered Therapy

A PERSON-CENTERED THERAPIST'S PERSPECTIVE ON RUTH by David J. Cain, Ph.D.

David Cain is founder and editor of the *Person-Centered Review* and founder and coordinator of the Association for the Development of the Person-Centered Approach. For more than 15 years he has been a client-centered therapist, teacher, supervisor, consultant, and frequent speaker and workshop presenter. He is a Diplomate in Clinical Psychology of the American Board of Professional Psychology and a member of the Center for Studies of the Person. He is in private practice in Carlsbad, California.

Assessment of Ruth

As a person-centered therapist I would not undertake any formal assessment of Ruth or attempt to establish a diagnosis for her unless she requested an assessment. Therefore, my "assessment" of her consists largely of my attempt to understand how she experiences herself and to assist her in seeing herself more clearly. In person-centered therapy self-assessment and self-definition are seen as part of the ongoing therapeutic process. Thus, I am especially attentive to the ways in which Ruth views herself. In this regard several components of her self-concept emerge from her autobiography. Most striking is that she views herself primarily as a caretaker for her family, a person whose identity, and probably self-esteem, hinges on attending to other people's needs and fulfilling their expectations of her. Self-descriptors such as "superwoman," "good wife," and "good mother" describe not only Ruth but also her life's focus. She is intent on giving to and pleasing others even at the cost of sacrificing her own needs and identity. In a real sense she is self*less,* without a clear sense of who she is.

At the same time, Ruth is in conflict with her present view of herself. By her own admission she doesn't like who she is. She dislikes her overweight body and the fact that her life is devoid of any joyful or meaningful activity apart from her roles as wife and mother. She can imagine that becoming a teacher would be fulfilling but places her own desires behind those of her family.

Her religious beliefs and values are changing and are in conflict with her earlier fundamentalist views. At present, however, her self-concept remains vague and tentative. She dimly perceives whom she might become, yet she is fearful that pursuing her own identity, interests, and needs will result in her losing her husband and family. But she has not given up. In recent years she has become a "questioner," and she holds onto the glimmer of hope that she can "begin to live before it's too late."

Key Issues

From a person-centered perspective a key issue with Ruth is the *incongruence* between the person she is and the person who is "trying" to emerge, though hesitantly and cautiously. Fear is her main obstacle to becoming a newer, fuller, and more gratified self. It is also her warning signal (symptom) that tells her that something is wrong with her life. She feels somewhat secure in her present life, though it is boring and unfulfilling in terms of personal growth and meaning. Yet she fears change because its consequences may be greater than she can or is willing to tolerate. This dilemma is complicated by her lack of trust in her own judgment ("I'm scared I'll make the wrong decisions") and resourcefulness ("I'm trapped and don't see a way out"). As a consequence her inclination is to look to others (God, her therapist) for guidance and direction instead of herself. She seems to feel that because she cannot be trusted, she will find someone else (superior to her) to take responsibility for her life. Paradoxically, she is as much afraid of living as she is of dying. Her numerous physical symptoms (panic, sleep disturbance, heart palpitations, headaches) seem to symbolize the turmoil of her present life. In a real sense her life is "sickening"—that is, depressing, constricted, and avoidant.

There are also hopeful signs in Ruth's current existence. She is restless, dissatisfied, and fearful that life is slipping by. She has a rather meek desire for something better and a vision of what she might become. Her desire to become a teacher seems to provide her with the possibility of achieving more of her potential, because it is a step toward finding personal meaning in her life.

Therapeutic Techniques

As I anticipate becoming Ruth's therapist, my focus is on the nature and quality of the *relationship* I hope to provide for her. Therefore, I do not have any specific techniques in mind as I attempt to assist her, although I will do my best to be fully present and to *listen.* I would like to offer her a trusting, supportive, encouraging relationship, a safe atmosphere for self-learning. If I am successful in creating the sort of relationship I would like, she will experience me as genuinely interested in her, sensitively perceptive of her feelings, and accurately understanding of her expressed and intended meanings. I would hope to communicate my belief in her resourcefulness and my optimism about her capacity to move forward in her life.

In such a therapeutic relationship I anticipate that Ruth will move tentatively at first, perhaps starting with her general sense of dissatisfaction with her life and her physical symptoms. She may well find the nondirective nature of our interaction to be somewhat disturbing at first, preferring that I lead her in the "right" direction, tell her what she needs to do, and "push" her to do it. I hope that my trust in her to determine her own directions and courses of action will enable her to consider that she may have more personal strengths and resources than she is aware of at present. If I can see her as she is and communicate my experience of her accurately, I believe that she will begin to see herself more clearly, including her assets and limitations.

As therapy progresses, Ruth will probably become increasingly aware of the incongruence she experiences between who she is (good mother and good wife) and the person she yearns to be (a teacher and more attractive person). Most probably she will experience guilt over what she perceives as selfishness and will fear a disruption of her marriage and family life if she attends more to her needs. As she expands and modifies her perceptual field, however, she may well come to believe that her own desires and goals are as deserving of attention as those of her family and others.

Ruth may wish to bring her husband into her therapy sessions in order to address this dilemma. Whether John is supportive of her change or not, she will have to wrestle with her own conflict about meeting her needs and becoming more of a separate, independent person. Her marriage will probably go through a dramatic transition if she pursues her hopes. It may improve as she becomes a fuller person or become more conflicted if her husband is threatened by her development.

If therapy is successful, Ruth will come to view herself in a more positive and differentiated way. She will feel more power and control in her life and will probably become more assertive. More of her satisfaction in life will be derived from her work and interests apart from, but not excluding, her roles of mother and wife. As she learns to listen to the messages of her feelings and her physical symptoms, she will attend to and identify her needs and draw on her resources more effectively to satisfy them. Gradually, she will learn that there is someone in her life on whom she can always depend—herself.

JERRY COREY'S WORK WITH RUTH FROM A PERSON-CENTERED PERSPECTIVE

Basic Assumptions

From a person-centered perspective I view counseling as being directed at more than merely solving problems and giving information. It is best aimed at helping clients tap their inner resources, so that they can better deal with their problems, both current and future. In Ruth's case I think that I can best accomplish this goal by creating a climate that is threat-free, one in which she will feel fully accepted by me. I work on the assumption that my clients have the capacity to lead the way in our sessions and that they can profit without my active and directive intervention. Therefore, I do not pin a diagnostic label on clients, for I think that such categories are limiting. I rarely make interpretations, because I believe that clients will be able to learn about themselves without such judgments from me. I will not direct Ruth to go into her past or point her in any other direction. The sessions will be focused on her, and she will be the one to decide the direction we take. Likewise, I will avoid any analysis of so-called transference. If she is having reactions to me, there is no reason to assume that she is reacting to me as she did to her mother; she may be reacting to me personally.

I do not operate on the assumption that Ruth will move forward in therapy only if she is pushed, rewarded, punished, or in some other way controlled. I have a deep faith in her capacity to identify her problems and to find the resources within herself to solve them, provided that I can create a climate of safety, respect, and trust. Thus, I assume that three attributes on my part are necessary and sufficient to release her growth force:

1. *Genuineness.* I am real, without a false front, during the therapy sessions. In other words, I am congruent: my outer expression matches my internal experience.
2. *Unconditional positive regard and acceptance.* My caring for Ruth is not contaminated by evaluation or judgment of her thoughts, feelings, and behaviors.
3. *Accurate empathic understanding.* I can sensitively and accurately comprehend her present experiencing and can convey this understanding to her.

If I genuinely experience these attitudes toward Ruth and successfully communicate them to her, she will decrease her defensive ways and move toward becoming her true self, the person whom she is capable of becoming. Therapy is not so much a matter of my doing something to her; rather, it is establishing a relationship that she can use to engage in self-exploration and ultimately find her own way.

Assessment of Ruth

In talking to Ruth I can see that she is disappointed with where she is in life and that she is not being herself around her friends or family. Her therapy is based on this concern.

As I review Ruth's autobiography, I see her as asking "How can I discover my real self? How can I become the person I would like to become? How can I shed my phony roles and become myself?" My aim is to create an atmosphere in which she can freely, without judgment and evaluation, express whatever she is feeling. If she can experience this freedom to be whatever she is in this moment, she will begin to drop the masks and roles that she now lives by.

Ruth exists largely in response to the demands of others. She seems to have no self of her own, and the source of her values lies outside of herself. She has spent much of her life attempting to think, feel, and behave in the way that others believe that she *ought* to think, feel, and behave. As a result, she is not in contact with what she really values and wants for herself. In order for her to discover her sense of self, she needs a place where she can look nondefensively at the way she is now.

Goals of Therapy

My basic goal is to create a therapeutic climate that will help Ruth discover the kind of person she is, apart from being what others have expected her to be. When her facades come down as a result of the therapeutic process, four of her characteristics should be enhanced: (1) her openness to experience, (2) a greater degree of trust in herself, (3) her internal source of evaluation, and (4) her willingness to live more spontaneously. These characteristics constitute the basic goals of person-centered therapy.

Therapeutic Procedures

When clients begin therapy, they tend to look to me to provide direction and magical answers. They often have rigid beliefs and attitudes, an internal blockage, a sense of being out of touch with their feelings, a basic sense of distrust in themselves, and a tendency to externalize problems. As therapy progresses, I find, they are generally able to express fears, anxiety, guilt, shame, anger, and other feelings that they have deemed too negative to incorporate into their self-structure. Eventually, they are able to distort less, express more feelings that were previously out of awareness, and move in a direction of being more open to all of their experience. They can be in contact, moment by moment, with what they are feeling, with less need to distort or deny this experience.

The Therapeutic Process

Elements of the process

During the early stages of her therapy Ruth does not share her feelings but talks instead about externals. To a large degree she perceives her problems as outside of herself. Somehow, if her father would change, if her husband's attitude would change, and if her children would present fewer problems, she would be all right. During one of our early sessions Ruth wonders whether I will be able to really understand her and help her if she does share her feelings. She indicates that she has some reservations about me because I am a man and that she isn't sure I can empathize with her struggles as a woman.

Exploring our relationship. Ruth lets me know how diffcult it is for her to talk personally to me, and she tells me that it's especially uncomfortable for her to talk with me because I'm a man. I feel encouraged because she is willing to talk to me about her reservations and brings some of her feelings toward me out in the open.

RUTH: I've become aware that I'm careful about what I say around you. It's important that I feel understood, and sometimes I wonder if you can really understand the struggles I'm having as a woman.

JERRY: Well, I like it that you're willing to let me know what it's like for you to attempt to trust me. I would hope that you don't censor what you say around me, and I very much want to understand you. Perhaps you could tell me more about your doubts about my ability to understand you as a woman.

RUTH: It's not what you've said so far, but I'm fearful that I have to be careful around you. I'm not sure how you might judge me or react to me.

JERRY: I'd like the chance to relate to you as a person, so I hope you'll let me know when and if you feel judged or not understood by me.

RUTH: It's not easy for me to talk about myself to any man; all of this is so new to me.

JERRY: What is it that you think I'd have a hard time understanding about you as a woman? And you might want to talk more about what makes it difficult to talk to me.

RUTH: So far, no man has ever been willing to *really* listen to me. I've tried so hard to please my father and then to please John. I suppose I wonder if you can understand how I depended so much on my father, and now on John, to give me a feeling that I'm worthwhile as a woman.

JERRY: Even though I'm not a woman, I still know what it feels like to want to be understood and accepted, and I know what it's like to look to others to get this kind of confirmation.

It is important that we pursue what might get in the way of Ruth's trust in me. As long as she is willing to talk about what she is thinking and feeling while we are together in the sessions, there is a direction that we can follow. Staying with the immediacy of the relationship will inevitably open up other channels of fruitful exploration.

Getting in touch with Ruth's feelings. In a later session Ruth talks about how it is so hard for her to really experience her feelings. She is not very aware of the nature of her feelings, for she blocks off any that she deems inappropriate. She does not permit herself to freely accept the flow of whatever she might be feeling. Notice how she puts it:

RUTH: It's hard for me to feel. Sometimes I'm not sure what it is that I feel.

JERRY: From moment to moment you're not aware of what feelings are flowing inside of you.

RUTH: Yeah, it's difficult enough for me to know what I'm feeling, let alone express it to someone else.

JERRY: So it's also hard for you to let others know how they affect you.

RUTH: Well, I've had lots of practice in sealing off feelings. They're scary.

JERRY: It's scary not knowing what you're feeling, and it's also scary if you know.

RUTH: Sort of . . . When I was a child, I was punished when I was angry. When I cried, I was sent to my room and told to stop crying. Sometimes I remember being happy and playful, only to be told to settle down.

JERRY: So you learned early that your feelings got you in trouble.

RUTH: Just about the time I start to feel something, I go blank or get confused. It's just that I've always thought that I had no right to feel angry, sexual, joyful, sad—or whatever. I just did my work and went on without complaining.

JERRY: You still believe it's better to keep what you feel inside and not express feelings.

RUTH: Right! And I do that especially with my husband and my children.

JERRY: It sounds as if you don't let them know what's going on with you.

RUTH: Well, I'm not so sure they're really that interested in my feelings.

JERRY: Like they really don't care about how you feel. [At that point Ruth begins to cry.] Right now you're feeling something. [Ruth continues crying, and there is a period of silence.]

RUTH: I'm feeling so sad and so hopeless.

JERRY: Yet now you're able to feel, and you can tell me about it.

In this interchange it is important for Ruth to recognize that she can feel and that she is able to express feelings to others. My acceptance of her encourages her to come in contact with her emotions. This is a first step for her. The more difficult task is for her to begin to recognize and share her emotions with the significant people in her life.

Exploring Ruth's marital problems. In another session Ruth brings up her marital difficulties. She explores her mistrust of her own decisions and her search outside of herself for the answers to her problems.

RUTH: I wonder what I should do about my marriage. I'd like to have some time to myself, but what might happen to our family if I made major changes and nobody liked those changes?

JERRY: You wonder what would happen if you expressed your true feelings, especially if your family didn't appreciate your changes.

RUTH: Yes, I guess I do stop myself because I don't want to hurt my family.

JERRY: If you ask for what you want, others are liable to get hurt, and there's no room in your life to think both about what's good for others and what's good for yourself.

RUTH: Yes, I didn't realize I was saying that it has to be either me or them. I do wonder if they'll be angry if I start doing some things for me.

Process commentary

We proceed with how Ruth's fear of others' anger keeps her from asking for what she really wants in her life. She then begins to seek answers from me. Not trusting that she knows what is best for herself, she thinks I have the experience and wisdom to provide her with at least some answers. She continues to press for answers to what she should do about her marriage. It is as though she is treating me as an authority who has the power to fix things in her life. She grows very impatient with my unwillingness to give her answers. As she puts it, she is convinced that she needs my "validation and approval" if she is to move ahead.

We return to an exploration of Ruth's feelings toward me for not giving her more confirmation and not providing reassurance that she will make correct decisions. She tells me that if I really cared about her, I would give her more direction and do more for her than I am doing. She tells me that all I ever do is listen, that she wants and expects more, and that I am not doing my job properly. I let her know that I do not like her telling me what I am feeling about her. I also tell her that I do care about her struggle but that I refuse to give her answers because of my conviction that she will be able to find answers within herself. I hope she will learn that I can be annoyed with her at times yet not reject her.

Ruth continues to risk sharing more of her feelings with me, and with my encouragement she also begins to be more open with her family. Gradually, she becomes more willing to think about her own approval. She demands less of herself by way of being a fixed product, such as the "perfect person," and allows herself to open up to new experiences, including challenging some of her beliefs and perceptions. Slowly she is showing signs of accepting that the answers to her life situation are not to be found in some outside authority but inside of herself.

Although it is not easy for me to refuse to provide answers and direction for Ruth, I believe that to do so would imply a lack of faith in her capacity to find her own way. Therefore, I do not rely on techniques, nor do I fall into the trap of being the guru. We focus on Ruth's feelings about not trusting herself, and she explores in depth the ways in which she is discounting her ability to take a stand in many situations. At times I become angry with her when I feel set up by her. I think it is important for her to learn that I can express my anger toward her and at the same time not feel disapproving of her. She learns that she can evoke feelings in others and that she can express her own feelings.

I do value support, acceptance, and personal warmth; yet at the same time I try to challenge Ruth to look at what she is saying and doing. If I am to be an influence in her life, I have to be more than a mirror that simply reflects back what she is projecting. Thus, I attempt to give of myself in our sessions. By relating to Ruth personally, I allow her to feel an increased freedom to express whatever she is thinking and feeling. This encourages her to explore the ways in which she feels judged by her parents, the feelings that she has denied or distorted, and her lack of confidence in being able to find her own answers. Ruth can actually use our relationship as the basis for her growth. As she grows, she can learn to be more accepting of herself, with both strengths and limitations.

Questions for Reflection

1. To what degree have you been willing to struggle with finding your own answers to life? Are there ways in which you have avoided this responsibility by looking to others to provide you with answers? How would your experience of searching within yourself for answers affect how you worked with Ruth?
2. Knowing what you do of Ruth, how would it be for you to develop a therapeutic relationship with her? Is there anything that might get in your way? If so, how do you think you would deal with this obstacle? To what degree do you think you could understand her subjective world?
3. Ruth confronts me with her doubts about my ability to understand her as a woman. Do you think that she would do better to see a female therapist? Would you recommend that I suggest a referral to a woman, especially since she brought up her concerns about my being a man? Do you think that a male counselor would have a more difficult time understanding her world and her struggles than a female therapist?
4. Ruth mentions that it is especially difficult to trust a man and that she feels judged by men. How could you work with this theme therapeutically?
5. What are some of your general reactions to the way in which I approached and worked with Ruth? What do you particularly like? What do you like least? What aspects of her therapy would you have duplicated? What would you have done differently?
6. In both this approach and the previous one (existential therapy) the client/therapist relationship is central, and the focus is on clients'

choosing their way in life. Do you agree that Ruth has this potential for directing her life and making wise choices? Would you be inclined to let her select the topics for exploration, or might you suggest topics? Would you be more directive than I was?

7. Do you think that understanding and caring are enough to lead to personality change? This particular approach assumes that if the therapist is genuine, accepts the client fully and unconditionally, and respects, cares for, and deeply understands the client, constructive change will occur. To what degree to you agree with this assumption? Do you think anything else is necessary? If so, what?
8. Staying within this model, show how you would continue to work with Ruth and what general direction you would expect your sessions to take.

DON: HE IS SURE HE HAS TO PROVE HIMSELF

Some Background Data

Don, a major in the Air Force, comes to see me on the basis of a referral from a military doctor. He is of Hispanic background, is married, and has two daughters and two sons. As a member of a minority group, Don feels under tremendous pressure to prove himself as an exceptional leader. He has encountered many obstacles in his attempt to rise through the military ranks. He is doing everything possible to get a promotion to lieutenant colonel, and ultimately he would like to be at least a "bird" colonel.

He consulted with his physician because of continuing chest pains. Even though he is only in his mid-30s, he has had two mild heart attacks. These resulted in his being hospitalized and having to take a leave of absence. He is about ten pounds overweight, has high blood pressure, has a high cholesterol level, smokes cigarettes, suffers at times from angina, and develops severe headaches that are chronic under stressful situations. His physician insisted that if he wanted to live, he would have to learn to relax and deal with stress more constructively. Because his doctor was convinced that Don needed psychological as well as medical treatment, he was referred to me.

Our First Session

At our first meeting Don fills me in on his medical problems. He also talks of his feelings about being sent to see a psychologist and of how he hopes to benefit from our contact. He lets me know how unusual it is for him to ask for help with his personal life. He cannot remember a time that he felt a need to talk about personal matters. As he puts it, "If there is a job to be done, you get to it and do it." It appears that the more challenging the task, the more merit in the accomplishment. However, it also seems that meeting continual challenges is certainly taking a toll on Don. It could literally kill him.

To give a flavor of his view of himself, as well as the manner in which I might work with him from the person-centered perspective, I will present the following dialogue. I emphasize that this will be my own style of working with this approach; I do not want to give the impression that it is necessarily characteristic of all those who identify themselves as person-centered counselors.

DON: Well, Doctor, it's really hard for me to admit that I have to ask for outside help. I mean, no offense or anything, but I don't need a shrink.

JERRY: I'd like to hear how it feels for you to be here now. Could you tell me in what ways seeing me is hard for you?

DON: Sure. I thought I'd never die, until I had my first heart attack, and then I realized that I might kick over long before my time. It's hard enough for me to admit that my body can't take it. Now to be told that I have mental problems that I also have to learn to deal with—that's too much.

JERRY: It seems easier to do something about your physical problems than to do something about your feelings.

DON: The physician I've been seeing says there's not much more he can do for me, besides giving me the medication. I know my job has stress. I'm under constant pressure from the upper brass to produce and keep my outfit in order. I'm responsible for a lot of other men in my unit, and that's what's hard to handle. I can handle my own responsibilities, but being expected to make sure that the other men under me follow through almost does me in. I worry constantly about whether they'll pull their end.

JERRY: As you talk, I hear how unsupported you feel, as well as how difficult it is for you to carry the weight for the rest of your men. You have all this burden on your shoulders.

DON: It's part of my job. I'm the top man in my unit, and I've gotta make sure that nobody under me messes up, because our unit is a vital unit in a chain. If we're a weak link, the rest of the chain will be useless. And it's my job to make sure that we're effective at all times and that there aren't any slipups! If I don't keep a close watch on the entire operation, everything is liable to go to pot. I can't live with myself knowing that I haven't done all that was expected of me—and then some. If I want to get that promotion I've been angling for, I can't afford any mistakes. It's so important that I get my promotion. I really want the recognition that comes with being at the top.

JERRY: As I look at you, I see the weariness in your face. You look *very* tired and extremely tense. Sitting with you here I can feel your tension. I'm getting tired just listening to you. It seems that you don't see any way out of assuming all this responsibility.

DON: Not really. That's why I'm coming to see you. I hope you can teach me some relaxation methods and some better ways of living with this stress that's a part of my job.

JERRY: Maybe you can tell me more about what this stress is like for you. Is it mainly at work or in other areas of your life?

DON: I carry my work home with me. I have so much to do that I have to bring hours of paperwork home every night. In the military filling out papers is what counts. I can't get behind in the paperwork whatever I do. Besides, even when I'm at home, I always get calls from my subordinates asking me my opinion on this or that matter that needs immediate attention.

JERRY: So you're on constant call. I feel the sense of how overwhelming all this is to you. No matter how hard you try to keep up, there are always other decisions to be made, more papers waiting for you to complete, and more responsibility than you can handle. There's no place you can go to escape those who depend on you.

DON: You hit on a good point. I do feel exhausted and very tight. That's just the way I am—and that's the way it has always been. But I don't know how to change that. I look at the other officers who have positions of command, and they seem to be able to deal with the stress far better than I do. It doesn't get to them. Most of the guys are much older, and they don't have heart problems.

JERRY: You say that it has always been that way. Has it been this way even before you entered the military?

DON: For sure. I came from a large family. I was the oldest son. We all had to work hard, and my father expected a lot from all of us kids. He was tough on me and never gave me any recognition. But I kept on trying to do what he expected so that he'd be proud of me.

JERRY: It's difficult to work so hard and then still not get the recognition you want.

DON [a long pause and then a sigh]: I just keep asking myself what's wrong with me that I can't take this stress more in stride. I *should* be able to get the job done without my body giving out on me. This is a hard one for me to take!

JERRY: It's hard for you to accept that your body has its limits and that you can push yourself only so far.

DON: Yeah. Why can't I be like the rest of the guys and handle things? Not only do I have trouble handling stress on the job, but I have a heck of a time dealing with stress at home.

JERRY: It's just the same at home?

DON: Yeah. I feel that I've got to be the one in charge there, too. I've got to plan for laying aside money to send my kids through college. I've got to be the one who keeps peace in the family. It's really important that I don't break down. I've *got* to be strong, and there's no room for weakness. If I'm not strong, everything in my life will fall apart. I've got to make sure that Millie, my wife, feels important and special. I've got to be the counselor for my kids and give them answers when they come to me with problems. I've got to ride herd on my teenage boys to do their chores properly, and I've got to keep nagging at my daughters to keep the house in order. Sure, I'm the one who's the head of the house, and it's up to me to see that our family functions smoothly. When there's a fight in the house between the kids, I can't stand the arguing. I feel it's *my* job to get them to resolve their differences. So I can't relax at home either.

JERRY: I'm struck with all the responsibility you take on yourself. You've got to do everything, or it won't get done right. There's no one you can trust to take responsibility. And all these responsibilities are weighing you down and creating trouble for you.

DON: Well, it's true! When I do trust others in the family to do something, inevitably things go sour. Then I've got to get involved and clean up the mess that others made. I don't like being in that position either. I'd like to change it, but I know it's easier said than done. But I tell you, I hate having to be the strong one *all the time!*

JERRY: Even though you'd like to change the way you are, you're at a loss to know where to begin. You hate being this superstrong person all the time, but you *have* to be this way. How would it be for you if you weren't so strong *some* of the time?

DON: I don't think you can understand. In my head I say to myself that a man is strong and doesn't buckle under with burdens. I'm the kind of guy who can't show feelings of weakness. I'm supposed to be able to meet these challenges of life. I can't afford to be weak and let down. I have to hang in there and make it.

JERRY: You have to hang in there at all costs?

DON: At all costs. Even if it kills me. I'm the kind of guy who can't stop running. Once I set out to do something, I'm determined to succeed. I can't let my body get the best of me.

JERRY: Your body is speaking a loud message, and yet you're not willing to listen to what it's telling you. I sense how hard it is for you to accept that you can't manage everything in life by yourself. And I see you as willing to hang onto the notion that somehow you'll find a way to be superhuman.

DON: You're hearing me! I don't mind being superman *some* of the time, but I don't like being superman *all* of the time.

Some Observations on Our Sessions

During this first session I'm interested in seeing the world through Don's eyes. I want to understand what it's like for him to feel driven to prove himself, to be consistently strong, to meet all his obligations (and then some), to take on the responsibilities of everyone, and to keep moving ahead even if it kills him. At the same time, I want him to know I have some understanding of how his life is. But I want to do more than merely reflect what I hear him saying.

In one of his sessions Don tells me something about his cultural background and his upbringing as a child that will be important in our work. Being Hispanic, Don feels that he must play clear roles if he is to preserve his sense of being a man. Growing up in a family with several brothers, he learned to compete and to be tough in all situations. A message he consistently heard was to be strong at all times. He is convinced that he should be able to handle any challenges, and to be faced with his body's resistance is hard for him to accept. Apparently, he learned his lessons well, for Don now has great difficulty in accepting or expressing feelings, which are manifestations of weakness in his eyes. He also learned that it was the man's place to take care of his wife and children by making a good living. His self-concept involves the notion that he needs to be on top of all of his responsibilities, that he cannot let down, and that there is no room for errors. I certainly do not want to challenge his assumptions quickly, and I want to find out which of his cultural values, if any, he is interested in modifying. He may not be interested in becoming more emotionally expressive. And he may decide that he wants to remain the strong and dependable man that he sees himself as being. My first task is to listen to him and to understand the meanings he puts on aspects of living such as "being strong" and "always being capable in every situation."

Yet I do want to get him to begin to look at the obvious signs that his body is sending him. I hope that he can allow himself to tune into his own tiredness and his own pain at always having to be strong. Without pushing my values on Don and encouraging him to assume goals that are mine, I hope that he can pay attention to what he is experiencing and the price he is paying for living in certain ways.

I do not think that he will change merely from my telling him that he *should* be different—that he should allow himself to be "weak," should delegate responsibilities, or should slow down and take it easy. He has heard this from his physician, and he *knows* (intellectually) that this is what he should do; yet he *feels* (emotionally) that he has to stay together at all costs. My assumption is that Don will be more open to change if I encourage him to share openly with me what it feels like for him to live the way he does. Without directly insisting that he be different from the way he is, I want to encourage him to talk more about his striving to be on top, to express his frustrations over his body's failure to stand up under the pressure, and to express his need to be strong and capable. At the same time, I am hoping that he will eventually consider whether he really does need to assume the responsibility for everyone else. I hope that he will begin to question how hard he is on himself and that he may eventually challenge himself on the necessity of maintaining such standards. He may decide to give up some of his burdens and to stop putting himself in the position of being completely responsible for the functioning of his family. It is possible for me to be respectful of his cultural framework yet also invite him to look at which attitudes and values are working for him and which are not serving him.

In getting Don to take this look at himself, I will share what is being evoked in me, especially my tenseness and tiredness as I try to be with him. If I am myself with Don, he is more likely to be himself with me. He may be willing to reveal whatever he is attempting to cover up by a show of strength. I do not need to give him answers, even though on some level he would like to know "the way" to cope with stress. If I can stay with him and encourage him to express whatever he is feeling, this expression will provide the needed direction for us to move in future sessions. He is giving plenty of clues to pursue, if I will listen and follow them. I do not need to rely on techniques to get him to open up or techniques to resolve his problems. The best I can offer to him is the relationship that we develop, regardless of how brief it may be. If I am able to accept him in a nonjudgmental way, I see a good chance that he will begin to listen to himself (including his body) and that he will grow toward self-acceptance, which can be the beginning of real change for him.

Follow-Up: You Continue as Don's Therapist

1. How do you see Don? What are the major themes of his life that need to be focused on and explored more fully? How do you personally respond to him?
2. Assume that I were to refer Don to you for continued therapy (in the person-centered style). How do you imagine that it would be for you to work with him? How might a person such as Don relate to you?
3. Assuming that you will be seeing Don for at least six more sessions, what are some specific issues that you most want to explore? How might you go about doing this with him?
4. Coming from a Hispanic cultural background, Don has certain notions of what it means to be a man. His self-concept and his masculine definition of self include being strong at all times, being able to handle his responsibilities, providing well for his family, not showing signs of weakness, and being able to keep up with the other men he knows. If you were working with Don, how might you separate his self-destructive beliefs and behaviors from certain messages he has received from his cultural upbringing? Would you expect to have any difficulty in respecting his cultural differences and at the same time challenging him to examine his beliefs? What other cultural variables would you want to consider in your counseling with Don?
5. If you have a different cultural background from Don's, would you initiate a discussion of your cultural differences? Would you ask him if he feels

willing to confide in you, especially if he has let it be known how strange it is for him to ask for help in dealing with his personal life? How would you feel, and what would you say to him, if he confronted you on not being able to understand him because of your differences?

6. Given the data that you have on Don, do you think he would do better with a female or a male therapist? Or does it make any difference?
7. This approach was characterized by my listening and responding to him rather than by my active, directive intervention with therapeutic procedures and techniques. Do you think you would feel comfortable in staying in such a role in your work with Don? Why or why not? Are there other techniques that you might want to introduce?
8. Don is driving himself relentlessly, and his body is telling him that he will probably kill himself if he does not change. Can you think of anything you might do or say to him to increase the probability that he will pay attention to the messages his body is sending him?

RECOMMENDED SUPPLEMENTARY READINGS

Dibs: In Search of Self (1976), by V. Axline (New York: Ballantine), gives a touching account of a boy's journey from isolation toward self-awareness and self-expression. It emphasizes the crucial effects of parent/child relationships on the development of a child's personality. It also describes how play therapy can be a tool for developing an autonomous individual.

On Becoming a Person (1961), by C. Rogers (Boston: Houghton Mifflin), compiles many of Rogers's significant essays on education, therapy, communication, family life, and the healthy personality. Case examples illustrate the process of person-centered therapy in action.

A Way of Being (1981), by C. Rogers (Boston: Houghton Mifflin), contains a series of updated writings on Rogers's personal experiences and perspectives, as well as chapters on the foundations and applications of a person-centered approach.

Focusing (2nd ed., 1981), by E. T. Gendlin (New York: Bantam Books), is a step-by-step approach to getting in touch with feelings by a person-centered therapist formerly associated with Rogers.

SUGGESTED READINGS

Belkin, G. (1987). *Contemporary psychotherapies* (2nd ed.). Pacific Grove, CA: Brooks/Cole. (Chapter 12)

Belkin, G. S. (1988). *Introduction to counseling* (3rd ed.). Dubuque, IA: William C. Brown. (Chapter 8)

Burke, J. F. (1989). *Contemporary approaches to psychotherapy and counseling.* Pacific Grove, CA: Brooks/Cole. (Chapter 8)

Corey, G. (1991). *Theory and practice of counseling and psychotherapy* (4th ed.). Pacific Grove, CA: Brooks/Cole. (Chaper 7)

Corsini, R., & Wedding, D. (Eds.). (1989). *Current psychotherapies* (4th ed.). Itasca, IL: F. E. Peacock. (Chapter 5)

Gilliland, B., James, R., Roberts, G., & Bowman, J. (1984). *Theories and strategies in counseling and psychotherapy.* Englewood Cliffs, NJ: Prentice-Hall. (Chapter 4)

Hansen, J., Stevic, R., & Warner, R. (1986). *Counseling: Theory and process* (4th ed.). Boston: Allyn Bacon. (Chapter 6)

Ivey, A. E., Ivey, M. B., & Simek-Downing, L. (1987). *Counseling and psychotherapy: Integrating skills, theory, and practice* (2nd ed.). Englewood Cliffs, NJ: Prentice-Hall. (Chapter 10)

Patterson, C. H. (1986). *Theories of counseling and psychotherapy* (4th ed.). New York: Harper & Row. (Chapter 14)

Prochaska, J. O. (1984). *Systems of psychotherapy: A transtheoretical analysis* (2nd ed.). Pacific Grove, CA: Brooks/Cole. (Chapter 4)

Wedding, D., & Corsini, R. J. (Eds.). (1989). *Case studies in psychotherapy.* Itasca, IL: F. E. Peacock. (Chapter 4)

CHAPTER SIX

Case Approach to Gestalt Therapy

A GESTALT THERAPIST'S PERSPECTIVE ON RUTH
by Rainette Eden Fantz, Ph.D.

Rainette Eden Fantz is one of the founders of the Gestalt Institute of Cleveland. She is chairwoman of the institute's Intensive Postgraduate Training Program and is engaged in the private practice of psychotherapy. She also teaches, works with groups, and conducts special-interest workshops. Fantz draws on her extensive background as an artist, musician, and actress to enrich her therapy. She has written chapters about the Gestalt approach in various books on psychotherapy and is on the editorial board of the Gestalt Institute Press.

Assessment of Ruth

It is fairly simple to give Ruth a diagnosis by addressing her case through her presenting problems, their history, her psychosocial history, and her "autobiography." Based on this information, I would classify her according to the DSM-III-R as 309.28, which is *adjustment disorder with mixed emotional features* (a fairly common, "wastebasket" diagnosis). However, if we regard all of the above factors through the lens of the Gestalt cycle of experience—namely, the need-fulfillment cycle—we become aware that her poor adjustment and the symptomatology accompanying it apply not only to Ruth's current situation but also to her entire life patterning. Examining the cycle and noting where Ruth's internal and external behavior interrupts the smooth progression of the cycle, so that her needs are never actually met and contact never actually made, we find the situation depicted in Figure 6-1.

We begin with unpleasant *sensations,* largely somatic in nature (10 o'clock on the figure), and an absence of pleasant sensations such as sensuality, warmth, pleasure, or fullness. These unpleasant sensations

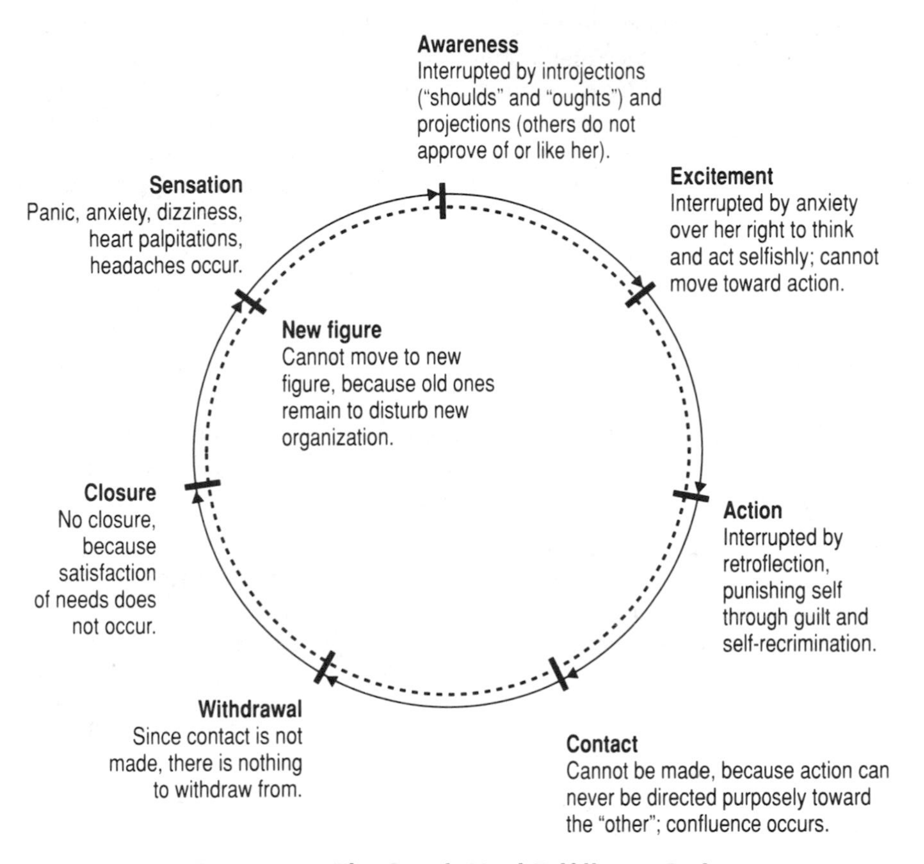

Figure 6-1. The Gestalt Need-Fulfillment Cycle

do move into *awareness,* but it is a very partial awareness inasmuch as Ruth's introjections and projections prevent her from knowing herself as other than a reification of her parents' and church's values. Consequently, she cannot look at her own ''wants'' and ''wishes'' because of the guilt they engender.

Ruth shows *excitement* over the possibility of teaching. Whenever this excitement begins to emerge, however, she becomes anxious and worries about her right to think and act selfishly. Her fear of losing her husband and her secure, though mundane, life prevent her from taking *action.* Whatever action she does begin to take is interrupted by her retroflection, turning her actions back on herself, so that her anger is *not* directed to her children, her husband, or her parents but to Ruth herself, with self-recrimination, self-deprecation, and guilt. Because she cannot make eye contact with the people she addresses, possibly out of the fear that they might actually know what she is harboring against them, she merely becomes confluent and goes along with them or placates. No *contact* is made.

Needless to say, since contact does not occur there is no way Ruth can complete the cycle, inasmuch as there is nothing there to *withdraw* from. She is plagued by numerous unfinished situations, which, in turn, prevent *closure* and the possibility of developing a fresh figure and starting a new cycle. (If both awareness and excitement are present and working together, the object of awareness becomes a sharper figure against an unnoticed background. This form of unified figure is called a "good Gestalt.")

Life Themes and Key Issues

In light of Ruth's lack of progress around the cycle and the reasons for her many interruptions, numerous major life themes and key issues present themselves. Among these life themes are:

- trying to please others and rarely succeeding
- overeating to the point of discomfort (which might stem from a need for rebellion and a need for an armoring of herself)
- always giving, yet never taking (no nourishment is derived; the well is empty)

Some of Ruth's key issues that we would be likely to explore in therapy are:

- her unsatisfactory relationship with her husband
- her lack of sexuality
- her distant, authoritarian father
- her largely critical and never-satisfied mother
- the little affection displayed between her father and mother
- her practice of caring for her younger siblings to gain approval
- her long-term guilt generated by playing "doctor" at age 6 and being caught by her father
- the fact that people see her as "weird"
- her fear of eternal punishment

Therapeutic Techniques and Interventions

Clearly we have a plethora of major themes and key issues to concentrate on in Ruth's psychotherapy. Given that Gestalt is an existential therapy, it behooves us to begin by attending to her *current process,* starting with attention and awareness. How and what does she see, hear, smell, taste, and feel in the present moment? For example, we could focus on the difference between seeing (passive) and looking (active). What is it like to allow her eyes to glaze over and let objects and persons infringe on her, rather than choosing things in the room to actively look at? What is it like to make eye contact with me? What does she see? How am I different from her? What is it like to close her eyes and allow the sounds from inside and outside to encroach on her, rather than attending only to the therapist's voice? What is it like to actually experience the support of the chair under her rather than sitting on its edge with her feet not planted, her body not centered? These are techniques we could use with *all* the senses.

Certainly it would be incumbent to attend to her sensations: her dizziness, her palpitations, her headaches, her depression. One way to work with these is to have her *become* her palpitations and her other physical symptoms and discover what these symptoms are saying to her. The palpitations might say: "You do not allow me to breathe. I am suffocating." The suggestion to breathe is certainly in order. This might allay her panic. If she spoke as her headache, she might say "I am going to continue to pound away at you until you stop giving yourself a hard time and allow yourself some choices." When she speaks as her depression, we might move into polarities and probably discover the anger that underlies it.

Polarities, indeed, are a tool par excellence to use with Ruth, inasmuch as they would tap the shadow side of her personality: anger rather than depression, resentment rather than guilt, being spontaneous rather than being controlled, taking rather than giving, and speaking forthrightly from her own needs rather than always appeasing and considering those of others.

In addition to polarities we could use other empty-chair work in which she might indulge in dialogues both with different facets of herself and with the different characters in her life—father, mother, husband, daughter, former peers—changing chairs and playing out each role.

All of these are important, but perhaps paramount is the side of Ruth that chooses to eat rather than allow herself to be slim and attractive and perhaps sexy. That might be fun (as well as threatening, since she is so armored against that part of herself). Some homework I might give her is to eat *very* slowly so that she could experience the satisfaction of tasting and the sensation of fullness. She does not appear to have achieved satisfaction in any area of her life.

I would notice how Ruth fidgets with her clothes and wonder, out loud, what else she might like (or not like) to do with her hands. For example, would she like to stroke, tear, hit, or clutch with her hands? I would encourage her to move into the area of retroflections and try to discover how to undo them. I would certainly expect resistance here.

It would be extremely interesting to move into the area of dreams or directed fantasy and find there her present existence, her exciting potential, and those elements she would not touch with a ten-foot pole. These are the missing parts of her *self,* which could possibly prove to be the most important aspect that we explore in her therapy.

Over time we would work extensively on Ruth's various life themes and her key issues, always exploring her sensations, her awareness, her beginning excitements, and her approach to action. I would hope, in time, to enable her to make better contact so that she could finish her unfinished situations, whether in fantasy or reality. I would share parts of myself with her when doing so would be pertinent and not intrusive, so that she could learn to share. I would be active and set up experiments, adjusting the risks so that they were tolerable yet at the growing edge. I would hope that we could approach our session with a focus on a particular "figure," so that we could develop themes and experiments and have a beginning, a middle, and an end.

Ruth impresses me as being very capable of growth, having both intelligence and feelings ready to emerge. I rather expect it would be a delight to work with her.

JERRY COREY'S WORK WITH RUTH FROM A GESTALT PERSPECTIVE

Basic Assumptions

Approaching Ruth as a Gestalt therapist, I assume that she can deal effectively with her life problems, especially if she becomes fully aware of what is happening in and around her. My central task as her therapist is to help her fully experience her being in the here and now by first realizing how she is preventing herself from feeling and experiencing in the present. My approach is basically noninterpretive; instead, I will ask her to provide her own interpretations of her experiences. I expect her to participate in experiments, which consist of trying new ways of relating and responding.

I will encourage Ruth to experience directly in the present her "unfinished business" from the past. (Unfinished business involves unexpressed feelings such as resentment, rage, hatred, pain, anxiety, grief, guilt, abandonment, and so on. Because these feelings are not fully expressed in awareness, they linger in the background and are carried into present life in ways that interfere with effective contact with oneself and others.) A basic premise of Gestalt therapy is that by experiencing conflicts directly, instead of merely talking about them, clients will expand their own level of awareness and integrate the fragmented and unknown parts of their personality.

Assessment of Ruth

Viewing Ruth from a Gestalt perspective, I see her as having the capacity to assume personal responsibility and to live fully as an integrated person. Because of certain difficulties in her development she devised various ways of avoiding problems, and she has therefore reached impasses in her quest for personal growth.

There are a number of ways in which Ruth is presently stuck. She has never learned that it is acceptable to have and to express feelings. True, she does feel a good deal of guilt, though she rarely expresses the resentment that she must feel. Any person who is as devoted to others as she is must feel some resentment at not having received the appreciation that she believes is due her. She does not allow herself to get angry at her father, who has punished her by withholding his affection and approval. She does not experience much anger toward John, despite the fact that here again she does not feel recognized. The same is true for both of her sons and both of her daughters. Ruth has made a lifetime career out of giving and doing for her family. She maintains that she gets little in return, yet she rarely expresses how this arrangement affects her. I think that keeping all of these feelings locked inside of her is getting in her way of feeling free. Therefore, I believe that she needs to embrace feelings that she is now excluding. A lot of her energy is going into blocking her experience of threatening feelings, sensations, and thoughts. Our therapy will encourage her to express her moment-by-moment experience so that her energy is freed up for creative pursuits instead of being spent on growth-inhibiting defenses.

Goals of Therapy

My goal is to challenge Ruth to move from environmental support to self-support and to assist her in gaining awareness of her present experience. With awareness Ruth will be able to recognize denied aspects of herself and thus proceed toward the reintegration of all her dimensions. Therapy will provide the necessary intervention and challenge to help her gain awareness of what she is doing, thinking, and feeling now. As she comes to recognize and experience blocks to maturity she can then begin experimenting with different ways of being.

Therapeutic Procedures

As a Gestalt therapist I work to foster clients' ability to stand on their own two feet. Thus, in my work with Ruth I will not do her seeing, nor will I listen for her, because she has eyes and ears. Although philosophically I accept the existential view of the human condition, I draw heavily on experiential techniques that are aimed at intensifying here-and-now experiencing. These techniques are designed to help clients focus on what is going on within their body and to accentuate whatever they may be feeling. In this sense I will be directive and active in my sessions with Ruth. I will take my cues from her, but I will also pay attention to what she is saying both verbally and nonverbally. From the cues I pick up, I will invent action-oriented techniques that will enable her to heighten whatever she is experiencing.

I have a bias against having clients simply *talk* about conflicts or situations in their life. In Ruth's case she could go on talking forever about issues and abstractly analyzing matters to death. Clients find that they do not get rid of feelings within them, but they can learn how to live with these feelings—love/hate, wanting to be tough/tender—even though such feelings may seem contradictory at times. In my sessions with Ruth we will work with some of these polarities that she generally does not express. For example, she tends to be critical and judgmental, so we may focus on the dimension of self-acceptance, which does not get recognized or expressed. In this way she will find sides of herself that can be developed and integrated.

Along this line I will be asking Ruth to carry out some experiments. These may entail giving expression to unexpressed body movements or gestures, or they may involve talking in a different tone of voice. I may ask her to experiment with rehearsing out loud those thoughts that are racing through her, ones that she usually keeps to herself. My style is to invite clients to try new behavior and see what these experiments can teach them. I assume that if clients learn how to pay attention to whatever it is that they are experiencing at any moment, this awareness itself can lead to change.

The Therapeutic Process

At one of our early sessions Ruth feels the necessity of bringing me up to date by decribing her history. I direct her to continue to talk but to act as if what she is saying is happening right now. She is somewhat resistant to getting into the present tense and keeps falling back into talking in the past tense. I let her know that when she speaks in the present tense, I experience her as more animated and easier to listen to. I give her a general rationale for the things I will be asking her to try. She initially has some difficulty in working with fantasy and bringing significant people in her life symbolically into the room with me, so we explore her fears of looking foolish and doing dumb things. Because she cannot see much value in carrying out the experiments I am suggesting, I spend more time preparing her for participating in Gestalt therapy. I ask her to risk trying experiments in the safety of the therapeutic setting and afterwards deciding for herself whether the new behavior works for her. I want her to trust her own direct experience, rather than relying on my judgment of the value of these techniques.

Elements of the process

Ruth works with her daughter Jennifer. Ruth brings up the topic of how guilty she feels about disappointing her daughter Jennifer, who is 18 and who lives at home.

JERRY: Ruth, rather than telling me about how guilty you feel over not having been the mother you think you should have been to Jennifer, would you simply list all the ways that you feel this guilt?

RUTH: Oh, that's not hard—there are so many ways! I feel guilty because I haven't been understanding enough, because I've been too easy on her and haven't set limits, because I haven't touched her enough, because I've been away at college when she needed me during her difficult years. And in some ways I feel responsible for her getting kicked out of school, for her drug problem—I could go on!

JERRY: So go on. Say more. Make the list as long as you can. [I am encouraging her to say aloud and unrehearsed many of the things that I assume she tells herself endlessly in her head. She continues to speak of her guilt.]

RUTH [letting out a deep sigh]: There! That's it!

JERRY: And what is that sigh about?

RUTH: Just relief, I suppose. I feel a little better, but I still have a sense that I've done wrong by Jennifer.

I am aware that Ruth is not going to rid herself forever of her guilt. If she does not let her guilt control her, however, she could make room for other feelings. Based on my hunch that behind guilt is usually resentment, I propose another experiment.

JERRY: If you're willing to go further, I'd like you to repeat your list of guilts, only this time say "I resent you for . . ." instead of "I feel guilty over . . ."

RUTH: But I don't feel resentment—it's the guilt!

JERRY: I know, but would you be willing to go ahead with the experiment and see what happens?

RUTH [after some hesitation and discussion of the value of doing this]: I resent you for expecting me to always be understanding of you. I resent you for demanding so much of my time. I resent you for all the trouble you got yourself into and the nights of sleep I lost over this. I resent you for making me feel guilty. I resent you for not understanding me. I resent you for expecting affection but not giving me any.

My rationale for asking Ruth to convert her list of guilts into a list of resentments is that doing so may help her direct her anger to the sources where it belongs, rather than inward. She has so much guilt because she directs her anger toward herself, and this keeps her distant from some people who are significant to her. Ruth becomes more and more energetic with her expression of resentments.

JERRY: Ruth, let me sit in for Jennifer for a bit. Continue talking to me, and tell me the ways in which you resent me.

RUTH [Speaking to her daughter directly, she immediately becomes more emotional and expressive.]: It's hard for me to talk to you. You and I haven't really talked in such a long time. [Tears well up in her eyes.] I give and give, and all you do is take and take. There's no end to it!

JERRY: Tell Jennifer what you want from her.

RUTH [There is a long pause, and then, with a burst of energy, Ruth shouts at Jennifer.]: I want to be more like you! I'm envious of you. I wish I could be as daring and as alive as you . . . Wow, I'm surprised at what just came out of me.

JERRY: Keep talking to Jennifer and tell her more how you're feeling right now.

With Ruth's heightened emotionality she is able to say some things to Jennifer that she has never said but has wished she could. She leaves this session with some new insights: her feelings of guilt are more often feelings of resentment; her anger toward Jennifer is based on envy and jealousy; and the things that she dislikes about Jennifer are some of the things that she would like for herself.

Exploring the polarities within Ruth. In later sessions we continue working with some of the splits within Ruth's personality. My aim is not to get rid of her feelings but to let her experience them and learn to integrate all the factions of her personality. She will not get rid of one side of her personality that she does not like by attempting to deny it, but she can learn to recognize the side that controls her by expressing it.

RUTH: For so many years I had to be the perfect minister's daughter. I lost myself in always being the proper "good girl." I'd like to be more spontaneous and playful and not worry constantly about what other people would think. Sometimes when I'm being silly, I hear this voice in my head that tells me to be proper. It's like there are two of me, one that's all proper and prim and the other that wants to be footloose and free.

JERRY: Which side do you feel most right now, the proper side or the uninhibited side?

RUTH: Well, the proper and conservative side is surely the stronger in me.

JERRY: Here are a couple of chairs. I'd like you to sit in this chair here and be the proper side of you. Talk to the uninhibited side, which is sitting in this other chair.

RUTH: I wish you would grow up! You should act like an adult and stop being a silly kid. If I listened to you, I'd really be in trouble now. You're so impulsive and demanding.

JERRY: OK, how about changing and sitting in the chair over here and speaking from your daring side? What does she have to say to the proper side over there?

RUTH: It's about time you let your hair down and had some fun. You're so cautious! Sure, you're safe, but you're also a very, very dull person. I know you'd like to be me more often.

JERRY: Change chairs again, talking back to the daring side.

RUTH: Well I'd rather be safe than sorry! [Her face flushes.]

JERRY: And what do you want to say back to your proper side?

RUTH: That's just your trouble. Always be safe! And where is this getting you? You'll die being safe and secure.

This exchange of chairs goes on for some time. Becoming her daring side is much more uncomfortable for Ruth. After a while she lets herself get into the daring side and chides that old prude sitting across from her. She accuses her of letting life slip by, points out how she is just like her mother, and tells her how her being so proper stops her from having any fun. This experiment shows Ruth the difference between thinking about conflicts and actually letting herself experience those conflicts. She sees more clearly that she is being pulled in many directions, that she is a complex person, and that she will not get rid of feelings by pretending that they are not inside of her. Gradually, she experiences more freedom in accepting the different parts within her, with less need to cut out certain parts of her.

A dialogue with Ruth's father. In another session Ruth brings up how it was for her as a child, especially in relation to a cold and ungiving father. I direct her not merely to report what happened but also to bring her father into the room now and talk to him as she did as a child. She goes back to a past event and relives it—the time at 6 years old when she was reprimanded by her father in the bedroom. She begins by saying how scared she was then and how she did not know what to say to him after he had caught her in sexual play. So I encourage her to stay with her scared feelings and to tell her father all the things that she was feeling then but did not say. Then I say to Ruth:

JERRY: Tell your father how you wish he had acted with you. [She proceeds to talk to her father. At a later point I hand her a pillow.] Let yourself be the father you wished you had, and talk to little Ruth. The pillow is you, and you are your father. Talk to little Ruth.

RUTH: [This brings up intense feelings in Ruth, and for a long time she says nothing. She sits silently, holding "Ruth" and caressing her lovingly. Eventually, some words follow.]: Ruth, I have always loved you, and you have always been special to me. It has just been hard for me to show what I feel. I wanted to let you know how much you mattered to me, but I didn't know how.

Process commentary

During the time that Ruth is doing her work, I pay attention to what she is communicating nonverbally. When she asks why I "make so much fuss over the nonverbals," I let her know that I assume that she communicates at least as much nonverbally as through her words. As she is engaged in carrying on dialogues with different parts of herself, with her daughter, and with her father, she feels a variety of physical symptoms in her body. For example, she describes her heart, saying it feels as if it wants to break; the knots in her stomach; the tension in her neck and shoulders; the tightness in her head; her clenched fists; the tears in her eyes; and the smile across her lips. At appropriate moments I call her attention to her body and teach her how to pay attention to what she is experiencing in her body. At different times I ask her to try the experiment of "becoming" her breaking heart (or any other bodily sensation) and giving that part of her body "voice."

When she allows herself to speak for her tears, her clenched fists, or her shaking hands, Ruth is typically surprised by what her body can teach her. She gradually develops more respect for the messages of her body. In the same manner, we work with a number of her dreams. When she feels free enough to become each part of a dream and then act out her dreams, she begins to understand the message contained in them.

Ruth exhibits some resistance to letting herself get involved in these Gestalt experiments, but after challenging herself and overcoming her feelings of looking foolish, she is generally amazed at what comes out of these procedures. Without my interpretations she begins to discover for herself how some of her past experiences are related to her present feelings of being stuck in so many ways.

A theme that emerges over and over in Ruth's work is how alive material becomes when she brings an experience into the present. She does not merely intellectualize about her problems, nor does she engage in much talking about events. The emphasis is on trying out action-oriented techniques and experiments to intensify whatever she is experiencing. In most cases when she does bring a past event into the present by actually allowing herself to reexperience that event, it provides her with valuable insights. Ruth does not need interpretations from me as her therapist, because by paying attention on a moment-to-moment basis to whatever she is experiencing, she is able to see the meaning for herself.

Ruth's awareness is by itself a powerful catalyst for her change. Before she can hope to be different in any respect, she first has to be aware of how she is. The focus of much of her work is on *what* she is experiencing at any given moment, as well as *how*. Thus, when she mentions being anxious, she focuses on *how* this anxiety is manifested in a knot in her stomach or a headache. I focus her on here-and-now experiencing and away from thinking about *why*. Asking *why* would remove Ruth from her feelings. Another key focus is on dealing with *unfinished business*. This case shows that unfinished business from the past does seek completion. It persists in her present until she faces and deals with feelings that she has not previously expressed.

Questions for Reflection

1. What do you think of Dr. Fantz's diagnosis of *adjustment disorder with mixed emotional features*? What behavior and personality patterns of

Ruth's either lend support to or negate this diagnosis? At this point what diagnosis do you think best fits Ruth? Why?

2. Dr. Fantz indicates that she would tend to focus on the following life themes and key issues: pleasing others, giving to the point that the well is dry, overeating, unsatisfactory marital and sexual relationship, and problems with parents. If you were to work with Ruth as a Gestalt therapist, what are some techniques that you might use in working with these themes? What are your reactions to some of the techniques and interventions that Fantz describes as a part of her work with Ruth?
3. Gestalt techniques are useful in working with the splits and polarities within a person. As you can see, Ruth has problems because she is not able to reconcile or integrate polarities: good versus bad, child versus adult, dependent versus independent, giving to others versus asking and receiving, feelings versus rational ideas, and the need for security versus the need to leave secure ways and create new ways of being. Are there any of Ruth's polarities that you are aware of struggling with in your life now?
4. Knowing what you do of Gestalt therapy, what kind of client do you imagine you'd be in this type of therapy? How free would you be to try experiments? to engage in fantasy dialogues? to allow yourself to intensify whatever you were feeling? to stay focused in the here and now? Do you see any connection between the type of client you'd be and the type of therapist you'd be within a Gestalt framework?
5. Can you think of some ways to blend the cognitive focus of Adlerian therapy with the emotional focus of Gestalt therapy in working with Ruth? Provide a few examples of how you could work with her feelings and cognitions by combining techniques and concepts from the two approaches.
6. How does the Gestalt approach work with Ruth's past differently from the psychoanalytic approach? Which style of dealing with the past do you prefer? Why?
7. What main differences do you see between the way in which Dr. Fantz worked with Ruth as a Gestalt therapist and the way in which Dr. Cain worked with her as a person-centered therapist? What about the differences in the way I counseled Ruth from these two perspectives? Which approach do you prefer? Why?
8. What did you particularly like and not like about the way in which I worked with Ruth as a Gestalt counselor? What are some other possibilities you see for working with her?
9. Think about Ruth as being from each of the following ethnic and cultural backgrounds: Native-American, Black, Hispanic, and Asian-American. How might you modify Gestalt techniques in working with her if she were a member of each of these groups? What are some of the advantages and disadvantages of drawing on concepts and techniques from Gestalt therapy in working with cultural themes in her life?

10. What are the specific areas of unfinished business that are most evident to you as you read about Ruth? Do any of her unexpressed feelings ignite any of your own unfinished business from the past? Are there any unresolved areas in your own life or any feelings that might interfere with your ability to work effectively with her? If so, what are they? How might you deal with these feelings if they came up as you were counseling her?

CHRISTINA: A STUDENT WORKS WITH HER FEELINGS TOWARD HER SUPERVISOR AND HER FATHER

To demonstrate the flavor of my personal style of working with a client, I dramatize a group session in which a client begins by saying she wants to work on her feelings toward me. I will use a dialogue to show how I draw on Gestalt concepts and employ Gestalt techniques. At the same time, I will give a running commentary on the process and my rationale for using the techniques I am using.

Some Background Data

Christina is a former student in my counseling practicum class. She says that she was constantly uncomfortable in the class, that the course and I threatened her, and that she would like to deal with some of the feelings she sat on during that entire semester. She has taken the initiative to ask for an individual counseling session to work on these feelings and on her relationship with me. The following imaginary dialogue is a sample of a typical way I would work if I were to stay within a Gestalt framework.

A Dialogue with Christina

JERRY: What would you like to get from this session, Christina?

CHRISTINA: I just get so down on myself for the way I let other people make me feel unimportant. I really became aware of this in your class. So I want to work on the feelings I had toward you then.

JERRY: Feelings you *had?* If you still have any of those feelings now, I'd like to hear more about them.

CHRISTINA: Oh, I suppose I still have those feelings, or at least it wouldn't be too difficult to get them back again. I just don't like the way you make me feel, Jerry.

JERRY: I still don't know what *those feelings* are, but I do know you're making me responsible for them. I *make* you feel? I don't like being put in that position.

CHRISTINA: Well, you *do* make me feel inadequate when I'm around you. I'm afraid to approach you, because you seem so busy, and I think you'll just brush me off. I don't want to give you the chance *not* to listen to me. I'm afraid that you'll have too many other things to do and that you wouldn't want to spend the time with me to hear my feelings. So that's why I stayed away from you that semester I had your class.

Without getting defensive, I want to let Christina know that *I* would like to be allowed to decide whether I have the time or the willingness to listen to her. I do not like being written off in advance or being told *who* I am and *how* I am without being given the chance to speak for myself. I let her know this directly, because I think my honest reactions toward what she is saying will be a vital component to building the kind of relationship between us that is needed to deal effectively with her feelings. Further, I call her on her unwillingness to accept responsibility for her own feelings, as expressed in her statements of "You make me feel. . ."

JERRY: So Christina, if you're willing, I'd like to try an experiment. Would you just rattle off all the ways that you can think of that you feel around me, and after listing each of them I'd like you to add *"and you make me feel that way!"* OK?

CHRISTINA: Sure, now I get my chance. This could be fun! Are you ready for this? When I'm around you, I feel so small and so inadequate—and you make me feel this way! When I'm around you, I feel judged. I feel that whatever I do isn't what you expect, and that whatever I do it won't be enough to please you—and you *make* me feel that way! [She seems more excited and is getting into the exercise with her voice and her postures and gestures.] I have to read all those damn books for the course. And then I feel I'll never be able to write papers that are clear enough for you and I'll feel stupid and inferior. And it's *your* fault that I feel this way—you *make* me feel this way! You're always rushing around doing so many things that I can't catch you long enough to get you to listen to me. Then I feel unimportant, and you *make* me feel this way.

I want Christina to say out loud many of the things that I imagine she has said silently to herself. As she lists all the ways she feels around me, as well as restating over and over that I make her feel those ways, I listen and encourage her to continue. I want her to become aware of her resentments and *experience her feelings,* not just to talk abstractly about them. I see this awareness as essential before any change can occur. While she is doing this, I pay attention to the *way* she is delivering her message, because her body provides excellent leads to follow up on. I listen for changes in the tone and pitch of her voice. I notice any discrepancies between her words and facial expressions. I pay attention to her pointed finger or to her clenched fist. I notice her tapping foot. I also notice her blushing, her moist eyes, and any changes in her posture. All of these provide rich possibilities for exploring in this session, and there are any number of possibilities that I can follow through on. All the while I will be frequently checking in with her on what she is feeling right now. This will determine the direction we take next.

JERRY: What are you experiencing now?

CHRISTINA: I'm afraid you're judging me.

JERRY: What do you imagine I'm saying about you?

CHRISTINA: You're thinking I'm really immature and stupid. I'm feeling small again. And I'm also feeling vulnerable . . . weak . . . helpless . . . but mostly like you're up there and I'm down here looking up at you. And I don't like feeling little and making you that important.

JERRY: What would your "littleness" say to me now?

CHRISTINA: I'm feeling hopeless. Like I'll never be able to touch you or really reach you. [A long pause follows.]

JERRY: What are you experiencing now?

CHRISTINA: I'm thinking about my father.

JERRY: What about your father? Let me be him, and you talk to me.

CHRISTINA: I'll never be able to touch you or really reach you. I feel so dumb with you. [another long pause]

JERRY: And what else do you want to say to your father right now?

CHRISTINA: I'd love to really be able to talk to you.

JERRY: You're talking to him right now. He's listening. Tell him more.

CHRISTINA: I've always been scared of you. I'd so much like to spend time with you and tell you about my pains and joys. I like that you're listening to me now. It feels so good.

JERRY: It feels good . . . What is it?

CHRISTINA [smilingly]: I feel good. [another pause]

JERRY: What do you want to do next?

CHRISTINA: I'd like to give you a hug, Dad. [She gives Dad a hug, sits down.]

JERRY: You look different now than you looked earlier.

CHRISTINA: I feel more at peace with myself.

JERRY: Anything else you'd like to say?

CHRISTINA: To my Dad or to you?

JERRY: To either or both of us?

CHRISTINA: You know, Jerry, right now you don't seem as much *up there* as you did. I think I could actually talk to you now and feel straight across with you—in fact, I'm feeling that way now. It feels good to me not to give you all that power, and the more I talk the less scared I feel. Like right now I'm feeling a real strength. I think you can see me for what I am, and I *am* worth something! I *am* important! And looking at you now, I feel that you're with me, and that you're *not* judging me and putting me down. I'm feeling good saying all this.

JERRY: Sitting across from you and looking at your face now and hearing you, I'm feeling good too. I don't like being put in unreachable places and then told how distant I am. I feel good sensing a quiet power in you and I really like the way you are with me.

I continue by telling her some of the observations I had of her work and sharing what I was feeling at different points in our dialogue. I also tell her how I experience her very differently when she is soft, yet direct and powerful, instead of whining and giving me critical glances. I again offer her support and recognize the difficulty of her work.

Commentary on the Session

I think Gestalt techniques are powerful ways to help bring feelings out and also into focus. There is a vitality to Christina's work as she lets herself assume the identities of various objects. She can begin to reclaim disowned sides of herself and to integrate parts within herself. She is doing far more than reporting in an abstract fashion details from the past. She is bringing this unfinished business from her past into the present and dealing with whatever feelings arise in her.

Although I value Gestalt techniques as a way to take Christina further into whatever she is experiencing, I want to stress that these techniques cannot be used as a substitute for an honest exchange and dialogue between us. I can use myself and my own feelings to enhance the work of the session. Even though I will be departing from "pure" Gestalt, I want to integrate some cognitive work by asking Christina to put into words the meaning of what she has experienced and encourage her to talk about any associations between her work in our session and other aspects of her life. She may continue to talk about her awareness of how she puts *all* authority figures up high and what this is like for her. In my view blending this cognitive work with her affective work seems to result in longer-lasting learning.

Follow-Up: You Continue as Christina's Therapist

Assume that Christina and I decide that it is best that she continue her counseling with another therapist, one with a Gestalt orientation. I refer her to you.

1. Overall, what are your general impressions of Christina? Does she evoke any reactions in you? Knowing what you know of yourself and of Christina, how do you imagine that she would respond to you?
2. How comfortable would you be using Gestalt techniques similar to the ones I demonstrated in my work with Christina? Are there any techniques I used that you would *not* use? Why? Are there other Gestalt techniques you would like to try in your sessions with her?
3. I put a lot of emphasis on helping Christina pay attention to whatever she was feeling or experiencing at the moment. Why do you think I did this? What value, if any, do you see, in this?

4. Does my work with Christina bring to the foreground any unfinished business in yourself that you recognize? How might any of your own conflicts affect your work with her?
5. Where would you go from here with her? How?

RECOMMENDED SUPPLEMENTARY READINGS

Gestalt Therapy Now (1970), by J. Fagan and I. Shepherd (New York: Harper & Row), has some excellent readings dealing with the theory, techniques, and applications of Gestalt therapy.

Gestalt Approaches in Counseling (1975), by W. Passons (New York: Holt, Rinehart & Winston), is a very useful resource for learning how Gestalt techniques can come alive in individual counseling sessions. The chapters contain many clear examples of dealing with fantasy, bringing the past or the future into the present, working with both verbal and nonverbal messages, and using techniques appropriately.

Gestalt Therapy Verbatim (1969), by F. Perls (Moab, Utah: Real People Press), is a useful book to get a flavor of Gestalt concepts and a first-hand account of the style in which Fritz Perls worked. Many examples of clients working with Perls provide a sense of how Gestalt techniques bring the past into the here and now.

You're in Charge: A Guide to Becoming Your Own Therapist (1979), by J. Rainwater (Los Angeles: Guild of Tutors Press), is an excellent self-help book based on principles and techniques of Gestalt therapy. The author suggests exercises to increase self-awareness. She has useful ideas for keeping a journal, the uses of autobiography, working with dreams, the constructive use of fantasy, and the art of living in the here and now.

Creative Process in Gestalt Therapy (1978), by J. Zinker (New York: Brunner/Mazel), is an exceptionally good book that captures the essence of Gestalt therapy as a combination of phenomenology and behavior modification. The author provides many excerpts from therapeutic sessions to show how the therapist functions much as an artist. The book shows how Gestalt therapy can be practiced in a creative and eclectic style.

SUGGESTED READINGS

Belkin, G. (1987). *Contemporary psychotherapies* (2nd ed.). Pacific Grove, CA: Brooks/Cole. (Chapter 14)

Belkin, G. S. (1988). *Introduction to counseling* (3rd ed.). Dubuque, IA: William C. Brown. (Chapter 8)

Burke, J. F. (1989). *Contemporary approaches to psychotherapy and counseling.* Pacific Grove, CA: Brooks/Cole. (Chapter 8)

Corey, G. (1991). *Theory and practice of counseling and psychotherapy* (4th ed.). Pacific Grove, CA: Brooks/Cole. (Chapter 8)

Corsini, R., & Wedding, D. (Eds.). (1989). *Current psychotherapies* (4th ed.). Itasca, IL: F. E. Peacock. (Chapter 9)

Gilliland, B., James, R., Roberts, G., & Bowman, J. (1984). *Theories and strategies in counseling and psychotherapy.* Englewood Cliffs, NJ: Prentice-Hall. (Chapter 5)

Hansen, J., Stevic, R., & Warner, R. (1986). *Counseling: Theory and process* (4th ed.). Boston: Allyn & Bacon. (Chapter 7)

Ivey, A. E., Ivey, M. B., & Simek-Downing, L. (1987). *Counseling and psychotherapy: Integrating skills, theory, and practice* (2nd ed.). Englewood Cliffs, NJ: Prentice-Hall. (Chapter 10)

Patterson, C. H. (1986). *Theories of counseling and psychotherapy* (4th ed.). New York: Harper & Row. (Chapter 13)

Prochaska, J. O. (1984). *Systems of psychotherapy: A transtheoretical analysis* (2nd ed.). Pacific Grove, CA: Brooks/Cole. (Chapter 5)

Wedding, D., & Corsini, R. J. (Eds.). (1989). *Case studies in psychotherapy.* Itasca, IL: F. E. Peacock. (Chapter 8)

CHAPTER SEVEN

Case Approach to Transactional Analysis

A TA THERAPIST'S PERSPECTIVE ON RUTH
by John M. Dusay, M.D.

John Dusay is a psychiatrist in private practice in San Francisco and is an associate clinical professor at the University of California, San Francisco. He was a protégé of Eric Berne and is a founding member and past president of the International Transactional Analysis Association. He has written and lectured extensively on transactional analysis, and he received the Eric Berne Memorial Scientific Award for his development of egograms and related energy theory.

Assessment of Ruth

A transaction is a stimulus from one person and a related response from another. The observation of a transaction—whether it occurs between therapist and patient in a dyadic setting, between husband and wife in couples therapy (or family members in family therapy), or between nonrelated clients in group psychotherapy—is the basic unit for analysis. The psychological assessment is an ongoing process and is not separate from treatment.

After saying hello and exchanging a few informal remarks, I beckon Ruth to choose where she wants to sit in the office. She nervously hesitates and asks me where to sit (there are several different chairs and a sofa). I tell her that it's up to her. Although seemingly insignificant, this interchange is her introduction to the attitude that she has the power to choose. She looks uncomfortable, hesitates, and looks toward me for guidance, which is not forthcoming; then she cautiously sits down.

Although Ruth's behavior during the first 45 seconds may seem to be a simple nervous attempt to find a place, I intuitively know that this is a capsule presentation of her personality and is perhaps a clue to her entire life course. She is insecure in being herself and seeks approval. She is uncomfortable in freely choosing what might be pleasant for herself, even at the superficial level of finding a suitable chair. I will reassess this initial intuitive hunch throughout the course of treatment.

Transactional analysis is a contractual treatment in which the client and the therapist agree on the goal. "How will you know—and how will I know—when you get what you are coming here for?" is a succinct expression of the contract and will suffice for Ruth's case. The development of a contract is a means not only to attain a mutual goal but also to reveal how Ruth proceeds to set the goal. This process is very important in her evaluation.

I then tell Ruth that in this first session an important priority is to find out what she is seeking and to decide whether her goal is reasonably attainable. I tell her that she has the opportunity to find out whether she wants to work with me, and I give her permission to be candid and say whatever she wants. Some people, depending on their unique personalities, find this challenge easy to respond to. Others, like Ruth, who is not accustomed to expressing what she wants, may find that this simple opening is difficult. If I say "Tell me what you are seeking," she may respond "Dr. McCole [the referring physician] said that you're very good and maybe could help me." Her statement is an attempt to portray me as a powerful helper and to represent her presence in the office as a transfer from one authority figure to another. Many other statements empowering me or my methods follow: "You must be successful" or "Transactional analysis can help me."

I repeat to Ruth "Tell me what you are seeking for yourself."

Trying to find what she can say or do to please me, she responds, in an exasperated tone, "What do you want me to say?"

I persist by telling her "It's OK to say what you want for yourself."

"I really don't know what I want," she says tearfully and meekly, with a bowed head.

A direct assertion of what she *wants to gain* is a laborious undertaking for Ruth; it's not the nature of her personality. She is not making crisp, clear, logical assertions, like an adult, but is more like an indecisive, unsure little girl, who won't venture to say what she wants for herself. She finds it easier to tell about what she wants to go away, such as her symptoms of panic, insomnia, and obesity, than to make positive assertions. Her posture is marked by pulling in her chin and gazing upward toward me; she pulls on her dress, and her inflections end high at the end of sentences, creating an inquisitive tone. She sounds unsure as she frequently says "You know, you know."

All transactional analysts work with ego states. I diagnose by visual observation and by listening to Ruth's tone and inflection, as well as her verbal content, that her predominant presentation of herself is as a child, not as a grown-up. Her little-girl part is labeled her Child ego state. (When referring to ego states in transactional-analysis literature, upper-case letters are used, and when referring to actual biological children, lower case is used.) An ego state is defined as a cohesive system of thoughts, feelings, and related actions. Every person has a basic trio of Parent, Adult, and Child. The Parent is the expression of values, morals, and "shoulds," which are introjected from actual parents or surrogates. The Parent is observed to use a downward eye gaze, a more erect chin, finger pointing when speaking, and an "absolute" vocabulary, such as *always, never, all,* and *none,* as opposed to more Adult words, such as *usually, probably,* and *occasionally.* Although Ruth suffered under the influence of her authoritative father, she will actually speak, feel, and act toward her own children in the same way that her father and mother acted toward her. She may be surprised, when confronted about her difficulties with her own daughter, that she is similar to her own parents. For example, when she disapproves of her daughter's wearing fashionable clothes, she is in her Parent ego state, although she infrequently expresses that state. Her Adult ego state is her logical, non-emotional, thinking state. When in her Adult ego state, she can add up her bank account (and get the correct balance), plan a menu, and perform well in school examinations. Under the stress of seeing a therapist for the first time, her Child is dominant. Under stress the most familiar, habitual part of the personality usually emerges.

The function of these basic ego states varies from one person to another. Ruth has much more energy in her Child ego state and, more specifically, in the Adapted Child function of her Child ego state. Adaptation refers to her learning how to exist with her father, how to please him, how to conform to his personality, and how to survive in her father-dominated biological family. Her mother also played an important role in her adapting to her father, as she seemed to set an example by being subservient and raising her daughter to be a good and pleasing little girl. Some children decide to rebel against authoritarian parents. Ruth chose to conform. More than 30 years later, this adapted little girl still lives in her Adapted Child ego state, as witnessed in my office. The other vital and very different function of the Child is that of freedom, autonomy, creativity, sexual pleasure, wanderlust, and growth. This is termed the Free Child ego-state, and it is what every individual is born with. This ego state was severely suppressed in Ruth, so much so that she was even uncomfortable in freely choosing a chair in the therapist's office. Not only does she have different ego states, but she also has different amounts of energy in the parts. Her Adapted Child is highly charged, and her Free Child is very low in energy.

I also note that Ruth's Parent ego state, like that of all other people, has functions of both nurturing and of criticizing. She is less critical, probably because her father seems to be the critic and keeper of the morals in the family. Her Critical Parent is low, but she is able to survive by developing the nurturing part of her Parent ego state. Ruth's unique profile of energies—low Critical Parent, higher Nurturing Parent, moderate Adult, extremely low Free Child, and very high Adapted Child—is the mosaic that is her personality.

Ego-state analysis is a fundamental consideration. At some point I will have Ruth reexamine the roots of her personality. This is most frequently done by a psychoregressive technique. I sense that Ruth is exhibiting a repetitive pattern in deciding what she wants. For example, she expresses discomfort in finding a seat, she is agitated in her attempt to form a contract, and she is afraid to advance her career out of the fear that she will provoke the wrath of her husband. I have her trace the feelings that are being expressed in the here and now of the consulting room back to their original source. While talking about her husband, she exhibits her telltale somatic signs: a furrowed brow, downcast chin, upward-gazing eyes, and nervously fidgeting hands.

I tell Ruth to close her eyes, and I may enhance her discomfort by pinching her already tightened brow and squeezing her hands to reinforce her discomfort. I tell her "Say how you are feeling."

Ruth replies, "I'm frightened. I'm afraid my husband won't let me work."

I then direct her: "Let those feelings go back, back in time." With this suggestive technique she goes further and further back in time as I offer many guiding comments. I allow several minutes for her to go back all the way to childhood, if possible.

Finally, I say "Say where you are." Ruth, in a very emotional state, has gone back to age 6, when her father discovered her playing doctor with a friend. I encourage her to be 6, to speak in the present tense as if she were 6 years old. She sobs and appears very frightened.

Ruth (age 6) says: "I'm bad. I should not play like this . . . "

I allow a full expression of her affect and then ask the most important question: "What are you deciding about yourself?"

Ruth (age 6) replies decisively: "I'll never do this again."

Although this was not the only time that she displeased her father by playing, being herself, and doing natural and free things, this recall is very dramatic. She decided at the young age of 6 that she would not be free again. In essence, her father repeatedly gave her the injunction "Don't be yourself" and she agreed, at age 6, "I won't be myself." That decision is the "it," the "real problem," that, like a self-fulfilling prophecy, has determined her life course of suppressing her desires. Thirty-three years later, she is still hanging on to this childhood decision. It is now so habitual and reinforced that she believes that this is just the way she is. This pattern is what transactional analysts call a script.

The process of reexperiencing those decisive childhood moments reveals the nature of the decision. A transactional analyst does not utilize regressive techniques primarily to discover information but, rather, to reopen the emotion of the learning situation for renegotiation. Ruth now has more options than when she was absolutely dependent on her physiological family for survival. This process is inspirational for Ruth, who is introduced to the notion that she is responsible for her life course and that she may actually have the power to change her mind. The transactional analyst's assumption is that anything that has been learned can be relearned. This assessment of the script is crucial, and it is usually made during the process of psychoregression rather than by historical questioning and data gathering.

Over the years Ruth has come to believe that she should please others, starting with her father when she was a little girl and culminating with a decision at age 6. From that point on she habitually proved that her self-decision was correct and reinforced it by playing psychological games. A game is an orderly series of transactions with two levels. One is an overt social level:

RUTH: Will you treat me for my problem?
THERAPIST: Yes, that is my speciality.

This is an overt Adult-to-Adult transaction. The two are discussing therapist/client business. The other level is a covert psychological one:

RUTH: How can I please you?
THERAPIST: Treat me as God.

This game fulfills her script needs to please the empowered authority figure and to forego being herself. (The therapist in this example, hopefully not a transactional analyst, has his or her own hidden ulterior agenda of being treated as a deity.)

The first clue to Ruth's game came when she attempted to empower me, by viewing herself as weak—"What do you want me to say?"—and by viewing me as strong—"Dr. McCole said you're very good." While on one level an Adult-to-Adult transaction revolved around getting treatment, she has a secret, hidden level of transaction: "How can I please you?" My needs are portrayed as more important than her needs.

Key Issues

The transactional analyst focuses on the three distinct facets of every patient in treatment—namely, the personality as revealed in the function of the *ego states,* the genesis of this personality as it unfolds in the *script,* and the lifelong reinforcing behaviors that have the qualities of a *game.* Like so many other innovators of the time, Eric Berne, the father of transactional analysis, was a trained Freudian analyst. From this background he developed his basic theory from an intellectual analytic route. His major objection to psychoanalysis was that it was time-consuming, complex, and poorly understood or communicated to patients.

Transactional analysts do not apologize for being concise, and they have chalkboards in their consulting rooms. This approach is especially useful to Ruth, who seems to have a love/hate relationship with authority figures, including me as her therapist. With the concise transactional analysis symbols she can understand what I understand—on an equal footing—allowing her to experience her own power and ability to change. Therapists, instead of being deifed and hiding behind big words, share their knowledge equally.

Three diagrams will highlight Ruth's key issues. The egogram (Figure 7-1) is a bar graph showing Ruth's personality functions (see figure). She is highly energized in the Adapted Child (AC) function and extremely low in Free Child (FC). Her seeking of treatment is a direct reflection of her desire to become more free and to raise this part of herself. She is also low in her Critical Parent (CP), the part that criticizes others, as she is more habitually comfortable in being criticized. This function is the part that stands up for her rights and desires and that is protective of her. Her Nurturing Parent (NP) and Adult (A) functions are about average.

Ruth's script matrix symbolizes from where her personality arises (see Figure 7-2). She introjects the values and morals of her father and mother into her developing Parent ego state. But on the Child level, from the Child in her father to her own Child, she receives many thousands of injunctions, both direct statements (symbolized by a solid line) of "Don't play like that" and indirect signs (dotted lines) such as a disapproving frown, saying "Don't be yourself." At age 6 these injunctions culminated in her script decision "I won't be myself," reflected in her resolve to please her father and snuff out the free proclivities with which she was born. Her mother reinforced this suppression by showing her how to please her father. To a 6-year old girl the father is the prototype of all men, and indeed she carried this decision into her marriage and through life, with male (and possibly female) authority figures.

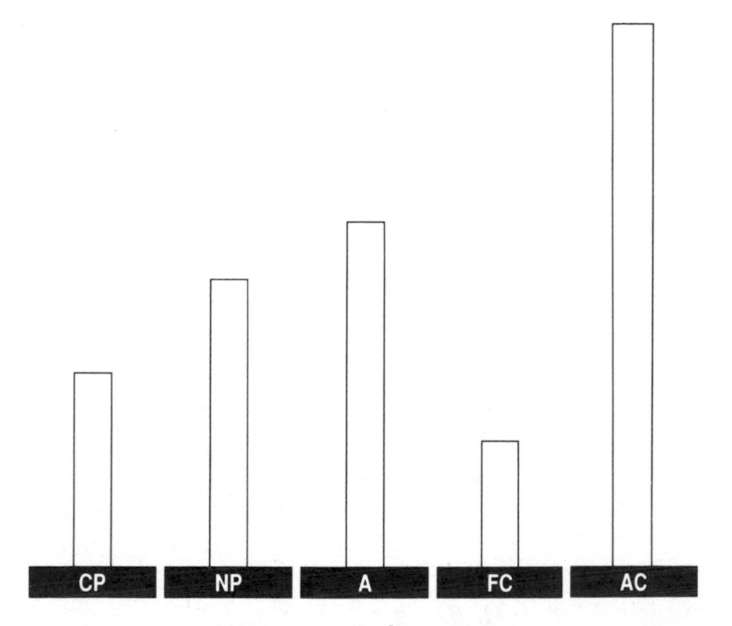

Figure 7-1. Ruth's Egogram

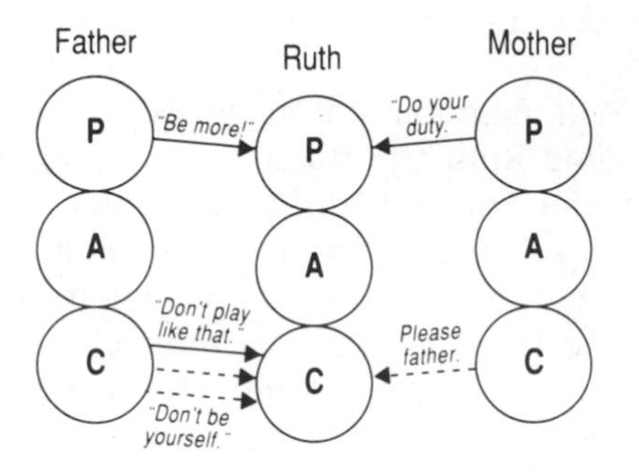

Figure 7-2. Ruth's Script Matrix

Although Ruth left her biological family, this learned behavior did not become extinct, as she reinforced the phenomenon by playing games, as seen in Figure 7-3. She recounts how she discussed her educational goals with her husband on the Adult-to-Adult level:

RUTH: I would like to go to college.
JOHN: That's fine with me.

But on the Child-to-Parent level she transacts in a hidden way:

RUTH: Will that please you?
JOHN: No, stay the way you are.

Both Ruth and John might deny the existence of the hidden level if I saw them as a couple. She might glance at him and seek approval, and he might look disgusted when she talked about being absent from the home.

Therapeutic Techniques

Two major advantages of transactional analysis as a psychotherapeutic approach are (1) there is a complete, crisp, and easily communicated theory of personality and (2) because of this solid foundation the therapist is quite

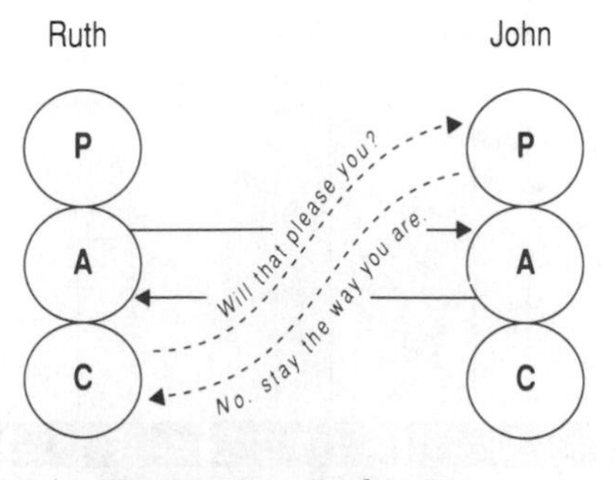

Figure 7-3. Ruth's Game

free to develop an innovative style of treatment utilizing his or her own strengths. Although Berne's treatment style was reminiscent of that of an intellectual analyst of the 1950s, his theories were greatly influenced by the evolving human-potential movement, especially in northern California, where he practiced in the 1960s. Following his death in 1970 these influences were rapidly incorporated into techniques for doing transactional analysis. Nowhere was this more evident than through the work of Robert and Mary Goulding at the Western Institute for Group and Family Therapy in Mt. Madonna, California. They married Berne's transactional analysis with the techniques of Fritz Perls's Gestalt therapy, along with others, and developed *redecision therapy.* This has been the predominant and major advance in transactional analysis after Berne.

Observing trained transactional analysts in action, you may see treatment styles ranging from a more "intellectual" cognitive approach to a highly emotive "feeling" display. At different times you may observe the transactional analyst using techniques such as hypnosis, psychodrama, and role playing. The same therapist may later be seen standing at a chalkboard offering a cognitive review that is so specific that the process and problems are actually being diagrammed with circles, arrows, and bar graphs. To a transactional analyst this apparent intellectual/emotional dichotomy is melded into a cohesive system in which neither thinking nor feeling is discounted or exalted as the primary vehicle.

Ruth's treatment began when she first contacted me. Her game of "How can I please you?" in which she had great difficulty in stating what she wanted for herself was gently but consistently confronted. When she became very emotional in discussing what pleased her husband, I initiated a redecision model. Ruth was asked to close her eyes and trace the "bad" feelings back into her past. She regressed to the incident at age 6 when she was discovered having fun in normal childhood sex play—in essence, *being herself*—and was abruptly shocked by her disapproving, critical father. "I will never play again" ("I will not be myself") became her resolve.

I intervene by placing an empty chair in front of Ruth. When her sobbing subsides, I ask her to come and sit in this other (curative) chair. As I direct her to the cure chair, I gently massage her tense shoulders, stroking her in a nurturing manner, unlike the pinching of her brow earlier to enhance the bad feelings.

DUSAY: Take care of the little girl who is so sad.
RUTH [cure chair]: Why are you so sad?
DUSAY: Switch back and respond.
RUTH [script chair]: I have disappointed my father.
DUSAY: Switch back.
RUTH [cure chair, sobbing again]: It's hard to please him. You must feel bad.

After a few of these switches I observe that Ruth seems to be getting nowhere; she is at an impasse. She seems unable to overcome the negative feelings of her Adapted Child, and she has actually slipped into an Adapted Child state while sitting in the curative chair. This, unfortunately, reinforces the bad-feeling script state, and therefore I am quick to intervene. I do so by having Ruth sit in another chair placed perpendicular to the script chair and the cure chair. She is then directed to comment on the process. This immediately allows her to cathect her observing Adult ego state. She may say something like: "I was sad in both chairs, like the blind leading the blind."

The TA therapist is like a consultant. Ruth and I have an Adult-to-Adult conversation. This is the technique to resolve the impasse. We may decide that she needs some practice in having fun, dancing, writing poetry, taking part in sexual counseling, or the like, by which she can raise the energy in her Free Child ego state.

After weeks or, sometimes, a few months of treatment focused on the strengthening of weaker ego states, she may reapproach the redecision model. In the curative chair she may spiritedly tell the Adapted Child: "To hell with your father! Do what you want to do."

When she switches back to the original chair she responds: "That feels good—to hell with him and with my husband, too, if he wants to be a fuddy-duddy."

Then she is cured! Cure means that she has redecided her script, that she is not here to please her father, her husband, me, or anyone else. From a personality standpoint her Free Child has gained energy relative to her Adapted Child, and she will no longer look for how she can please others. Her habitual game has abated.

There is rarely a dramatic redecision in the first attempt. But by separating ego states, opposing the forces against each other, and strengthening the weaker growth forces, the client and therapist can achieve at least gradual results and, occasionally, dramatic breakthroughs. The cure is in the process itself. Note that though the transactional analyst is quite active in structuring the session, is an active catalyst for the redecision, and confronts impasses (slippages into the Adapted ego state), the client does all of the actual work. The patient has the power to change negative childhood decisions and does so by developing and then using more positive ego-state forces. The use of multiple chairs is similar to J. L. Moreno's pioneering psychodrama, done as early as 1924 in Vienna. What happens in the different chairs is that Ruth is able to utilize different forces that were always present in her head.

A final note is that John may be invited to couples therapy and may be able to have a deeper understanding of why Ruth seems rebellious toward him as she participates in her regressions and exposes her childhood decision. He is able to recognize that the problem started long before he even met her. He may also explore why he is so afraid of letting go of his tendency to control by tracing his own "fear of abandonment" back to his own childhood. Transactional analysts frequently encourage joint psychoregressive sessions for couples therapy, and Ruth and John can become allies rather than adversaries in a different, but growing, marriage.

JERRY COREY'S WORK WITH RUTH FROM A TA PERSPECTIVE

Basic Assumptions

Transactional analysis emphasizes the cognitive, rational, and behavioral aspects of personality and is oriented toward increasing awareness so that the client will be able to make new decisions. TA is rooted in an antideterministic philosophy and asserts that we are capable of transcending our conditioning and early programming. It acknowledges that we were influenced by the expectations and demands of significant others, especially because our early decisions were made at a time in life when we were highly dependent on others. But these decisions can be reviewed and challenged, and, if they are no longer appropriate, new ones can be made. As I review Ruth's case, it becomes readily apparent that she accepted many parental injunctions that still have control over her life.

Assessment of Ruth

Perhaps the clearest way to describe my initial assessment of Ruth is to present in shortened and modified form her responses to the TA *personal life-script questionnaire.* Early in the course of TA therapy, beginning with the intake interview, I start asking for information that forms the basis of the life script of a client. I ask Ruth the following questions as the basis for this general assessment, and I expect that from a summary of this information we can develop a therapeutic contract that will give structure and direction to the course of therapy.

1. *How do you see yourself now?* As a person who has made a lifetime career out of thinking of and serving others.
2. *Three things that I'd most like to change about myself are:* Being able to feel that I was worth getting affection; being able to have fun; and being able to think of myself and do what I want without feeling guilty.
3. *What has prevented me from changing these things is:* My sense of duty and obligation to other people in my life and my fear of the consequences if I don't carry out my duties.
4. *To what degree are you living up to the expectations of others?* I have done what others expect of me for so long that I don't have a clear idea of what I want for myself or what is right for me.
5. *How do you see your mother?* As a self-sacrificing martyr who had no life of her own.

6. *How are you like your mother?* We are both serious, and we both have lived to serve others.
7. *How are you unlike your mother?* I am not satisfied with my present state, and I am motivated to change.
8. *When my mother compliments me, she says:* "You're a good person."
9. *When my mother criticizes me, she says:* "Don't be so selfish" and "You're not trying hard enough."
10. *Her main advice to me is:* To follow the Bible and not make a fuss.
11. *What could you do to make her happy?* Do everything that was expected—but even then she was not happy with me!
12. *What could you do to disappoint her?* Bring shame to the family. We all had an image to live up to, and, if we didn't, she showed her displeasure by her sad face.
13. *How did you see your father?* As a stern, authoritarian, hard-working man who was quick to criticize.
14. *How are you like your father?* We both are very concerned about what people think.
15. *How are you unlike your father?* I want to have fun, and he thinks having fun is a sin.
16. *When my father compliments me, he says:* His compliments are so rare that I don't remember what he says.
17. *When my father criticizes me, he says:* "You could have done much better if you had tried harder."
18. *His main advice to me was:* "Always do what is right, and you'll find true happiness."
19. *I could disappoint him by:* Giving up my religion.
20. *Some of the main* do's *that I have learned and accepted are:* Do follow the Bible. Respect the Lord. Do for others, and ask nothing in return. Do suffer in silence, and offer it up as atonement for your sins. Live in a moral and decent manner. Be proper. There is virtue in not complaining about the crosses that you must carry in this life.
21. *Some of the main* don'ts *that were programmed into me were:* Don't be close. Don't be a child. Don't be frivolous. Don't be sexy. Don't get angry. Don't think for yourself.
22. *One important early decision I made as a child was:* I'll strive for perfection so that someday I'll be loved and accepted.
23. *One early decision that I feel I have changed is:* Well, I am still struggling with the one about thinking I have a right to get an education, which is something I've really wanted.
24. *What is one new decision that you would like to make?* That I could treat myself as well as I treat others.
25. *What I most like about myself is:* My determination. I just won't give up.
26. *What I least like about myself is:* How scared of life I am.
27. *What did your mother tell you (either directly or indirectly) about*
    a. *you?* That I had to earn my place in life.

b. *life?* That it was given by God.
c. *death?* That it comes like a thief in the night and I should always be prepared.
d. *love?* That is has to be earned.
e. *sex?* That is is a necessary means of procreation.
f. *marriage?* That it is the expected path and a sacred union.
g. *men?* That I shouldn't get too close or too friendly.
h. *women?* That they are meant to have children and to serve.
i. *your birth?* That I was extremely difficult and caused her much pain.

28. *What did your father tell you (either directly or indirectly) about*
    a. *you?* That I did not count in his life.
    b. *life?* That it was to be lived in accordance with the word of the Lord.
    c. *death?* That it ushers the way to either heaven or hell.
    d. *love?* That it doesn't involve sex.
    e. *sex?* That it is the source of many a person's downfall.
    f. *marriage?* That it is a serious matter, never to be broken.
    g. *men?* That they are the head of the house.
    h. *women?* That they reach their zenith by bearing children.
    i. *your birth?* I have no idea!
29. *How did you see yourself as a child?* As compliant, quiet, obedient, hard-working, striving to please, scared, lonely, lost.
30. *How did you see yourself as an adolescent?* As scared, without friends, responsible, mature, hard-working, studious, eager to please.
31. *How did you see yourself five years ago?* As the supermother, superwife, and one who simply did what was expected of her.
32. *How would you like to see yourself five years from now?* As a professional woman with satisfactions both in the home and outside of it.
33. *What are you doing to make that ideal become real?* I am beginning therapy, which is difficult for me to do.
34. *If you were to write your own epitaph, what would it say?* Here lies Ruth who thought about everyone, yet she forgot about herself.
35. *What words do you fear might appear on your tombstone?* I fear that there will be no tombstone—that I will be forgotten.
36. *What do you wish your mother had done differently?* I wish she had shown me affection and let me know that she appreciated all my efforts in taking care of my sisters and brother.
37. *What do you wish your father had done differently?* I wish he had been more gentle with me, hugged me, and told me that he approved of me.
38. *What do you most want out of life?* To feel really alive—to be able to have fun and still to accomplish.
39. *If you could have three wishes, what would they be?* That John would appreciate the changes I am making and support me in them; that I could become a teacher; and that I could dump the guilt I so often feel.
40. *What was a critical turning point in your life?* A few years ago, when I decided to enroll in college.

After Ruth has answered this questionnaire, we look for patterns. Many of her injunctions fit together. It becomes clear that she accepted most of the parental messages uncritically. A major injunction was for her not to think, question, or to have a life of her own. By way of summary, *the major message she received from her father* was: live in a moral and decent manner; emotions will lead you astray, so keep on the right path and pray for guidance to always be strong. *From her mother, the main message* was: suffer in silence; never let people know how difficult things are for you; there is virtue in not complaining about the crosses you must carry in this life. United, her parents would say: be proper; whatever you do, don't shame us.

In terms of stroking, or signs of recognition, Ruth got mainly ''conditional strokes.'' She had to earn recognition. Yet even when she lived up to the expectations set by her parents, she did not typically feel appreciated or recognized by them.

A review of Ruth's responses will point the way to areas that she can consider changing. First, she will have to decide which specific changes she wants to make, and then together we will establish a therapeutic contract.

Goals of Therapy

Specific goals are defined by Ruth and stated in her contract. After reviewing the life-script questionnaire, she says she does not want to act out the rest of her life by her parents' design and end her life according to their plan. One of the points of her contract is to talk directly to her husband and to tell him specific ways in which she wants their marriage to be different. She agrees that she is willing to risk displeasing him by saying how she would like to change their family life.

Therapeutic Procedures

Transactional analysis attempts to take the mystery out of the therapeutic process, for the client and therapist work together on goals that are mutually agreed on. Ruth's contract is not a rigid and legal document; it is a procedure that puts the responsibility on her to state what she is willing to initiate in the sessions. Her contract can be modified as she goes along, and in this sense it is an open one. It will prevent me from digging into her past like an archaeologist looking for interesting artifacts.

I like to teach my clients about the fundamentals of transactional analysis so that we have a simple common vocabulary. In this way clients are half of the therapeutic partnership, as opposed to my being the ''expert'' and keeping what I know about them to myself. I will ask Ruth to read a few books that describe how TA actually works and this reading will help her apply these concepts to herself. We will be working with the ego states of

Parent, Adult, and Child, which she will learn to recognize in herself, so that she can choose which one to function in at any given time. We will look at any games that she plays. These are "crooked" transactions between her and others that prevent intimacy from occurring and result in bad feelings. We will explore in depth the ways in which she has programmed herself and how she behaves now as a result of some of her early decisions. I hope that she can see that some of her decisions may have been needed for her survival at one time but that she may be clinging to decisions that are both archaic and nonfunctional. Working with her life script will be a large part of what we do in the sessions.

Transactional analysis integrates the cognitive and the affective (feeling) dimensions. It is fair to say that I emphasize the cognitive aspects of therapy, yet I realize that changing entails actually experiencing feelings. In my view, however, experiencing feelings alone is not enough to bring about a substantive change in behavior.

The Therapeutic Process

Elements of the process

When I first mention to Ruth that our work will be defined by a therapeutic contract, she seems resistant. She thinks it sounds so formal and legalistic, and she wonders why it is necessary.

JERRY: A contract sets the focus for TA therapy. As the client you decide what specific beliefs, emotions, and behaviors you plan to change in order to reach your stated goals.

RUTH: But I'm not quite sure what I want to change. After we went through that life-script questionnaire, I was counting on *you* to point out to me what I should work on. There's so much to change, and frankly I'm at a loss where to begin.

JERRY: Part of our work here will be for you to take increasing responsibility for your own actions.

Helping Ruth define her goals. At this point Ruth and I discuss this issue in some detail. The essence of what I let her know is that TA is based on the expectation that clients focus on their goals and make a commitment. It emphasizes the division of responsibility and provides a point of departure for working.

RUTH [after some exploration]: I just want to be me. I want to be happy. I'm tired of taking care of everyone else, and I want to take care of me.

JERRY: That's a start, but your statements are too global. Can we narrow them down? What would make you happy? What do you mean by taking care of yourself? How will you do this? And in what ways are you not being you?

I work with Ruth until she eventually comes up with clear statements of what she wants from therapy, what steps she will take to get what she wants, and how she will determine when her contract is fulfilled. After much discussion and a series of negotiations, she is able to come up with a list of changes she is willing to make.

RUTH: For one, I'm willing to approach my husband and tell him what I feel about our relationship. I know you say that I can't change him and that I can only change myself, so I'll tell him what I intend to do differently. And later, I would like to deal directly with my four children. They all take advantage of me, and I intend to change that. I can begin by telling them what I'm willing to do and what I'm no longer willing to do.

Although the above list is more specific than her original goals, there is still a need for greater specificity. Thus, I proceed by asking her exactly what she does want to change about each area she has mentioned, including what she intends to do differently. One part of her contract involves asking her husband to attend at least one of the sessions so that she can tell him the specific things she most wants to change in their relationship.

Role-playing Ruth's marriage. In another session Ruth and I do some role playing in which I stand in for John. Ruth tells me, as John, how frightened she is of making demands on me, for fear that I might leave. Out of that session she begins to be aware of how intimidated she has allowed herself to become. I point out to her that she has made John her Critical Parent. She continues to set him up to punish her by giving him the power to make her feel scared and guilty. As a homework assignment I ask her to write a letter to him, saying all the things she really wants him to hear, but not to mail it. The writing is geared to getting her to focus on her relationship with him and what she wants to be different. (In an earlier session I gave her a similar assignment of writing a detailed letter to her father, which she agreed not to send him but to bring in for a session with me.) I make the observation to Ruth that in many ways she is looking to John for the same things she wanted from her father as a child and adolescent. Further, she assumed the role of doing whatever she thought would please each of them, yet she typically ended up feeling that no matter how hard she tried, she would never succeed in pleasing them. From here I try to show her that she will have to change her own attitudes if she expects change in her relationships, rather than waiting until her father or her husband might change. This is a new discovery for her, and it represents a different direction for her.

Holding a joint session with John. Later I remind Ruth of her contract, and I suggest that she ask John to attend a therapy session with her so that we can deal directly with some of the issues that surface. Initially, she gives a list of reasons why she is sure that he will never come in. After some discussion with me she does agree to ask him directly and clearly to attend at least one session (which we will also role-play first). To her surprise he agrees to join her. What follows are a few excerpts from this initial joint session.

RUTH: I brought John here today even though I don't think he really wanted to be here. [Notice that she speaks for him.]

JERRY: John, I'd like to hear from you about what it's like to attend this session.

JOHN: When Ruth asked me, I agreed because I thought I might be of some help to her. I know I don't need therapy for myself, but I couldn't see any harm in giving it one shot.

RUTH: Now that he's here, I don't know what to say.

JERRY: You could begin by telling him why you wanted him here.

RUTH: It's that our marriage just can't go on this way much longer. Things are no longer satisfactory to me. I know that for many years I never complained—just did what was expected and thought that everything was fine—but the truth is that things are not fine by me.

JOHN [turning to me]: I don't know what she means. Our marriage has always seemed OK by me. I don't see the problem. If there's a problem, *she's* got it [said in a manner like a critical parent].

JERRY: How about telling Ruth this? [I want Ruth and John to talk *to* each other directly, rather than talking *about* each other. My guess is that at home they are very indirect. By having them speak to each other in this session, I get a better sense of how they interact.]

RUTH: See, *that's* the problem. Everything is fine by John—I'm the one who's crazy! Why is he so contented while I'm so discontented?

JERRY: Tell John. You're looking at me. He needs to hear from you, not me.

RUTH: Why, John, am I the only one who is complaining about our marriage? Can't you see anything wrong with the way we're living? Do you really mean that everything is just fine by you? Why is everything on me?

JERRY: Wait a minute, Ruth, I hear lots of questions. Rather than asking all these questions of John, tell him what you really want him to hear.

RUTH [again turning to me and addressing me]: But I don't think he ever hears me! That's the trouble—I just don't think he cares or that he listens to me when I talk about our life together.

JERRY: I can understand why he might not hear you. You're not telling him what you want, and you're not giving him a chance. You know, Ruth, part of the problem I'm seeing is that you aren't telling him about you. If this is the way it is at home, I can see why you feel you're not listened to. Are you willing to hang in there with him and tell him directly what you say you'd like him to hear?

RUTH [with raised voice and a great deal of emotion]: John, I'm tired of being the perfect wife and the perfect mother, always doing what's expected of me. I've done that for as long as I can remember, and I want a change. I feel that I'm the only one holding up our family. Everything depends on me, and all of you depend on me to keep things going. But I can't turn to any of you for emotional support. I'm the nurturer, but no one nurtures me. And there are times that I need to know that I matter to you, and that you recognize me.

JOHN: Well, sure—and I appreciate your hard work. I know you do a lot in the home, and I'm proud of you.

JERRY: How does it feel to hear John say that to you?

RUTH: But you never say that—you just don't tell me that you appreciate me. I need to hear that from you. I need to feel your emotional support.

JERRY: Ruth, you still didn't tell John how you were affected by what he said to you. [I am calling to Ruth's attention that in this brief interaction, for one short moment, her husband responded to her in a way that she says she would like him to. She does not acknowledge it and instead continues with her litany of complaints. I am letting her know that John may be more likely to change if he gets some positive stroking.] How could you stroke John right now?

RUTH: I like it when you tell me that you're proud of me. It means a lot to me.

JOHN: I'm just not used to talking that way. Why make a lot of useless words? You know how I feel about you.

JERRY: John! That's just the problem. You don't tell Ruth how you feel about her and what she means to you, and she is not very good in asking that from you. Both of you are very stingy with each other in giving strokes.

RUTH: Yeah, I agree. It hurts me that you think I want to hear useless words. I'm missing affection from you. It's so hard for me to talk about my life with you—about you and me—about our family—oh! [Ruth's eyes grow moist, she lets out a sigh, and then she grows quiet.]

JERRY: So, don't stop now, Ruth. Keep taking to John. Tell him what your tears and that heavy sigh are about. [My hunch is that Ruth often feels defeated and stops there, seeing herself as misunderstood. I am encouraging her to stay with herself and continue to address John. Even though he is looking very uncomfortable at this point, he seems receptive.]

JOHN: Sometimes I find it hard to talk to you because I feel criticized by you. It's as if you were a victim of my insensitivity. But how can I be sensitive when you don't tell me what you want?

JERRY: Sounds like a reasonable request. Will you tell him?

RUTH: You may not know how important going to college really is for me. I so much want to finish and get my credential. But I can't do that and be responsible for the complete running of our house. I need for the kids to pitch in and do their share, instead of always expecting me to do everything. I need some time to myself—time just to sit and think for a few minutes—when I'm at home. And I would like to be able to sit down with you, John, after dinner and just talk for a bit. I miss talking to you. The times we do talk, the topic is household maintenance.

JERRY: What are you hearing, John, and how does this sound to you?

JOHN: Well, we have to talk about chores. I just don't understand what she wants me to say. [John continues for a time with a very critical voice, in many ways belittling Ruth. Yet eventually he does admit that the children don't help as much as they could and that he might be willing to do a bit more around the house.]

RUTH: Well, I'd really like your help at home. And what about spending time with me? Do you want to talk with me?

JOHN: Yes, I do, but too often I just want to relax after busting my butt at work all day. I want it to be positive at home after a long day.

JERRY: It sounds like both of you would like to talk to each other. Would you be willing to set aside some time during the next week when you can have some uninterrupted conversation?

Together we develop a realistic contract that specifies when, where, and how long they will spend uninterrupted time with each other. John agrees to come in for another joint session. In the meantime I ask Ruth to monitor what she actually does at home for two weeks and to keep these notes in her journal. I suggest that she write down a specific list of the changes she wants at home, along with what she could do to make these changes happen.

Process commentary

As part of Ruth's therapy I ask her to keep a daily journal so that she can record specifics of how she is meeting her contract. Toward the end of her therapy, which lasts eight months, I request any summary statements that she can make so that I can get a glimpse of her view of her basic progress. We devote the last two therapy sessions to reviewing the progress she has made as well as making specific plans for what she can do now that she is ending therapy. She agrees to call within two months to give a follow-up report on how she is carrying out her plans. Below are the summary statements that she excerpts from her journal:

> I've completed eight months of TA therapy with Jerry, and as a result I've changed some of the decisions I made *for life* as a child. Much of the latter stages of my therapy focused on redecision work. One of the most significant redecisions I've made is to stop trying to be the perfect person, my father's "good girl"—all in the hope that he'll one day give me his love. My therapy taught me that I can't directly change him into a loving person. I see how for so many years I hung onto my unhappiness in order to get Father to change; now I see that I'm responsible for myself and for finding love in my own life, and I'm not waiting around forever for him to learn to give me this love. Another important lesson for me was that I now believe that there isn't necessarily something basically wrong or evil about me that makes me unlovable. My father's inability to show love is *his problem,* not a fault of mine.

I've worked on many parental messages that I accepted, and I've changed some of the decisions I made in response to those messages. At one time I accepted the injunction "Don't think." So I decided not to think for myself. Who was I to make a decision? I now realize that I can think for myself and come up with pretty good decisions! "Don't be sexy"—that one still gives me trouble, but I'm making progress. I'm able to say to the parents inside me that you had your standards, but I don't want them for me. I've learned that there are many new decisions I *can* make—that I don't have to be bound by some of the inappropriate ones I made when I felt helpless as a child. And I'm learning how to ask for more for myself, and feel good about asking and getting!

Ruth and I spend several sessions working with her part in creating and maintaining the difficulties she is experiencing in her marriage. Rather than focusing on John and what he can do to change, I challenge her to change her own attitudes and behaviors, which will inevitably lead to changes in her relationship with John. Eventually, she sees how she has made him into a Critical Parent and has become an Adapted Child around him. She begins to see how difficult it is for her to make requests of him or ask him for what she needs emotionally. Although she initially resists the idea of telling him directly what she wants with him and from him, she eventually sees some value in learning to ask for the strokes she wants. One of the games that she has been playing is deciding in advance that he (and others) will not take care of her emotionally, and with this expectancy she has blocked off possibilities of feeling emotionally nourished by others. There are many times when she becomes aware of ways in which she is slipping into old patterns, many of which were developed as a child, yet she becomes increasingly aware of when she is about to fall into these traps and is able to behave in more effective ways.

I do a fair amount of teaching with Ruth, because TA is a didactic therapy. Although her therapy does involve reliving earlier events that are associated with intense emotions, I am interested in helping her to cognitively understand the nature of certain decisions that she made as a child. The majority of our sessions consist of reviewing and critically examining these early decisions, with the aim of determining the degree to which they are still functional. When I am working with early scenes that Ruth recalls from her childhood, what I have in mind is to provide her with an opportunity to recreate these situations with as much emotional intensity as she felt at that time. Yet our work does not stop with this role playing and reliving of past events; instead, I continually challenge her to think about what she decided about herself and her place in life at these moments. Before her therapy she was not aware of the parental messages she had incorporated. By the end of her therapy she has given considerable thought to both the implied and expressed messages she accepted from her parents. She has also developed a clearer perspective on how she has been perpetuating many of these injunctions and how she has still been trying to live up to the standards of her father. I consistently ask that she raise the question "Will I wait forever for my father's approval, or will I begin to work for my own approval?"

Questions for Reflection

1. What general reactions do you have to the ways in which Dr. Dusay and I worked with Ruth? What differences, if any, do you see between our focuses and styles?
2. What are some things you like about the TA approach? What do you like the least? How might you approach Ruth differently from either Dusay or myself but still stay within the TA model?
3. Dr. Dusay paid particular attention to Ruth's behavior patterns and mannerisms during the first few minutes of the initial session. How much importance do you place on your initial reactions to a client? How might you have interpreted Ruth's mannerisms as described by Dr. Dusay if you were meeting her for your first session?
4. In Dr. Dusay's selection Ruth had a great deal of difficulty in expressing what she wanted for herself, and she was unclear in defining a therapeutic contract. If you were working with Ruth as a TA therapist, how might you assist her in getting a clearer focus on what she wanted? What would you do if she put pressure on you to tell her what she *should* work on in her therapy?
5. What do you think about the idea of beginning therapy with a clear contract, one that spells out what the client wants from the process and states the functions and responsibilities of the therapist? What differences are there between working with a contract and not using one? Which is your preference? Why?
6. Dr. Dusay integrated concepts from the theory of TA with several Gestalt techniques. If Ruth were your client, what possibilities would you see in blending TA theory with Gestalt experiments?
7. What injunctions of Ruth's do you recognize in yourself, if any? Did you make any early decisions that resemble hers? If so, what are they? What have you done to challenge your early decisions? To what degree do you think that your potential effectiveness with Ruth would directly depend on how well you know your own injunctions?
8. What techniques might you introduce to help Ruth work on some of the injunctions and early decisions that she mentioned?
9. What major differences do you see between Dr. Dusay's TA approach to working with Ruth and Dr. Blau's psychoanalytic approach? Dr. Bitter's Adlerian approach? Dr. Polkinghorne's existential approach? Dr. Cain's person-centered approach? Dr. Fantz's Gestalt approach?
10. In reviewing the TA life-script questionnaire, how would you answer some of the questions yourself? If you were a TA client, what would it be like for you to begin therapy with an extensive survey such as this

questionnaire? What kind of contract would you draw up, based on these life-script data?

11. How might you work with Ruth's cultural injunctions from a TA perspective? What value do you see in drawing on TA concepts as a way of helping you understand how her cultural experiences have affected her?
12. What are some of the main themes in Ruth's life that you would pursue in her therapy sessions? What kinds of information from the questionnaire could you tap and use in therapy?
13. Compare the TA life-script questionnaire in this chapter with the lifestyle-assessment questionnaire in the Adlerian chapter. What similarities and differences do you notice?
14. Do you see any similarities between Ruth's injunctions and early decisions (TA) and her "basic mistakes" (Adlerian)? Can you think of ways to combine an Adlerian and a TA perspective as you explore the major themes in her life?

ADA: ALMOST A DOCTOR

Some Background Data

Ada Chan, who is 32, came to Chicago from Hong Kong to pursue graduate study in social work. Her ultimate goal is to return to Hong Kong to work in the management of social-service agencies. She sees a great need for counseling and social work there and is committed to helping her people. Ada is convinced that she would be in a good position to understand the needs of her clients, many of whom struggle to achieve a balance between their Chinese identities with the Westernized urban setting where they live. She has completed all her course work in the doctoral program in social work. To complete her degree, she needs to write her dissertation, which is almost finished. Of course, she will have an oral examination in which her doctoral committee questions her about the dissertation. She has been putting off the final phase of this project for well over a year despite promptings from her chairperson.

During the intake interview Ada tells me that she had a negative experience with a prior therapist, which made it extremely difficult for her to seek help again. She feels that her former therapist was not at all sensitive to her cultural background and did not understand the nature of her struggles. Moreover, she felt a great deal of pressure to accept his views on life, because, as she puts it: "He was pushy in getting me to do things I wasn't ready for. He'd tell me that it's about time that I grow up and think about myself, and forget what my parents and family want of me. He just would not listen to me when I tried to explain that in my Chinese family you simply don't say aloud everything you think and feel." Because I am not Chinese and her experiences with her previous therapist were not satisfactory, she is concerned about my ability to relate to her situation. However, she decided to come to me because she knew that transactional analysis was my orientation. She had a particular interest in TA, both personally and professionally. She even chose to study one facet of TA as the basis for her dissertation. Assuming a TA orientation, I will demonstrate the way I might proceed in working with her during the first few sessions.

The Contract as a Starting Place

As a TA counselor I stress a therapeutic contract setting the focus for counseling. Ada will have to decide specifically what beliefs, feelings, and behaviors she wants to change. The contract will identify *what* she plans to change about herself and *how* she will go about accomplishing her stated goals.

However, Ada is vague in stating what she wants. She tells me that she is confused about her wants. Then, after more questioning from me, she finally says that she wants to get rid of "parental tapes" and that she wants to change her "life script." She appears to have a difficult time in asking for what she wants for herself. It becomes apparent that she has learned about TA on an intellectual level but has not integrated her insights on an emotional level. Although she has studied therapeutic approaches, she lacks a personal awareness of her internal conflicts.

One way in which I can assist Ada in becoming more personal is asking her specific questions that call on her to use descriptive language. I could ask her, for example: "What do you hear your parents telling you now? When you say you want to change your life script, what would you most want to change? What aspects of your life don't you like?" Such questions show respect for Ada, yet at the same time she is learning how to think in more personal and concrete terms.

We stay with the issue of defining what Ada wants and what she is willing to do to get it. After we work together to narrow down her goals, she finally comes up with a clear statement: "I want to take whatever steps are necessary to complete the writing of my dissertation and to apply for my oral and written doctoral examination." She agrees to do this within a particular period, and together we outline specific steps that she will take to accomplish her objectives. As important as it is, however, completing her doctoral dissertation is not the total answer to her problems. She recognizes her pattern of avoiding completion of projects. She very enthusiastically initiates diverse projects, and then, just as she is at the point of successfully completing them, she typically finds some way to put off whatever is needed for completion. As a part of her contract she wants to explore the meaning and the implications of this behavior pattern.

We Work with Ada's Life Script

In working on the latter part of her contract, dealing with her choice to explore the meanings of her failure to complete projects, we review the components of her life script. In this script, or plan, many life events have had an impact on her. She has accepted and learned definite roles, and she now rehearses and acts out these roles according to the script. This script outlines where she will go in life and what she will do when she gets there. From a TA perspective there is a compelling quality that drives her to live out her life plan. The significant components of her life script include parental messages she has incorporated, early decisions she made in response to such messages, the patterns of stroking she received, the games she plays to maintain her decisions, and the *rackets* (collections of old familiar feelings such as depression, guilt, and anger) she uses to justify her decisions. The focus of TA therapy will consist of working with the interrelated factors of this life script.

Injunctions and early decisions. In TA work we pay attention to how parental injunctions teach children what they have to do or be in order to get stroked (to gain recognition). Ada has probably heard many verbal and direct messages as well as some subtle ones that she inferred from her parents' actions.

We will certainly want to take into account the power that cultural injunctions continue to play in Ada's life today. For instance, simply coming to therapy proved to be extremely difficult. She initially explains: ''In my culture, to talk about one's personal problems is to demonstrate weakness. It's shameful for me to have to ask for help. I feel that revealing my problems to you is making myself vulnerable. It's very hard for me to express my feelings, especially to show tears or to show you what I consider my weakness.'' Merely coming to therapy goes against her cultural grain. Although it is acceptable for her to study psychotherapy and practice it with others as a helper, she feels it is not acceptable for her to need this help or to reveal her deeper problems to others. Her negative experiences with her previous therapist compounded her reluctance to explore her own psychological world.

Ada realizes that she has internalized many traditional Chinese values. This is fine with her, for there is much in her culture that she appreciates. At the same time, her experiences in the United States have given her another perspective, which has led to her fear that she may not feel at home in either Hong Kong or the United States.

Ada says that growing up in the Chan family she heard a lot of ''Don't make it'' or ''Don't succeed'' messages. One of the cultural injunctions she grew up with was the notion that education was for boys more than it was for girls, that her place was to create an identity by being a homemaker, that having a profession was not necessary, and that she should be loyal to the traditional ways of her family. In our work together Ada and I identify and explore some of these injunctions in our early sessions by reviewing selected events that she remembers from her childhood and adolescent years. She was actually stroked for *not* succeeding; and on those occasions when she did succeed, she was *negatively* stroked (which, in essence, says "I don't like you"). Together we review memories of past events, and she reports that in many situations her parents ignored her when she was successful. In one situation her folks responded with a polite "That's very nice, dear" when she was chosen to study in the United States. Her perception is that she was not supposed to go on to college and succeed academically or professionally. Her parents actively encouraged and supported her two older brothers' educational and professional endeavors, and both of them became highly successful, one as a physician and the other as an architect. For the daughters in the family, however, higher education was viewed as unnecessary. Her parents could not understand Ada's striving for a profession and for graduate education. They conveyed their expectations that she should get a well-paying job in business for a time, save her earnings, and then marry and settle in Hong Kong. They were extremely distressed when she was determined to go to the United States for her studies. Ada gave this report:

> Both of my parents, and especially my mother, would tell me that it was a waste of my time to think of going on to college. They thought is was fine that I had graduated from high school, but they asked what I was trying to prove when I kept up my interest in college. To their way of thinking I should learn all the domestic talents, and I should set my sights on some desirable and successful man. Marriage was seen as the ultimate in my parents' plan for me. Any hint on my part that I wanted to get not only a bachelor's degree but also a doctorate in social work was unthinkable. They didn't want to hear about any of my academic accomplishments. In so many ways I tried to get my parents to understand how important my profession was to me. When I tried to tell them about professional opportunities that I'd accepted as a social worker, they abruptly changed the subject, often talking about the successes of my brothers.

A major injunction of Ada's was "Don't make it!" Based on this strong parental message, we discover, she made an early decision: "While I'll go ahead and do what I want, I won't complete important ventures in life." This decision follows her to this day. Even though she is mostly finished with a doctoral program, which far exceeds the programming in her life by her parents, she finds some way *not* to ultimately succeed. In this way she never has to admit failure. She can always use as an excuse that she is not yet finished with something and that *if* she did finish, *then* she would be successful. Although she incorporated certain drives and ambitions from her family, she also made an early decision not to fully experience the satisfaction that comes from completing projects. It is clear that she is afraid of how others would react if she were truly successful.

Fear of success. We devote some time to looking at Ada's anxiety over going beyond what her parents actually accomplished in their own lives and beyond their *expectations* of her. Furthermore, we look at the power of the cultural messages that reinforced the injunctions of her parents and played down professional success. We talk about the many ways in which she sabotaged herself so that she would somehow fail to succeed in endeavors that had meaning for her. This involved looking critically at her games. (In TA a game is a series of transactions that ends in at least one of the players feeling bad. It develops for the purpose of supporting an original decision—in this case, "I won't finish anything, and that way I won't have to enjoy success." And it is a basic part of one's life script, necessary to survive in the world.)

One of Ada's games that we analyze is her encouraging people to push her to complete a project, at which time she resists all the more, telling herself that she is not going to do something *because* they want her to. Another game consists of her convincing herself that those people who are not pushing her obviously do not care enough about her to give her a nudge. Therefore, she does nothing, and then she blames others for what happens. We explore some of the typical games she played as a child and as an adolescent, and we see the parallel between those and the ones she is playing now. For example, she sees important connections between her past and the present in her chairperson's pressure on her to complete her doctoral project and her own increasing defiance against complying with reasonable requirements or deadlines. We also talk about how she dealt with a therapist she considered "pushy."

We Move toward Action

Understanding the patterns that fit into Ada's life script is one matter. Yet if she hopes to change, she will have to take *action* and do something about changing, not merely talk about the prospects of change. Thus, because TA is an action-oriented therapy, she and I think of ways in which she can practice some behavior that will challenge the early decisions she made. We begin to plan for how she can, for a change, actually complete a very meaningful project, her doctorate. The therapy involves going through each of the steps and practicing what she has typically done to procrastinate and what she can do differently now. Also, I encourage her to predict problems with her typist in finishing her dissertation. She looks at ways to overcome barriers that will prevent her from completing this important task. We explore her fears of the board of examiners and predict the worst of outcomes. She is convinced of the importance of finishing her dissertation, and she makes a commitment to stick to her contract.

A Closing Commentary

Depending on the number of our sessions, I would work with Ada on the *redecision* process. The heart of therapy involves going back, both emotionally and intellectually, to an early scene in which she made her decision not to enjoy the satisfaction that comes with completing significant goals. From the psychological frame of reference she would make a different decision—this time, one that is more effective. In her case this could be: "I am going to make it professionally and academically. Even if it's not what you want or what you have in mind for me in life, this is what I want and what I'll get." At least our work will move her closer to being able to make such a redecision.

Another important aspect of our work would be to help Ada find some way to satisfactorily blend Chinese and American cultural values into a new synthesis. My hope would be that she could find some way to remain true to the values she acquired in Hong Kong yet also be able to modify some traditions that are not meaningful for her. If she wants to pursue a profession, she will probably have to come to grips with the reality that her culture does not put a great deal of emphasis on individuality, autonomy, and thinking about what is best for oneself. She will surely have some conflicts when she attempts to integrate some of her American ways with her life back home. If she chooses to, this would be a fruitful area for her to explore in future therapy sessions. If we have more time together, I'd like to draw on Gestalt techniques as a way of assisting her to become clearer about what she wants and as a tool to help her work toward an integration of the many sides of her personality. Using Gestalt techniques within the theoretical framework of TA offers some exciting possibilities in this case.

Follow-Up: You Continue as Ada's Therapist

Assume that Ada continues counseling with the goal of working toward making a *new decision.* On my referral she comes to see you. Show how you would work with her from a TA perspective.

1. Ada really lives in two cultures. Do you have any thoughts on how you might help her work through what seem to her to be conflicts without a resolution? How might you help her respect and appreciate the values she acquired from her experiences in both Hong Kong and Chicago?
2. Do you have any ideas of how you might proceed if what Ada wanted was diametrically opposed to what would be acceptable in her culture? What might you suggest if you saw that her progress in attaining her personal goals was alienating her from her family and from her culture?
3. What ethical and clinical issues are involved in dealing with Ada's negative reactions to her previous therapist? If she told you that she

was reluctant to get involved in therapy with you because she wondered if you could understand her struggles with her culture, how would you address her concern?

4. What specific knowledge would you want to have about Chinese traditions and the culture in which Ada grew up as a child and as a youth? What mistakes might you make if you attempted to counsel her strictly within the framework of an American perspective?
5. Assume that you talked to a colleague about Ada's case and this person said: "She needs to realize that if she is going to live and study in Chicago, she will have to give up many of her Chinese ways. After all, she has to face reality." What attitudes might your colleague be expressing? What would you want to say to this person?
6. Do you think there is a way to help Ada make the transition when she leaves the United States and goes back home to work?
7. Do any of Ada's injunctions and early decisions touch off any associations with your life? To what degree have you faced, or do you now face, similar issues? How do you think they will either facilitate or interfere with your work with her?
8. Can you see different directions from mine in which you would like to take Ada? What are some of the most pressing themes in her life that you think need attention? What TA techniques might you draw on in helping her in this exploration?
9. What advantages and disadvantages do you see to beginning Ada's therapy with a contract? If she failed to complete her dissertation by the time she had said she would, what might you say and do?
10. TA tends to stress the cognitive aspects of therapy. What advantages, if any, do you see to integrating affective dimensions into the cognitive work Ada is doing? How might you blend these two dimensions of human experience?

RECOMMENDED SUPPLEMENTARY READINGS

What Do You Say After You Say Hello? (1975), by E. Berne (New York: Bantam Books), demonstrates how we learn certain scripts that determine our present behavior and how we can change them.

Changing Lives through Redecision Therapy (1979), by M. Goulding and R. Goulding (New York: Brunner/Mazel), is an excellent presentation of the major concepts of TA. This text deals, in depth, with concepts such as injunctions, early decisions, and redecisions. Many examples of therapy sessions show how TA concepts can be integrated with techniques from many other therapeutic approaches.

The Power Is in the Patient (1979), by R. Goulding and M. Goulding (San Francisco: TA Press), is a collection of essays on personal growth from a TA perspective. Articles deal with the therapeutic impasse, basic concepts of TA, methods of helping clients make new decisions, and various techniques in action.

Redecision Therapy: Expanded Perspectives (1985), by L. B. Kadis (Watsonville, CA: Western Institute for Group and Family Therapy), contains a range of articles on the theory, techniques, and applications of redecision therapy.

Born to Win: Transactional Analysis with Gestalt Experiments (1971), by M. James and D. Jongeward (Reading, MA: Addison-Wesley), is a readable guide to combining TA concepts with Gestalt exercises for the goal of personal growth. Topics include scripts, games, early decisions, injunctions, and autonomy.

SUGGESTED READINGS

Belkin, G. (1987). *Contemporary psychotherapies* (2nd ed.). Pacific Grove, CA: Brooks/Cole. (Chapter 18)

Belkin, G. S. (1988). *Introduction to counseling* (3rd ed.). Dubuque, IA: William C. Brown. (Chapter 9)

Burke, J. F. (1989). *Contemporary approaches to psychotherapy and counseling.* Pacific Grove, CA: Brooks/Cole. (Chapter 7)

Corey, G. (1991). *Theory and practice of counseling and psychotherapy* (4th ed.). Pacific Grove, CA: Brooks/Cole. (Chapter 9)

Corsini, R., & Wedding, D. (Eds.). (1989). *Current psychotherapies* (4th ed.). Itasca, IL: F. E. Peacock. (Chapter 11)

Gilliland, B., James, R., Roberts, G., & Bowman, J. (1984). *Theories and strategies in counseling and psychotherapy.* Englewood Cliffs, NJ: Prentice-Hall. (Chapter 6)

Hansen, J., Stevic, R., & Warner, R. (1986). *Counseling: Theory and process* (4th ed.). Boston: Allyn & Bacon. (Chapter 5)

Patterson, C. H. (1986). *Theories of counseling and psychotherapy* (4th ed.). New York: Harper & Row. (Chapter 12)

Prochaska, J. O. (1984). *Systems of psychotherapy: A transtheoretical analysis* (2nd ed.). Pacific Grove, CA: Brooks/Cole. (Chapter 8)

Wedding, D., & Corsini, R. J. (Eds.). (1989). *Case studies in psychotherapy.* Itasca, IL: F. E. Peacock. (Chapter 10)

CHAPTER EIGHT

Case Approach to Behavior Therapy

A BEHAVIOR THERAPIST'S PERSPECTIVE ON RUTH by Arnold A. Lazarus, Ph.D.

Arnold Lazarus is a Distinguished Professor in the Graduate School of Applied and Professional Psychology at Rutgers University. He has written numerous books and professional papers. He developed the multimodal approach, a broad-based, systematic, and comprehensive approach to behavior therapy, which calls for technical eclecticism but remains firmly grounded in social-learning theory.

The multimodal orientation assumes that clients are usually troubled by a multitude of specific problems that should be dealt with by a wide range of specific techniques. Its comprehensive assessment, or therapeutic modus operandi, attends to each area of a client's BASIC ID (B = behavior, A = affect, S = sensation, I = imagery, C = cognition, I = interpersonal relationships, and D = drugs and biological factors). Discrete and interactive problems throughout each of the foregoing modalities are identified, and appropriate techniques are selected to deal with each difficulty. A genuine and empathic patient/therapist relationship provides the soil that enables the techniques to take root.

Multimodal Assessment of Ruth

In Ruth's case more than two dozen specific and interrelated problems can be identified by using the following diagnostic, treatment-oriented BASIC ID methodology:

Behavior

fidgeting, avoidance of eye contact, rapid speaking
poor sleep pattern
tendency to cry easily
overeating
various avoidance behaviors

Affect
anxiety
panic (especially at night when trying to sleep)
depression
fear of criticism and rejection
pangs of religious guilt

Sensation
dizziness
palpitations
fatigue and boredom
headaches
tendency to deny, reject, or suppress her sexuality

Imagery
ongoing negative parental messages
residual images of hellfire and brimstone
unfavorable body image and poor self-image
view of herself as aging and losing her looks

Cognition
self-identity questions (Who and what am I?)
worrying thoughts (death and dying)
doubts about her right to succeed professionally
categorical imperatives ("shoulds," "oughts," "musts")
search for new values

Interpersonal
unassertiveness (especially putting the needs of others before her own)
fostering of her family's dependence on her
limited pleasure outside role as mother and wife
problems with children
unsatisfactory relationship with husband (yet is afraid of losing him)

Drugs and biological factors
overweight
lack of an exercise program
various physical complaints for which medical examinations reveal no organic pathology

Selecting Techniques and Strategies

The goal of multimodal therapy is not to eliminate each and every identified problem. Rather, in concert with Ruth, I would select several key issues. Given the fact that she is generally tense, agitated, restless, and anxious, one of the first antidotes might be the use of relaxation training. Some people respond with paradoxical increases in tension when practicing relaxation, and it is necessary to determine what particular type of relaxation will suit an individual client (for example, direct muscular tension/relaxation contrasts, autogenic training, meditation, positive mental imagery, diaphragmatic breathing, or a combination of methods). There are no a priori reasons to believe that Ruth would not respond to deep muscle relaxation, positive imagery, and self-calming statements.

The next pivotal area on which to focus might be her unassertiveness and self-entitlements. I would employ behavior rehearsal and role playing. Our sessions would also explore her right to be professional and successful. Cognitive restructuring would address her categorical imperatives and would endeavor to reduce the "shoulds," "oughts," and "musts" she inflicts on herself. Imagery techniques might be given prominence. For example, I might ask her to picture herself going back in a time machine so that she could meet herself as a little girl and provide her alter ego with reassurance about the religious guilts her father had imposed. One of her homework assignments might be the use of this image over and over until she felt in control of the situation.

If Ruth and her husband agreed to it, some marital counseling (and possibly some sex therapy) would probably be recommended, followed, perhaps, by some family-therapy sessions aimed at enhancing the interpersonal climate in the home. Indeed, if she became a more relaxed, confident, assertive person, John and her children might need help to cope with her new behaviors. Moreover, I could try to circumvent any attempts at "sabotage" from him or the children.

If Ruth felt up to it, I would teach her sensible eating habits, and she would embark on a weight-reduction and exercise regimen. Referral to a local diet center might be a useful adjunct.

Comment

The multimodal approach assumes that lasting treatment outcomes require one to combine various techniques, strategies, and modalities. A multimodal therapist works with individuals, couples, and families as needed. The approach is pragmatic and empirical. It offers a consistent framework for diagnosing problems within and among each vector of personality. The overall emphasis is on fitting the treatment to the client by addressing factors such as the client's expectancies, readiness for change, and motivation. The therapist's style (for example, degree of directiveness or nondirectiveness and supportiveness or nonsupportiveness) varies according to the needs of the client and situation. Above all, flexibility and thoroughness are strongly emphasized.

JERRY COREY'S WORK WITH RUTH FROM A BEHAVIORAL PERSPECTIVE

Basic Assumptions

A basic assumption of the behavioral approach is that therapy is best conducted along systematic and scientific lines. Although behavior therapy represents a variety of principles and therapeutic procedures, its common denominator is a commitment to objectivity and evaluation. Because of the above-mentioned diversity it is difficult to enumerate a set of agreed-on assumptions and characteristics that apply to the entire field. Some general characteristics, however, are part of all the behavioral approaches:

1. As a behavioral practitioner I value a good client/therapist relationship. Without a sense of rapport there is no real assessment or treatment. Although I see the quality of this relationship as having a bearing on therapeutic outcomes, I do not place primary emphasis on these relationship variables.
2. I begin therapy with an assessment of the client, as a way of determining present problems, personal liabilities, and major strengths. The assessment focuses mainly on current influences on behavior, as opposed to past influences. I am primarily concerned with how the client is functioning and the stimuli that are maintaining present behavior.
3. Treatment goals are established in specific and concrete terms.
4. After the client and I identify the goals for therapy, we work out a treatment plan, which includes a set of procedures or techniques designed to attain these goals.
5. Assessment and evaluation are a part of the entire therapeutic process. Procedures are continually evaluated, so that if they are not working, new techniques can be tried.

Assessment of Ruth

I very much like beginning with a general assessment of a client's current functioning. Assessing Ruth on the seven modalities used in multimodal therapy is excellent (see Lazarus's assessment of Ruth in his section). As a behavior therapist I typically use some type of questionnaire. In Ruth's case I select Lazarus's multimodal life-history questionnaire, which is reproduced in the Appendix of his book *The Practice of Multimodal Therapy.* My purpose is to obtain a comprehensive picture of Ruth's background for use in designing and carrying out any therapeutic program. This assessment begins with the intake session and continues during the next session if necessary. The following are some areas of information tapped by this questionnaire:

1. general information
2. a description of the presenting problems
3. a personal and social history, including information about family, childhood, and adolescent years, past problems, and current ambitions
4. an analysis of the current problems

This fourth section is designed to identify specific problems in some detail so that therapy can be tailored to the needs of the client. Each area of human behavior is followed by a list that the client can underline if applicable. This analysis is done in the following areas: behavior, feelings, physical sensations, images, thoughts, interpersonal relationships, and biological factors. For each of these areas, specific questions are asked so that a comprehensive assessment of the client's current functioning is possible.

Gathering these data on Ruth takes two sessions. By way of summary, she and I come up with the following problem areas that she wants to focus on: (1) She feels tense to the point of panic much of the time and wants to learn ways to relax. (2) From the standpoint of her interpersonal relationships, she does not have the skills to ask for what she wants from others, she has trouble in expressing her viewpoints clearly, and she often accepts projects that she does not want to get involved in. (3) She says she has battled a weight problem for years, with very little success. She would like to take weight off and keep it off.

Goals of Therapy

After making the assessment of Ruth's strengths and weaknesses, I clarify with her the behaviors that she wants to increase or decrease in frequency. She will now set specific goals in her three problem areas. Before treatment we establish *baseline data* for those behaviors that she wants to change. The baseline period is a point of reference against which her changes can be compared during and after treatment. In working on weight control, for example, she would chart factors such as her weight, foods that she eats, times and circumstances of eating, and size of her portions. For a week or so, she might simply record her eating habits and also pay attention to her thoughts and feelings associated with eating. Does she tend to eat more when she is depressed? What does she tell herself when she overeats? By establishing such baseline data we will be able to determine therapeutic progress. There is continual assessment throughout therapy to determine the degree to which her goals are being effectively met.

The general goal of behavior therapy is to create new conditions for learning. I view Ruth's problems as related to faulty learning. The assumption underlying our therapy is that learning experiences can ameliorate problem behaviors. Much of our therapy will involve correcting faulty cognitions, acquiring social and interpersonal skills, and learning techniques of self-management so that she can become her own therapist. Based on my initial assessment of her and on another session in which she and I discuss the matter of setting concrete and objective goals, we establish the following goals to guide the therapeutic process:

- to learn and practice methods of relaxation
- to learn stress-management techniques
- to learn assertion-training principles and skills
- to develop a behavioral self-management program to control her weight

Therapeutic Procedures

Behavior therapy is a pragmatic approach, and I am concerned that the treatment procedures be effective. I will draw on various cognitive and behavioral techniques to help Ruth reach her stated goals. If she does not make progress, I must assume much of the responsibility, because it is my task to select appropriate treatment procedures and use them well. As a behavior therapist I am continually evaluating the results of the therapeutic process to determine which approaches are working. Ruth's feedback in this area is important. I will ask her to keep records of her daily behavior, and I will expect her to become active to accomplish her goals, including working outside the session.

I expect that our therapy will be relatively brief, for my main function is to teach Ruth skills that she can use in solving her problems and living more effectively. My ultimate goal is to teach her self-management techniques, so that she will not have to be dependent on me to solve her problems.

The Therapeutic Process

Elements of the process

The therapeutic process begins with gathering baseline data on the specific goals that Ruth has selected. In her case much of the therapy will consist of learning how to cope with stress, how to be assertive in situations calling for this behavior, and how to develop a self-directed weight-control program.

Learning stress-management techniques. Ruth indicates that one of her priorities is to cope with tensions more effectively. I ask her to list all the specific areas that she finds stressful, and I discuss with her how her own expectations and her self-talk are contributing to her stress. We then develop a program to reduce unnecessary strain and to cope more effectively with the inevitable stresses of daily life.

RUTH: You asked me what I find stressful. Wow! There are so many things. I just feel as if I'm always rushing and never accomplishing what I should. I feel pressured so much of the time.

JERRY: List some specific situations that bring on stress. Then maybe we can come up with some strategies for alleviating it.

RUTH: Trying to keep up with my schoolwork and with the many demands at home at the same time. Dealing with Jennifer's anger toward me and her defiance. Trying to live up to John's expectations and at the same time doing what I want to do. Getting involved in way too many community activities and projects and then not having time to complete them. Dealing with how frazzled I feel in wearing so many hats.

Feeling pressured to complete my education. Worrying that I won't be able to find a good teaching job once I get my credential . . . How's that for starters?

JERRY: That's quite a list. I can see why you feel overwhelmed. We can't address all of them at once. I'd like to hear more about what being in these stressful situations is like for you. Tell me about one of these situations, and describe what you feel in your body, what you're thinking at the time, and what you actually do in these times of stress. [I want to get a concrete sense of how she experiences her stress, what factors bring it about, and how she attempts to cope with it.]

RUTH: Well, I often feel that I wear so many hats—I just have so many roles to perform, and there's never enough time to do all that's needed. I often lie awake at night and ruminate about all the things I should be doing. It's awfully hard for me to go to sleep, and then I wake up in the morning after hours of tossing and turning feeling so tired. Then it's even harder for me to face the day.

JERRY: Earlier you mentioned that you have panic attacks, especially at night. I'd like to teach you some simple ways to use the relaxation response just before you go into a full-scale attack. You'll need to identify the cues that appear before a panic attack. I'd then like to teach you some simple and effective relaxation methods. Instead of wasting time lying there trying to sleep, you could be practicing a few exercises. It's important that you practice these self-relaxation exercises every day, for 20 minutes.

RUTH: Oh my! That's 20 minutes of one more thing I have to cram into my already busy schedule. It may add to my stress.

JERRY: Well, that depends on how you approach it.

We talk at some length, because I am afraid that she will make this practice a chore rather than something that she can do for herself and enjoy. She finally sees that it does not have to be a task that she does perfectly but a means of making life easier for her. I then teach her how to concentrate on her breathing and how to do some visualization techniques, such as imagining a very pleasant and peaceful scene. Then, following the guidelines described in Herbert Benson's book *The Relaxation Response,* I provide her with these instructions:

JERRY: Find a quiet and calm environment with as few distractions as possible. Sit comfortably in a chair and adopt a passive attitude. Rather than worry about performing the technique, simply let go of all thoughts. Repeating a mantra, such as the word *om,* is helpful. With your eyes closed, deeply relax all your muscles, beginning with your feet and progressing up to your face. Relax and breathe.

A week later, Ruth tells me how difficult it was to let go and relax.

RUTH: Well, I didn't do well at all. I did practice every day, and it wasn't as bad as I thought. But it's hard for me to find a quiet place to relax.

I was called to the phone several times, and then another time my kids wanted me to do their wash, and on and on. Even when I wasn't disturbed, I found my mind wandering, and it was hard to just get into the sensations of feeling tension and relaxation in my body.

JERRY: I hope you won't be too hard on yourself. This is a skill, and like any skill it will take some time to learn. But it's essential that you block off that 20 minutes in a quiet place without disturbances.

Ruth and I discuss how difficult it is for her to have this time for herself. I reinforce the point that this is also an opportunity to practice asking others for what she wants and seeing to it that she gets it. Thus, she can work toward another of her goals: being able to ask for what she wants.

As our sessions go on, Ruth sticks by her relaxation practice fairly well, and it is working for her. It does reduce stress considerably but does not eliminate it. One day Ruth comments that she would love to have a professional massage. I suggest a homework assignment. Knowing how difficult it is for her to treat herself to any luxuries, I recommend that she spend one day in a spa and get a massage. Although she finally does so, and loves it, she first experiences reluctance. She thinks it is silly, she complains about one more thing to do, and she feels guilty about spending money on herself in this way. But finally, after going through this list, she agrees to do something she wants, something that will be for herself. Of course, the following week we get therapeutic mileage out of her experience. We explore all the things she tells herself that are self-defeating, and I suggest some new sentences that she can practice in place of these old and ineffectual ones.

Learning how to say no. Ruth tells me that she has been a giver all of her life. She gives to everyone but finds it difficult to ask anything for herself. We have been working on the latter issue, with some success. Ruth informs me that she does not know how to say no to people when they ask her to get involved in a project, especially if they tell her that they need her. She wants to talk about her father, especially the ways in which she thinks he has caused her lack of assertiveness. I let her know that I am not really interested in going over past experiences in childhood or in searching for reasons for her present unassertiveness. Instead, I ask her to recall a recent time when she found it difficult to say no and to describe that scene.

RUTH: Last week my son Adam came to me late at night and expected me to type his term paper. I didn't feel like it at all, because I had had a long and hard day, and besides, it was almost midnight. He begged me, saying that it was due the next day and that it would only take me an hour or so. I got irked with him for giving it to me so late, and at first I told him I wasn't going to do it. Then he got huffy and pouty, and I finally gave in. Then I didn't sleep much that night because I was mad at myself for giving in so quickly. But what could I do?

JERRY: You could have done many things. Can you come up with some alternatives?

I want Ruth to search for alternative behaviors to saying yes when it is clear that she wants to say no. She does come up with other strategies, and we talk about the possible consequences of each approach. Then I suggest some behavioral role playing. First, I play the role of Adam, and she tries several approaches other than giving in and typing the paper. Her performance is a bit weak, so I suggest that she play Adam's role, and I demonstrate at least another alternative. I want to demonstrate, by direct modeling, some behaviors that she does not use, and I hope that she will practice them.

As the weeks progress, there are many opportunities for Ruth to practice a few of the assertive skills that she is learning. Then she runs into a stumbling block. A PTA group wants her to be its president. Although she enjoys her membership in the group, she is sure that she does not have time to carry out the responsibilities involved in being the president. In her session she says she is stuck because she doesn't know how to turn the group down, especially since no one else is really available. We again work on this problem by using role-playing techniques. I play the role of the people pressuring her to accept the presidency, and I use every trick I know to tap her guilt. I tell her how efficient she is, how we are counting on her, how we know that she won't let us down, and so on. We stop at critical points and talk about the hesitation in her voice, the guilty look on her face, and her habit of giving reasons to justify her position. I also talk with her about what her body posture is communicating. Then we systematically work on each element of her presentation. Paying attention to her choice of words, her quality of voice, and her style of delivery, we study how she might persuasively say no without feeling guilty later. As a homework assignment I ask her to read selected chapters of the paperback book *Your Perfect Right,* by Alberti and Emmons. There are useful ideas and exercises in this book that she can think about and practice between our sessions.

The next week we talk about what she has learned in the book, and we do some cognitive work. I especially talk with her about what she tells herself in these situations that gets her into trouble. In addition to these cognitive techniques I continue to teach her assertive behaviors by using role playing, behavioral rehearsals, coaching, and practice.

Working on Ruth's weight problem. Ruth brings up her struggle with her diet as follows:

RUTH: Ever since I can remember, I've had a weight problem. When I get depressed, I eat even more, which gets me even more depressed, and then I get down on myself. I really would like to do something about taking off the pounds and then keeping them off.

JERRY: You sound pretty determined about making this change. As you know, we usually attack problems such as this in a systematic way.

RUTH: Well, I *am* determined, but I'm always this way at first, and then when things don't work out, I get discouraged and drop the program. I'm afraid I'll repeat history.

JERRY: Your thinking sounds fatalistic, as if you're setting yourself up for failure. [I discuss with her negative expectations and self-fulfilling prophecies. We then explore new statements that she can make, in the hope that she can program herself for success instead of for defeat.]

RUTH: I need some help in working out a program, and then I need you to push me to stick with it.

JERRY: Well, I'm willing to work with you on developing a self-management program to control weight, and I'll negotiate a contract with you. But I'm not comfortable in assuming the role of pushing you.

I tell her why my pushing might end up defeating her purposes, and then I explain the nature of the program. First of all, I ask her to get baseline data by recording her eating habits for a one-week period. Ruth agrees to keep an accurate record of the number of calories she consumes daily, any between meal snacks, the kinds of foods she eats, and other specific factors relating to her eating patterns. At the same time, we agree on realistic goals. At first she declares that she will lose 20 pounds in a month. I recommend that she consult with her physician before embarking on a weight-control program. I also express my fears of her setting unrealistic goals and then getting discouraged and giving up the entire program. After getting a physical examination and discussing the matter with her doctor, she finally agrees to lose 5 pounds (or more) in a month's period.

We then discuss what eating behaviors Ruth will need to change. This is where her self-monitoring phase is of real value, for we look at when she eats, what she eats, how she eats, and events leading up to her wanting to eat. She decides on specific behaviors that she wants to increase or decrease. Coupled with her monitoring of food intake and cutting certain high-calorie foods out of her diet, she also agrees to resume riding her bicycle daily. At first she will ride for 15 minutes each day, then work up to 25 minutes, and then discuss with me whether she will ride 45 minutes daily. She is learning not to set herself up to fail. Now she is agreeing to smaller subgoals and then increasing them after enjoying success. All during this period she keeps charts and graphs of her eating patterns and continues to weigh herself daily. In this way she has feedback on how well she is meeting her goals.

Another technique I use with Ruth is bibliotherapy. I suggest a number of self-help books for her to select from, especially books that will help her control her weight. She selects a book that describes the advantages of a combined approach focusing on both diet and exercise. Since she is also concerned about her health, these readings on topics of diet, nutrition, exercise, and general wellness are timely. We spend some time talking about what she is learning from her reading and ways in which she can continue to apply the suggestions to herself. Through her readings and her outside homework, she is getting more mileage out of her therapy experience.

With the help of a structured program and what she learns from her readings, Ruth sticks to her plan. By the end of the month she has lost eight pounds, which is three pounds more than the minimum she contracted for. She is proud of herself for following through with the program, and she comments that she liked the reinforcement and support she got from me along the way. She is looking trimmer and feeling better. As a reward she treats herself to another visit to the spa, which is still difficult for her, because she is not used to spending money on herself in such a fashion!

Process commentary

As part of teaching Ruth a method of self-monitoring and as a way of keeping track of her progress toward meeting her goals, I suggest that she keep a journal in which she records how she acts in certain situations (as well as how she feels and what she is thinking as she faces problematic situations). In the final phase of her therapy she summarizes some of the major things she has learned and describes some of her reflections on her work:

> I just finished three months of behavior therapy, and I thought I'd write down a few notes on what that was like for me. I see that I have gained a lot more control over my behavior than I thought I could. Reading those books on assertion training, relaxation methods, and plans for weight loss were extremely helpful. It also helped greatly to be listened to by Jerry and to be taken seriously. I often felt that I was exaggerating my problems and that I should be grateful for the good life I have. Working with Jerry these few months has shown me that I have it within my power to actually change those behaviors I want to change. I don't know about changing the person I am, but I'm surely doing something about some of the things that really bugged me about myself. I've lost those eight pounds, and I'm losing more. I'm staying in the weight-loss program, and this is the first program that I've ever stuck to. I feel good about that. I'm continuing my relaxation exercises each day, and I'm also taking a course in meditation. I'm pleased to report that I'm much less uptight over finishing everything on time; I don't have as many panic attacks in the middle of the night as I used to. And when I do, I've learned to use deep-breathing exercises. I learned that I make matters worse by breathing in a shallow way, and how I actually hyperventilate. I'm also aware of changing some of the things that I tell myself. I seem less hard on myself, and I'm learning how to argue back with the critical voices that go on in my head. It's helping me to debate those self-destructive messages that I listened to for so long. At those times that I don't meet my goals or live up to my own expectations, I tell myself that I'm only human and that progress is not always smooth. There are still many problem areas in my life that I don't feel are taken care of. I still wonder what I want to do with my life besides what I've done. But I'm meeting some practical problems better than I ever have.

In this approach Ruth is clearly the person who decides what she wants to work on and what she wants to change. She makes progress toward her self-defined goals because she is willing to become actively involved in challenging her assumptions and in carrying out behavioral exercises, both in the sessions and in her daily life. For example, she is disciplined enough to practice the relaxation exercises I have taught her. She learns how to ask for what she wants and to refuse those requests that she does not want to meet, not only by making resolutions but also by regularly keeping a record of the social situations in which she was not as assertive as she would have liked to be. She takes risks by practicing in everyday situations those assertive skills that she has acquired in our therapy sessions. Her willingness to carry out homework assignments is also instrumental in increasing her assertive behavior, which in turn helps her in the area of weight control; *she* decides that losing weight is a priority. Rather than speculating about the causes of her overeating or creating excuses for her weight problem, she accepts the problem and follows through with a regular action program designed for self-change. Although I help her learn *how* to change, she is the one who actually chooses to apply these skills, thus making change possible.

Questions for Reflection

1. What are some of the features that you like best about my approach? What do you like least? How might you have proceeded differently, still working within this model, in terms of what you know about Ruth?
2. This model assumes that the therapist's technical skills are essential to behavior change. What are your reactions to this assumption in light of the assumption of some other approaches that the therapeutic relationship itself is a sufficient condition for change?
3. What is your reaction to my attempt to get Ruth out of therapy as fast as possible so that she can apply self-management skills on her own? What skills can you think of to teach her so that she can be more self-directed?
4. What reactions do you have to my lack of interest in exploring the past? Do you think that Ruth's present personal issues can best be taken care of by focusing on learning coping skills? Do you think that for change to occur in her current situations she must go back to her past and work out unfinished business?
5. Using other behavioral techniques, show how you might proceed with Ruth if you were working with her. Use whatever you know about her so far as well as what you know about behavior-therapy approaches to show in what directions you would move with her.
6. What specific behavioral changes do you want to make in your life? What behaviors would you like to eliminate or decrease? acquire or increase? Applying behavioral methods to yourself, which specific techniques would be most helpful to you in making these changes?
7. How would you go about designing a self-management program in your own life? Identify some behaviors that you want to control or modify, and then describe the specific steps in a behavioral self-management program aimed at your goals. Knowing what you do of yourself, how would you cooperate and follow through with the program? What problems and obstacles would you encounter?

8. Do you see any possibilities of integrating some of the feeling dimensions from the experiential therapies (Gestalt, person-centered, and existential therapy) with the focus on behavior and cognition in this approach? How might you integrate several of these approaches?

SALLY: HOPING TO CURE A SOCIAL PHOBIA

Sally is 27 years old, single, and Hispanic, and she comes from a family of eight children. She supervises employees at a large office of the Internal Revenue Service. She has come to a community mental-health center on the recommendation of a close friend. Although she had many reservations about admitting to herself that she had personal problems, let alone admitting it to someone else, she felt reassured after talking with her friend about her experience in counseling. Sally still has mixed feelings about seeking professional help, for this is not something that she ever saw herself as doing. In her culture it is acceptable to talk about personal concerns with family members, with a priest, or perhaps to a very close friend. However, it is considered a taboo to talk about such matters with outsiders.

Sally's major presenting problem could be labeled a *social phobia.* She has a persistent and exaggerated fear of being exposed to scrutiny by others in social situations. She fears that she may act in ways that will be humiliating or embarrassing, so she tends to avoid social gatherings. Another major problem is her insomnia. Even though she is tired when she goes to bed at night, she tosses and turns and becomes highly anxious because of her inability to sleep. She goes to work utterly exhausted in the morning and then feels like nodding off when she needs to be alert.

Sally's fears and difficulties in coping with the demands of everyday living are becoming so pressing that she feels she must defy her cultural injunctions and seek professional help. When she told her parents that she wanted to go to counseling, they were offended and took it personally. They tried to persuade her to see the parish priest instead. She respectfully, but with some guilt, declined to follow their advice.

Sally's Self-Presentation

On meeting the counselor Sally lists many of the fears that she would like to conquer and shares some key themes going on in her life:

It seems as if I'm afraid of *everything!* I'm very afraid of being in this office now, and my fear of coming here almost kept me from doing it. A good friend who's been to counseling here gave me the push I needed. Actually, she practically forced me to come, at least for one session. I'm afraid of new situations, because I have no idea how I'll react. I'm afraid to go to work, because I have a hard time feeling good about the decisions I make. I'm afraid of speaking out in our staff meetings and expressing my opinions on an issue. I'm so afraid that I'll do some dumb thing and totally embarrass myself. When I have to tell any of the employees that I supervise that they're not doing an adequate job, it takes every bit of my courage to sit down with them. And even then, I worry about what I'll say and how it will come across. If someone at work confronts me, I begin to doubt myself and start backpedaling.

Although I have this trouble at work, it's even more difficult for me to get involved in social situations. I panic at the thought of going to parties or going on a date. I just don't know how to act around people. I break out in a cold sweat just thinking about being in a social situation. Generally, I'm very quiet and unassuming in these situations, because I've been taught that it's not appropriate for a woman to be too assertive. So I keep a lot of what I feel and think to myself.

What else? I guess that I think that by 27 a woman should be married. Often I dream of how nice it would be for me to have a man in my life that I really cared for and who cared for me in return. I'd love to have a family, also. My parents are pressuring me to get engaged to a family friend, Ramon, whom they see as an eligible bachelor. They keep telling me that he's a nice Latino man with a great job. I know they would be so pleased if I got engaged to Ramon, yet I've never felt attracted to him in that way. He's a nice guy and we go out on dates once in a while, but I have a hard time feeling really close to him. Someday I really would like a close friendship with a man. Most of my fears have to do with not knowing what's appropriate or expected of me when I'm with people—especially when I'm with men.

My Way of Working with Sally as a Behavior Therapist

I view the therapeutic relationship as a collaborative one. I do not view therapy as merely a matter of my being the all-knowing expert who makes decisions for a passive client. Instead, from our first until our final session, Sally and I will work together toward goals that we have agreed will guide our sessions—if, in fact, she decides to enter counseling with me. At the outset my procedures will include the following:

- During the initial session I will explore with Sally what it is like for her to come to the center for counseling as well as her expectations, reservations, and hopes.
- I will explain the nature and purpose of counseling goals, and the importance of making those goals specific and concrete.
- Sally will decide on the specific changes or goals she desires as a result of her relationship with me.
- Together we will explore the feasibility of her stated goals.
- Both of us will identify and discuss any risks associated with these goals.
- Together we will discuss the possible advantages of counseling as a way of meeting these stated goals.
- By the end of the initial session, I hope, Sally and I will have made one of the following decisions: to continue counseling for a specified number of sessions, to reconsider her goals, to evaluate whether counseling is appropriate at this time and whether she is willing to actively work at

achieving her goals (both in the sessions and in her daily life), or to seek a referral to another therapist or another agency.

Dealing with Sally's immediate feelings and thoughts. There are some things that I know about Sally that would be important to attend to during the first session. I am aware that she comes to the office with some reluctance and only after the goading of a close friend. As a place to begin, I'd ask her how it was for her to call and make the appointment and what it was like for her as she walked into the waiting room. Building trust with her would involve talking about her reservations about seeking counseling, about talking to a "stranger," and about the difficulties that she had to overcome simply to be in the office now. Some questions that I may ask are: "What would you most hope to get from this session or from the next several sessions? What is going on in your life now that prompted you to take the action of coming here today? What expectations did you have in mind after you talked to your friend?"

After we have had a chance to talk for a time, I am likely to invite her to let me know how she feels about our exchange so far. This is especially important because I know she has difficulty in encountering men and because she said that she could never see herself talking personally to a "stranger." In several ways I could be a stranger. She is a 27-year-old, Hispanic, female administrator and I am a 53-year-old, White, male psychologist of Italian background. The fact that we differ in age, cultural background, and gender could influence a counseling relationship. Although I do not automatically assume that she would feel more comfortable with a younger, Hispanic, female counselor, I still need to be alert to her reactions to me and my reactions to her. This certainly may not be discussed fully at the first session but it may be introduced as a topic for discussion if it seems appropriate.

Goal setting and deciding on a course of action. As I have indicated, one of our first tasks is to develop clear and specific goals, so that we are able to determine what kind of treatment plan we will design. This plan includes the possible procedures and techniques we will use as well as the criteria for determining how well the procedures are accomplishing Sally's stated goals.

Sally and I work at narrowing down her goals. Like many other clients she is approaching her therapy with global and fuzzy aims. It is my task to help her formulate clear and concrete goals, so that she and I will know what we are working toward and will have a basis for determining how well the therapy is working. When I ask her what she wants from therapy, for example, she replies with statements such as these: "I want to learn to communicate better. I want to be able to state my opinions without being afraid. I don't do very well in social situations. I'd like to get over feeling scared all the time. I wish I could go to bed and sleep instead of just lying there."

Although her goals are general, they do relate to becoming more effective in social situations. I can facilitate her moving from global to specific goals by asking her: "Whom in your life do you have trouble talking to? Are there any particular people to whom you find it difficult to say what you'd like to say? What are some situations in which you have problems in being assertive? In what social situations don't you do well? How would you like to change in these situations? Would you tell me about a few specific fears you experience? When you are frightened, what do you tell yourself? And what do you do at these times? What would you like to do differently? When you are unable to sleep, what are some of the things that you feel or think? If you were able to sleep better, how do you think your life would be different?" My line of questioning is aimed at helping her translate fuzzy goals into clear statements pertaining to what she is thinking, feeling, and doing (and ways that she would like to think, feel, and behave differently).

Eventually, Sally and I draw up a contract that is geared to helping her develop a course of action to attain her goals. We determine that the basis of her contract will be the following goals: She will work on *identifying* and *lessening* (or, ideally, removing) her unrealistic fears. She will identify specific manifestations of unassertive behaviors on her part, which include her difficulty in expressing her opinions, in making contacts with people, in turning down others when that is what she wants to do, and in making her wants and needs clearly known to others. She will experiment with new behaviors, both in the therapy sessions and in daily life. Practicing these behaviors will lead to *increasing* her repertoire of social skills, especially her *assertive behavior.*

Because it will take some time to learn and practice skills related to Sally's stated goals, we discuss a realistic time frame for therapy. She decides to commit herself to a series of six one-hour individual counseling sessions. This kind of structuring will encourage her to evaluate her progress after each session and will serve to keep her focused.

Sally learns systematic desensitization. Sally initiates a discussion about dealing with her fears relating to men. She tends to avoid men, mainly because she is frightened of them. She is both put off by them and attracted to them, and she has the dual fear of being rejected by them and being accepted. She thinks that she can handle rejection easier than acceptance; she wonders what she would do if a man actually liked and desired her and if he wanted an intimate relationship.

At this point I work with Sally on clarifying her values. Before using behavioral techniques, I believe, it is essential that she become clear about what she wants, so that she is freely deciding on her behavioral goals. After examining her values she says that she respects her parents and that it hurts her that she does not meet their expectations. Specifically, she feels guilty that she is not engaged to Ramon, yet she knows that this is not what she wants. We discuss possible ways in which she can show regard for her family yet at the same time do what is right for her. Here, role playing is useful. I invite her to talk to me as her father, which gives us an opportunity to deal further with her self-talk about pleasing him. This role playing helps her sort out her values from what her father wants for her.

Sally also says that she would like to be free enough to go to parties, to accept dates, and to initiate social contact with selected men. It is clear to her that initiating these contacts is particularly difficult because of her socialization, which has taught her that "proper" women do not behave in this manner. She hopes to learn how to assertively say what she wants and does not want, which is also going against her cultural conditioning. Although she is now frightened over the possibility of a man's making a sexual advance or even an offer, she would like to learn to avoid being unduly anxious over this prospect.

We then proceed with systematic-desensitization procedures, which start with a behavioral analysis of situations that evoke anxiety in her. We then construct a hierarchy of her anxieties by ranking them in order, beginning with the situation that evokes the least anxiety and ending with the worst situation that she can imagine. The following is her hierarchy of fears:

1. She sees a man across the room to whom she is attracted.
2. They are sitting together in a room.
3. They are sitting together, and he initiates a conversation with her.
4. He invites her to go on a date.
5. She accepts the date.
6. She goes on a date.
7. He asks her to go to his apartment after a party.
8. They are in his apartment kissing and embracing.
9. They have sex, and she leaves and never hears from him again.
10. They have sex, and he says that he hopes this is only the beginning of an intense relationship.

I then teach Sally some basic relaxation procedures, which she practices until she is completely relaxed in the session. I ask her to select a peaceful scene where she would like to be. She picks a lake in the forest. We proceed with the relaxation exercise until she is fully relaxed, has her eyes closed, and has the peaceful scene in her mind.

I describe a series of scenes to Sally and ask her to imagine herself in each of them. I present a neutral scene first. If she remains relaxed, I ask her to imagine the *least anxiety-arousing* scene she set up in her hierarchy (seeing a man whom she found pleasant on the far side of a room). I move progressively up the hierarchy until she signals by raising her index finger that she is experiencing anxiety, at which time I ask her to switch off that scene and become very relaxed and imagine herself at her lake. We continue until we progress to the *most anxiety-arousing* scene in her hierarchy (imagining a sexual relationship with a man who wants to continue the relationship).

In our therapy sessions we continue the desensitization procedure until Sally is able to imagine this ''worst'' scene without experiencing anxiety. Basically this procedure consists of combining an incompatible stimulus and response. We pair the relaxation exercises and the imagining of a pleasant scene with scenes that evoke anxiety, until gradually the anxiety-provoking stimuli lose their potency. Now that we have successfully desensitized her of her fears of relating to a man she perceives as attractive on an imaginary level, we hope that she is ready to try new behavior in a real-life situation.

Sally Goes on a Date

As a behavior therapist I believe in the value of assignments. These are not activities that I pick out as good for Sally. Rather, *she* decides on some new behaviors that she would like to experiment with outside of our sessions. Then she applies what she has learned in therapy to a social situation in the hope of acquiring new social skills and overcoming her inhibitions and negative self-talk. She tells me that she has decided to ask Julio, whom she met through her friend, to the upcoming office Christmas party.

Before she actually carries out this assignment, we examine what she is telling herself before inviting him. She recognizes that she is setting herself up for failure by telling herself that he probably will not want to go and that if he does accept, it is only because he feels sorry for her. So we do some additional cognitive work that will lead to positive expectancies on her part. Before she asks Julio to the party, she practices her relaxation exercises and calms herself so that anxiety will not interfere with what she wants to do.

When Sally returns to her session the next week, she reports that all went well. She is feeling an increasing sense of confidence and is willing to tackle new social situations that are more difficult.

A Commentary

Sally's therapy began with assessment, and at our last session we assess the degree to which she has met her goals. We also review what she has learned in these sessions as well as what she has done in various situations at school, at work, and at home. Our focus now is on consolidating what she has learned and helping her translate it into future real-life situations. I suggest that she continue by reading self-help books, doing her daily relaxation exercises, giving herself behavioral assignments, monitoring and assessing her behaviors, and keeping a behavioral log in her journal. Finally, she agrees to join a ten-week assertion-training group designed to help students improve their social skills. In this way she is able to continue what we have begun in these sessions.

Follow-Up: You Continue as Sally's Therapist

After my six individual sessions with Sally, she enters the ten-week assertion-training group. Assume that she has now finished this group and consults you for further counseling.

1. What are your reactions to the very structured approach I used with Sally? To what degree would you be comfortable using such an approach, and how effective do you think you would be?
2. What are your reactions to the specific techniques that I employed with Sally? What other (behavioral) techniques can you think of that you might use? What general direction do you see yourself taking with her?
3. What cultural variables might you be alert to in this case? Some of the clues provided initially are these: Sally is reluctant to talk about her personal problems to people outside of her family; she has mixed feelings about admitting that she needs professional help; she has a desire to follow the traditions and expectations of her family; and she is struggling with a cultural injunction that says that women should not be too direct and too assertive. How might you work with any of these themes?
4. What advantages, if any, would there be if Sally saw a female therapist? What factors would determine whether it might be best that she see a Hispanic therapist?
5. If you are of a different gender and have a different ethnic background from Sally, how might this be for you as a counselor? Given what you know of her case, would you anticipate any difficulties in establishing a rapport with her?
6. What factors in yourself do you see that might contribute to or detract from your effectiveness in working as Sally's therapist?

RECOMMENDED SUPPLEMENTARY READINGS

Your Perfect Right: A Guide to Assertive Behavior (5th ed., 1986), by R. E. Alberti and M. L. Emmons (San Luis Obispo, CA: Impact), is my recommendation for those who want a single book on the principles and techniques of assertion training.

The Relaxation Response (1976), by H. Benson (New York: Avon), was a national best-seller. It is a readable and useful guide to developing simple meditative and other relaxation procedures. Particularly helpful are the author's summaries of the basic elements of meditation (pages 110–111) and methods of inducing the relaxation response (pages 158–166).

Helping People Change (3rd ed., 1986), edited by F. H. Kanfer and A. P. Goldstein (New York: Pergamon Press), is a collection of major behavioral strategies in current use, including fear-reduction methods, self-management methods, biofeedback, modeling, cognitive restructuring, and aversion methods.

The Practice of Multimodal Therapy (1989), by A. A. Lazarus (Baltimore: Johns Hopkins University Press), is interesting, easy to read, and highly informative. A wide variety of behavioral techniques is described, and the author shows how such diverse techniques can be integrated into an eclectic framework.

Self-Directed Behavior: Self-Modification for Personal Adjustment (5th ed., 1989), by D. L. Watson and R. G. Tharp (Pacific Grove, CA: Brooks/Cole), is aimed at helping readers achieve control over their life. Specific steps are described for setting up behavioral self-management programs.

SUGGESTED READINGS

Belkin, G. (1987). *Contemporary psychotherapies* (2nd ed.). Pacific Grove, CA: Brooks/Cole. (Chapters 6, 7, 8, 9, 10, 11, & 15)

Belkin, G. S. (1988). *Introduction to counseling* (3rd ed.). Dubuque, IA: William C. Brown. (Chapter 10)

Burke, J. F. (1989). *Contemporary approaches to psychotherapy and counseling.* Pacific Grove, CA: Brooks/Cole. (Chapters 4 & 5)

Corey, G. (1991). *Theory and practice of counseling and psychotherapy* (4th ed.). Pacific Grove, CA: Brooks/Cole. (Chapter 10)

Corsini, R., & Wedding, D. (Eds.). (1989). *Current psychotherapies* (4th ed.). Itasca, IL: F. E. Peacock. (Chapters 7 & 13)

Gilliland, B., James, R., Roberts, G., & Bowman, J. (1984). *Theories and strategies in counseling and psychotherapy.* Englewood Cliffs, NJ: Prentice-Hall. (Chapter 7)

Hansen, J., Stevic, R., & Warner, R. (1986). *Counseling: Theory and process* (4th ed.). Boston: Allyn & Bacon. (Chapter 8)

Ivey, A. E., Ivey M. B., & Simek-Downing, L. (1987). *Counseling and psychotherapy: Integrating skills, theory, and practice* (2nd ed.). Englewood Cliffs, NJ: Prentice-Hall. (Chapter 9)

Patterson, C. H. (1986). *Theories of counseling and psychotherapy* (4th ed.). New York: Harper & Row. (Chapters 5, 6, & 7)

Prochaska, J. O. (1984). *Systems of psychotherapy: A transtheoretical analysis* (2nd ed.). Pacific Grove, CA: Brooks/Cole. (Chapter 10)

Wedding, D., & Corsini, R. J. (Eds.). (1989). *Case studies in psychotherapy.* Itasca, IL: F. E. Peacock. (Chapter 12)

CHAPTER NINE

Case Approach to Rational-Emotive Therapy and Other Cognitive-Behavioral Approaches

A RATIONAL-EMOTIVE THERAPIST'S PERSPECTIVE ON RUTH
by Albert Ellis, Ph.D.

Albert Ellis is the founder and director of the Institute for Rational-Emotive Therapy in New York. He is considered the grandfather of the other cognitive-behavioral approaches and he continues to work hard at developing RET. Ellis is a prolific writer, having published about 600 journal articles and authored or co-authored over 50 books.

Rational-emotive therapy (RET) assumes that people like Ruth do not get disturbed by the unrealistic and illogical standards they learned during their childhood (from their family and culture) but that they largely disturb themselves by the dogmatic, rigid "musts" and commands that they creatively construct *about* these standards and values and *about* the unfortunate events that occur in their lives. Ruth is a good case in point, because she not only has accepted some of the fundamentalist ideas of her parents (which innumerable fundamentalist-reared children adopt *without* becoming disturbed) but also rigidly *insists* that she *has to* follow them while simultaneously *demanding* that she *must* be herself and *must* lead a self-fulfilling, independent existence. She could easily neuroticize herself with *either* of these contradictory commands. By devoutly holding *both* of them, she is really in trouble! As RET shows, transmuting *any* legitimate goals and preferences into absolutist musts will usually lead to self-denigration, rage, or self-pity, and Ruth, as I show below, seems to overtly or covertly have all these neurotic feelings.

Assessment of Ruth

Ruth has a number of goals and desires that most therapies, including RET, would consider legitimate and healthy, including the desire to have a good, stable marriage, to care for her family members, to be thinner and more attractive, to keep her parents' approval, to be a competent teacher, and to discover what she really wants to do in life and largely follow her personal bents. Even though some of these desires are somewhat contradictory, they would probably not get her into serious trouble as long as she only held them as *preferences,* because she could then make some compromises and not get into much trouble with herself or others.

Thus, Ruth could choose to be *somewhat* devoted to her husband and children, and even to her parents, but *also* determined to pursue a teaching career and to follow her own non-fundamentalist religious views and practices. She would then fail to lead a *perfectly* conflict-free and happy life but would hardly be in great turmoil. However, like practically all humans (yes, whether they are reared very conservatively or liberally), she has a strong (probably innate) tendency to take some of her *important* values and to dogmatically *sacredize* them. From early childhood onward she anti-scientifically concluded: "Because I *want* my parents' approval, I completely *need* it!" "Because I *love* my children, I *have* to be thoroughly devoted to them!" "Because I *enjoy* thinking for myself and doing my own thing, I *have to* do so at practically all times!" "Because I'd *like* to be thinner and more attractive, I've *got* to be!"

With grandiose, perfectionist fiats like these, Ruth takes her reasonable, often achievable, goals and standards and transmutes them into absolutist "musts." She thereby almost inevitably makes herself—that's right, *makes* herself—panicked, depressed, indecisive, and often inert. Additionally, when she sees that she feels emotionally upset and is not acting in her best interests, she irrationally upsets herself about *that.* She strongly—and foolishly—tells herself "I *must*n't be panicked" instead of "I wish I were not panicking myself, but I am. Now how do I *un*panic myself?" She then feels panicked about her panic. And she rigidly insists "I *have to* be decisive and do my own thing." Then she feels like a worm about her worminess! This self-castigation about her neurotic symptoms makes her even more neurotic. And it makes her less able to see exactly what she is thinking and doing to create these symptoms and then extirpate them.

As a rational-emotive therapist I would assess Ruth's problems and her belief system about these problems as follows. She asks certain questions that lead to practical problems:

- "How much shall I do for others, and how much for myself?"
- "How can I exercise and keep on a diet?"
- "How can I be a teacher and still get along well with my husband?"
- "How can I get along with my parents and still not follow their fundamentalist views?"
- "How can I benefit from therapy and live with the things I may discover about myself when undergoing it?"
- "How can I be myself and not harm my husband and kids?"

She has certain rational beliefs that lead to appropriate feelings of concern and frustration:

- ''If I do more things for myself, people may not like me as much as I want them to. Too bad!''
- ''Exercising and dieting are really difficult. But being fat and ugly is even more difficult!''
- ''If I get a teaching job, I may antagonize my husband. But I can stand that and still be happy.''
- ''My parents will never like my giving up fundamentalism, and that's sad. But it's not awful!''
- ''If I find out unpleasant things about myself in therapy, that'll be tough. But I can also benefit from that discovery.''
- ''Being myself at the expense of my husband and kids is selfish. But I have a right to a reasonable degree of selfishness!

She has certain irrational beliefs that lead to inappropriate feelings of anxiety and depression and to self-defeating behaviors of indecision and inertia:

- ''I *must* not do more things for myself and *dare not* antagonize others.''
- ''Exercise and dieting are *too* hard and *shouldn't* be that hard!''
- ''If my husband hated my getting a teaching job, that would be *awful!*''
- ''I can't *stand* my parents criticizing me if I give up fundamentalism.''
- ''I would be a *thoroughly rotten person* if therapy revealed bad things about me.''
- ''I must *never* be selfish, for if I am, I am no damned good!''

She has certain irrational beliefs that lead to secondary disturbances (panic about panic, depression about depression):

- ''I must not be panicked!''
- ''It's awful to be depressed.''
- ''I'm no good for being indecisive!''

Key Issues

The key issues in most neurotic feelings and behaviors and those that are suspected and looked for by me and other RET practitioners are (1) self-deprecation, stemming from the irrational belief that ''*I* must perform well and be approved by significant others''; (2) an irrational insistence that ''*you* [other people] must treat me kindly and considerately''; and (3) the irrational idea that ''the *conditions* under which I live have to be comfortable and easy.''

Ruth clearly seems to have the first of these disturbances, because she keeps demanding that she be very giving and lovable, that she be thin and beautiful, that she be a good daughter, that her ''badness'' not be uncovered in therapy, and that she make only good and proper decisions. With these kinds of perfectionist commands, she leads a self-deprecating, anxious existence.

Ruth also seems to have some unacknowledged (and sometimes overt) rage, stemming from her underlying insistence that her husband not expect her to be a "good wife," that her parents not demand that she be a fundamentalist, and that everyone stop criticizing her for trying to be herself.

Finally, Ruth has low frustration tolerance and self-pity, resulting not from her desires but from her *dire needs* to lose weight without going to the trouble of dieting and exercising, to have a guarantee that she won't die, to have the security of marriage even though she has a boring relationship with her husband, to be sure that therapy will be comfortable, and to have a magical, God-will-take-care-of-me solution to her problems.

Because Ruth strongly holds the three basic irrational ideas (dogmatic "musts") that RET finds at the root of neurosis and because some of her demands—like those that she be herself *and* be quite self-sacrificial—are contradictory, I would guess that she will be something of a DC (difficult customer!) and require about a year of individual therapy and perhaps some additional group therapy. But since she has already taken some big risks and worked at changing herself, I would predict a good prognosis despite her strong tendency to create irrational beliefs.

Therapeutic Techniques

RET invariably includes a number of cognitive, emotive, and behavioral methods. If I worked with Ruth, I would probably use these main methods:

Cognitive techniques of RET. I would show Ruth how to discover her rational preferences and distinguish them from her irrational "musts" and demands. Then I would teach her how to scientifically dispute these demands and change them back into appropriate preferences. I would encourage her to create some rational coping statements and inculcate them many times into her philosophy—for example, "I want to be a caring mother and wife, but I also have the right to care for myself." I would help Ruth do RET "referenting"—that is, make a list of the disadvantages of overeating and think about them several times each day. I would have her do reframing, so that she could see that losing some of her husband's and children's love has its good as well as its bad sides. I would encourage her to use some of RET's psychoeducational adjuncts: books, pamphlets, cassettes, lectures, and workshops. I would show her the advantages of teaching RET to others, such as to her husband, children, and pupils, so that she would better learn it herself. I would discuss with her the advantages of creating for herself a vital, absorbing interest in some long-range project, such as helping other people guiltlessly give up their parental fundamentalist teachings.

Emotive techniques of RET. I would recommend that Ruth use some of the main emotive, evocative, and dramatic methods that I have found effective in RET, such as these:

1. *Forcefully* and *powerfully* telling herself rational coping statements: "I do *not* (definitely *not*) *need* my parents' approval, though I would certainly prefer to have it!"
2. Taping a *rigorous* debate with herself, in which she very *actively* disputes one of her irrational "musts," and then listening to her disputation to see not only if its content is good but also if its *force* is effective.
3. Doing rational-emotive imagery, by imagining one of the worst things that could happen to her—for example, her father strongly berating her for her non-fundamentalist views—and working on her feelings so that she first gets in touch with her horror and self-downing and then changes them to the appropriate feelings of sorrow and regret.
4. Doing some of the famous RET shame-attacking exercises, in which she first publicly does something she considers shameful, foolish, or ridiculous and simultaneously works on herself *not* to feel ashamed while doing it.
5. Receiving unconditional acceptance from me, no matter how badly she is behaving in and out of therapy, and being shown how to always—yes, always—accept herself, *whether or not* she does well.
6. Doing role playing, in which I play her irate father and she plays herself, to see how she can cope with his severe criticism. We stop the role playing from time to time to see what she is telling herself to make herself anxious and depressed.
7. Practicing reverse role playing, in which I stick rigidly to some of her irrational beliefs and encourage her to vehemently argue me out of them.
8. Using humor to rip up some of her irrational beliefs, especially singing to herself some of my rational humorous songs.

Behavioral techniques of RET. As I do with virtually all RET clients, I would stress several behavioral methods with Ruth, including these:

1. I would show her how to select and perform *in vivo* desensitization assignments, like registering for education courses despite her anxiety about her family's disapproval.
2. I would encourage her to do what she was afraid to do—for example, talk to her husband about her career goals, many times, implosively rather than gradually, until she thoroughly lost her irrational fears of his disapproval.
3. I would encourage her to reinforce herself with some enjoyable pursuits, such as reading or music, only after she completed her difficult-to-do homework; and if she were truly lax about doing it, sometimes to penalize (but never *damn*!) herself with an unpleasant chore, such as getting up an hour earlier than usual.
4. I would plan with her, and supervise her carrying out, practical goals such as applying for graduate school or arranging for help with her household tasks.

5. If she started getting over her emotional hangups but had skill deficiencies, I would help her acquire missing skills through assertiveness training, communication training, or decision making.

In using any or all of these RET techniques with Ruth, I would try to help her not only ameliorate her presenting symptoms (panic, guilt, and indecisiveness) but also make a profound philosophical change. My goal would be for her to acknowledge her own construction of her emotional problems, minimize her other related symptoms, maintain her therapeutic progress, rarely redisturb herself again, and, when she did so, quickly use RET once more to overcome her reinstated disturbances. In other words, by the time my therapy with Ruth ended, I would hope that she had strongly internalized and kept using regularly the three main insights of RET:

1. "I mainly emotionally and behaviorally upset myself *about* unfortunate conditions in my life, and I largely do so by constructing rigid 'musts' and commands about these conditions."
2. "No matter when I originally started to upset myself and no matter who helped me do so, I am *now* disturbed because of my *present must*urbatory beliefs."
3. "To change my irrational thinking, my inappropriate feelings, and my dysfunctional behaviors, I'd better give up all magical solutions and keep working and practicing—yes *keep working and practicing*—for the rest of my life!"

If Ruth (and neurotics like her) will learn and keep working to uphold these antidisturbance theories and practices of RET, I can't guarantee that she will significantly change and stay changed. But I can confidently accord her a high degree of probability.

JERRY COREY'S WORK WITH RUTH FROM AN RET PERSPECTIVE

Basic Assumptions

Rational-emotive therapy is a highly didactic, cognitive, behavior-oriented approach that stresses active practice by clients to combat irrational, self-indoctrinated ideas. RET and the other cognitive-behavioral therapies focus on the role that thinking and belief systems play as the root of personal problems.

RET is grounded on the philosophy that individuals are born with the potential for rational thinking but tend to fall victim to an uncritical acceptance of irrational beliefs that are perpetuated through self-reindoctrination. It also shows that individuals are born with a potential for creating their own absolutist "shoulds" and "musts" and that even without indoctrination from others, they would create many of these irrational ideas themselves. Although the indoctrination from others *helps* them do so, it doesn't *make* them do so. RET assumes that thinking, evaluating, analyzing, questioning, doing, practicing, and redeciding are at the base of behavior change. It is a system that is both *disputational* and *reeducational,* in that it teaches clients how to dispute their irrational and perfectionistic "shoulds," "oughts," and "musts" and also how to replace self-defeating ideologies with a rational philosophy of life. I draw on a range of cognitive, emotive, and behavioral techniques to demonstrate to my clients that they are causing their own emotional disturbances by the beliefs they have uncritically accepted. As a cognitive therapist I operate on the assumption that it is not an event or a situation in life that actually causes negative emotions such as guilt, depression, hostility, and so forth. Rather, it is the evaluation of the event and the beliefs that people hold about it that get them into trouble.

Assessment of Ruth

As I review Ruth's intake form and her autobiography, it becomes evident that the majority of her problems are self-induced and self-maintained. True, as a child she was subjected to many absolutist and moralistic beliefs, some of which were irrational. Yet she is still clinging to these beliefs and living by them as though they were tested and proven values. The trouble is that she uncritically and unthinkingly accepts these values, many of which rely on guilt as a main motivation to control behavior. She probably invented or created some of her irrational thinking herself, as well as accepting some of it from her parents and culture. So she is not actually making clear decisions based on self-derived values; rather, she is listening to archaic and intimidating voices in her head that tell her what she should and ought to do. In short, she is the victim of *must*urbatory thinking.

As Ellis mentions in his commentary, Ruth has a basic and underlying irrational belief that she must be perfect in all that she attempts. If she is not perfect, the results are horrible, for this means that she is a rotten person who deserves to suffer and feel guilty. She is continually rating her performances, and she gives herself low ratings because of her unrealistically high standards. I do not see her problems as stemming from the adverse situations that she writes about in her childhood. Instead, it is her evaluation of these events that directly contributes to her emotional disturbances. Therefore, what she needs is to learn practical ways of thinking critically and reevaluating her experiences as she changes her behavior. This will be the focus of my therapy with her.

Goals of Therapy

The basic goal of RET is to eliminate a self-defeating outlook on life and acquire a rational and tolerant philosophy. Thus, I will teach Ruth how to uproot her faulty beliefs and replace them with constructive beliefs. To do so, I will teach her the A-B-C theory of personality. This theory is based on the premise that the activating events (A) do not cause emotional consequences (C); rather, it is *mainly* her beliefs (B) about the activating events that are the source of her problems. (Ellis goes into greater detail on the goals that would guide his interventions with Ruth.)

Therapeutic Procedures

In working with Ruth, therefore, I expect to employ a very directive and action-oriented approach. Functioning as a teacher, I will focus on what she can learn that will lead to changes in the way she is thinking, feeling, and behaving. I will stress the value of applying logical analysis to evaluating the assumptions and beliefs that she lives by. It will help if she reads rational-emotive and cognitive-therapy literature as an adjunct to these sessions. For instance, I'll strongly recommend that she read and study books such as Ellis's *How to Stubbornly Refuse to Make Yourself Feel Miserable about Anything—Yes, Anything!* and Aaron Beck's *Cognitive Therapy and the Emotional Disorders.* Furthermore, like any other form of learning, therapy is *hard work.* This means that if she expects to successfully change her beliefs and thus change her behavior, it will be necessary to practice what she is learning in therapy in real-life situations. I will stress completing of homework assignments. And I will ask her to fill out an RET Self-Help Form that has her analyze activating events, her beliefs about these events, the consequences of those beliefs, her disputing and debating of her irrational beliefs, and the effects of such disputing. I teach this A-B-C method of understanding problems to all my clients in anywhere from 1 to 10 sessions. Some clients take 20 or more sessions to learn these A-B-Cs and some never learn it.

Ruth's *real* work, then, consists of doing homework in everyday situations and then bringing the results of these assignments into our sessions for analysis and evaluation. I am concerned that she not only recognize her irrational thoughts and feelings but also take steps to abandon them. My main function is to confront her if I see her clinging to these deeply ingrained beliefs. Ultimately, my goal is to challenge her to develop a rational view of life so that she can avoid becoming a victim of future irrational thinking.

The Therapeutic Process

To achieve the goal of helping Ruth achieve a rational philosophy of life, I perform several tasks as her therapist. First of all, I challenge her to evaluate the self-defeating propaganda that she originally accepted without question.

I also urge her to give up her irrational ideas and then to incorporate sound beliefs that will work for her. Throughout the therapeutic process my attempt is to actively teach her that self-condemnation is the basis of emotional disturbance, that it is possible for her to stop rating herself, and that with hard work, including behavioral homework assignments, she can rid herself of the irrational ideas that have led to her disturbances in feeling and behaving. There are two other factors in emotional disturbance: damning other people for their poor behavior and damning external conditions when they are not as good as the individual thinks they must be.

Elements of the process

Beginning therapy. We begin by my teaching Ruth some of the basic principles that I think will make for effective therapy. I provide structure and direction from the outset. She hears about how we incorporate irrational beliefs and then continue to indoctrinate ourselves with them, and I go through the A-B-C model. She quickly learns that reading, writing, thinking, and carrying out activity-oriented homework assignments are part and parcel of this therapeutic approach. She grumbles a bit about being asked to read self-help books and keep a record of her daily events. She tells me that she already has more schoolwork than she can fit into her overstuffed schedule. I do not give her much sympathy at this point, and I clearly let her know that if she intends to change, therapy means plenty of work and effort. She will not uproot old patterns easily.

Working on Ruth's "musts." Ruth does cooperate, and she writes a list of some of the beliefs that she is living by. She brings them to the following session, and we work on a few of them.

RUTH: Here's my list. I'll read a few of the "musts" that I came up with during the week. I *must* be perfect in everything I do. I *must* be the perfect mother, the perfect wife, the perfect daughter, the perfect student, the perfect client, and on and on. And I believe that if I'm not perfect, the consequences are going to be very painful. If I'm not the perfect wife, my husband may leave me, and I'm not sure I could stand that. If I'm not the perfect mother, my children will suffer, and I'll feel guilty for failing them. I came up with a few more: I *must* not have sexual desires for other men. I *must* not make wrong decisions. I *must* constantly be striving for more.

JERRY: That's quite a list. Did you encounter any situations during the week when you started thinking about how these "musts" get you into trouble?

RUTH: Yeah! In my speech class I've been putting off giving my impromptu talk for weeks now. In fact, I thought about dropping the class, but once I start something, I hate to quit in the middle.

JERRY: Is that another "must"? That under no circumstances should you change your mind once you make a decision?

RUTH: Well, I suppose so. At any rate, I'm not dropping speech, but that impromptu assignment is worrying me sick. I can't sleep thinking about it at times. Going to that class is a pain. I worked myself up so much that I got diarrhea.

JERRY: So what are you telling yourself? What do you see as so horrible about giving an impromptu speech?

RUTH: It's only a five-minute speech, but what agony in thinking about it! If I could prepare it and use notes, it wouldn't be so bad. What I'm afraid of is that I'll get up there and forget what I want to say. Then I'll stutter, and make a complete fool of myself.

JERRY: How would you make a complete fool of yourself? You might act foolishly, but this is not the same as *being* a fool. And then, if all that did happen, what would be so horrible? Would you fail the class?

RUTH: Oh, I've got an "A" so far, so that wouldn't hurt me much. What's horrible is that I'd look dumb and be laughed at.

JERRY: I don't know if you're ready for this, but I'd like you to do a homework assignment. In RET we call this a "shame-attacking exercise." What I have in mind is for you to step into a crowded elevator at school and tell everyone how glad you are that they could attend this meeting you have called. In fact, you might spend your lunch hour riding up and down this elevator and continue your exercise!

RUTH: Oh, I just don't think I could ever . . .

JERRY: And what would stop you?

We explore how her fear of making a fool of herself stops her from doing so many things. She then says that she would love to square-dance but has not because she is afraid of being clumsy and looking like a jerk. She would love to ski but avoids it for fear that she will fall on the "bunny hill" and break a leg—and then really look like a fool. I explain to her that the purpose of the shame-attacking exercise is to challenge her worst fears and to test them. Chances are, she will survive the embarrassment and will not die of shame. In these shame-attacking exercises, moreover, I want her to work on herself so that she either does not feel ashamed when she does the exercises or quickly gets rid of the feeling of shame after she does it and first feels ashamed.

RUTH [next week]: I hate to say it, but I didn't follow through. I went to the elevator door and stood there for the longest time, but I just couldn't walk into the elevator and make a fool of myself.

JERRY: Couldn't? At least say "I would not!" You could have done it, but you chose not to. Any idea why you didn't do it?

RUTH: I was just too afraid of being that far out. But I've decided to go ahead with that impromptu speech this week.

JERRY: Good, let's work on that. But let's talk some about your reactions to standing outside that elevator door.

Even though she did not do the assignment, there is plenty of therapeutic potential in what she put herself through. So we explore her thinking, her catastrophic expectations, and what she might do differently. One of her great fears, for example, was that people would think she was crazy. Finally, we begin talking about her upcoming speech.

RUTH: I'm just afraid I'll freak out or, worse yet, chicken out.
JERRY: So let's go through it right now. Close your eyes and imagine that you're giving the speech, and all the worst things you can imagine happen.

After her fantasy of catastrophic expectations we take them one by one and try to demolish them. I am working with her on her evaluation of events and her prediction that she will fail. All the time, I want her to see that even if she fails, she can still stand the outcomes. They may be unpleasant but surely not absolutely horrible.

We continue for a couple of months, with Ruth agreeing to do some reading and also carrying out increasingly difficult homework assignments. Gradually she works up to more risky homework assignments, and she does risk looking foolish several times, only to find that her fantasies were much worse than the results. She gives her speech, and it is humorous and spontaneous. This gives her an increased sense of confidence to tackle some other difficult areas she has been avoiding.

Dealing with Ruth's beliefs about herself as a mother. Ruth is feeling very guilty about letting one of her daughters down. Jennifer is having troubles at school and, Ruth says, is "going off the deep end." Ruth partially blames herself for Jennifer's problems, telling herself that she must be a better mother than her own mother was.

RUTH: I don't want Jennifer to suffer the way I did. But in so many ways I know I'm unloving and critical of her, just as my mother was of me at that age.
JERRY: What are you telling yourself when you think of this? [Again, I want Ruth to see that her self-defeating thoughts are getting her depressed and keeping her feeling guilty. My hope is that she will see that the key to eliminating needless anxiety and guilt lies in modifying her thinking.]
RUTH: I feel guilty that I didn't help Jennifer enough with her schoolwork. If I had tutored her, she would be doing well in school. I tell myself that I'm the cause of Jennifer's problems, that I should have been a better mother, that I could have cared more, and that I've ruined her chances for a good life.

JERRY: Do you see that this absolutist thinking doesn't make sense? What about Jennifer's role in creating and maintaining her own problems?

RUTH: Yes, but I've made so many mistakes. And now I'm trying to make up for them so she can shape up and change.

JERRY: I agree that you may have made mistakes with her, but that doesn't mean it will be the ruination of her. Can you see that if you do so much for her and make yourself totally responsible for her, she doesn't have to do anything for herself? Why should she accept any responsibility for her problems if you're blaming yourself? [My attempt is to get her to dispute her own destructive thinking. She has continued this pattern for so long that she now automatically blames herself, and then the guilt follows.]

RUTH: Well, I try to think differently, but I just keep coming back to these old thoughts. What would you like me to say to myself?

JERRY: When Jennifer does something wrong, who gets the blame for it?

RUTH: Me, of course. At least most of the time.

JERRY: And those times that Jennifer does well, who gets credit?

RUTH: Not me. Anyway, I dwell so much on what she's not doing that I don't often see that she does much right.

JERRY: How is it that you're so quick to place blame on yourself and just as quick to discount any part you have in Jennifer's accomplishments?

RUTH: Because problems occupy my mind, and I keep thinking that I should have been a better influence on her.

JERRY: I'd just hope that you could stop damning yourself and *should*ing yourself to death. Do you think you can begin to be kinder to yourself? What I'd like you to consider saying to yourself is something like this: "Even though I've made mistakes in the past and will probably continue making mistakes, that doesn't mean I've ruined Jennifer or will. It doesn't mean I'm the same kind of mother to her that mine was to me. I'll lighten up on myself and be more forgiving, because if I don't, I'll drive myself crazy." What I want you to see is that even if you have acted badly to your daughter and were pretty much the same kind of mother that your mother was to you, that still wouldn't make you a rotten person. It would merely mean that you might be rotten at mothering.

RUTH: That sounds pretty good . . . If only I could say those things and mean them, and feel them!

JERRY: Well, if you keep disputing your own thinking and learn to substitute constructive self-statements, you're likely to be able to say and mean these things—and you'll probably feel different, too.

Process commentary

As can be seen, my major focus with Ruth is on her thinking. Only through learning to apply rigorous self-challenging methods will she succeed in freeing herself from the defeatist thinking that led to her problems. I place value on behavioral homework assignments that put her in situations where she is forced to confront her irrational beliefs and her self-limiting behavior. I also consistently challenge her to question her basic assumption that she needs the approval of others in order to feel adequate.

Toward the conclusion of her therapy Ruth brings in the following excerpt from her journal, which is a glimpse of her experience in RET:

> Well, now that six months has passed, my sessions with Jerry are ending. I'm writing a review of what this time has been like for me and what I have learned from my therapy. My therapist has shown me that I need to rid myself of my anxiety, guilt, and depression by fully accepting myself as a worthwhile human being in spite of my imperfections. I'm acceptable whether or not I succeed at all the tasks and performances in my life and whether or not significant people like Father and Mother approve of me and love me. I've worked very hard to come to this line of thinking, because all my life I've been programmed to think the opposite. I now see that I have indeed kept alive this indoctrination that my parents began by telling myself that I *had* to be all the ways in which they told me I *should* be.
>
> Jerry always accepted me personally, though at the same time he constantly confronted my distortions in thinking. He told me that I had *childish demands* and that I needed to replace them with *preferences.* I can see that although I'd still like for my father to approve of me and love me in the way I want him to, I can live without his love. Life doesn't have to be exactly the way I demand it to be. I realize that my insistence that life be fair at all times has contributed to my feeling as anxiety-ridden as I have. So I'll continue to work on eliminating my many irrational notions.

Questions for Reflection

1. What are your general reactions to Dr. Ellis's approach to working with Ruth? What do you like best? like least? After reading his description of his assessment and treatment of Ruth, what aspects of her life would you focus on if you were to continue as her counselor?
2. Contrast the way in which an RET therapist works with Ruth to the way in which the psychoanalytic therapist worked with her. Which style do you prefer in Ruth's case? What differences do you see between the RET therapist and the person-centered therapist? the existential therapist? Again, which do you prefer in Ruth's case? Why?
3. Assume that you suggested a technique to Ruth (such as a shame-attacking exercise, keeping a journal, or reading self-help books) and that she refused by simply telling you that what you were asking of her was too much to expect. What might you say to her?
4. What common irrational beliefs do you share with Ruth, if any? To what degree have you challenged your own irrational thinking? How do you think that it would affect your ability to work effectively with her?

5. Using RET concepts and procedures, show how you might proceed in counseling Ruth in terms of what you know about her. What would be the focus in your sessions?
6. RET assumes that by changing our beliefs about situations we also change our emotional reactions to such events. How valid do you find this assumption to be for you? Can you come up with examples of how changing your beliefs and interpretations of events has changed your ways of feeling and acting?
7. Working with Ruth very forcefully and in a confrontational manner could raise some ethical issues, especially if you attempted to impose your values by suggesting what she should value. As you review Dr. Ellis's work with her and my work with her, do you have any concerns that we are "pushing values"?
8. What might you do if Ruth were from a cultural background where her "musts," "oughts," and "shoulds" came from her cultural conditioning? What if she insisted that she felt guilty when she dared to question her upbringing and that in her culture doing so was frowned upon? Might you adjust your confrontational techniques? If so, how would you challenge her *must*urbatory thinking (or would you)?
9. Can you think of possibilities of using the Adlerian lifestyle questionnaire to detect basic mistakes and then working with them using an RET framework and RET techniques?
10. How comfortable would you be in employing RET techniques in your therapy with Ruth? Do you think you could be confrontive enough to uproot her faulty thinking and encourage her to begin to think in different ways? What would you say?
11. What ideas do you have for using RET concepts and procedures in conjunction with Gestalt techniques? Can you think of examples from Ruth's case in which you could work on her feelings (with Gestalt techniques) and then proceed to work with her faulty thinking (by using RET techniques)?

MARION: A WOMAN WHO LIVES BY "OUGHTS" AND "SHOULDS"

Some Background Data

Marion, age 37, is a Black physician who has lived by a series of "shoulds" and "oughts" for most of her life. Among the things she is now telling herself is that she *must* succeed in her profession. From her perspective succeeding means being *far* better than most of her colleagues in her professional specialty, family medicine. She constantly berates herself for not being able to publish more research articles, for not keeping up with all the reading in her field, and for sometimes failing to live up to the expectations her patients have for her. One of her beliefs is that she should take care of everyone: her family, her friends, her colleagues, and her patients. It is essential for her to always be in control. Even without the benefit of therapy, she is aware that a key motivating force in her life is to demonstrate her success both as a Black person and as a woman. There is not much room in her life for making mistakes. Her perfectionistic strivings are literally making her sick. She experiences frequent migraine headaches, chronic constipation, stomach pains, and dizziness. Although her body is sending her clear messages that she is driving herself relentlessly, she keeps forging ahead, thinking that she *must* meet all of her standards. Unfortunately, these standards are unrealistically high, and she will never be able to attain them. No matter what her level of achievement, she persistently puts herself down for not having done better or done more. On top of all this she feels guilty about having all of her physical symptoms, because as a physician, she thinks that she should be in better control of her physical and mental state.

Marion judges herself constantly in all areas of her life. She gives herself grades for her performances, and typically her grades are low, for she demands so much of herself. Although her grades during medical school were consistently high (mostly "A"s with an occasional "B"), when she reflects on her record, she rates herself as a "C" student. In the area of being a wife she gives herself a low "C" at best. She does not cook fancy meals the way her mother or her husband's mother did. She feels that she is neglecting her husband, Byron. In her sex life she gives herself an "F." Byron complains that she is not responsive enough, not playful, way too serious, and too prudish. She almost never experiences an orgasm, because she is so worried about her performance and Byron's approval. It is next to impossible for her to relax and enjoy having sex. Of course, she sees it as her fault that she is not as sexually responsive as she thinks she ought to be. In her social life she gives herself a "C." She keeps telling herself that she ought to entertain her husband's clients more often, that she ought to have friends over for dinner more often, and that when she does, she ought to be a far better hostess than she is now. Marion struggles with feeling uncomfortable in social situations. She typically tells herself that she is not an interesting person and wonders how other people could enjoy her.

The reality is that Marion is deeply committed to her medical practice in a community health center. Both her colleagues and her patients have a great deal of respect for her. She puts in long hours and rarely takes any time off from work. When she is not working or achieving something, it is almost unbearable for her. The drive to accomplish more and more in a shorter amount of time keeps her from being able to relax. Often she says that she cannot afford the luxury of free time because there are so many important things to do.

In her family of origin Marion learned that it was not enough for Blacks to be simply good or even excellent but that they must be *outstanding* in everything they attempted. Her parents frequently told her that if she followed through with her plans to go to medical school, she would certainly encounter more than her share of discrimination on the grounds of both her race and her gender. She would have to prove herself time and again. She has accepted this view of life; moreover she feels a great deal of pressure to live up to the high expectations of her parents and not to disappoint them.

How I Would Proceed with Marion from the Perspective of RET and Other Cognitive-Behavioral Methods

Marion presents herself voluntarily for therapy, for she recognizes that her pressurized lifestyle is killing her. She would like to continue doing her best, but she does not want to feel that she *always* has to be the best in *every* aspect of her personal and professional life. It has finally come down to a matter of her feeling somewhat desperate: she feels miserable both physically and emotionally and has not been able to change her situation in spite of her most determined efforts. It is clear to her that she is driving herself in self-destructive circles. She says that she wants to break this chain, learn to modify her perfectionism, and begin accepting herself as a worthwhile person in spite of her limitations. She would like very much to be able to enjoy her work, without telling herself that she *should* and *must* do more. She has told herself that she ought to be less judgmental of herself than she is, yet this does little good. She finally seeks professional help.

Exposing Marion's irrational beliefs. In essence, I want to show Marion that it is her irrational beliefs that are the direct cause of her psychological and physiological problems. Further, I will show her that *she* is the one who is feeding herself these irrational and unrealistic assumptions and that she alone is the one who can change her misery by learning to uproot and demolish them. Together we will identify and actually write down the "musts," "shoulds," and "oughts" that keep her the driven and unhappy person she is. Finally, I will work with her to create a new set of assumptions and a rational set of attitudes.

Drawing on some of Beck's notions in cognitive therapy, I also focus on Marion's internal communications. I assume that she monitors her thoughts, wishes, feelings, and actions. In social situations she probably keeps score of how other people are reacting to her. Her thinking is also polarized in many respects. She sees things in terms of good or bad, wonderful or horrible. Further, she engages in some "catastrophizing," in which she anticipates negative outcomes of her ventures. In sum, she is contributing to her emotional problems by what she is telling herself, by the assumptions she is making, and by her belief system. Some of her faulty assumptions, along with the dire consequences that she tells herself will occur unless she follows her "shoulds," are as follows:

- I *must* perform well sexually so that I can meet Byron's expectations. If I fail, this confirms that I am sexually dead, unattractive, and incapable of giving anyone sexual pleasure. I won't be able to bear this thought.
- I *must* be the very best physician at the community health center. I *must* live up to all the expectations of all of my colleagues—and then I *should* go *beyond* what they expect! If I fail, it means that I'm basically incompetent.
- Because I am a Black female physician, I *must* be far better than my White male colleagues, or they will never respect me. If I don't get their respect, I simply don't think I will ever be able to feel like a worthwhile and competent person.
- I must be *thoroughly competent* in anything and everything I attempt. If I can't, I must avoid trying anything new. I couldn't *stand* making any mistakes, because that would prove to me and to the world that I'm deficient as a person.

To more clearly identify her faulty cognitions, I use the RET Self-Help Form as one of the main homework assignments. First of all, I ask Marion to write down an activating event (A), such as one of the times she made a mistake. Next she writes down the consequence (C), which is her guilty feelings or self-defeating behavior that she would like to change. Then, using the RET form, I ask her to keep track of all of her irrational beliefs (IBs) that led to the consequence. The activating event was a situation in which one of her patients got very upset and complained to her that she was not helping him and that he would be switching physicians. Initially Marion says, she felt devastated. Although she had tried as hard as she could, her patient was a chronic complainer. Yet her beliefs about his displeasure over his medical care led her to feel depressed and inadequate. Below is a partial record of her irrational beliefs (IBs), followed by a dispute (D) for each irrational belief, which is followed by an effective rational belief (RB) to replace her irrational belief:

IB: "All of my patients should feel satisfied, and I must please all of them all of the time."

D: "Who told me this nonsense to begin with? And what's more, why must I continue telling myself that it's true?"

RB: "Although I'd like all of my patients to appreciate me, I can live with the fact that not all of them will like my care."

IB: "I must do very well."

D: "And this is the very belief that keeps me stressed out and makes me sick."

RB: "I'd like to do as well as I can, but I'm imperfect, and I can tolerate my shortcomings."

IB: "If I make a mistake, this proves that I am an incompetent person."

D: "Where is the evidence that my worth as a person hinges on being totally competent in everything I do?"
RB: "I'm a competent physician in spite of the fact that one of my patients thinks I'm incompetent. Furthermore, even if I were incompetent at times, it wouldn't mean I was incompetent as a person."

By keeping a record of the irrational beliefs that crop up, along with taking the time to dispute each one and substituting a rational belief, Marion begins to learn how to refuse to feel miserable.

As an adjunct to homework assignments for Marion, I ask her to keep a journal in which she will record her thoughts and feelings in various situations. I also ask her to devote some time to evaluating her own progress. (The practice of keeping a journal is an effective technique that could be used with any therapeutic approach.) Questions such as the following are useful: "What are some of the irrational beliefs that I fed myself this week? When I became aware that I was engaged in this self-indoctrination process, what did I actually *do?* How did it feel to be in situations that brought up anxiety? And how did I react to these situations? Did I risk trying new behavior? Or did I stay with old and safe behavior? What gains am I making in uprooting specific attitudes and beliefs that I see as irrational? What new things have I been telling myself this week, and what are the consequences?" Through various other techniques of an active/directive nature (such as didactic teaching, role playing, behavioral rehearsal, coaching, modeling, confrontation, and desensitization, to mention a few), Marion progresses toward learning how to challenge her thinking and how to incorporate a constructive philosophy of life.

Another strategy that I employ is the rational-emotive imagery procedure, which consists of asking Marion to intensely imagine herself thinking, feeling, and acting exactly as she would like to think, feel, and behave in daily situations. This is a good method for helping her imagine all the specific ways in which she would like to be different. What feelings would she like to experience more often? What thoughts would she like to decrease? And what are the beliefs and thoughts that she would like to have? How would she like to behave differently? She can be whatever she wants to be in fantasy, and with this imagery procedure she creates an ideal world. Later we can explore what she is doing to thwart her getting what she would like to have.

A typical session. During a typical session Marion and I follow through with a critical evaluation of one of her irrational notions. She relates several situations in which older, White, male patients have expressed doubts about her ability to help them. She believes that she has had to face and struggle with the reality of prejudice and discrimination all of her life and that she must still contend with prejudice from some of her patients. Together we explore this reality that she continues to face, and we begin to sort out realistic and unrealistic conclusions. Given the reality of prejudice and discrimination against minorities, I still challenge Marion to change her thinking when it is not possible to change her environment. After discussing the many instances of discrimination she has experienced and her reactions to these events, we proceed to explore her belief that she must be an outstanding physician largely because she is a Black woman. I ask her to show me the evidence for her conclusion that because she is a Black woman, she must constantly prove herself. I confront her in this way: "Who is telling you these things now? Why do you burden yourself with *having* to live up to those expectations? Do you get tired of always having to be in control and taking care of everyone? In your mind do you think there is anything you could do to prove your worth to yourself? What would be so terrible about doing a fine job without being perfect? And what would be absolutely horrible and devastating about being less than outstanding?" I hope Marion will come to see that all the catastrophic thinking and expectations of doom are not nearly so unbearable as she thinks. It might not be pleasant for her to be imperfect, but I hope that she will learn to accept herself as a fallible human.

During this session Marion confronts me with being too hard on her and tells me that maybe her "irrational beliefs" about having to prove herself as a competent Black female physician may be more rational than I am willing to admit. She tells me "You are a White male psychologist, and I wonder if you can really understand the irrational world that I have had to struggle with in being a minority on two counts!" She tries to convince me that her convictions have helped her get through some difficult times and that she has to constantly fight to create her place in the professional arena. We spend some time talking about our differences, because if she does not trust me, there will be little that I can do or say to help her. She eventually accepts that I can understand her struggles and her feelings, in spite of the fact that I have not experienced the discrimination that she has lived with.

Integrating techniques. As our sessions continue, I draw on a variety of diverse methods of a cognitive, affective, and behavioral nature. I employ an eclectic approach suited to Marion's individual problems. If a technique does not seem to work in a session, I find alternative procedures that will work. As I mentioned earlier, Marion's progress will be determined in large part by her willingness to work hard outside of the sessions. Thus, I ask her to give herself homework assignments to practice in confronting her irrational thinking. The aim here is to learn how to deal with anxiety by resolving difficult situations that are anxiety-provoking. For example, she has said that she feels inadequate as a wife. She is burdening herself with the conviction that she has to please Byron in all respects. As a matter of fact, her work schedule is far more demanding than his, so eventually she challenges her notion that it is her duty to be a full-time housewife as well as maintaining a demanding professional life. She begins to take a critical look at her assumptions about her role as a woman in a dual-career family, and as a result she changes some of her reactions to "neglecting her husband." Instead, she begins to see that on many counts it is she who is being neglected by *him.* Yet instead of moaning about her fate she begins to take action at home to bring about the changes that she wants. One of these changes consists of her hiring a person to clean the house, do most of the time-consuming chores, and even to cook most of the dinners. Even though Byron resists this change, she persists in restructuring her beliefs about the absolute necessity of always pleasing him. She is learning to please herself, even if she does not receive support for this change.

Employing techniques of cognitive behavior modification. Marion continues to monitor her thoughts during a typical week by writing down specific situations that produce stress for her. She is getting better at noticing those factors and she is also improving her ability to detect self-statements that increase her level of stress. As a part of her homework she records what she *tells* herself in problematic situations, what she then *does,* and how she *feels.* During her sessions we go over her written analysis of her thinking, behaving, and feeling patterns in various situations. We then discuss alternative statements that she could make to herself, as well as ways that she could actually behave differently.

A *bibliotherapy* program, which is a supplement to Marion's sessions, is helping her become a more astute observer of her own experience. I suggest that she read books such as *A New Guide to Rational Living,* by Ellis and Harper, and *Cognitive Therapy and the Emotional Disorders,* by Beck. As she begins to apply to herself what she is learning from her readings, she also takes a more active role in her sessions with me. At this time I introduce her to the work of Donald Meichenbaum, as set forth in his book *Cognitive Behavior Modification.* I operate on the assumption that reorganizing her cognitive structures (her thoughts and self-statements) will result in a corresponding reorganization of her behavior in interpersonal situations. At the same time, I assume that forcefully and vigorously changing her behavior will change her irrational thinking.

The beginning step in Marion's changing consists of continued observation of her behavior in interpersonal situations. Thus, we go over her week as she recorded it to see what we can learn about the ways she is contributing to her fears in social situations through her negative thoughts. She reports that she has become aware of how many times in various social situations she sets herself up for failure by telling herself that people will not be interested in her.

The second step in changing Marion's cognitive processes involves my teaching her how to substitute *adaptive behavioral* responses for the maladaptive behaviors she now displays. If she hopes to change, what she says to herself must initiate a new behavioral chain, one that is incompatible with her maladaptive behaviors. Thus, we look at positive self-talk that can generate new expectations for her. She considers saying to herself: "Even though I'm nervous about meeting new people, I will challenge my assumption that people find me boring. I can learn to relax, and I can tell myself that I do have something to say." As an RET therapist I also try to get Marion to see that even if she didn't have anything interesting to say, she could always fully accept herself as a person and never damn or condemn herself for being inept. She is beginning to learn some new internal dialogues, and she is learning how to create positive expectations to guide new behavior.

The third phase of Marion's cognitive modification consists of learning more effective coping skills, which can be practiced in real-life situations. In this case I teach her a standard *relaxation exercise* used in the cognitive-behavioral approaches. I ask her to practice it twice a day for about 20 minutes each session. I teach her some training procedures in breathing and deep-muscle relaxation, ones that she can apply to many of the situations she encounters that bring about anxiety. As she practices more effective coping skills, she notices that she is getting different reactions from others, which reinforce her to continue with new patterns of behavior.

A Commentary

By using a combination of rational-emotive techniques and other cognitive-behavioral methods, Marion gradually develops a conceptual framework that helps her understand the ways in which she responds to a variety of stressful situations. First, through Socratic questioning she learns to become astute at monitoring maladaptive behaviors that flow from her inner dialogue. Second, she learns a variety of behavioral and cognitive coping techniques that she can apply in difficult situations. She acquires and rehearses a new set of self-statements. Eventually, she makes fewer negative and self-defeating statements to herself and substitutes positive and realistic self-statements. In RET she would largely use realistic rather than positive and reinforcing self-statements. She would have a new problem-solving and accepting philosophy rather than resorting to positive thinking. Third, she learns that merely learning to say new things to herself is not enough to result in behavioral change. It is necessary for her to practice these self-statements in real-life situations that present actual threats. Having become proficient in some cognitive and behavioral coping skills, she practices behavioral assignments on a graded level. As she experiences some success in carrying out these assignments in daily life, the assignments become increasingly demanding. In teaching her a method of thinking and behaving differently, I make the assumption that she will begin to feel better about herself.

Follow-Up: You Continue as Marion's Therapist

Consider the concepts and techniques I drew on and the style in which I did so as you think about how you might work with Marion further. What would you do differently?

1. Do any of Marion's "shoulds," "oughts," and "musts" remind you of messages that you tell yourself? How successful do you see yourself in identifying and working through some of your major irrational beliefs?
2. How do you imagine it would be for you to work with Marion? What might you do if she persisted in clinging to certain self-defeating notions and refused to see the irrationality of some of her beliefs?
3. Are there any ways in which you might work with Marion differently than you would with a White female physician? or with a White male physician? What special issues might you want to explore with her that are related to her gender and race?
4. How might you react if Marion were to say to you: "How can you understand my problems if you are not a Black woman who happens to be involved in a male-dominated medical profession?" What problems, if any, do you think you'd have in establishing an effective therapeutic relationship with her?
5. How comfortable would you be using RET methods? How effective do you imagine you would be?
6. Most of Marion's work with me consists of identifying irrational and self-defeating notions and learning to dispute them, both in the session and through activity-oriented homework assignments. In RET I am trying to get her to see how her irrational beliefs lead to self-defeating thoughts, feelings, and actions. What do you think of this approach? Do you think it is sufficient to produce lasting change? If not, what else do you think might be needed?
7. To what degree do you find it helpful to integrate the cognitive-behavioral perspective of Beck and Meichenbaum with the RET approach?
8. What are some cognitive-behavioral methods that you'd want to employ with clients?

RECOMMENDED SUPPLEMENTARY READINGS

Cognitive Therapy and the Emotional Disorders (1976), by A. Beck (New York: New American Library [Meridian]), is a very useful book illustrating how emotional disorders often have their roots in faulty thinking. Beck clearly outlines the principles and techniques of cognitive therapy, giving many clinical examples of how the internal dialogue of clients results in various emotional and behavioral problems.

Growth through Reason: Verbatim Cases in Rational-Emotive Therapy (1973), by A. Ellis (Hollywood, CA: Wilshire Books), is a recording of actual cases in RET.

It gives the reader a good grasp of how the rational-emotive therapist actually works with a wide range of clients.

Handbook of Rational-Emotive Therapy: Vol. 2 (1986), edited by A. Ellis & R. Grieger (New York: Springer), is one of the most comprehensive, up-to-date overviews of RET theory and practice. It is especially good on the application of RET principles to problems pertaining to anger, self-acceptance, love, lack of motivation, and depression.

A New Guide to Rational Living (rev. ed., 1975), by A. Ellis and R. Harper (Hollywood, CA: Wilshire Books), shows how to apply the principles of RET to problems of everyday living. An easy-to-read and interesting book.

How to Stubbornly Refuse to Make Yourself Miserable about Anything—Yes, Anything! (1988), by A. Ellis (Secaucus, NJ: Lyle Stuart), is a self-help book that shows how to translate insights into action by uprooting irrational beliefs and learning functional beliefs. The book presents the A-B-Cs of RET in a simple and interesting way.

Feeling Good: The New Mood Therapy (1981), by D. Burns (New York: New American Library [Signet]), is a practical self-help book based on the principles of Beck's cognitive therapy. The focus is on learning how to cope with everyday stresses and to control our feelings and actions by becoming aware of and changing our self-defeating thinking.

Intimate Connections (1985), by D. Burns (New York: New American Library [Signet]), represents an application of Beck's cognitive therapy to relationships, both building them and learning how to deal with losses.

Cognitive Behavior Modification: An Integrative Approach (1977), by D. Meichenbaum (New York: Plenum), is an excellent source for learning about cognitive-behavioral techniques such as cognitive restructuring, stress-inoculation training, and self-instructional training. The author does a good job of discussing how cognitive factors are related to behavior. He develops the theme that clients have the power and freedom to change by observing their behavior, telling themselves new sentences, and restructuring their belief system.

***A Practitioner's Guide to Rational-Emotive Therapy* (1992),** by S. Walen, R. DiGiuseppe, & W. Deyden (New York: Oxford University Press), is a practical manual; describing specific methods for teaching clients the basics of RET. It shows ways to design homework for client's, and it presents a variety of different styles of practicing RET.

The Principles and Practice of Rational-Emotive Therapy (1980), by R. A. Wessler & R. L. Wessler (San Francisco: Jossey-Bass), is a useful book designed for practitioners. It contains an expansion of the A-B-C model, RET's clinical theories and findings, and an inventory for evaluating one's own rational therapeutic skills.

SUGGESTED READINGS

Belkin, G. (1987). *Contemporary psychotherapies* (2nd ed.). Pacific Grove, CA: Brooks/Cole. (Chapter 17)

Belkin, G. S. (1988). *Introduction to counseling* (3rd ed.). Dubuque, IA: William C. Brown. (Chapter 9)

Burke, J. F. (1989). *Contemporary approaches to psychotherapy and counseling.* Pacific Grove, CA: Brooks/Cole. (Chapters 5 & 10)

Corey, G. (1991). *Theory and practice of counseling and psychotherapy* (4th ed.). Pacific Grove, CA: Brooks/Cole. (Chapter 11)

Corsini, R., & Wedding, D. (Eds.). (1989). *Current psychotherapies* (4th ed.). Itasca, IL: F. E. Peacock. (Chapters 6 & 8)

Gilliland, B., James, R., Roberts, G., & Bowman, J. (1984). *Theories and strategies in counseling and psychotherapy.* Englewood Cliffs, NJ: Prentice-Hall. (Chapter 8)

Hanson, J., Stevic, R., & Warner, R. (1986). *Counseling: Theory and Process* (4th ed.). Boston: Allyn & Bacon. (Chapter 10)

Ivey, A. E., Ivey, M. B., & Simek-Downing, L. (1987). *Counseling and psychotherapy: Integrating skills, theory, and practice* (2nd ed.). Englewood Cliffs, NJ: Prentice-Hall. (Chapter 11)

Patterson, C. H. (1986). *Theories of counseling and psychotherapy* (4th ed.). New York: Harper & Row. (Chapters 1, 2, & 8)

Prochaska, J. O. (1984). *Systems of psychotherapy: A transtheoretical analysis* (2nd ed.). Pacific Grove, CA: Brooks/Cole. (Chapter 7)

Wedding, D., & Corsini, R. J. (Eds.). (1989). *Case studies in psychotherapy.* Itasca, IL: F. E. Peacock. (Chapters 5 and 7)

CHAPTER TEN

Case Approach to Reality Therapy

A REALITY THERAPIST'S PERSPECTIVE ON RUTH
by William Glasser, M.D.

William Glasser is the founder and president of the Institute for Reality Therapy in Canoga Park, California. He presents many workshops each year, both in the United States and abroad. His practical approach continues to be popular among a variety of practitioners. He has written a number of books on reality therapy and control theory.

Everything I suggest below should be the product of a dialogue in which all the following points are brought up through the process of good reality therapy questioning. From experience I know that all of it can be done, but I can't teach the actual techniques here except to say that Ruth is asked to evaluate these suggestions.

Assessment of Ruth

As Ruth presents herself, it is obvious that she has never been able to satisfy her needs. In terms of the basic human needs, the only one that she is satisfying now is her need for survival. She does not feel that she has love, power, fun, or freedom in her life, and her *anxieting, panicking,* and *psychosomaticizing* are her way of expressing her extreme frustration. These symptoms keep her anger from bursting forth, and they "scream," *Help me!*

Ruth hasn't the strength to come out and say what she wants: a life far different from the one she has. So her symptoms and her complaints are her only way to express her intense dissatisfaction with her life. If she does not get the counseling she needs, which will lead her to a more satisfying life, she will choose more and more symptoms and will ultimately become disabled by them. She will also grow fat because eating (a survival need) is her only satisfaction, and she will probably choose *phobicking* to the point at which she will say she is not able to leave the house alone.

Key Issues and Themes

First of all, Ruth needs someone who will listen to her and not criticize her for what she says. She has never had this, and she needs it desperately. She will, however, present her story and continually ask for criticism by saying things like "It's wrong for me to complain; I have so much; I'm acting like a baby." She will make a whole family of comments like this. She knows how to "guilt," and the counselor must not get involved in the process. My most important task as her therapist is to listen to her and tell her that she has a right to express herself, that she does not deserve to be criticized, and that I will never criticize her no matter what she does or fails to do.

Then, it is important for Ruth to learn about her basic needs. It is essential that she learn how to satisfy these needs and that she recognize that she can do this without hurting her husband or children. If her parents disapprove of what she does and say they are hurt, this is their choice, and she can do nothing about it. I can ask over and over "How does your being miserable help you or anyone else?" Although Ruth can be kind to her parents and others when she talks to them, it is important that she tell them firmly that she is going to do what she believes is right for her life.

Ruth should be encouraged in her choice to go to work, although it would be a good idea to discuss with her the choice to become an elementary schoolteacher. This is a very giving role, and she may not do well at this now. She may need to work among adults and to be appreciated for her adult qualities by her peers. She needs a job where she does not have to be a "good" person to be appreciated. A large office where there is a lot of sociability would be ideal. It would be good for her to survey the job market.

Ruth's weight, diet, or symptoms should not be discussed in detail. If she wants to talk about them, I will listen but not encourage her. Talking about her problems or failures will lead her to choose to guilt, because she will not be able to solve them quickly. My approach will be to focus on her getting out of the house and finding a satisfying place in the adult world. When she does this, her complaints and symptoms will disappear, and her weight will be possible to control.

Ruth's finances would be discussed. What she earns for the first several years might be spent on herself and on doing things with her husband and children that are especially enjoyable to her. She should be encouraged not to save her money, give it to charity, or spend it on necessities unless that is what she really wants to do. It would be helpful to constantly encourage her to do what is right for her, not what is right for others or "good" for the world. She needs to learn to be a little selfish; she does not have to worry about becoming too selfish.

Finally, when Ruth has made progress, her marriage should be discussed, and her husband could be encouraged to be a part of this discussion. There is every reason to believe that she has little love in her marriage, but through marriage encounter or some such help this lack may be remedied. It may be that she will divorce, as she fears, but this is not an immediate issue. If it comes to this, she will be ready at that time.

Every session will end in a concrete plan for her to do something that will get her some love, power, fun, or freedom. What she plans need not be a big deal, but she has to learn, through doing things that satisfy her, that she is in control of her life and can use this control for her benefit.

Therapeutic Techniques

It is important that I be warm and uncritical and teach Ruth to be accepting of herself. In fact, I may say to Ruth: "In here we will not criticize anyone and will focus only on what you can do for yourself, first, and then what you can do for the others around you."

It would be useful for Ruth to carefully read my book *Control Theory* and we could discuss it in each session until she is well aware of these concepts and how they apply to the life she has and is still choosing to live.

It is best that plans be discussed, written out, and checked off. Ruth is competent, but her competence is never used for herself. She can be asked over and over "How will your satisfying your needs hurt anyone else?" and "How may doing this actually help others? Let's talk about this, because the answers to these questions are important for your life."

As much as possible, humor in the sessions would be helpful. Ruth is overdue for a laugh or two, and laughter will allow her to let go of her psychosomatic symptoms more quickly than anything else she can do.

There can be an emphasis on her good points, which are many, and at each session she might be encouraged to tell what she did that was good for her and what she accomplished that she never thought she would be able to.

It would be good for Ruth to consider the idea of inviting friends in and making a social life. She needs people. If her husband does not want to help, she can be encouraged to do this by herself. If she has a job, she might get hired help in to do the housework, which is something that this woman probably has never done or even dreamed of doing. The idea of spending money for enjoyment is worth a lot of therapy time.

Ruth can be encouraged to talk about her children and apply the ideas of control theory to them. I will ask her what she thinks she needs to do to get along with her daughter Jennifer, and I will advise her to stop telling her daughter what to do. Also, Ruth can be challenged to stop criticizing Jennifer completely, no matter what Jennifer or any of her other children say or do. Instead, Ruth might go out with her daughter for a good time, tell her she likes her the way she is and say, jokingly, that she should not model herself after an unhappy mother, only a happy mother.

I can teach Ruth that it is her life and that it is up to her, not anyone else, to make what she wants of it. Whenever she says that she can't do something, I can ask her why she can't, ask her to give all the reasons why she could do it, and then compare the two sets of reasons.

What Ruth needs is freedom. She has locked herself in a prison of her own making for most of her life, and there should be a discussion of who can let her out. My job is to persuade her through good reality-therapy questioning to throw away the key. If she is locked in, it is because she won't open the door.

This woman will need at least a year of one counseling session a week, but she will emerge as a vastly different and more happy person. Group counseling with others like her would also be a very helpful supplement. I would say that the chance of her achieving this better life through the use of reality therapy is about 100%. I wish I had the opportunity to see her personally, as people like her are a delight to counsel.

JERRY COREY'S WORK WITH RUTH FROM A REALITY-THERAPY PERSPECTIVE

Basic Assumptions

Reality therapy is active, directive, practical, and behavioral. As a reality therapist I see my task as helping clients clarify their wants and perceptions, evaluate them, and then make plans to bring about change. My basic job is establishing a personal relationship with my clients that will give them the impetus to make an honest evaluation of how well their current behavior is working for them. Reality therapy concentrates on total behavior (which includes doing, thinking, feeling, and physiological components). The focus is on what people are doing and thinking, because these components of behavior are the easiest to change.

I hold a number of basic assumptions that will guide my intervention strategies with Ruth. One is that people strive toward gaining better control of their lives and achieving a "success identity." Those who achieve this kind of identity see themselves as being able to give and accept love, feel that they are significant to others, experience a sense of self-worth, get involved in a caring way, and meet their needs in ways that are not at the expense of others. By contrast, people who seek therapy often have a "failure identity": they see themselves as unloved, believe that they are incompetent to make and stick with commitments, and feel powerless to change their life. Because reality therapy assumes that people are largely able to shape their destiny by what they choose to do, its focus is on helping clients learn behavior that will lead to a success identity.

Another basic premise underlying the practice of reality therapy is that *behavior* controls our perceptions. Although we may not be able to control what actually is in the real world, we do attempt to control our perceptions to meet our own needs. Applied to Ruth, this means that she creates her own perceived world. Her behavior has four components: acting, thinking, feeling, and physiology. Because I make the assumption that controlling feelings and thoughts is more difficult than controlling actions, the focus of therapy is on what she is doing—behaviors that are observable. She will find that it is typically easier to force herself to *do* something different than to feel something different. Although it is acceptable to discuss feelings, this is always done by relating them to what she is doing and thinking.

Assessment of Ruth

Rather than merely focusing on Ruth's deficits, problems, and failures, I am interested in looking at her assets, accomplishments, and successes. Initially I ask her questions such as these: "What do you want? How might your life be different if you had what you wanted now? What do you consider to be your major strengths? What are the qualities that you most like about yourself? What have you done that you are proud of? What resources can you build on?" From Ruth's autobiography and intake form, I know that she has several apparent strengths. She has graduated from college and is in a teacher-education program at the graduate level. She has done this against many odds. Her parents could see no real reason why she should get a college degree. In her current situation her husband and children have not been supportive of her efforts to complete her education. She has been involved in numerous community groups and made some contributions there, she has managed to keep up her family life and still have time for her education, and she has set some career goals that are meaningful to her. Now she needs to develop a clear plan for attaining her *personal* objectives.

Goals of Therapy

As implied above, the basic goals of reality therapy are to help clients clarify what they really want and why, to guide them toward making value judgments about their present behavior, and to assist them in deciding on a constructive plan of responsible behavior change that will lead to taking effective control of their lives. Ruth's present behavior is not working as well as it might. She is unproductively dwelling on unfortunate events from her past, and she is paying too much attention to feelings of guilt and anxiety and not enough to those things that she is doing to actually create these feelings. In short, she is making herself anxious and guilty by what she is doing and not doing in everyday life. I try to direct her attention toward these actions, because they are the most easily controlled parts of her life. I continue challenging her to make an honest assessment of how well her current behavior is getting her what she wants. Then I help her make plans to bring about change.

Therapeutic Procedures

I will ask Ruth to develop plans to change failure behavior into success behavior. I will expect her to make a commitment to carry out these plans, for if she hopes to change, *action* is necessary. It is essential that she stick with her commitment to change and not blame others for the way she is or give excuses for not meeting her commitments. Thus, we will work with a therapeutic contract, one that spells out what she wants from therapy as well as the means by which she will attain her goals.

If Ruth says that she is depressed, I will not ask *why* she is depressed, nor will I ask her to dwell on feelings of depression. Instead, I will ask what she has *done* that day to contribute to her experience of *depressing.* Changes in behavior do not depend on changing one's attitudes or gaining insights. On the contrary, attitudes may change, as well as feelings, once clients begin to change their behavior. I am also concerned about Ruth's *present,* not her past. Why should I dwell on the unsuccessful person that she has been? I would rather focus on the successful person that she can be. Also, I do not pay heed to psychoanalytic factors such as transference, unconscious dynamics, dreams, and early memories. Through my real involvement with Ruth I hope to help her to choose more effective behaviors aimed at fulfilling her realistic wants, thereby satisfying her needs for belonging, power, fun, and freedom.

The Therapeutic Process

Ruth's therapeutic journey consists of my applying the procedures of reality therapy to help her meet her goals. Although the principles may sound simple, they must be adapted creatively to the therapeutic process. It should be noted that although these principles are applied progressively in stages, they should not be thought of as discrete and rigid categories. Each phase builds on the previous stage, there is a considerable degree of interdependence among these principles, and taken together they contribute to the total process that is reality therapy. This process weaves together two components, the counseling environment and specific procedures that lead to changes in behavior. We will now look at a few of the highlights and turning points in Ruth's therapy.

Elements of the process

Establishing the relationship. During our initial sessions my main concern is to create a climate that will be conducive to Ruth's learning about herself. The core of the counseling environment consists of a personal involvement with the client, which must be woven into the fabric of the therapeutic process from beginning to end. I convey this involvement through a combined process of listening to Ruth's story and skillful questioning. This process increases the chances that she will evaluate her life and move in the direction of getting what she wants. I obtain involvement by attempting to understand her, affirming a belief that she can experience success, and communicating an attitude of caring. At this time I listen carefully to her to get a sense of why she is seeking therapy and what she wants from me. Without pushing her I try to discover as much as possible about her perceived and internal worlds. She seems relatively open and appears sincere in wanting more from life and taking more control of her actions. She is also somewhat frightened and tells me that changing seems so difficult, adding that for years she has made firm resolutions to change the course of her life, only to slip back again. I detect some discouragement, so we pursue how she might create self-fulfilling prophecies of success, rather than of doom.

In some of our early sessions Ruth wants to talk about occasions when she experienced failure in her childhood and youth. She quickly wants to blame past negative experiences for her fears. She seems a bit stunned when I tell her that I do not want to go over her past failures and that if we are going to talk about the past at all, I am more interested in hearing what went right for her. From that topic she jumps to complaining about feeling anxiety, depression, and some physical symptoms. I ask her to describe what she would be doing if she were not depressing. This focus begins a process of redirection and gets her to think about other alternatives besides depressing. I do not encourage her to focus on feelings related to negative experiences. Part of her present problem is that she is already stuck in some negative feelings, and I do not want to reinforce her in continuing this pattern.

Challenging Ruth to evaluate her behavior. After getting a picture of how Ruth sees her world, I encourage her to try something different: to take a hard look at the things she is doing and see if they are working for her. After some debating she agrees with my suggestion that she is depressing herself by what she is doing. Questions that I pose to her are: "What are the things you've done today? What did you do this past week? Do you like what you're doing now? Are there some things you would like to be doing differently? What are some of the things that stop you from doing what you say you want to do? What do you intend to do tomorrow?" Let me stress that I do not bombard her with these questions one after another. The early sessions are, however, geared to getting her to consider this line of questioning. Rather than looking at her past or focusing on her attitudes, beliefs, thoughts, and feelings, I want her to know that we will be zeroing in on what she is doing today and what she will do tomorrow.

I believe that Ruth will not change unless she makes some assessment of the constructiveness or destructiveness of what she is doing. I assume that if she comes to realize that her behavior is not working for her and that she is not getting what she wants, there is a real possibility that she might choose other alternatives. Here is a brief excerpt of a session:

RUTH: So what do you think I'm doing wrong? There are times I want to give up, because I don't know what to do differently. [She is very much wanting me to make a value judgment for her.]

JERRY: You know how important it is for you to be the one who makes a judgment about your own behavior. It's your job to decide for yourself what is and isn't working. I can't tell you what you "should" do. [For me to simply tell her that some of her present ways are ineffective will not be of much value to her.]

RUTH: Well, I do want to go out and get some practice with interviews for part-time or substitute teaching. I often find lots of reasons to keep me from doing that. I keep telling myself that I'm so busy I just don't have time to set up these interviews.

JERRY: And is that something you'd like to change? [My line of questioning is to ascertain how much she wants what she says she wants. I am attempting to assess her level of commitment.]

RUTH: Yeah, sure I want to change it. I want to be able to arrange for these interviews and then feel confident enough to have what it takes to get a part-time job.

We look at how Ruth stops herself (not why) and explore ways in which she might begin to change behavior that she calls "sitting back and waiting to see what happens." She says that she does not like her passivity and that she would like to do more initiating. One of the factors we talk about is how she lets her family get in the way of her doing some of these things she says she wants to do.

Planning and action. We devote a number of sessions to identifying specific behaviors that Ruth decides are not working for her. A few of these ineffective behaviors are procrastinating in arranging for job interviews; sitting at home feeling depressed and anxious and then increasing these feelings by not doing anything different; allowing her 19-year-old son, Rob, to come home after squandering money and then taking care of him; allowing her daughter Jennifer to control her life by her acting out; and continually taking on projects that she does not want to get involved in. Knowing that we cannot work on all fronts at once, I ask her what areas she wants to do something about.

Ruth decides first to line up some interviews for jobs. She makes it clear that her life is boring, stale, and without much challenge. Then she tries to convince me that everything she has to do for her family makes it next to impossible for her to get out of her boring rut. I reply "If things are as bad as you say, do you expect them to change if you keep doing what you have been doing?" We gradually work out some realistic plans, which include her filing an application with school districts and setting up interviews. Interestingly enough, after taking these beginning steps she reports that she is already feeling much better.

We also develop some plans to set clear limits with Ruth's family. She has a pattern of doing things for her children and then resenting them and winding up feeling taken advantage of. Part of her plan calls for sitting down with each of her sons and each of her daughters and redefining their relationships. I suggest that it would be a good idea to have at least one session with her family. The idea both excites and frightens her. Yet she actually surprises herself when she is successful in getting John and her four children to come in for a two-hour session of family therapy. At this session we mainly negotiate some changes in roles after Ruth has told each family member specific changes that she would like and has been striving for. One of her sons and one of her daughters is not at all excited about some of the proposed changes, and they want to know what is wrong with the way things are. What I had in mind when I suggested this family session was to give Ruth an opportunity to ask for what she wants and to witness her negotiating for these changes. The session helps me see how she relates to her family, and it helps Ruth ask for what is important to her.

Other phases of Ruth's therapy. Most of our work together consists of developing realistic and specific plans and then talking about how Ruth might carry them out in everyday life. When she does not stick with a subgoal or carry out a plan for the week, I do not listen to any excuses that she might offer. Instead, I simply say: "Ruth, do you want to do it or not? When will you do it?" In a few cases in which she persistently does not follow through with an agreed-on plan, we then discuss whether what she has planned is something she really wants or something she thinks she should want. Several times she returns looking sheepishly at me, almost expecting to be punished or yelled at. I try to get across that as long as she keeps coming in, I do not intend to give up on her, nor will I get into a punishing stance with her. Instead, I want her to deal with the consequences of her actions and then be her own judge.

Eventually, Ruth gets better at setting smaller goals and makes more realistic plans. She stops and says "Now I wonder if I really want to do this, or am I hearing someone else tell me that I should want it?" Before finishing her therapy she fills out a form evaluating her progress over the months. Her comments are reproduced below.

> After two months of weekly visits with a reality therapist I have a better idea of what I can do to get out of the boring rut I've been in for so long. I've gotten a lot of miles out of complaining and feeling helpless, but I must say this is something that Jerry just would not tolerate. He quickly told me when I whined that if I was really interested in being different, I'd be taking steps to see that I became different.
>
> I remember the time I agreed to begin a daily exercise and jogging program as one way of losing weight. For several weeks I had complained to Jerry that I couldn't stand the way I looked. He worked with me to develop a realistic program for losing weight—and then I didn't follow through with the plans. Jerry said he didn't want to listen to my rationalizations for having failed. I tried to convince him that I had gone on another eating binge because my husband was ignoring me and I got depressed. Then I ate out of defiance. I said to myself "Why should I lose weight

for John if he's going to treat me so mean?'' When I told Jerry this, he countered with: ''Whom are you losing weight for, *yourself* or John? Whom are you hurting with your eating behavior?'' That got me to thinking about how I so often make others responsible instead of putting the responsibility on me, where it belongs. I do see that if I don't like my weight, or anything else in my life, matters won't be different until I get in there and take action.

By the way, I interviewed for the job, and I did get part-time work as a substitute. This shows me that I'll get nothing unless I make an attempt.

Process commentary

As a reality therapist I do not tell Ruth what she should change but encourage her to examine her wants and determine her level of commitment to change. It is up to her to decide how well her current behavior is working for her. Once she makes a value judgment about what she is actually *doing,* she can take some significant steps toward making changes for herself. She has a tendency to complain of feeling victimized and controlled, and my intention is to help her see how her behavior actually contributes to this perceived helplessness. Rather than focusing on her feelings of depression and anxiety, I choose to focus on what she does from the time she wakes up to the time she goes to bed. Through a self-observational process she gradually assumes more responsibility for her actions. She sees that what she does has a lot to do with the way she feels.

After Ruth becomes clearer about certain patterns of her behavior, I encourage her to develop a specific plan of action that can lead to the changes she desires. Broad and idealistic plans are bound to fail, so we work on a concrete plan for change that she is willing to commit herself to. Once she makes a commitment to a certain course of action, I do not accept excuses if she does not follow through with her program. I simply ask her to look at her plans again to determine what has gone wrong. Through this process she learns how to evaluate her own behavior to see ways in which she might adjust her plans and experience success.

Questions for Reflection

1. In Dr. Glasser's assessment of Ruth he says ''If she does not get the counseling she needs, which will lead to a more satisfying life, she will choose more and more symptoms and will ultimately become disabled by them.'' What are the main symptoms that she presents? What are your thoughts about the manner in which Glasser deals with her symptoms and the key themes that she presents?
2. In Dr. Glasser's commentary on Ruth he suggests asking, over and over, ''How does your being miserable help you or anyone else?'' To what

extent do you think that she is choosing her misery? How would you be inclined to work with her on this score?

3. Dr. Glasser seems very directive in pointing out the themes that Ruth should explore, and he is also fairly directive in suggesting what she should do outside of the sessions. For example, he suggests that she consider a job in a large office where there is a lot of sociability, he says that her finances should be discussed, and he indicates that her marriage should be discussed. What are your reactions? Would you be inclined to bring up these topics (and other themes that you thought were important) if Ruth did not specifically mention them?
4. Do you have any concerns that a reality therapist might impose his or her values on the client? Do you see this as potentially happening with either the way Glasser works with Ruth or the way I work with her?
5. What are your general impressions of the way I work with Ruth? What do you like best about my approach with her? like least? What are some specific things you might have done differently?
6. What are your reactions to the lack of focus on matters such as Ruth's early childhood experiences? her unconscious dynamics? her dreams? her feelings of being bound by her parents teachings? her feelings of guilt? Do these have a place in reality therapy ? If so, what is it? What are the major differences you see between reality therapy and psychoanalysis? Which do you think is more appropriate for Ruth?
7. What similarities do you see between reality therapy and existential therapy? transactional analysis? behavior therapy? rational-emotive therapy? Adlerian therapy?
8. Assume that you are Ruth's therapist and she wants to present you with the reasons that she has failed in a particular plan for action. How might you respond? What do you think of the reality therapist's view of *not accepting excuses* and of *not blaming the past* for the way one is today?
9. Show how you would proceed with Ruth on the basis of what you know about her, staying within the framework of reality therapy.
10. Apply the procedures of reality therapy to what you know of Ruth. Systematically show how you would get her to focus on what she is doing, on making an evaluation of her behavior, and on helping her formulate realistic plans.
11. Assume that you are a client in reality therapy. How would you describe your current behavior? How well is it working for you? Are you getting what you want from life? If not, what specific behaviors do you think you would have to change in order to do so? Can you come up with a plan for changing a particular behavior you really want to change?

MANNY: A LOSER FOR LIFE?

The scene is a U.S. Army base in Germany. The army has a mandatory counseling program for drug and alcohol rehabilitation of personnel with addictive personalities. I am called in as a consultant to train the counselors who are a part of this program. I mention that I would like to get some feel for the clients they work with, and I am quickly given an opportunity. They know that my theoretical orientation is reality therapy, and because the army is very supportive of this approach to rehabilitation programs, I am sent a client to interview for one session.

My Approach with Manny

Manny, at 27, has made the military his career. He approaches the session in a high state of anxiety and displays many nervous bodily mannerisms. After we briefly introduce ourselves, our exchange goes this way:

MANNY: I really don't want to be here, you know. The only reason I'm here is because my commanding officer told me "You will report to Dr. Corey at 1600 hours on 7 July at the health clinic."

JERRY: If you don't want to be here, how come you're here?

MANNY: What do you mean, man? I *had* to show up. The commanding officer didn't give me any choice!

JERRY: Well, you walked through the door by yourself. Nobody brought you here. What would have happened if you hadn't shown up?

MANNY: They gave me one more chance, and then they're booting me out.

JERRY: So you *did* decide to come and see me rather than get kicked out.

MANNY: Yeah, I don't know what good this will do, but it's better than getting my walking papers.

JERRY: Well, I'm not sure how much good counseling will do unless we both agree to do what's needed to make it work. But you're here, and how you use this time is largely up to you.

MANNY: I don't want them to discharge me, especially since I have all those years in toward retirement.

JERRY: So I'd like to hear more about what might be the consequences if they do discharge you and about what you see that you can do to prevent this from happening.

Initially, Manny does not want to be in the office. Rather than fighting his resistance, I go with it by engaging him in a discussion of the possible consequences of both seeing me and not seeing me. My hope is that he will find it easy enough to talk with me, that I will not appear overly threatening to him, and that I will be able to lay the foundations for more meaningful *involvement* with him. Note that even though he sees himself as an involuntary client, I challenge him a bit on the fact that he indeed chose to come and see me rather than suffering the consequences of not keeping his appointment. He could have been more difficult and more resistant by simply saying: "Hey, why am I talking to you? I don't want to talk to you." Examples of facilitative remarks would be: "And who would you rather talk to?" "Where would you rather be right now?" "Maybe we can talk more about what is likely to happen if you don't come for counseling.'' ''Are you willing to say why you are here?'' Again, if I let him lead the way and go with his resistance, he can provide me with useful information about himself that will help me understand his current situation. My aim is to help him acquire a new perspective about a situation in which he sees himself as an involuntary client, so that he might perceive some payoffs in choosing to participate in counseling.

At some point Manny will surely remind me that he does not want to attend therapy sessions. Then I am likely to tell him what we will be doing in the sessions and what he can expect of me. But I will also tell him what I expect of him. I am not willing to see him unconditionally, nor am I willing to sit with him silently or try to pry things out of him. It is probable, for example, that I will see him three times to explore the possibilities of what counseling can offer him. If he agrees to come in for three sessions, the time will be used mainly to teach him about the counseling process, to get him to look at what he is *doing* now, and to decide how well it is working for him. Notice that I am not determining what he will talk about, but I will insist that on some level he address his present behavior. If he agrees to these limited terms, we can then proceed in the first session as follows:

JERRY: I'd like to talk more about why you were sent here and what you might get from this one session today. Are you willing?

MANNY: You're calling the shots. Whatever you say. I'm here because the army thinks I have a big problem with drugs—Big H and all that stuff—and they think you're supposed to put my head on straight. My problem isn't the drugs. It's the army and all those Mickey Mouse rules.

JERRY: What about the army and its rules?

I want to give Manny some slack in saying what problems he has, if any. Unless *he* sees that he has a problem, one that is getting in the way of living, he may do nothing to change any of his behavior. It is one thing for his commanding officer to order him to seek counseling for a problem he sees with Manny and quite another matter for Manny to accept that he does indeed have a problem. At this point he sees his locus of control as being outside of himself. Part of creating the involvement process consists of helping him find ways of gaining more effective control of his life. My aim is to help him look at what specific areas he has control over and what areas are outside of his control. I facilitate this process by encouraging him to explore his wants, needs, and perceptions.

MANNY: Sure, I've got my share of problems. You'd have some problems if you grew up the way I did. My old man kicked me out of the house when I was a kid, and I had to go and live with an uncle in East Los Angeles. I got in with a gang and started being a loser then. I got kicked out of school for peddling dope and gang activity. Never was able to hold a job. I mean, man, I've had a rough life. If you had all the things happen to you that I've had to go through, you might not have made it as far as I have. I'm a loser, but at least I'm still alive. I mean, Doc, you don't look like the type who's been with gangs and had to put up with the kind of life that I did. How can you understand what I'm going through?

I need to exert some caution here not to become defensive. Also, I do not want this to become a session in which Manny tells me that he is not to blame for all his woes. In reality therapy we do not want to encourage a pattern of blaming, in which clients absolve themselves of any personal responsibility for the way they are, nor do we want to encourage a recitation of past history as an explanation of current behavior. But another issue is that Manny is again trying to take the focus off of himself and telling me that I am not able to understand what he has been through. I must deal directly with the question of my ability to understand him.

JERRY: You're right, I haven't been through all that you have. I'm not sure I'd have survived. That doesn't necessarily mean that I can't understand you. I'd like for you to give me that chance. Even though I've had different life experiences from yours, I may still be able to have some of your feelings and see things the way you do. I'd like an opportunity to make contact with you, even for this single meeting.

MANNY: Well, before you can understand the way I am, you need to know about what I've lived through. My old man was never there, I got beat up all the time, I failed at everything I tried—I was a real loser. A loser from the word go. And it's mostly because I never had the things in life most normal kids have.

Again, there are some rich leads here. I can get some idea of what it is like to be Manny if I let him talk in more detail of what his life was like, as well as what he is facing now. But there is the danger that we can lose sight of his *present behavior*—what he is doing now—if we dwell on the adversity he has faced and the loser that he has been in the past. I want to focus him on the present by beginning to examine if what he is doing is working for him. If, from his vantage point, he does not like what he has in his life, the doors are open for counseling to proceed.

JERRY: You know, Manny, the way I work I prefer to look at what you're doing *right now* in your life and what this behavior is actually getting you. I think we can easily get sidetracked if we go back into your past with all the details of the negative things that happened to you. I'm not so much interested in hearing about the loser you've been all your life as I am in getting you to think about the winner you can be in your future. I'd like to hear you talk about what you can have *some* control over *now.*

MANNY: But I want to figure out why my head is all messed up the way it is. Don't you need to know about my childhood to help me? Don't

I need to know what's caused my problems before I can straighten them out?

JERRY: I don't think that talking about the past is important or that it will help you much, *unless* we discuss how your past relates to what you see as being a problem for you currently. What I'm after is to get you to look at your life to see in what ways it is or isn't working for you now. With what time we have left today, I'd be very willing to discuss with you what your present behavior is getting you. Are you willing to take this look?

MANNY: Well, it's not getting me much except heaps of trouble. I've spent time in the military jail because of my drug trip, and things don't look too rosy for the future. There are times when I'd like to be different, but I don't know how to do it.

Where I'd Proceed with Manny from Here

Assuming that Manny is willing to at least take a look at the results of his behavior, I ask him if he is committed to a better life for himself and how much he really wants change in his life. I ask him to talk more about some of the ways in which he has been a failure, and I challenge him to see if there are any ways in which he has contributed to his setbacks. However, my focus is on helping him see what steps he can now take toward becoming a successful person. Thus, our work together is grounded on the assumption that his behavior is an attempt to fulfill his basic needs for belonging, power, freedom, and fun. It is crucial that I do not judge his present behavior for him but that I continue to challenge *him* to do this. Thus, my attempts will be directed toward getting him to realistically appraise his behavior.

My main concern at this point is for Manny to simply see that nothing in his life will change unless he sees the need for change. He says that although there are times when he would like to be different, he does not know how to go about it. This provides an excellent lead for a discussion of specific plans that could lead to constructive changes for him. Therefore, I will at least begin by exploring with him some of the things he can do well, some of the things he likes, and some of the ways he would like to be different. This includes encourging him to talk about the mental pictures he has about the life he would like. My hope is that he will begin to consider possibilities for himself that he has previously ruled out. For example, in our discussion I find out that he would like to specialize in electronics, and he even admits to having some talent in this area. So I talk with him about the chances of enrolling in the army's electronics program. If he agrees to look into the program, this will be a responsible action, for he will not just be moaning about his ill fate but doing something about changing this fate.

My job is to help him make plans that are immediate and realistic. Such plans can even begin during the session. I hope that before our session ends, he will at least have some plan for checking out the program. This could even involve his making a phone call during the session to inquire about it. It is a good idea to write these plans down. If he agrees to short-range plans, we can discuss how he can best carry them out and what he might do if he encounters difficulties in doing what he says he would like to do. It would also be a good idea to ask him to consider what he might get from some further counseling sessions.

Follow-Up: You Continue as Manny's Therapist

Assume that Manny does do something about his life and decides to give short-term counseling a try. He consults you and asks you to continue where he and I left off, using reality therapy as a base. How might you proceed with him?

1. First of all, how do you perceive Manny? What are your personal reactions to him? Does it make any difference that he has sought counseling with you voluntarily, rather than being sent by his commanding officer? How might you be affected by him differently if he were an involuntary client? Would you want to work with him? Why or why not?
2. What are your general impressions of the way I worked with Manny? What would you do to further this work? What differences can you see between your style and mine in dealing with him (still staying in the reality-therapy perspective)?
3. From what was presented, what kinds of "pictures," or perceptions, does Manny have about his life now? What might you do or say to increase the chances that he would look at his behavior and make a value judgment about it?
4. To what degree have you had life experiences that would allow you to identify with Manny's drug problem and his failures? If you have not had similar feelings of being a "loser," do you think you could be effective with him?
5. How might you respond to Manny as your client if he reacted to you in a flip and sarcastic manner?
6. Manny wants to talk about his past and the experiences that he thinks contributed to the person he is today. I keep focusing him on the present and on what he might do about his future. What do you think of such an approach? What are its possible merits and demerits?
7. This approach stresses the importance of a concrete plan of action and a commitment from the client to follow the plan. What might you say and do if Manny neither developed a concrete plan for change nor committed himself to the process of behavioral change?
8. In my session with Manny I make it clear that I am interested mainly in his actions, not in his feelings, not in changing his attitudes and

beliefs, and not in helping him to acquire insight. What do you think of an approach that focuses so exclusively on one domain—in this case, what he is doing today?

9. Manny was not identified with respect to cultural and ethnic background or to his race. Consider how you might work with him differently depending on his specific cultural and ethnic background. What variables might you attend to if his background were different from yours? How might you proceed with him if he were Black? White? Native American? Hispanic? Asian American?

RECOMMENDED SUPPLEMENTARY READINGS

What Are You Doing? How People Are Helped through Reality Therapy (1980), edited by N. Glasser (New York: Harper & Row), is a casebook that gives readers a good sense of how reality therapy can be applied to working with a diverse range of clients.

Control Theory in the Practice of Reality Therapy: Case Studies (1989), edited by N. Glasser (New York:Harper & Row), shows how control theory is applied to the practice of reality therapy with a diverse range of clients. It brings the concepts of reality therapy up to date by illustrating how practitioners integrate the concepts of control theory into their practice. These cases demonstrate how the key ideas of control theory actually work in helping clients ask themselves the question "Is what I am choosing to do now getting me what I want?"

Control Theory (1985), by W. Glasser (New York: Harper & Row), is a useful source for readers wanting an update of Glasser's thinking. The author develops the thesis that we always have control over what we do and that if we come to understand how our behavior is an attempt to meet our needs, we can then find ways of taking control of our life.

Using Reality Therapy (1988), by R. Wubbolding (New York: Harper & Row), extends the principles of reality therapy by presenting case studies that can be applied to marital and family counseling, as well as individual counseling. The author has summarized control theory into five clear principles. This book is very clearly written with many practical guidelines for implementing the principles of reality therapy in practice. There are many excellent questions and brief examples that clarify ways of using reality-therapy concepts. There are chapters on guidelines for creating an effective counseling relationship as well as on specific procedures used by the reality therapist to facilitate change. The author has extended the scope of practicing reality therapy by describing other procedures such as paradoxical techniques, humor, skillful questioning, supervision, and self-help. He presents reality therapy as a philosophy of life rather than a doctrinaire theory or set of prescriptions.

SUGGESTED READINGS

Belkin, G. (1987). *Contemporary psychotherapies* (2nd ed.). Pacific Grove, CA: Brooks/Cole. (Chapter 16)

Belkin, G. S. (1988). *Introduction to counseling* (3rd ed.). Dubuque, IA: William C. Brown. (Chapter 9)

Corey, G. (1991). *Theory and practice of counseling and psychotherapy* (4th ed.). Pacific Grove, CA: Brooks/Cole. (Chapter 12)

Gilliland, B., James, R., Roberts, G., & Bowman, J. (1984). *Theories and strategies in counseling and psychotherapy.* Englewood Cliffs, NJ: Prentice-Hall. (Chapter 9)

Hansen, J., Stevic, R., & Warner, R. (1986). *Counseling: Theory and process* (4th ed.). Boston: Allyn & Bacon. (Chapter 9)

Ivey, A. E., Ivey, M. B., & Simek-Downing, L. (1987). *Counseling and psychotherapy: Integrating skills, theory, and practice* (2nd ed.). Englewood Cliffs, NJ: Prentice-Hall. (Chapter 11)

Prochaska, J. O. (1984). *Systems of psychotherapy: A transtheoretical analysis* (2nd ed.). Pacific Grove, CA: Brooks/Cole. (Chapter 3)

Bringing the Approaches Together and Developing Your Own Therapeutic Style

This chapter focuses on how to work with the themes of Ruth's life from a variety of therapeutic perspectives. I want to emphasize that one approach does not have a monopoly on the truth. There are many paths to the goal of providing Ruth with insight and mobilizing her resources so that she can take constructive action to give new direction to her life. These therapeutic perspectives can actually complement one another.

Before demonstrating my own eclectic style with Ruth, I will discuss working with her from a family-therapy perspective (or systems approach) and from a multicultural perspective. Then I will review some of the major themes that have been addressed in her therapy so far. I will accentuate several differences in working with these themes from various theoretical orientations. Some brief dialogues, with process commentaries, should give you a sense of the direction that each therapist is taking. Although this format will highlight contrasts in therapeutic style, look for ways in which you might develop your own style by combining the concepts and techniques of various approaches.

WORKING WITH RUTH FROM A FAMILY-THERAPY PERSPECTIVE

One of the reviewers of this book, Mary Moline, who has doctorates in marital and family therapy and in health sciences, commented to me that all the approaches to Ruth focused on her as an individual. Dr. Moline, the coordinator of Loma Linda University's Marriage and Family Therapy Program, maintained that readers would benefit from being introduced to the systems approach. I enthusiastically agreed, and we decided to illustrate a co-therapy model of working with a family.

There is a rationale for working with the family, even if the context is counseling an individual client. It is extremely helpful to witness the dynamics of the client's family as these patterns emerge when all family members are present. Such a session produces valuable data that can be more fully explored in individual sessions.

Presenting Ruth with the Idea of Family Therapy

I recommend to Ruth that she consider bringing her entire family into the therapeutic process. After exploring her individual psychodynamics in depth, she has made some significant changes. However, she still complains that members of her family are not changing and, as a matter of fact, tend to resist her changes. They prefer the ''old Ruth'' and do not want their lives to become unsettled.

Based on our discussion of the merits of family therapy, Ruth decides to ask her family to participate in her therapy. She has been arguing with her husband about her 16-year-old son, Adam. She agrees that she has been working hard in individual therapy and has made some significant changes but that these changes have had an effect on her relationship with John and her children. Because family therapy is not my expertise, I suggest that I would like to bring in a colleague (who teaches family therapy) to co-lead these family sessions. Ruth thinks that this is a good idea and consents to this arrangement.

My colleague, Mary Moline, insists that it is essential to have the entire family (all those presently living with Ruth) attend the first session. According to Ruth, John is willing to come if it will be helpful to her, but he does not see a reason for therapy for himself. The two of them have been arguing about their 16-year-old son, Adam, who has become a ''nuisance'' at home. John thinks that it would be a good idea for the therapists to address Adam's change in attitude. All of Ruth's children agree to participate in family therapy. However, the elder son, Rob, is reluctant. He feels that he does not have any problems, and he cannot understand why he should attend.

The First Session

Mary (my co-therapist) thanks the family for coming and asks the members to be seated where they want. She says that the purpose of this first meeting is to (1) establish the goals for treatment and (2) assess whether further sessions will be necessary for the family. We also discuss the limits of confidentiality and the reporting laws for the state.

The presenting complaint. When the entire family shows up, it is apparent that there is some confusion over why everyone needs to be present. Therefore, we ask Ruth to explain her concerns to the family and her hopes for these sessions.

RUTH: Since I've been in therapy, I've seen this family change. For example, Adam, you've become more moody. Your father and I are arguing more, and usually we're arguing over you.'' [She turns to the therapists.] ''But

I want you to know that our marriage is basically good. I also see that the rest of the children seem to be arguing more with their father, especially since I've been staying out of these arguments. I'd like to see this family get along more and argue less.

Mary and I observe that Ruth and Adam sit next to each other. John sits off to one side. Rob sits somewhat off to the other side. The other two siblings, Jennifer, 18, and Susan, 17, sit together. Mary and I ask each member for his or her observations regarding the family. We also ask them: "If you could get something from this session for yourself, what might that be? Would you like to have a different relationship with anyone in your family?"

The family interaction. What follows are excerpts of a dialogue among the family members, Mary, and me during this first session:

JOHN: We're here because my wife asked us to come. If we can help, we'd be glad to do that. I personally have no goals for myself. But the wife and I are concerned about the boy, Adam. Since Ruth began this counseling stuff, Adam has become less obedient and cooperative. Yesterday, he yelled at Jennifer, and when I tried to punish him, his mother told me to leave him alone and let them work it out by themselves. I disagree with her new idea of how to discipline these children. I think they should be punished if they do something wrong. I was brought up never to disobey my parents.

ROB [interrupting]: This is weird! We never talk about family stuff. The only time we ever get together is when we go to church. Sometimes I'm glad that Mom is more independent. She's not on my case as much as she was before.

JERRY: Rob, would you tell your mother what you mean by "being on your case"?

ROB: She would always want to know where I was going and what I was doing. Mom would always tell me if she didn't like the girls I was going with.

JERRY: Rob, you're talking about your mother as though she weren't in the room. How about talking directly to her over here?

ROB: That's kinda hard for me to do. It's not something that I usually do.

MARY: That's OK, Rob. But in these sessions I'd like you to address her directly. It would be good if everyone in here would address one another directly, rather than talking about someone.

ROB: I also want to say something about my Dad. I feel he's too hard on Adam.

JERRY: So, Rob, there sits your dad. Will you tell him directly what you mean by your statement that he's "too hard on Adam"?

ROB: Dad, you're always upset when Adam starts arguing with his sisters or me. And also, you're getting on my case lately. If I'm not home by

10, you get all bent out of shape, just like Mom used to be. You're right, Dad, Adam has become a real pain in the neck since mother began seeing a counselor. But can't you show a little patience with him?

JERRY: John, how is it for you to hear what Rob is saying to you? Would you let Rob know your reactions?

JOHN [looking to Mary]: I don't believe I have to take this. I never corrected my father.

MARY: How does this affect you to hear what Rob just said to you?

JOHN: It upsets me.

MARY: Would you be willing to tell that to Rob?

JOHN: Well, it does get me upset. Don't you know how much your mother and I care for you?

MARY: It seems that the two of you have much more to talk about. I'm hoping we can continue this dialogue at some future time, but I'd like to make sure that we get to each person in the family. [She turns to Jennifer.] What would you like to say about being here, and what you would like for yourself in these sessions?

JENNIFER [looking to Ruth and Susan]: Susan and I like the idea of coming here, because this family seems so different since Mom went to counseling. Susan and I feel that Mom has abandoned the family.

JERRY: Would you tell your mother what you mean by "abandoning the family"?

JENNIFER: Well, Mother, you don't do our wash anymore. You tell us to do our own wash. And we have to make our own lunches. You seem to have many more opinions now that are different. I agree with Rob that you and Dad argue more, but I stay out of those arguments and leave the house when you guys start bickering.

MARY: Ruth, what's it like for you to hear what Jennifer just said to you?

RUTH: It's hard to hear Jennifer disapproving of my going to college. I think that's why it's so difficult for me to get a job outside the home. I'm torn between making myself happy or my family happy.

MARY: How do you respond to what your mother just said, Jennifer?

JENNIFER: I'd rather not respond right now.

MARY: That's OK, you don't need to respond right now. Hopefully, we can get back to what's going on between you and your mother later in this session. [She turns to Susan.] How, specifically, would you like things to be different for yourself with each member of your family?

SUSAN: Jennifer and I would like more of Mom's time.

JERRY: Instead of talking for Jennifer, perhaps you could talk for yourself. Later, Jennifer can say what she would like to be different.

MARY: Susan, is there anything more that you want to add?

SUSAN: Well, I would like to say that I agree with Rob that Dad is not as nice as he used to be since Mom got into counseling and . . .

JOHN [interrupting Susan]: How can you say that I'm not nice to you? I work my butt off for this family, and nobody appreciates what I do.

JERRY: Is that what you were trying to tell your father, Susan? Did he hear you right?

SUSAN [turning to Jerry]: No.

JERRY: Would you mind telling your father what you'd like from him?

SUSAN [with tears in her eyes]: Dad, it's not that we don't appreciate how hard you work. It's just that I never hear anything nice from you.

MARY: Susan, if you could have one thing different with your father, what would that be?

SUSAN: That we could do something together without getting into a fight.

MARY: How would that be for you, dad?

JOHN: Well, if I could find the time, I'd like to do more with Susan.

MARY: If you could find the time, what would you like to do with Susan?

JOHN: I don't know. What does a father do with a 17-year-old daughter?

MARY: Why don't you ask her?

JOHN [looking at Susan, after a long pause]: Well, what do you think?

SUSAN: We could go to a movie.

MARY: Is that something that you'd like to do with Susan?

JOHN: Yeah, if we could ever agree on a movie.

MARY: It sounds good, and I hope the two of you will make the time to talk with each other about what both of you want. [She turns to Adam.] Adam, what would you like to say about yourself?

ADAM: I think it's unfair that my family picks on me.

MARY: Who in this room picks on you, and would you tell them directly?

ADAM: Susan, you've been picking on me. And Jennifer just sits around and smiles. And, well [fidgeting and looking to the floor], Dad has been upset with me a lot lately and . . .

JOHN [interrupting]: When have I been upset with you that you haven't deserved it?

RUTH [interrupting and turning to John]: I think you ought to leave Adam alone.

MARY: Ruth, how about letting John speak for himself. [She looks to John.] What would you like to say to Adam?

JOHN: I feel that everyone is picking on me, and it's getting me mad! We're supposed to be here for Ruth, not me!

JERRY: John, I can understand that you might feel as if you're being picked on. But another way to look at this is by considering that what they're telling you is a sign that they trust you enough to be open and honest with you about their feelings. Maybe these are things that they haven't been able to express to you until now.

JOHN: Well . . . I don't know . . . But I do want my kids to be able to talk to me.

JERRY: John, if you could be more open with them, that would allow them to be more open with you. A short time ago, Adam said some things to you, and you seemed to be very emotionally moved. Is there anything you'd like to say to Adam?

JOHN: It's very difficult to hear what you had to say, Adam. [He turns to Jerry laughingly.] Did I do it right this time?

JERRY [smiling]: I hope you'll continue to talk. [He addresses all the family members except for Ruth.] Several of you have mentioned that your mother's counseling has affected your lives. Some of you have even said that you felt abandoned by her. Would each of you be willing to talk to your mother?

SUSAN: Mom, it's hard to see you being different. I was so used to you taking such an interest in us and doing so much for us, but I guess you have a life of your own, too.

ROB: I think you're right on, Susan!

JOHN: I think Susan has made a good point.

ADAM: Mother, I miss you not sticking up for me more.

JENNIFER: I like talking like this. We never do this at home, and we're not even fighting right now.

MARY [turning to Ruth]: How is it to hear what is being said to you?

RUTH: It feels good to see my family talking about themselves and realizing that I don't have to take so much care of them anymore.

JERRY: Our time is almost up, but before we close I'd like to ask each of you if there are reasons you might want to return.

All of the family members feel that it is important to return, because they like what has happened during the session. They are all agreeable to attending another session next week. Mary then explains to them the value of doing some homework before the next session. Because the family members are open to this idea, she suggests the following assignments.

- For Ruth: "Avoid interfering when each child is attempting to interact with John."
- For Susan and John: "Decide on an activity that you're willing to do together before the next session."
- For Rob: "Take some more time to let your father know what you'd like with him. It's important that you don't tell him how *he* should be different, but instead talk about yourself with him."
- For Jennifer: "Take the initiative to ask your mother to do something with you before next week, such as going shopping or spending 20 minutes."
- For Ruth and John: "Be aware of how often you fight about the children, and when you do focus on one of the children, try instead to talk about yourselves to each other."

The family members are asked if they have any objections to these assignments and if they would be willing to follow through with them before next week. All feel that they can complete the assignments.

Process Commentary

Mary and I set out to observe the structure of the family by (1) allowing the members to sit where they wanted and (2) attempting to get a clearer picture of the family's transactional patterns. We assume, in observing this structure, that Ruth's change has produced stress in the spousal subsystem. Because Ruth and John have been unable to discuss the sources of this stress, they have detoured their tensions onto their youngest child, Adam. Ruth's changes have also led to stress between this spousal subsystem and the sibling subsystem (Rob, Jennifer, Susan, and Adam). According to family therapy, if change occurs in one part of the system, change will occur in other parts. In other words, change in Ruth has affected the equilibrium of this family. Thus, it is important to have a system enter treatment so that the change that occurs is productive for the system as well as the individual.

In this family there is an overdependency among family members. They lack a clear sense of their individuality and roles in the family. Families such as this are prone to conflict and confusion, and the behavior of one member (in this case, Ruth) immediately affects the other members of the family.

Through individual therapy Ruth is learning not to maintain her role as peacemaker. As a result the other family members are being forced to learn to deal with one another. Up to this session they have been increasing the conflict among themselves in order to bring Ruth back into her previous role as mediator. In family-therapy terms this is known as an attempt to maintain homeostasis.

This system (family) is relatively functional. Its members were able to make some strides in communicating in the session, especially considering that they have not expressed their own feelings with one another as a general rule. Even John demonstrated some flexibility by his willingness to consider my suggestion that the children were not showing disrespect to him when they shared their feelings.

Mary had a specific purpose in mind when she used the strategy of suggesting homework assignments. It is important that families work on issues outside of therapy as well as during therapy. In this way they can observe that they have the strength to make their own changes. By taking this responsibility they empower themselves. The only family member not given an assignment was Adam. This was an attempt to keep the other family members' focus away from him and onto themselves.

This family has an excellent chance of making structural changes. These include:

- being able to become more direct with one another
- taking the focus off of Adam as the source of the problem
- adjusting to Ruth's changes
- becoming more independent themselves

It is likely that future sessions will not always include the entire family. Rather, therapy may include parts of the system (John and Rob), the spousal subsystem (Ruth and John), or the sibling subsystem (Rob, Jennifer, Susan, and Adam). John appears to be having trouble adjusting to Ruth's independence. He was reared to be a traditional husband and to take care of the family financially. Ruth is asking him to change his perception of this traditional role. Obviously, he has a hard time sharing or accepting feelings or feedback from other family members. He may not have revealed to Ruth his innermost feelings about how her changes are affecting him.

This brief illustration and discussion of family therapy cannot begin to capture the complexity of working with families. For teaching purposes Mary and I have condensed into this initial meeting what might have taken place during several sessions. In an initial session a family therapist might not have made as many structural moves, such as asking members to be more direct with one another. Instead, he or she would have spent more time watching the family members interact in their typical mode. Moreover, many families might not have made as many productive interactions as this family did during the initial session. It should be noted that a typical family in today's society is not intact, as Ruth's is. For example, many families are of the following types: single-parent family, stepfamily, and reconstituted family. However, family therapy is a useful modality regardless of the family structure.

Mary and I want you to become aware of how the individual you are counseling can be affected by others. Also, other people are frequently affected by the client's changes. If you fail to address other parts of a person's system, you can easily miss crucial dynamics that will have lasting effects on your client and those in the client's life. We hope that you get a sense of how integral family therapy is in the treating of an individual and that you seriously consider this approach when counseling individuals.

If you are not qualified to treat families, Mary and I recommend that you refer appropriate clients to a family therapist and work closely with him or her. If family therapy is not your area of expertise, you could also consider co-leading family groups with a qualified family therapist as I did with Mary in this example. Course work and supervision in family therapy are some steps you can take to learn more about the practice of this fruitful approach to understanding the individual in a system.

Questions for Reflection

At this point consider the following questions:

1. What differences do you see between working with Ruth in individual counseling and using family therapy? Do you think that including her

family in a few sessions will promote or inhibit her progress in individual therapy?

2. If Ruth were your client, what advantages and disadvantages might there be if you discontinued seeing her individually and instead met with her and John as a couple on a regular basis? or met with the entire family and focused on changes within the system?
3. What possible ethical issues are involved if you do not suggest family therapy for Ruth, given clear indications that some of her problems stem from conflicts within her family? or that her family relationships are being affected by her work in individual therapy?
4. If you were to be involved in family therapy in this case, whom would you consider your primary client? Would your client be the family as a system? Ruth? John? Jennifer? Adam? Susan? Rob? Can you see any ethical binds if you develop an alliance with certain members of this family?
5. How do you think that your own relationships in your family of origin might either help or hinder you in working with this family? Can you see any possible sources of countertransference? If you become aware that you have unfinished business with either your family of origin or your present family, what course would you probably take?
6. If you were working with this family, with whom might you be most inclined to form an alliance? With which person do you think you would have the most difficulty in working, and why?
7. What do you think you would do if the tension within Ruth's family increased as she continued to make changes for herself? If she decided to file for a divorce or said that she intended to leave her family, what reactions would you have?
8. At this point in your professional development, how ready are you to work with the entire family? If Ruth requested either marital therapy or family therapy and if you did not feel competent in these areas, what would you say to her?
9. Do you see any difference between individual counseling and family therapy in their goals for therapy? Do you notice any differences between the interventions that were made in these family sessions and those in her individual sessions?
10. If you and Ruth were from different cultures, what factors would you as a family therapist want to address with both her and the members of her family? What role might cultural factors play in understanding the structure of this family? How might the interventions you make vary depending on the cultural background of the family involved in the therapeutic process?

WORKING WITH RUTH FROM A MULTICULTURAL PERSPECTIVE

I discussed Ruth and other cases in this book with Jerome Wright, Ph.D., a colleague who teaches human services and counseling at California State

University at Fullerton, specializing in courses in cultural diversity. Dr. Wright conceived of a way to encourage the students in a graduate course to appreciate the subtle aspects of working with cultural themes in the lives of clients. He gave Ruth's case to his students and asked them to form small study groups to research the cultural variables that would apply to Ruth if she were from each of these ethnic groups: Asian American, Hispanic, Black, and Native American. The students were also asked to think of issues that would be involved if she were being counseled from a feminist perspective and special issues to consider if she were a lesbian. Each of the study groups had the freedom to present its findings in any way it saw fit, so long as the members did so as a group. I attended my colleague's class for two weeks and heard each of the group's presentations. Some did role-playing situations, others invited guest speakers who represented the group they were studying, and others found interesting ways to involve the class in their presentation. I was impressed with the value of this approach in teaching multicultural awareness to counseling students, and it gave me some new ideas for the revision of Ruth's case. Before exploring themes in her life and demonstrating my eclectic approach to working with her, I'd like to raise a few issues that should be considered if she and her therapist were from different cultural backgrounds. Issues such as race, ethnicity, gender, age, socioeconomic status, religion, lifestyle, and sexual orientation are crucial when establishing a therapeutic relationship with clients.

Becoming immersed in the study of cultural diversity is not without its dangers, however. There is a problem in accepting stereotypes and applying general characteristics of a particular group to every individual within that group. Indeed, the differences among individuals within a given ethnic group can be as great as the differences between various populations. What is important to keep in mind is that knowledge about the client's culture provides counselors with a conceptual framework that they can use in making interventions. But knowledge of a client's cultural values is only the beginning. Counselors need to be aware of the ways in which their own culture has influenced their current behavior. It is especially important that counselors be aware of their assumptions and biases and how these factors are likely to influence the manner in which they work with clients who differ culturally from them. Counseling across cultures is personally demanding, but it can also be exciting.

A guiding principle that I try to build into my practice is that I allow my client to teach me what is relevant to our relationship. It would be impossible for me to have comprehensive and in-depth knowledge of the cultural backgrounds of all of my clients. However, it is not unrealistic to expect my client to teach me about those aspects of his or her culture that are important for us to attend to in our work together. I have become convinced that universal human themes unite people in spite of whatever factors differentiate them. Regardless of our culture, we have a need to receive and give love, to make sense of our psychological pain, and to make significant connections with others. Besides these universal themes that transcend culture there are also specific cultural values of which we need to be aware as we are counseling people of other cultures. This discussion is not limited merely to cultural differences but to any kind of difference between the counselor and client that has the capacity to create a gap in understanding. Thus, differences in age, gender, lifestyle, socioeconomic status, religion, and sexual orientation are all essential to explore within the context of the client/therapist relationship.

The Many Faces of Ruth

Let's assume that Ruth is an Asian American. Depending on her degree of acculturation, I would want to know something about the values of her country of origin. I may anticipate that she has one foot in her old culture and another foot in her new one. She may experience real conflicts, feeling neither fully Asian nor fully American, and at some points she may be uncertain about the way to integrate the two aspects of her life. She may be slow to disclose personal material, but this is not necessarily a reflection of her unwillingness to cooperate with the counseling venture. Rather, her reluctance to express her feelings is likely to reflect a cultural tradition that has encouraged her to be emotionally reserved. Knowing something about her case and about her background, I am aware that shame and guilt play a significant role in her behavior. Talking about family matters is often considered to be something shameful and to be avoided. Furthermore, in her culture stigma and shame may arise over experiencing psychological distress and feeling the need for professional help.

As another example, consider the importance of accurately interpreting nonverbal behavior. Let's assume now that Ruth is Hispanic and that she is cautious in attempting to maintain eye contact because her therapist is a man. I would probably err if I assumed that this behavior reflected resistance or evasiveness. Instead, she is behaving in ways that she thinks are polite, for direct eye contact could be seen as disrespectful. Also, I would need to be patient while developing a working alliance with her. As is true of many ethnic groups, Hispanics have a tendency to reveal themselves more slowly than do many Anglo clients. Again, this does not mean that Ruth is being defensive, but it can reflect different cultural norms. She may not relate well to a high level of directness, because in her culture she has learned to express herself in more indirect ways.

If Ruth were a Native American and if I were unfamiliar with her culture, I could err by interpreting her quiet behavior as a sign that she was stoic and unemotional. Actually, she may have good reason to be emotionally contained, especially during the initial meeting with a non-Indian. Her mistrust does not have to be a sign of paranoia; rather, it can be a realistic reaction based on numerous experiences that have conditioned her to be cautious. If I did not know enough about Ruth's culture, it would be ethically imperative that I either learn some of its basic aspects or that I refer her to a counselor who was culturally skilled in this area. I don't burden myself with the unrealistic standard that I should know everything. It would be acceptable to admit to her that I lacked knowledge about her culture and then proceed to find a way to remedy this situation. Openness with a client can certainly be the foundation for a good relationship. Ruth can educate me about what would be important to know about her cultural background.

If Ruth is a member of a minority group, as distinct from being a member of the WASP majority, she is likely to have encountered her share of discrimination based on being different. This factor will need to be addressed if her counselor is of a different ethnic or racial group. As a Black, Hispanic, American Indian, Asian American, or Pacific Islander, Ruth will share the experience of institutional oppression. She will know what it means to struggle for empowerment. Chances are that being both a woman and a member of one of these minority groups, she will experience a compounding of the problems that have previously been described in her case. This experience is bound to be reflected in the dynamics of our therapeutic relationship. I will need to somehow demonstrate my good faith and my ability to enter her world and understand the nature of her concerns. If I ignore these very real cultural realities, the chances are that she will not stay in therapy with me very long. However, I cannot emphasize enough the guiding principle of letting her provide me with the clues for the direction of therapy. In our initial encounter I will want to know what it was like for her to come to the office and why she is there. Rather than having prior conceptions of what we should be doing in this venture, I will ask her what she wants and why she is seeking help from me at this time in her life. If cultural issues are present, I expect that they will emerge very soon if I am listening sensitively to her and attempting to understand her world. As you read about the themes in Ruth's life in the following pages, be aware of how cultural variations could easily be woven into the fabric of the counseling process.

Questions for Reflection

At this point consider the following questions:

1. If your cultural background and life experiences are very different from Ruth's, do you see it as presenting any particular problems in establishing a therapeutic relationship? If you do differ from her on any of these dimensions—race, culture, ethnicity, socioeconomic status, value systems, religion, lifestyle, or sexual orientation—would you feel a need to discuss these differences with her? From your perspective might any of these differences incline you to refer her to another therapist? If you were to make a referral, what are the ethical and legal considerations?

2. In examining your own belief system and life experiences, do you think you would have any difficulty working therapeutically with any particular racial, ethnic, or cultural group? If you expect that you might have difficulty, what are your concerns, and what might you do about them?
3. What specific aspects about each culture do you feel a need to understand in order to develop a therapeutic alliance and work effectively with a client? If you do not have this knowledge, how could you go about acquiring it?
4. From your perspective how important is it that you be like your client in each of the following areas: age? gender? race? ethnicity? culture? socioeconomic status? religion? values? sexual orientation? education? marital status? family status?
5. How would you respond if a client said to you that he or she would not see you because you were from a different cultural or ethnic background?
6. Are you aware of referral sources for clients from various ethnic and cultural backgrounds? If so, what are they? If not, how could you find out about such referrals?
7. If you and Ruth were from different cultures and if you had to select one to three theoretical orientations from which to work with Ruth, which approaches might you select? Why?

THEMES IN RUTH'S LIFE

A few of the major themes that have therapeutic potential for further exploration are revealed in the following statements that Ruth made at one time or another:

1. "You seem so distant and removed from me. You're hard to reach."
2. "In spite of my best attempts, I still feel a lot of guilt that I haven't done enough."
3. "I just don't trust myself to find my own answers to life."
4. "I'm afraid to change for fear of breaking up my marriage."
5. "It's hard for me to ask others for what I want."
6. "I feel extremely tense, and I can't sleep at night."
7. "All my life I've tried to get my father's approval."
8. "It's hard for me to have fun. I'm so responsible."
9. "I've always had a weight problem, and I can't seem to do much about it."
10. "I'm afraid to make mistakes and look like a fool."
11. "My daughter and I just don't get along with each other."
12. "I give and give, and they just take and take."
13. "I've lived by the expectations of others for so long that I don't know what I want anymore."

14. "I don't think my marriage is the way it should be, but my husband thinks it's just fine."
15. "I'm afraid to tell my husband what I really want with him, because I'm afraid he'll leave me."
16. "I fear punishment because I've given up my old religious values."
17. "I wear so many hats that sometimes I feel worn out."
18. "There's not enough time for me to be doing all the things I know I should be doing."
19. "I'm afraid of my feelings toward other men."
20. "When my children leave, I'll have nothing to live for."

Look over the list of Ruth's statements above. Select the ones that you find most interesting. Here are three suggestions for working with them: (1) For each of the themes you select, show how you would begin working with Ruth from *each* of the nine perspectives. (2) If you prefer, take only two contrasting approaches and focus on these. (3) You might want to attempt to combine several therapeutic models and work with Ruth using this synthesis.

Attempt to work with a few of Ruth's statements *before* reading about my eclectic way of working with her in this chapter. *After* you have read the examples provided below and after you have completed the chapter, you could return to a few of her statements and try your hand at working with her again. This would make interesting and lively material for role playing and discussion in small groups. One person can "become" Ruth while others in the group counsel her from the vantage point of several different therapeutic perspectives. Practicing a variety of approaches will assist you in discovering for yourself ways to pull together techniques that you consider to be the best.

Below I select four of Ruth's themes and show how several therapeutic perspectives could be applied to each.

Theme: "I'm Afraid of My Feelings toward Other Men"

Psychoanalytic therapist's perspective

RUTH: I'm afraid of my feelings toward other men.
THERAPIST: What feelings come up as you think about men?
RUTH: Wanting to be close, but afraid of being put down.
THERAPIST: And being close would involve what?
RUTH: Oh, I'd be held, but I'd have to watch out that is doesn't go too far too fast.
THERAPIST: So you want to have a relationship with a man, but you're afraid of what might happen if you do. You're scared something will go wrong.
RUTH: Yes, and then I would feel as if I had caused it to go bad.

Then the analyst can ask Ruth to identify the roots of the theme embodied in her statement. The therapist will also make appropriate and timely interpretations. In this situation an interpretation could be that her emotions involving other men are resulting in guilt feelings that are related to her feelings toward her father.

TA therapist's perspective

RUTH: I'm afraid of my feelings toward other men.
THERAPIST: When you have feelings such as these, whose voices do you hear?
RUTH: My parents'.
THERAPIST: Whose voice is stronger?
RUTH: My father's.
THERAPIST: Quickly, without rehearsing, what are all the things he tells you?
RUTH: Don't be sexual. Don't feel. Sex is sacred and for marriage only. Don't have fun. Don't let me down. Don't shame the family.
THERAPIST: How old do you feel right now?

The therapist is pursuing early injunctions and helping her identify the ego states in which she is functioning.

Gestalt therapist's perspective

RUTH: I'm afraid of my feelings toward other men.
THERAPIST: I'm a man. How do you feel toward me? [A long silence follows.] Your face is flushed. Your hands are shaking. What are you experiencing now?
RUTH: I want to run and hide.
THERAPIST: Why don't you do that? Where do you want to run to?
RUTH: Behind the couch.
THERAPIST: OK, go over there and talk to me from there.
RUTH: Now I really feel foolish.
THERAPIST: So tell me about that.

The therapist stays in here now and goes with what is obvious, and he makes some assumptions. Rather than talking about other men outside, he focuses the attention on the fact that he is a man and makes the assumption that she may have feelings toward him because of their special relationship. He pays attention to her body language, makes no interpretations, and lets her tell him what her body language means. He does not push her to talk about her feelings toward him but goes with the flow of her feelings of foolishness.

Behavior therapist's perspective

RUTH: I'm afraid of my feelings toward other men.
THERAPIST: What feelings?
RUTH: Well, you know! [silence]

THERAPIST: No, I don't know.
RUTH: Well, I'm scared of my sexual feelings.
THERAPIST: Can you give an example of some recent sexual feelings?
RUTH: Well, I find one of the men in my class very attractive.
THERAPIST: And what do you do?
RUTH: Nothing—I avoid him.
THERAPIST: What would you like to do?
RUTH: I would like talk to him, but I'm too scared.
THERAPIST: Close your eyes and imagine you're in that class. He sits in the chair next to you. What are you thinking, and what do you want to do? List some of the things that you want to say to him.
RUTH: [She makes a list.]
THERAPIST: Out of this list, is there anything you'd be willing to say to him directly by next week?
RUTH: I'd be willing to say hello.
THERAPIST: Good, that's a start.

The therapist is paying attention to her lack of assertiveness and is establishing levels of fear and avoidance. After formulating specific plans the therapist would help her role-play assertive behaviors to be carried out in the real world.

Rational-emotive therapist's perspective

RUTH: I'm afraid of my feelings toward other men.
THERAPIST: And what are these feelings?
RUTH: Well, ah—sexual ones.
THERAPIST: So what about these sexual feelings?
RUTH: You know—you shouldn't have such feelings, especially if you're married.
THERAPIST: Why not? Where is it written?
RUTH: You shouldn't, because having sexual feelings could lead to something.
THERAPIST: You're *shoulding* on yourself. Where did you get all those "shoulds"?
RUTH: Well, my parents told me all my life . . .
THERAPIST: Just because your parents told you that you shouldn't have sexual feelings doesn't mean they're unquestionably right. I wonder what stops you from examining more closely what they told you and why you don't think and decide for yourself. Do you really accept everything that they told you? How does this affect your life?

Ruth is being challenged to critically evaluate beliefs that she clings to and now reindoctrinates herself with. Specifically, the challenge is to confront the irrational idea that having feelings of sexual attraction will actually lead to having sex, which she is implying. The therapist is likely to instruct Ruth to carry out a homework assignment to confront her fears. She could be asked to approach three men in her classes whom she finds attractive and then proceed to initiate a conversation with them. She is confronting an anxiety-producing situation in the hope that she will discover that her catastrophic expectations are groundless.

Theme: "You Seem So Distant and Removed from Me. You're Hard to Reach"

Person-centered therapist's perspective

RUTH: You seem so distant and removed . . .

THERAPIST: I hear you saying that it's hard for you to get close to me and that I'm contributing a lot to that.

RUTH: Yeah, and in some ways I just feel removed from you. Like you're way up there, and I can't reach you.

THERAPIST: So I'm above you, and we don't have equal standing.

RUTH: I suppose if I knew more about you, I might feel closer to you.

THERAPIST: Somehow knowing me would reduce that distance. I wish you did feel closer to me.

The therapist's rationale is that accurate reflection is assumed to lead to clarification, identification, expression, and deeper self-exploration of feelings. This therapist is likely to engage in relevant self-disclosure as a way to facilitate Ruth's self-exploration.

Existential therapist's perspective

RUTH: You seem so distant and removed . . .

THERAPIST: I'm surprised to hear you say that, since I like you and feel very open to you.

RUTH: Really? Well, somehow that didn't come across to me.

THERAPIST: I'm a little uncomfortable with the way you see me, but I'm glad you feel free enough to bring this up. I encourage you to go further with this, because I see it as an important issue.

The therapist engages in appropriate self-disclosure and facilitates Ruth's discussion of how she sees and feels about their relationship. This relationship is what is central, not any technique that he might come up with at this point.

Psychoanalytic therapist's perspective

RUTH: You seem so distant and removed . . .

THERAPIST: Hmm . . . [pausing pensively]

RUTH: See, you don't tell me much. I feel as if you're judging me now.

THERAPIST: Is that a feeling you've had often before?

A noncommital response is fostering the transference. The assumption is that Ruth is in some ways projecting onto the therapist qualities she felt toward other significant people in her life, particularly her father. The therapist will encourage her to express her feelings and then eventually interpret her reactions.

Gestalt therapist's perspective

RUTH: You seem so distant and removed . . .

THERAPIST: If you were to move me physically right now, where would I be that would express how you see me in relationship to you?

RUTH: You'd be standing on top of your mahogany desk, looking down on me.

THERAPIST [standing on the desk and looking down on Ruth]: And how is it for you to look up at me?

The therapist is going with the clue Ruth has provided and is exaggerating a feeling. He may have her talk to him from below, he may ask her to guess what he is thinking and feeling about her, and so forth. He is likely to follow leads that she provides and ask her to get involved in experiments to see what she can learn about herself. His aim will be for her to take responsibility for her own feelings of distance, rather than making him responsible for how she feels.

Rational-emotive therapist's perspective

RUTH: You seem so distant and removed . . .

THERAPIST: And what would be so terrible if I didn't feel close to you?

RUTH: Well, I wouldn't like that. I want you to like me and feel close to me. I want your approval.

THERAPIST: This is just the type of thinking that's getting and keeping you in trouble. You think others must like and approve of you.

The therapist will show Ruth how her irrational beliefs about the necessity of being liked and approved of are now contributing to the negative feelings she has and how such beliefs stop her from taking many actions in the real world. The challenge will be for her to risk being not liked and not approved of.

Theme: "When My Children Leave, I'll Have Nothing to Live For"

For this theme, the probable approach of therapists from all nine disciplines is summarized in Table 11-1.

Table 11-1. How nine therapists might deal with Ruth's concern about her children's leaving

Theory	*Therapist's General Direction*
Psychoanalytic therapy	Therapist may focus on unconscious meanings of children in Ruth's life. What are her fears of being without her children? How does taking care of her children ward off anxiety?
Adlerian therapy	Therapist may work with Ruth's general purpose in life. What are her goals? What are her strivings? How has she made a lifestyle of taking care of and serving others? Focus could also be on what she learned in her parents' family.
Existential therapy	Therapist may want to share his or her experiences and views with Ruth. They will engage in dialogue, as the client/therapist relationship is central in helping her search for a meaning in life. How will she create meaning without children?
Person-centered therapy	Therapist trusts that Ruth can find her own direction, that she will be able to establish a new meaning in her life once her children leave. This approach will stress listening and understanding as she shares her struggles and fears.
Gestalt therapy	Therapist is likely to ask what Ruth is experiencing now as she reports that she will have nothing to live for when her children are gone. Direction depends on the verbal and nonverbal clues that she provides. If she begins to cry, therapist may ask her to stay with her tears and feel fully whatever she is experiencing.
Transactional analysis	Therapist is likely to explore messages that Ruth has accepted about being a mother. What early decisions did she make about her worth as a person apart from serving others? How is taking care of her children fitting into her life script? Does she want to make a new decision? What kind of contract is she willing to make?
Behavior therapy	Therapist may zero in more carefully on what it specifically means to Ruth that she "will have nothing to live for" when her children are gone. Concrete goals need to be established, and only then can treatment proceed.
RET and other cognitive-behavioral approaches	Therapist is likely to challenge Ruth's beliefs about having no purpose in living. What assumptions is she making? Are they rational and realistic? Focus will be on how her thinking influences her feelings, not just on dealing with the children's leaving.
Reality therapy	Therapist may get Ruth to look at what rewards she receives from living for her children. She will be helped to determine if such behavior is working well for her. If she determines that she would like to find meaning apart from her children, therapist will work with her to develop a plan that will lead to doing something else.

Adlerian therapist's perspective

RUTH: When my children leave, I'll have nothing to live for.

THERAPIST: How did you get to the point that you would make such a statement? What does making such a statement do for you?

RUTH: Well, all my life I've lived for my children.

THERAPIST: How have you done this?

RUTH: I've always been more interested in them than myself. I've worked very hard to make life better for them than I had it. I've never made time for myself.

THERAPIST: It sounds to me as if once your children leave, you'll have a lot of time for yourself.

RUTH [unenthusiastically]: Yeah, I know.

THERAPIST: How is it that having more time for yourself in the future is making you sad rather than excited?

RUTH: When they're gone, I'm afraid there will be a void.

THERAPIST: So together let's be creative and see how we can fill this void. As a starter, how would you finish this sentence? "Something I always wanted to do and never had time for is . . ." [This therapist is interested in Ruth's goals for her future. Rather than going with her sense of discouragement, the counselor emphasizes creating new goals that will give meaning to life. The encouragement process helps her formulate new purposes to replace values that are no longer functional.]

RUTH: Something I always wanted to do and never had time for is going hiking and camping in the Smoky Mountains with friends.

THERAPIST: Awhile back, I saw seven out of ten waterfalls in the Smokies on a one-day hike I took with a friend. So this sounds good to me. I'm wondering what has stopped you from doing this.

RUTH: Hmm—I don't even know if I have any friends who would want to do that with me.

THERAPIST: Do you have any idea how you could find out?

RUTH: I suppose I could ask them.

THERAPIST: When are you going to do so, and whom will you ask?

The therapist is pursuing the importance of *social interest,* which Ruth has neglected. This would be a good place to continue discussing ways that she could become reacquainted with old friends, make new friends, and broaden her interests.

Reality therapist's perspective

RUTH: When my children leave, I'll have nothing to live for.

THERAPIST: What are you living for now?

RUTH: My children, of course. For years I've lived for them and done everything I could for them. [Ruth then goes on, with much energy, listing all the ways in which she has been a devoted mother.]

THERAPIST: Stop, Ruth. It's not very helpful to you to talk about how you've been in the past. What's more important is for you to take a look at what you're *doing now.* If your behavior isn't bringing about the results you want, we can talk about how you'll change.

RUTH: But I don't know what to do differently.

THERAPIST: Well, first of all, do you really want to change the way things are?

The therapist does not let Ruth bemoan the past but quickly gets her to look at how well her present behavior is working for her. Once she makes the decision that her life is not the way she wants it, therapy can begin. She first determines what she wants to change, and then together they make realistic plans pertaining to the "what," "how," and "when" of these changes. It is essential that she make a commitment to follow through with her plans.

Existential therapist's perspective

RUTH: When my children leave, I'll have nothing to live for.

THERAPIST: I know what you mean. I myself have had to struggle with finding a new purpose to life after having lost someone.

RUTH: They're not even gone yet, and I'm already missing them.

THERAPIST: Tell me some of the ways in which you'll miss them.

RUTH: I'll miss hearing about their ups and downs. Even my sons come to me with their problems and want my advice. And when they're gone . . . [After a heavy silence she tearfully continues.] It's so hard to let them go.

THERAPIST: I know, it never is easy.

RUTH: It feels good that you understand.

THERAPIST: And I'm glad I can be with you.

The therapist here offers the gift of presence and understanding and engages in selected self-disclosure.

TA therapist's perspective

RUTH: When my children leave, I'll have nothing to live for.

THERAPIST: What tape are you playing now?

RUTH: Without my kids I'm nothing.

THERAPIST: How is this tape working for you?

RUTH: Not very well. It's just that I feel as if I want to die when I think of them gone from my life. Who will I be without them?

THERAPIST: You say your decision to live for your children isn't paying off for you. Do you want to make a different tape?

RUTH: It just seems so hard. I'm not sure I can get rid of these voices in my head. Sometimes I get so down I just don't want to be alive anymore.

THERAPIST: Can you tell me more?

RUTH: It's hard for me to talk about, because some of my thoughts scare me. You know, sometimes it seems that life is so complicated, and I wonder what it would be like if I didn't have to struggle anymore.

THERAPIST: Have you thought about ways you would end your life?

RUTH: Not really. It's just a fleeting thought. You know, I would never actually take my own life.

The therapist attempts to establish whether she is seriously suicidal by asking further questions pertaining to her fantasies as well as any previous suicidal plans or attempts.

Theme: "I Had a Dream Last Week That I Want to Share"

Rational-emotive therapist's perspective

RUTH: I had a dream last week that I want to share. I was in San Francisco. I think I was with my brother-in-law. There were some other people in the dream. I think my kids were there. I was walking up a very steep street. It was very dangerous. I was afraid I was going to fall. I kept on going up. Nobody else seemed to be scared. The street ended at the top of the hill against a house. The only way I could cross the street was to hold onto holes and handles on the house wall. It was very scary. The handles seemed to come loose, and there were things in the holes. One time I thought I saw a snake, but I'm not sure. I think there were spiders. I was afraid and I wondered why I was putting myself through this. I was looking inside a window, and I saw a man in there reading. I wondered if he would be mad at me for intruding on his privacy. But he didn't look at me, and I didn't know who it was. When I finally crossed the street, I realized that I had left my purse on the other side. I again walked across to get my purse. I wondered why I was all alone and where everyone else had gone. There was something else about a funeral procession that I was going to watch, but I don't remember any more.

THERAPIST: Well, for the life of me, I don't know why you're telling me all this. Is this the way you want to spend your money in here?

RUTH: That makes me mad. Why did you listen to my dream if you weren't interested in it?

THERAPIST: Well, frankly I wasn't really listening, but *you* seemed to enjoy it. [It is obvious that this therapist is not therapeutically interested in listening to her dreams and is willing to let her know about his lack of interest and boredom.]

RUTH: Now I feel horrible. I shouldn't have gotten mad at you.

THERAPIST: Why not?

RUTH: You know what you're doing. And besides, I feel foolish.

THERAPIST: You mean you have no right to get angry at me? And what's so bad about feeling foolish? I know you don't feel great right now, but is the world going to end because of what just happened?

The therapist changes direction away from the dream and toward her beliefs about expressing anger and feeling foolish.

Gestalt therapist's perspective

RUTH: I had a dream.
THERAPIST [interrupting]: Ruth, continue telling me the dream, but speak as if it were happening right now.

The therapist listens to the dream, paying close attention to Ruth's non-verbals. She notices that Ruth shows the most emotion on realizing that everyone has gone and that she is all alone. The therapist brings her back to that moment and asks her to relive it. She instructs Ruth to talk out loud to the people who have left her, telling them how she feels. Later on, she asks Ruth to "become" those people who are not there and let them speak to Ruth. The therapist is tuned in to Ruth's emotional energy as a place to explore the dream. She goes not only with Ruth's energy but also with her own interest. None of the directions is right or wrong, for all aspects of Ruth's dream are a projection of herself. Ruth can learn a lot from giving voice to and "becoming" the people and the inanimate objects in the dream. The purse, the steep street, the holes, the handles, the things that she does not remember, the blocked-out funeral—all of these parts have significance. She will learn the meanings of her dream by becoming all these parts and acting them out. She discovers the meaning of her own dream, not the therapist's interpretation of it.

Psychoanalytic therapist's perspective

RUTH: [She recites the dream.]
THERAPIST: Ruth, you said something about a funeral in your dream, but you don't remember. Close your eyes and say whatever comes to mind.

The therapist encourages her to ramble without censoring while he pays close attention to any hesitancy on her part, changes in her voice, repetition of themes, and blockings. He is likely to be interested in the parts in her dream that she is not sure about or has forgotten, for to him these indicate resistance. The focus may be on the unknown man in the room or her fear of having interrupted him, the lack of certainty about her children and brother-in-law having been there, the snake and spiders that she thinks were there, the vague memory of the funeral, and so forth. He is likely to make interpretations about the symbolism of her dream, which will foster her insight into her unconscious fears and wishes. It is the therapist who points out parallels and meanings in Ruth's dream, rather than her.

Adlerian therapist's perspective

RUTH: [She recites the dream.]
THERAPIST: Does this dream fit into any of your other dreams?
RUTH: Yeah, I often have the feeling that I'm in dangerous situations, but I'm the only one who feels scared. Other people don't seem to think the situation is so dangerous.
THERAPIST: Are there any other patterns here that reoccur in your other dreams?
RUTH: I often forget parts of my dreams. There are many times that I feel left alone in my dreams. And I often wake up crying and scared.
THERAPIST: So there is some consistency with this and other dreams. Let's talk more about how your dream might be connected to the present course of your life.

The therapist sees dreams as purposeful, as reminders of what the person is about and what the person expects to do. Dreams are seen as valuable in that they are rehearsals for future behavior, and they express the unity and consistency of the individual. It is assumed that if Ruth wants to postpone action, she will forget the dream. Thus, attention could be directed to what actions she is hesitating over and what she is afraid of in her future. Identifying her dreams could serve the purpose of bringing problems to the surface and pointing to her movement in therapy.

MY APPROACH TO WORKING WITH RUTH

I will now work toward an integration of concepts and techniques from the various schools of therapy by demonstrating the progression of Ruth's counseling. I will then ask you to work with her by drawing particular aspects from each of the models and applying them to her.

Each therapy approach has something unique to offer in understanding Ruth. My attempt will be to use a combination of approaches by working with her on a *thinking, feeling,* and *behaving* basis. Table 11-2 shows what I am likely to borrow from each of the therapies as I conceptualize Ruth's case. As I describe how I imagine I would proceed with her, based on the information presented in her autobiography and the additional data from the nine theory chapters, I will make parenthetical comments that indicate from what theoretical orientations I am borrowing concepts and techniques in any given piece of work. Thus, in addition to seeing a sample of my style of working with Ruth, you will have a running commentary on what I am doing, why I am using particular techniques, and what directions I am going

Table 11-2. Major areas of focus in Ruth's therapy

Orientation	*Areas of Focus*
Psychoanalytic therapy	My focus will be on ways in which Ruth is repeating her early past in her present relationships. I have a particular interest in how she brings her experiences with her father into the session with me. I will concentrate on her feelings for me, because working with transference is a major way to produce insight. I am also interested in her dreams, any resistance that shows up in the sessions, and other clues to her unconscious processes. One of my main goals is to assist her in bringing to awareness buried memories and experiences, which I assume have a current influence on her.
Adlerian therapy	My focus is on determining what Ruth's lifestyle is. To do this, I will examine her early childhood experiences through her early recollections and family constellation. My main interest is in determining what her goals and priorities in life are. I assume that what she is striving toward is equally as valid as her past dynamics. Therapy will consist of doing a comprehensive assessment, helping her understand her dynamics, and then helping her define new goals.
Existential therapy	My focus is on challenging the meaning in Ruth's life. What does she want in her life? I am interested in the anxiety she feels, her emptiness, and the ways in which she has allowed others to choose for her. How can she begin to exercise her freedom? I assume that our relationship will be a key factor in helping her take actual risks in changing.
Person-centered therapy	I will avoid planning and structuring the sessions, because I trust Ruth to initiate a direction for therapy. If I listen, reflect, empathize, and respond to her, she will be able to clarify her struggles. Although she may be only dimly aware of her feelings at the beginning of therapy, she will move toward increased clarity as I accept her fully, without judgment. My main focus is on creating a climate of openness, trust, caring, understanding, and acceptance. Then she can use this relationship to move forward and grow.
Gestalt therapy	My focus will be on noticing signs of unfinished business for Ruth, as evidenced by ways in which she reaches impasses in her therapy. If she has never worked through her feelings of not being accepted, it is likely that these issues will appear in her therapy. I will ask her to bring them into the present by reliving them, rather than by merely talking about past events. I am mainly interested in helping her experience her feelings fully, instead of developing insight or speculating about why she behaves as she does. The key focus is on *how* she is behaving and *what* she is experiencing.

in. As you read, think about what you might do that is similar to or different from my approach.

Table 11-2. Major areas of focus in Ruth's therapy *(continued)*

Orientation	*Areas of Focus*
Transactional analysis	My focus will be on reviewing with Ruth the messages she received and the early decisions she made in response to those parental injunctions. I hope she will be able to understand the life script that was written for her by others, so that she can begin to write this script anew.
Behavior therapy	My initial focus is on doing a thorough assessment of Ruth's current behavior. I will ask her to monitor what she is doing so that we can have baseline data. We will then develop concrete goals to guide our work, and I will draw on a wide range of cognitive and behavioral techniques to help her achieve her goals—for example, stress-reduction techniques, assertion training, role rehearsals, modeling, coaching, systematic desensitization, and relaxation methods. I will stress learning new coping behaviors that she can use in everyday situations. She will practice these in our sessions and elsewhere.
RET and other cognitive-behavioral approaches	My interest will be focused on Ruth's internal dialogue and her thinking processes. I will uncover the ways in which she is creating her own misery through self-indoctrination and retention of beliefs that are not rational or functional. By use of Socratic dialogue, I will try to get her to spot her faulty thinking, to learn ways of correcting her distortions, and to substitute more effective self-statements and beliefs. I would be willing to use a wide range of cognitive, behavioral, and emotive techniques to accomplish our goals.
Reality therapy	Our focus will be guided by the principles of control therapy. First we will become friends, or work on our relationship. Key questions are "What are you doing now?" and "Is this behavior helping you?" Once Ruth has made a value judgment about her own current behavior, we will make plans. I will get a commitment from her to follow through with these plans and will never accept excuses.

Initial Stages of Work with Ruth

I often feel somewhat anxious as I think about meeting a new client. I wonder what the experience will be like, for both of us. I wonder to what degree I will be present for the person and how I might be instrumental in helping him or her become aware of the choices that are possible. I imagine that if I had read Ruth's autobiography before our initial session, I would feel excited about working with her. I like her ability to pinpoint many of her concerns, and the data she provides are rich with possibilities. From these data alone I do not have a clear idea of where our journey together will take us, for a lot will depend on *how far* she wants to go and *what* she is willing to explore. From the data alone, though, I do have many ideas of how I want to proceed.

Our beginning. I assume that Ruth, too, has some anxiety about initiating therapy. I want to provide her with the opportunity to talk about what it is like for her to come to the office today. That in itself provides the direction for part of our session. I surely want to get an idea of what has brought her to therapy. What is going on in her life that motivates her to seek therapy? What does she most hope for as a result of this venture? I structure the initial session so that she can talk about her expectations and about her fears, hopes, ambivalent feelings, and so forth. Because I will be an important part of the therapy process, I give her the chance to ask me personally and professionally how I will work with her. I do not believe in making therapy into a mysterious adventure. I think that clients have a right to know about the process that they are about to become involved with. Further, I think that Ruth will get more from her therapy if she knows how it works, if she knows the nature of her responsibilities and mine, and if she is clear on what she wants from this process. (This way of thinking is typical of models such as transactional analysis, Adlerian therapy, behavior therapy, rational-emotive therapy, and reality therapy.)

The contract. Again drawing on the above-mentioned models, I begin formulating a working contract, one that will give some direction to our sessions. As a part of this contract, I discuss what I see as my main responsibilities and functions, as well as Ruth's responsibilities in the process. I want her to know at the outset that I expect her to be an *active* party in this relationship, and I tell her that I function in an active and directive way (which is characteristic of most of the cognition/behavior/action-oriented therapies).

I see therapy as a significant project—an investment in the self, if you will—and I think that Ruth has a right to know what she can expect to gain as well as some of the potential risks. I begin by getting some sense of her goals, and though they are vague at first, I work with her to get them as specific and concrete as possible. (This process is especially important in TA, Adlerian therapy, behavior therapy, rational-emotive therapy, and reality therapy.) I will come back to goals in a bit.

Letting Ruth tell her story. I do not begin with a gathering of life-history data, though I do think this is important. I see value in first letting Ruth tell her story in the way she chooses. The way in which she walks into the office, her nonverbal language, her mannerisms, her style of speech, the details that she chooses to go into, and what she decides to relate and not to relate provide me with a valuable perspective from which to understand her. I am interested in how she perceives the events in her life and how she feels in her subjective world. (This is especially important in the existential and person-centered models.) If I do too much structuring initially, I interfere with her typical style of presenting herself. So I give everything to listening and letting her know what I am hearing (something that person-centered therapists put a premium on, and something I especially value in the initial stages of therapy). I want to avoid the tendency to talk too much during this initial session. It is not easy giving my full attention to Ruth, yet doing so will pay rich dividends in terms of the potential for therapy. If I listen well, I will get a good sense of what she is coming to therapy for. If I fail to listen accurately and sensitively, there is a risk of going with the first problem she states instead of waiting and listening to discover the depth of her experience.

Gathering data. I mentioned earlier that I would not begin the session by asking Ruth a series of questions pertaining to her life history. After letting her tell her story in her way, I ask questions to fill in the gaps. This method gives a more comprehensive picture of how she views her life now, as well as events that she considers significant in her past. Rather than making it a question-and-answer session, I like the idea of using an *autobiographical approach,* in which she writes about the critical turning points in her life, events from her childhood and adolescent years, relationships with parents and siblings, school experiences, current struggles, and future goals and aspirations, to mention a few. I ask her what she thinks would be useful for her to recall and focus on and what she imagines would be useful to me in gaining a better picture of her subjective world. In this way she does some reflecting and sorting out of life experiences outside of the session; she takes an active role in deciding what her personal goals will be for therapy; and I have access to rich material that will give me ideas of where and how to proceed with her. (This unstructured, or open-ended, autobiography could fit into existential and the person-centered models, in which the emphasis is on the subjective world of the client. Also, psychoanalytic practitioners would want to know a lot about her developmental history.)

In addition to asking Ruth to write an autobiography, I find value in a structured questionnaire in which she can complete sentences about the course of her life. (For such an exercise I use a modified version of the life-script questionnaire used in transactional analysis.) I suggest that Ruth do both the autobiography and the life-script questionnaire *at home.* Then, as a follow-up procedure, we discuss what this was like for her and anything that it brought up in her. This process helps her clarify issues that face her, and it gives me a clear picture of the life forces that have influenced her.

From the Adlerian perspective I am interested in getting background information about Ruth's experiences in her family. Of special interest are her early memories and her perceptions of her family life. I pay attention to the factors that shaped her style of life. We focus on her life goals and how she has sought ways to compensate for her perceived inferiority as a child. Together we summarize the material from her lifestyle assessment, interpret her basic mistakes, and discuss her assets as well as her limitations. Then we develop a contract to guide our work.

Therapy Proceeds

I favor integrating cognitive work into therapy sessions, and because I see therapy as a *learning* experience, I recommend some books to Ruth to supplement her therapy. These may include novels, books that deal with central areas of concern to her personally, and something on the nature of therapy. For example, I suggest that she read some books about women (and men) facing midlife crises, about parent/child relationships, about enhancing one's marriage, about sex, and about special topics related to her concerns. (This is consistent with approaches such as TA, behavior therapy, reality therapy, and, especially, rational-emotive therapy.) I find that this type of reading provides a good catalyst for self-examination, especially if these books are read in a *personal way*—meaning that Ruth would apply their themes to her life.

Clarifying therapy goals. During the beginning stages I assist Ruth in getting a clearer grasp of what she most wants from therapy, as well as seeing some steps she can begin to take in attaining her objectives. Like most clients she is rather global in stating her goals in her autobiography, so I work with her on becoming more concrete. When she looks in the mirror, Ruth says, she does not like what she sees. She would like to have a better self-image and be more confident. I am interested in knowing specifically *what* she does not like, the ways in which she now lacks confidence, and what it feels like for her to confront herself by looking at herself and talking to me about what she sees.

Ruth reports that she is unassertive and would like to be more assertive. She can be helped to pinpoint specific instances in which she is not assertive and to describe what she actually does or does not do in such circumstances and how she feels at these times. We consistently move from general to specific, for the more concrete she is, the greater are her chances of attaining what she wants. (It is from behavior therapy that I have learned the value of specifying goals. Also, TA stresses the necessity of a contract, which includes a clear statement of what the client wants from therapy.) I do not hold rigidly to the idea of a contract, although I do think that this is a good place to begin with Ruth. As therapy proceeds, then, we both have a frame of reference for evaluating the degree to which she is getting what she came to therapy for.

Importance of the client/therapist relationship. I am convinced that one of the most significant factors determining the degree to which Ruth will attain her goals is the therapeutic relationship that she and I will create. (This element is given primary emphasis in the person-centered, existential, Adlerian, and Gestalt approaches. Therapy is not seen as something that the therapist *does to* a passive client. It is much more than implementing skills and techniques. It is a deeply *personal* relationship that Ruth can use for her learning.) Thus, I think that the person who I am is just as important as my knowledge of counseling theory and the level of my skills. Although I see it as essential that I am able to use techniques effectively—and that I have a theoretical base from which to draw a range of techniques—this ability becomes meaningless in the absence of a relationship between Ruth and myself that is characterized by a mutual respect and trust. (I am influenced by the person-centered approach, which emphasizes the personal characteristics and attitudes of the therapist. Some questions I see as vital are the following: To what degree can I be real with Ruth? To what degree can I hear what she says and accept her in a nonjudgmental way? To what degree can I respect and care for her? To what degree can I allow myself to enter her subjective world? To what degree am I aware of my own experiencing as I am with her, and how willing am I to share my feelings and thoughts with her?) I can help her to the degree that I am authentic myself with her. This relationship is vital at the initial stages of therapy, but it must be maintained during all stages if therapy is to be effective.

Working with Ruth in Cognitive, Emotive, and Behavioral Ways

As I mentioned earlier, my eclectic style is a blend of concepts and techniques from many therapeutic approaches. As a basis for selecting techniques to employ with Ruth, I look at her as a *thinking, feeling,* and *behaving* person. Although for purposes of teaching in this illustration I may have to describe the various aspects of what I am doing separately, do keep in mind that I tend to work in an integrated fashion. Thus, I would *not* work with Ruth's cognitions, then move ahead to her feelings, and finally proceed to behaviors and specific action programs. All of these dimensions would be interrelated. When I am working with Ruth on a cognitive level (such as dealing with decisions she has made or one of her values), I am also concerned about the feelings generated in her at the moment and about exploring them with her. And in the background I am thinking of what she might actually *do* about the thoughts and feelings she is expressing. This *doing* would involve new behaviors that she can try in the session to deal with a problem and new skills that she can take outside and apply to problems that she encounters in real-life situations. (As a basis for this eclectic style of working with Ruth I am drawing on the cognitive and emotional insight-oriented approach of psychoanalysis; on the experiential therapies, which stress the expression and experiencing of feelings; on the cognitive therapies, which pay attention to the client's thinking processes that affect behavior and to beliefs; and to the action-oriented therapies, which stress the importance of creating a plan for behavioral change.)

Exploring Ruth's fears related to therapy. Ruth begins a session by talking about her fears of coming to know herself and by expressing her ambivalent feelings toward therapy:

RUTH: Before I made the decision to enter therapy, I had worked pretty hard at keeping problems tucked away neatly. I lived by compartmentalizing my life, and that way nothing became so fearsome that I felt overwhelmed. But this reading that I'm doing, writing in my journal, thinking about my life, talking about my feelings and experiences in here—all this is making me uncomfortable. I'm getting more and more anxious. I suppose I'm afraid of what I might find inside of me if I keep searching.

I see this anxiety as something realistic, and I surely do not want to merely reassure Ruth that everything will turn out for the best if she will only trust me and stay in therapy. I want to explore in depth with her the *decision* that she must *now* make. Looking at her life in an honest way is potentially frightening. There *are* risks attached to this process. Although Ruth has security now, she is paying the price in terms of boredom and low self-respect. Yet her restricted existence is a safe one. The attractions of getting to know herself better and the possibilities for exercising choice and control in her life can be very exciting, yet also frightening. At this point I hope that she will look at this issue and take a stand on how much she wants for herself and the risks that she is willing to take in reaching for more. The following dialogue between Ruth and me will give you a sense of how I pursue this issue:

RUTH: I want to stay in therapy, but I'm wondering if I want to go through all the pain I'm afraid I'll have to face.

JERRY: What is this pain you fear?

RUTH: The pain of feeling empty so much of the time. And the fear that if I take a good look, I'm going to find that I'm nothing but a hollow reflection of what everyone expects of me. There will be nothing of *me*!

JERRY: I'd like for you to imagine that what you fear *does* come true. What's the most horrible thing you can imagine you'd find?

RUTH: That what I am is nothing. Like an onion—I keep peeling away layers, only at the center there's no substance. I just keep peeling away layers of pretenses.

JERRY: OK, with your eyes closed let yourself peel away layer after layer of pretenses. Each layer you peel off, say out loud what you're peeling away.

RUTH: I'm peeling away my niceness. I'm polite on the outside, but on the inside I don't feel so nice.

JERRY: Keep peeling away as many layers as you can.

RUTH: Now I'll peel away my "good-girl" mask. I appear so good. I'd never do or say anything to offend or shock anyone. I'll be exactly what Father expects. But that's a mask so you can't see what's inside of me. Next layer—I'm peeling away the "devoted-mother" mask. All my life I've given and sacrificed for the sake of my children, getting nothing from it for myself.

JERRY: How about peeling away more of those masks.

RUTH: I'm peeling away my layers of fat. I hide behind my fat. I'm so fat that you won't look at me.

JERRY: You're smiling. Is that funny?

RUTH: That's another layer. I hide behind my smile. That way people won't see what's inside. I don't want people to see my hurt—so I'll smile.

JERRY: What are you feeling now?

RUTH: I'm scared. I've peeled away some layers, and now you can see me. And I'm scared you won't like what you see.

JERRY: What are you *most* scared of? Will you let yourself talk about your worst fear?

RUTH: I'm most afraid that what's inside of me is ugly—that inside of me is an evil witch, filled with poison.

JERRY: OK, let yourself be that evil witch and hex me. Talk to me from that side. What would you be saying to me?

RUTH: I'm evil—and deadly. If I get near you, I'll put a curse on you. I'll make you think I'm lovely, and when you get near me, then I'll trap you in a web, and I'll strangle you. And I'm afraid of becoming so dependent on you that if you leave or desert me, I'll be left with even more emptiness.

JERRY: Would you open your eyes and look at me and tell me what's going on inside of you now?

RUTH: That's the side of me I'm afraid to show anyone. If I show you what's inside of me, you may hate me. So I work hard at hiding—from you and from me. And I'm so tired of being afraid that you'll discover what I'm really like.

So far I have been working with Ruth to *experience feelings* that she keeps locked up for fear that she will see her own hate and vengeance. At this point we talk over how it feels for her to have come into contact with a part of her that she hides and how it feels to have shown me that side of her. (I have relied heavily on experiential techniques, especially Gestalt ones, as a way of getting her in contact with parts of herself that she represses.) I discuss with her the fact that she does have a choice—to stay in therapy and face those demons or not to look at them. (I am working within an existential framework that puts choice and responsibility in a central place.)

Ruth decides to continue. Being in therapy is a series of choices. Not only does therapy open Ruth up to new possibilities by expanding her awareness and thus widening the brackets of her freedom to choose, but she makes choices all during the therapy process itself. I respect her choices, and I support her when she is struggling with difficult ones; I also push her gently and invite her to ask for more and take more risks. Ultimately, she is the one who decides many times during our sessions the depth to which she is willing to go. (This is very much an existential concept.)

Ruth works to become free. Assume that Ruth says: "All my life I've felt unfree. I've had to be the person that my parents wanted me to be, I've had to be the wife that John expected me to be, and I've had to be what my kids expected as a mother. I'd like to be free and feel that I can live for me, but so far I don't seem to be able to."

There are any number of ways that I might go further with Ruth's feeling of being unfree. I suggest the following to her:

JERRY: Ruth, between now and our next session I'd like to suggest that you do several things. In your journal let yourself imagine all the ways you've felt unfree in your life. Just write down phrases or short sentences. It might help if you could write down messages that you've heard from your parents. What have they said they wanted of you? It might help if you actually imagine that you *are* for a time your father and just write as fast as you can all the things he might say about all he expects. Then let yourself write to Ruth as your mother. Again, without thinking much, just let her words and thoughts come to the paper. If you do that several times this week, we can pursue it more next week.

Here is the idea of "homework assignments," borrowed from the cognitive and behavioral therapies; only I am stressing the feelings that go with such an exercise. In this way Ruth can review some parental messages, and I hope she will stir up some old feelings associated with these memories.

At the following session Ruth brings her journal and says she would like to talk about what it was like to write herself letters (as her father and as her mother), saying all that was expected of her. I ask her to share what this was like, and I pay attention to her body as well as her words. (Like the Gestalt therapist, I think that the truth of one's messages is conveyed in voice inflections, postures, facial features, and the like. If I listen *only* to her words, I am likely to miss a deeper level of meaning. Like the person-centered therapist I value *listening* to what she is feeling and expressing.) Although I think it is important that I reflect and clarify (a person-centered technique), I deem it crucial that I bring myself into a dialogue with Ruth. If I am having reactions to what she is saying or if she is touching something within me, sharing with her my present experience can facilitate her work. (This is valued in both the existential and the person-centered approaches.) My own disclosure, at timely and appropriate moments, can lead to a deeper self-exploration on Ruth's part. I must take care not to disclose merely for its own sake; nor is it well to take the focus off of Ruth. But even a few words can let her know that I understand her.

Ruth is talking about her mother's messages to her. As I listen to her, I notice that there is a critical tone and a sharpness to her voice, and she makes a pointing gesture with her finger. I get an idea that I want to pursue, and I say:

JERRY: Ruth, would you sit in this red rocking chair? Actually rock back and forth, and with a very critical voice—pointing your finger and shaking it—deliver a lecture to Ruth, who is sitting in this other chair.

RUTH: I want you to work hard and never complain. Look at how I've slaved, and look at how moral I've been. Life is hard, girl, and don't forget that. You're put on earth here to see if you can pass the test. This life is merely a testing place. Bear all your burdens well, and you'll be rewarded in the next life—where it counts! Work hard! Keep pure—in mind, spirit, and body. Look what I've done in life—you can too.

There are many possibilities of places to go from here. (So far I have been using a Gestalt technique of asking her to "become" her mother in the hope that she can actually *feel* what this brings up in her as she relives the scene.) I ask her to sit in the other chair and be Ruth and respond to her mother's lecture. The dialogue can continue with an exchange between Mother and Ruth, and finally I ask her to stop and process what has gone on. This technique can also be done with her father.

We work on Ruth's cognitions. I see Gestalt techniques as very useful for assisting Ruth to get an experiential sense of what might be called "toxic introjects." These are the messages and values that she has swallowed whole without digesting them and making them her own. My goal is to help her externalize these introjections so that she can take a critical look at them. If what she has swallowed is toxic, she is poisoning herself and killing herself. I have an investment in getting her to look at this process and make her values truly her own. (This is very much an existential notion. Authenticity consists of living by one's own values, not living blindly by values given by others.)

So I ask Ruth to identify as many messages as she can that she recalls having received as a child. She recollects parental messages such as "Don't think for yourself." "Follow the church obediently, and conform your will to God's will." "Never question the Bible." "Live a moral life." "Don't get close to people, especially in sexual ways." "Always be proper and appropriate."

In addition to working with Ruth's feelings I find it essential to work with her *cognitive structures,* which include her belief systems, her thoughts, her attitudes, and her values. (In transactional analysis attention would be given to "parental tapes," or injunctions, and early decisions; in behavior therapy attention would be given to beliefs and assumptions that have an influence on her behavior; in rational-emotive therapy attention would be paid to irrational beliefs and self-indoctrination; in Adlerian therapy we would look at her basic mistakes; and in reality therapy the focus would be on values.) Whatever terms are used, I tend to focus on the underlying messages that Ruth pays attention to now in her life. I assume that her self-talk is relevant to her behavior.

Ruth brings up her father. As we explore the messages that Ruth was reared with, one theme seems to emerge. She has lived much of her life in ways that were designed to get her father's approval. She feels that unless she gets her father's acceptance and approval, she will never have "arrived." She reasons that if the father who conceived her could not love her, then nobody ever could. If *this* man does not show her love, she is doomed to live a loveless life! I proceed by getting her to look at the Adlerian, TA, and rational-emotive concepts and techniques to get her to critically evaluate some invalid assumptions she continues to make.)

As much as possible without pushing Ruth away, I challenge and confront her thinking and her value system, which appear to be at the root of much of her conflict. It is not so much a matter of my imposing my values on her; rather, it is a matter of getting her to look at beliefs and values that she has accepted to determine if she still wants to base her life on them. Does she want to spend the rest of her life in a futile attempt to "win over" her father? Does she want to continue making all men into her father? What will it take for her to finally gain her father's acceptance and love—if this is possible? What might she think of the person she had to become to gain his acceptance? I take this line of questioning in an attempt to get her to *think,* to *challenge* herself, and to *decide* for herself her standards for living. (This is an existential concept, and therapies such as rational-emotive therapy and TA are based on this kind of critical evaluation. I want Ruth to see that she does not have to live forever by the decisions she made as a child and by the beliefs that she uncritically accepted out of fear. TA would stress making new decisions, or the redecision process. Rational-emotive therapy would stress demolishing irrational beliefs, interrupting the self-indoctrination process that keeps them alive now, and replacing them with a sane and rational philosophy of life. In working with Ruth I am very heavily influenced by such concepts.)

Dealing with Ruth's past in understanding her decisions. I have been talking about some of the early decisions that Ruth made in response to messages that she received from her parents. I very much value the exploration of a client's early childhood experiences as a basis for understanding present pressing issues. (The psychoanalytic approach emphasizes a reconstruction of the past, a working through of early conflicts that have been repressed, and a resolution of these unconscious conflicts.) I accept that Ruth's childhood experiences were influential factors in contributing to her present development, although I do not think that these factors have *determined* her or that she is fixed with certain personality characteristics for life unless she goes through a long-term analytic reconstructive process. (I favor the Gestalt approach to working with her past.) I ask her to bring any unresolved conflicts from her past into the here and now through fantasy exercises and role-playing techniques. In this way her past is being dealt with in a powerful way as it is being manifested in her current problems.

In Ruth's attempt to face her past I expect some *resistance*—hesitation, defenses, and barriers at certain anxiety-provoking points. (Psychoanalysis has resistance as a central concept; Gestalt therapy mentions the "impasse.") In working with resistance I attempt to respect it. In other words, I see that Ruth's resistance is an inevitable part of how therapy proceeds. To some extent it is healthy to resist. Resistance shows that she is aware of the risks of changing and the anxiety that coming to terms with unknown parts of herself brings up. Thus (in a psychoanalytic view), I do not see resistance necessarily as conscious defiance or unwillingness to cooperate. (Behavior therapists often assume that "resistance" is an excuse on the therapist's part for poor management of techniques. They see it as a function of failure by the therapist to make a correct assessment and apply an appropriate treatment plan. I agree with the psychoanalytic concept of resistance as a fundamental part of therapy and as something that needs to be recognized and dealt with.)

Overall, Ruth is a very willing and motivated client. She is insightful, courageous, able to make connections between current behavior and past influences, willing to try risky behaviors both in the session and out of the session, and willing to face difficult issues in her life. Even under such favorable (and almost ideal) circumstances I still think that she will experience some resistance. She debated about whether to continue therapy; at times she blames her parents for her present problems, and at other times she chooses to stay comfortable because of her fear of plunging into unknown territory. In short, I work with whatever resistance she shows by pointing out its most obvious manifestations first and encouraging her to talk about her fears and explore them. I think an effective way to deal with resistance is to recognize it and deal with it directly. This can be done in a gentle yet confrontational way, along with providing support to face issues that she might otherwise avoid.

Working toward redecisions. As much as possible I structure situations in the therapy session that will facilitate new decisions on Ruth's part. I think that her redecisions have to be made on both the emotional and cognitive levels. It is not enough that she merely intellectually resolve to stop seeking parental approval; it is essential that she make this new decision from the feeling state (as she did when she made her early decision as a child). (In encouraging Ruth to make new decisions I draw on cognitive, emotive, and behavioral techniques. I use role-playing procedures, fantasy and imagery, assertion-training procedures, and Gestalt techniques, to mention a few. Ruth can spend years in getting insights into the cause of her problems, but what I think is more important is that she commit herself to some course of action. Here I like the Adlerian and reality-therapy reality-therapy emphasis on getting the client to decide on a plan of action and then make a commitment to carrying it out.)

Encouraging Ruth to act. In many ways I look at therapy as a place of safety where clients can experiment with new ways of being to see what behavioral changes they really want to make. The critical point consists of actually taking what is learned in the sessions and applying it to real-life situations. I consistently encourage Ruth to carry out homework assignments geared to having her challenge her fears and inhibitions in a variety of practical situations. Thus, if she says that she is yearning for a weekend alone with her husband yet fears asking for it because she might be turned down and the rejection would hurt, I challenge her: "If you don't bother to ask, chances are you won't have this weekend you say you want with John. You've constantly brought up in here that you don't ask for what you want, suffer in silence, and then end up depressed and unloved. Here's your chance to actually *do* something different instead of what you typically do. What stops you from asking for what you want?"

Ruth has a long list of excuses to justify her lack of willingness to initiate a weekend alone with John. A few of them are that they do not have the money, their children would miss them, John is too busy, and they might find that they were bored with each other's company. In reality-therapy fashion I tell Ruth that I don't want to settle for excuses. I argue with her on each point, attempting to convince her that if she does want to change her situation, she has to actually take risks and try new behavior. (This fits into most of the action-oriented behavioral approaches.) I ask Ruth to decide if she *really* wants to make changes in her life or merely *talk about* making changes. Because she sincerely wants to be different, we use session time in much role playing and behavioral rehearsal, and then I ask her to try out her new learning in different life situations. For me translating what is learned in the sessions into daily life is the essence of what therapy is about.

Evaluating Ruth's Therapy Experience

My style of counseling places emphasis on continuing assessment by both the counselor and the client from the initial to the final session. In my work with Ruth I bring up from time to time the topic of her progress in therapy. We openly discuss the degree to which she is getting what she wants from the process (and from me). If she is not successfully meeting her objectives, we can explore some factors that might be getting in the way of her progress. I could be a restricting factor. This is especially true if I am reacting to her strictly from a technical approach and am withholding my own reactions from her. If I am being inauthentic in any way in the sessions, I am certain that this will show up in a failure on her part to progress to the degree to which she might.

I also explore with Ruth some of the circumstances in her life that might be contributing to what appears to be slow or nonexistent progess. She may have done a lot of changing, which may itself be creating new problems in her home relationships, and she may feel a need to pull back and consolidate her gains. There may be a plateau for a period of time before she is ready to forge ahead with making other major life changes. Still another factor determining her progress or lack of it lies within herself—namely, her own decision and commitment of how far she wants to go in therapy. Is she willing to make some basic changes in her personality and create a new identity for herself? Is she willng to pay the price that changing entails? Does she merely want to solve some pressing problems on the surface, while remaining personally unchanged? These are but a few of the factors that we have to consider in understanding any failure in the therapy process.

How do Ruth and I determine the degree to which she is progressing? What criteria do we use to make this determination? (Behavior therapy is built on the assumption that assessment and evaluation are basic to the therapy process. Techniques must be continually verified to determine if they are working. *Behavior changes* in the client are a major basis for making this evaluation.) From my vantage point I look at Ruth's work in the sessions and what she is doing outside of them as a measure of the degree to which therapy is working. Another important index is our relationship. If it is one of trust and if she is dealing with difficult personal issues in her therapy and also working on these issues outside of the sessions, then therapy is working. Also, her own evaluation of how much progress she sees and how satisfied she is by the outcomes is a major factor in assessing therapeutic results.

When is it time for Ruth to terminate therapy? This, too, is a matter that I openly evaluate at appropriate times. Ultimately, I see it as her choice. My hope is that once she attains a degree of increased self-awareness *and* specific behavioral skills in meeting present and future problems, she might well be encouraged to end formal therapy and begin to become her own therapist. (This is a cognitive-behavioral approach.) To keep her beyond this point could result in needlessly fostering her dependence on me, which is not too unlike the problem she entered therapy for in the first place.

How Would You Work with Ruth Using Your Own Approach?

At this time you are challenged to try your hand at achieving some synthesis among the nine approaches by drawing on each of them in a way that seems meaningful to you—one that fits your own personality and your view of people and the nature of therapy. I am providing some questions to help you organize the elements of your approach.

1. What would you be thinking and feeling as you approached your initial session with Ruth? Use whatever you know about her from the material presented about her and her autobiography in the first chapter, from

the nine chapters on her work with various therapists, and from my eclectic approach in working with her in this chapter.

2. Briefly state how you see Ruth, in terms of her current dynamics and most pressing conflicts. How would you feel in working with her as a client? How do you view her capacity to understand herself and to make basic changes?
3. How much direction do you see Ruth needing? To what degree would you take the responsibility for structuring her sessions? Where would you be on a continuum of highly directive to very nondirective?
4. Would you be inclined toward short-term therapy or long-term therapy? Why?
5. What major themes do you imagine that you would focus on in Ruth's life?
6. In what ways might you go about gathering life-history data in order to make an initial assessment of her problems and to determine which therapy procedures to use?
7. How might you help Ruth in clarifying her goals for therapy? How would you help her make her goals concrete? How would you assess the degree to which she was meeting her goals?
8. How much interest would you have in working with Ruth's *past* life experiences? her *current* issues? her *future* aspirations and strivings? Which of these areas do you favor? Why?
9. What value do you place on the quality of your relationship with Ruth? How important is the client/therapist relationship for you as a determinant of therapeutic outcomes?
10. Would you be more inclined to focus on Ruth's *feelings*? her thought processes and other *cognitive factors*? her ability to take action as measured by her *behaviors*?
11. How supportive might you be of Ruth? How confrontational might you be with her? In what areas do you think you would be most supportive? most confrontational?
12. How much might you be inclined to work toward major personality reconstruction? toward specific skill-development and problem-solving strategies?
13. How might you explore Ruth's major fears, both about therapy and about her life?
14. What life experiences have you had that would most help you in working with Ruth? What personal characteristics might hinder your work with her?
15. How might you proceed in dealing with Ruth's parents and the role she feels that they have played in her life? How important would it be to focus on working through her attitudes and feelings toward her parents? Do you think that this can be done symbolically (through role playing), or for her to resolve her problems is it necessary that she deal directly with her parents?

16. How much might you structure outside-of-therapy activities for Ruth (homework, reading, journal writing, and so forth)?
17. What values do you hold that are similar to Ruth's? How do you expect that this similarity would either get in the way of or facilitate therapy?
18. What specific techniques and concepts might you draw from the psychoanalytic approach? from the experiential approaches? from the cognition/behavior/action-oriented approaches?
19. To what degree would you view Ruth's therapy as being a didactic and reeducative process? To what degree do you see therapy as being a teaching/learning process?
20. Would you orient Ruth's therapy more toward insight or toward action? What balance might you seek between the cognitive aspects and the feeling aspects? How might you make the determination of when Ruth was ready to end therapy?

RECOMMENDED SUPPLEMENTARY READINGS

Now that you have studied nine contemporary theories and seen their applications to cases, you may be interested in sources that will help you develop a basis for integrating these diverse approaches and books dealing with counseling in a multicultural context.

Counseling Today's Families (1990), by H. Goldenberg & I. Goldenberg (Pacific Grove, CA: Brooks/Cole), deals with the family as a social system and the process of appraising family functioning. The book offers a useful perspective on counseling families with alternative lifestyles. The authors discuss implications for counseling practice of the following family structures: the single-parent family, the remarried family, cohabiting heterosexual couples, gay and lesbian couples, and the dual-career family.

Counseling across Cultures (1989), by P. B. Pedersen, J. G. Draguns W. J. Lonner, & J. E. Trimble (Honolulu: University of Hawaii Press), contains a diversity of helpful articles on general considerations in cross-cultural counseling and specific ethnic and cultural considerations in working with Asian Americans, Native Americans, and Hispanics.

A Handbook for Developing Multicultural Awareness (1988), by P. Pedersen (Alexandria, VA: American Association for Counseling and Development), is based on the assumption that all counseling is to some extent multicultural. The author contends that we can choose either to attend to the influence of culture or to ignore it. In this useful handbook the author deals with topics such as developing multicultural awareness, becoming aware of our culturally biased assumptions, acquiring knowledge for effective multicultural counseling, and learning skills to deal with diversity.

Counseling American Minorities: A Cross-Cultural Perspective (3rd ed., 1989), edited by D. R. Atkinson, G. Morten, & D. W. Sue (Dubuque, IA: William C. Brown), has excellent sections dealing with counseling for American Indians, Asian Americans, Blacks, and Latinos, and it contains some helpful case illustrations.

Eclectic Psychotherapy: A Systematic Approach (1983), by L. E. Beutler (New York: Pergamon Press), is an excellent source for readers who want to develop an integrated approach. The author describes a systematic eclectic psychotherapy, which can be applied in a relatively consistent and reliable fashion. He attempts to define the ingredients of effective therapy by matching clients to both therapists and techniques.

The Practice of Multimodel Therapy (1989), by A. A. Lazarus (Baltimore: Johns Hopkins University Press), represents a practical approach that is highly readable. The author develops his own systematic and comprehensive therapy and describes a wide variety of techniques. He endorses and expands on the stance he calls "technical eclecticism."

The Counseling Experience: A Theoretical and Practical Approach (1982), by M. E. Cavanagh (Pacific Grove, CA: Brooks/Cole), develops the basic principle that counselors should use what works and discard what does not work. Endorsing a pragmatic viewpoint, the author explores some of the following topics pertaining to the nature of counseling: stages in the therapeutic process, the person of both the client and the counselor, cognitive and emotional factors in counseling, communication in counseling, resistance, and problems facing counselors.

Therapeutic Psychology: Fundamentals of Counseling and Psychotherapy (5th ed., 1989), by L. Brammer, E. Shostrom, & P. J. Abrego (Englewood Cliffs, NJ: Prentice-Hall), presents an "actualizing model" of counseling. The authors maintain that their creative synthesis of various counseling theories goes beyond popular eclecticism. They provide a concise summary of the theoretical foundations of counseling practice. They draw on a combination of theories as they discuss topics such as the therapeutic process, assessment and diagnosis in counseling, the client/therapist relationship, transference, countertransference, resistance, and the role of values in therapy.

Handbook of Eclectic Psychotherapy (1986), edited by J. C. Norcross (New York: Brunner/Mazel), is an excellent collection of various eclectic approaches. It also deals with the underlying assumptions of eclecticism; its possibilities, promises, and problems; training eclectic therapists; and future directions in the integration of psychotherapy.

Casebook of Eclectic Psychotherapy (1987), edited by J. C. Norcross (New York: Brunner/Mazel), is a compendium that was designed as an extension of the *Handbook of Eclectic Psychotherapy.* The 13 case histories presented in this book concretely illustrate the practice of a systematic eclectic therapy in its varied manifestations.

CHAPTER TWELVE

Additional Cases for Practice

This chapter is divided into two segments: Cases 1–9, *identified cases,* are designed to be analyzed within the framework of a particular therapeutic approach. Cases 10–20, *unidentified cases,* are designed to give you some practice in deciding which approach works best for each case, to help you combine approaches, and to give you opportunities to apply what you have learned in the previous chapters. There are a number of suggested class activities, including role-playing possibilities and discussion questions. Think creatively about ways of comparing and contrasting the approaches, of integrating several theories, and of borrowing techniques from all of the nine models as you work with these cases. Remember, there are no "right" answers. The real challenge is to think through why you would use certain interventions with different cases and to be able to describe what you see going on in each of these cases.

1. TIM: A CHILD MOLESTER (PSYCHOANALYTIC)

Assume that you are working in a state mental hospital for the rehabilitation of mentally disordered sex offenders. The psychiatrist who is the head of your ward and also your supervisor maintains that a psychoanalytic perspective is most useful for understanding the dynamics of the child molesters on the ward. Although she realizes full well that most members of the treatment staff are limited both in available time and skill in using pyschoanalytic techniques, she also believes that the staff can draw on pychoanalytic *concepts* to guide the therapy with their patients. She contends that you can think in psychoanalytic terms even though you do not practice in strict psychoanalytic ways. With this in mind she presents a case study at a staff meeting, summarizing the psychological development of a client named Tim.

Some Background Data

Tim's mother was overprotective and overpossessive and controlled him with guilt. Even now she reminds him of all she gave and sacrificed and of how he was a "difficult child" from birth on. She almost died delivering him, and she tells him that she has been suffering because of him for many years. Tim was the only boy in a family of five children. Psychosexually, he eventually decided to become a neuter in an effort to become what he thought his mother wanted of him. He became quite overweight, developed a very passive and unassertive style (especially with women), and has avoided developing lasting relationships with women for 50 years.

Tim saw his father as being extremely weak and uncaring. He reports that he cannot remember any events in which he and his father did anything together. His father showed no interest in him, and his typical way of dealing with Tim was to ignore him. Tim's father was controlled by Tim's mother and grandmother (who lived with the family). Tim recalls tension between his mother and his grandmother (the mother of Tim's father), each fighting to run the house in the way she saw fit. They had very different ideas about how the family should be, so conflict was a continual pattern in the home. Things Tim did to please his mother often upset his grandmother, and the reverse happened when he tried to please the older woman.

As a child Tim envied his sisters because he thought they were treated more fairly than he was. Eventually, the discriminatory treatment he felt he was receiving changed his envy to resentment. He grew to fear women who were older than he, for he continually felt that they could and would dominate him. His relationships with others have been inadequate, and he has never been able to form and maintain satisfactory relationships with adults of either sex.

Tim discovered that he felt relatively comfortable around small children, especially boys. They seemed to take a liking to him, they did not make demands on him, and he did not feel inadequate around them. For a while during his early adult life he worked as a teacher's aide in an elementary school. He began his pattern of molesting young boys in this job. He would invite some of these children to climb onto his lap, and he would then stroke their hair and cuddle them. Eventually, he progressed with several boys to the point of touching their genitals; he also encouraged them to touch him. His pattern continued, and eventually he was arrested.

During the rest of his adult life he has been in and out of state hospitals for sex offenders a number of times. When he "finishes his time" as stipulated by the court, he is released, goes into the community, and then reoffends. He feels that he never hurts his victims and that he is typically "very nice and kind" to them. He even rationalizes that they often enjoy the attention and physical affection he demonstrates. Yet at times he also feels that what he does is wrong, and he feels guilty over his deeds. He does not think that his actions are normal, yet he worries about how he will deal with the impulses he might feel toward certain children. He has made resolutions to control himself, yet he has often acted on his impulses. He says he would like to learn to control his desires and be able to relate well with adults.

Questions for Reflection

By attempting to think psychoanalytically, show how you might proceed in your contacts with Tim by addressing yourself to these questions:

1. What value do you see in knowing Tim's developmental history, family background, experiences as a child and adolescent in school, work history, and other key adult experiences? Do you think that knowing this information will help you be a more effective therapist? How might you proceed differently with him if you had no prior knowledge about his past and instead simply relied on what you could learn about him through your contacts with him on the ward and observing his behavior? What advantages and disadvantages do you see in having prior knowledge about a client?
2. From the summary notes about Tim alone, how might you react to a person like him? What reactions does it evoke in you when you think about a middle-aged man who has a pattern of sexual molestation of children? In what ways can you predict that your own reactions to a person such as Tim could affect your ability to work with him therapeutically? How might you be able to deal with your own feelings so that they would not be a barrier between you and him?
3. Tim says that he feels guilt and sorrow over what he recognizes are his offenses and also that he would like to learn how to control his impulses. How might you be able to tell the degree to which this is so? Might he be saying what he feels he is expected to say so that he will obtain a release from the hospital? How do you think that either your belief or lack of belief in what he is saying will affect your work with him?
4. Do you think that Tim can change (stop his child-molesting behavior) without gaining insight into the causes of his problems? How much importance might you put on factors such as his understanding of his early childhood? his resolution of psychic conflicts with his mother and grandmother? a resolution of his feelings toward his father? If you see value in focusing on the above issues, *how* might you do this within the limited time that you would have to work with him?
5. Do you see Tim as a victim of his early experiences? Or do you see that even though he has had adverse experiences in growing up, he could do something to change his behavior now? Again, how do your answers to the above questions determine how you will work with him in therapy?
6. As you proceed with Tim, what would be your major goals for him? Merely stopping his antisocial behavior? Changing his basic personality

structure? Merely seeing that he has a choice in doing something about the problem that keeps him in the hospital?

2. THE KLINES: WORKING WITH THE FAMILY OF AN IDENTIFIED PATIENT (ADLERIAN)

Assume that a person in the agency where you work has done an intake interview and that you are given the following information.

Some Background Data

The Kline family consists of Gail and George, their two daughters (Jessie, 10, and Jaimi, 12), and their son (Gary, 16). George called for the intake interview. He said that his son had got into trouble for stealing and dealing in drugs. Gary is on probation, and the court ordered him to undergo therapy. It was suggested that the entire family be involved in some kind of family therapy.

George is following the suggestion of the court and involving the entire family in counseling sessions. However, he does not have much hope that therapy will be of great help. According to him, the one who is responsible for the family's problems is his wife, who, he says, is an alcoholic. George, a businessman who does a great deal of traveling, is convinced that he is doing all he can to hold the family together. He comments that he is a good provider and that he does not understand why Gail insists on drinking. He feels that Gary has gotten everything that he ever wanted, and he maintains that the young people of today are "just spoiled rotten." The father says that his elder daughter, Jaimi, is the best one of the bunch, and he has no complaints about her. He sees her as being more responsible than his wife as well as being more attentive to him. He views his younger daughter, Jessie, as pampered and spoiled by her mother, and he has little hope for her.

George is willing to give family counseling a try and says he hopes that the therapist can straighten them all out. He says that he, Gail, and Jessie are all willing to come in for a family session. Jaimi does not want to attend, however, because she says she has no problems and sees no purpose in therapy for herself. Gary is very reluctant to appear, even for one session, because he feels sure that the others in the family will see him as the source of their problems. To satisfy the conditions of his probation, Gary would rather choose "the lesser of two evils" and see a therapist privately.

The counselor who did the intake interview saw only the father for an initial session. He suggests that you see the entire family for at least one session and then decide how to proceed.

Questions for Reflection

1. What are your initial reactions after reading the intake interview? What are the themes that interest you the most in this case? Why?
2. How would you proceed as an Adlerian therapist in an initial session if you saw the entire family? What issues would you want to discuss with this family at the first meeting?
3. George does not seem very open to looking at his role in contributing to the problems within his family. If you were to see him as your client, how would you go about establishing a relationship with him?
4. If you believed in the value of seeing the family as a unit for one or more sessions, how might you go about getting the entire family to come in? Assume that all agreed to attend one session. What would be your focus, and what would you most want to achieve in this family session?
5. What are the key dynamics of the family as a system? What does the family atmosphere seem like? How would you interpret what is going on in this family from an Adlerian perspective?
6. What speculations do you have about George's dynamics? From the vantage point of an Adlerian how would you explain his behavior? Do you have ideas of how you'd work with his resistance?
7. Do you see any aspects of yourself in this case? Can you identify with any of the family members? How do you think this similarity or dissimilarity would help or hinder you in working with this family?
8. Assume that the mother and father wanted to come in for a number of sessions. Would you be inclined to gather life-history data from each of them? Why or why not? In what ways might you use this information as an Adlerian therapist?
9. What would your major goals be in working with this family? How would you go about increasing the social interest of each of the members?
10. Show how you would work with this family, and discuss any problems that you might expect to encounter. Say how you would deal with these problems.

3. PAULINE: A YOUNG WOMAN FACING DEATH (EXISTENTIAL)

The existentialist views death as a reality that gives meaning to life. As humans we do not have forever to actualize ourselves. Thus, the realization of the fact that we will die jolts us into taking the present seriously and evaluating the direction in which we are traveling. We are confronted with the fact that we have only so much time to do the things we most want to do. Thus, we are motivated to take stock of how meaningful our life is. With this existential perspective in mind, assume that a young woman of 20 comes to the center where you are a counselor.

Some Background Data

Pauline has recently found out that she has leukemia. Though she is in a period of remission, her doctors tell her that the disease is terminal. Pauline is seeking counseling to help herself deal with this crisis and at least get the maximum out of the remainder of her life. She is filled with rage over her fate; she keeps asking why this had to happen to her. She tells you that at first she could not believe the diagnosis was correct. When she finally got several more professional opinions that confirmed her leukemia, she began to feel more and more anger—toward God, toward her healthy friends, whom she envied, and generally toward the unfairness of her situation. She tells you that she was just starting to live, that she had a direction she was going in professionally. Now everything will have to change. After she tells you this, she is sitting across from you waiting for your response.

Questions for Reflection

Attempting to stay within the frame of reference of an existential therapist, what direction would you take with her? Think about these questions:

1. What do you imagine your immediate reactions would be if you were faced with counseling this client? What would be some of the things that you would initially say in response to what you know about Pauline?
2. What are your own thoughts and feelings about death? To what degree have you reflected on this reality as it applies to you? Do you avoid thinking about it? In what ways have you accepted the reality of your eventual death? How do you think that the answers to the above questions will affect your ability to be present for Pauline?
3. What goals would you have in counseling with her?
4. In what ways would you deal with the rage that Pauline says she feels?
5. Pauline tells you that one of the reasons that she is coming to see you is because of her desire to accept her fate. How would you work with her to gain this acceptance? What specific things might you do to help her find ways of living the rest of her life to its fullest?
6. Do you see any possibilities for helping Pauline find meaning in her life in the face of death?

4. DORIS: LEAVING HER HUSBAND AND CHILD (PERSON-CENTERED)

Doris comes to a community counseling center at the recommendation of a friend, who expresses concern that Doris intends to leave her child. The friend thinks she is confused and needs professional help.

Some Background Data

Doris was born and reared in Arkansas. Her father is a reformed alcoholic who drank heavily when the client was a child. Both parents are religious, and the father is described as a strict fundamentalist. Doris has a younger brother who is now an enlisted man in the army and is described as the family favorite. She says her parents were stricter with her than with their son and emphasized the importance of marriage as well as the woman's dependent and inferior role in that relationship.

Doris is a "sweet" girl who dropped out of high school in the tenth grade. She worked as a manicurist in Arkansas until marrying and moving to Kentucky three years ago. She then worked as a waitress. Her husband says that they have had no fights or arguments during their three-year marriage, and the client agrees. Six months ago Doris gave birth to a baby boy. There were no medical complications, and she maintains that she adjusted well to the baby, but she reports just not being able to feel much of anything except tired. Two months ago she and her husband moved to Houston so that he could join an amateur band. She began working as a cashier at a drugstore. In the course of her work she began to have series of brief sexual affairs with fellow workers as well as customers. At the same time, although her husband is happy with the band, he has not been able to find a steady job. He has asked her to try to find a second job or to take overtime hours at the drugstore.

Doris is considering leaving her husband and her child, although she is uncertain how she would continue to support herself financially. She is also concerned with what would happen to her son, because her husband has no means of support. She insists that she does not want to take the child with her.

Questions for Reflection

1. Would you be inclined to accept Doris as a client? Do you think that you could empathize with her situation? Explain.
2. What is your attitude about her wanting to leave her husband and her child? What are your values on this matter, and how would they influence the way you would work with her?
3. Would you want to see Doris and her husband together? Would you want to see him individually? see her individually? see them on an individual basis and also as a couple? Explain your rationale, showing what you would probably focus on in each instance.
4. Assume that Doris asked you for your advice regarding her plan to leave her husband and child. What would you say? To what degree do you think Doris can function without advice?

5. If you accepted Doris as a client, in what ways do you think you could be of most help to her?
6. Are there feelings about herself and her husband that Doris is currently unwilling to accept? How would a person-centered approach help with acceptance of feelings and with denied parts of the self?
7. By staying with a person-centered framework, do you feel that you could respond to her in a way you would like? Do you feel limited by this theory in any way. If so, how?
8. What are some of the advantages of working with Doris within a person-centered framework?

5. LINDA: IN CRISIS OVER HER PREGNANCY (GESTALT)

Assume that you are a counselor in a community mental-health clinic, that you have a Gestalt orientation, and that the counselor at the local high school tells you about Linda, a 15-year-old client he has seen several times. He feels that she needs further counseling, but he is limited by a school policy that does not permit personal counseling of any duration. He would like for you to see her for at least three months, as she is facing some difficult decisions. Here is what you learn about her from the counselor.

Some Background Data

Linda comes from a close-knit family, and in general she feels that she can seek her parents out when she has problems. But now she says that she just *cannot* turn to them in this time of crisis. Even though she and her boyfriend had been engaging in sexual intercourse for a year without using birth-control measures, she was convinced that she would not get pregnant. When she did learn that she was pregnant, she expected that her 16-year-old boyfriend would agree to get married. He did not agree, and he even questioned whether he was the father. She felt deeply hurt and angry over this. On the advice of a girlfriend she considered an abortion for a time. But she decided against it because she felt she could not deal with the guilt of terminating a life within her. The possibility of putting her child up for adoption was suggested to her. But she felt this to be totally unacceptable, because she was sure she could not live knowing that she had created a life and then "abandoned" the child. She considered having her baby and becoming a single parent. Yet when the counselor pointed out all the realities involved in this choice, she could see that this option would not work—unless she told her parents and lived with them, which she was *sure* she could not do. Her pregnancy is moving toward the advanced stages, and her panic is mounting.

Questions for Reflection

Linda agrees to work with you for several months, and you will be using Gestalt procedures with her.

1. What do you imagine would be your initial reactions and responses to the counselor's account? What might your first words be to Linda after you were introduced to her? What do you think you would *most* want to say to her?
2. What might be some of your goals in working with Linda? Check any of the following that apply:
   ___ I hope that she will tell her parents about her situation.
   ___ I hope that she will reconsider the possibility of having an abortion, and I might be inclined to push this alternative.
   ___ I hope that she will reconsider the possibility of having the child and then putting it up for adoption, and I might be inclined to push this alternative.

   Can you suggest other goals?
3. What are *your values* as they relate to the above matters, and what role do you see your values playing in the approach you will take with Linda? Might you be inclined to share your values, so that Linda knows where you stand? Might you be inclined to push your values and thus steer counseling in a particular direction?
4. At some point you might work with Linda's feelings of anger and hurt toward her boyfriend. What Gestalt techniques can you think of to help her explore these feelings? What techniques could you use to work with her feelings of guilt over not having lived up to her parents' high expectations? What other Gestalt approaches might you use (with what expected outcomes) to explore with Linda her other feelings associated with being pregnant?
5. As you proceed with Linda, you become aware of the following body messages:
   - Whenever she talks about having a baby, she puts her hands to her face, almost as though she were hiding it.
   - As she talks about her fear of telling her parents and expresses her guilt over letting them down, her voice changes to a very soft and almost pleading tone.
   - Her mouth is extremely tight when she mentions her boyfriend, and her eyes become moist.
   - She often has teary eyes and a slight smile at the same time.

   Can you think of some Gestalt-oriented techniques that you would build on to work with the body messages you observe in Linda? How might you use her nonverbal clues as a way of helping her experience her feelings more fully?

6. Below are some Gestalt-oriented techniques that you might consider using. Check any of them that you think you would use, and show how you would go about implementing them. What outcomes do you expect from each technique? What do you hope will be achieved through the use of each?
   ___ I will ask her to have a dialogue between *herself* and her *boyfriend,* using the empty-chair technique.
   ___ I will ask her to have a similar dialogue with her father.
   ___ I will ask her to have a similar dialogue with her mother.
   ___ I will ask her to fantasize, with her eyes closed, the worst possible situation and describe it, along with what she is experiencing as she does so.
   ___ I will ask her to write a letter to her boyfriend (or to her parents, or to her unborn child) and say anything that comes to her without censoring it—and I will ask her *not* to mail it.
7. How comfortable would you feel in using techniques such as the above with such a client? How would you prepare Linda for such exercises, so that she would be open to experimenting with some Gestalt fantasy work?
8. Some states have a law requiring parental permission for counseling a minor if she is pregnant. How do you think this requirement would affect your relationship with Linda?
9. What are the limitations, if any, of staying within a Gestalt framework in this case? Do you feel that you could say and do what you would like within this theory?
10. What are some advantages of using a Gestalt perspective in this case?

6. HAROLD: A CLIENT IN SEARCH OF A FRIEND (TA)

Harold presents himself for treatment at a community mental-health clinic.

Some Background Data

The client is 55 years old and has been a client for six weeks. Harold is divorced, has no children or other family, and has no real social connections in the city. He has been living a very isolated existence in a hotel in the downtown area. The client receives approximately $400 a month in Supplemental Security Income and does not work. He is a chronic alcoholic who passes through various phases of sobriety and inebriation. He appears to be a very alienated, depressed individual.

As you talk with him, you become aware that he has accepted injunctions such as "Don't be." "Don't be close." "Don't succeed." In response to these and other messages, he made early decisions such as "I am a born loser." "I don't deserve to feel good." "I won't feel close to anyone." He gives little evidence of having questioned the messages he has internalized and is living by.

Harold is in therapy attempting to qualify for more financial aid as a psychiatrically disabled person. Despite the fact that he initiated therapy as a ploy to receive financial support, you sense that a relationship is developing between the two of you in your weekly sessions. He arrives punctually, is animated and communicative, and often seems in good spirits. He reports, however, that he does not have enough money to live in the hotel, that he is out on the street, and that he needs somewhere to stay. He goes so far as to ask if he can use your office. That evening, he is waiting by your car and asks for a ride to a location a few miles away. You suggest that he take a bus. A week later, this behavior is repeated. In therapy, meanwhile, he becomes withdrawn and depressed.

Questions for Reflection

1. Initially knowing that Harold wants to "beat the system," would you be willing to see him? To what degree would you cooperate with his goals? What legal or ethical issues, if any, would you want to address?
2. Is there anything about this case that would cause you to take immediate action? If so, what specifically needs to be done?
3. Would you comply with his wish that you become his friend? Do you see any inconsistency between his injunction of "Don't be close" and his wanting a friendship?
4. If you were to establish a contract with Harold, what might it entail? How would you go about developing a contract with him?
5. How, if at all, would you deal with his concerns over living arrangements and financial matters?
6. What limits do you think would be important to establish in this case? To what degree might you have difficulty in enforcing limits?
7. How would you deal with his change in moods?
8. In what ways would you approach working with Harold as a TA therapist? Specifically, what are some therapeutic procedures that you would probably employ?
9. What are some of the ways in which you would work with his injunctions and early decisions? What kind of redecision do you hope he would make?
10. Do you have any guesses about what life script Harold might be living out? What games does he play? What are the possible payoffs of such games?

7. KATHRINA: LEARNING TO COPE WITH ANXIETY (BEHAVIORAL)

Kathrina, a Native American in her early 20's, comes to the clinic where you are a behaviorally oriented therapist. Assume that this is your initial meeting with her and that you know nothing else about her. Also assume that she would very much like to become involved in short-term behavioral counseling, mainly to deal with chronic anxiety that is getting in the way of her personal and professional life.

Some Background Data

During the initial interview Kathrina tells you:

> I've just *got* to learn how to cope with stress. I feel as if there's a dark cloud over my head—a constant feeling of apprehension. I'm so worked up during the day that when I try to go to sleep, I just toss and turn most of the night, ruminating over everything that happened to me that day. I keep telling myself that I've got to get to sleep or I won't be worth a damn the next day. I just lie there and can't seem to stop thinking of what I did or will do the next day. When I do get up the next morning, I'm a basket case. I sell real estate, and lately I'm getting more anxious about my future. I'm fearful of contacting people, afraid I'll say the wrong thing and blow the potential sale, and afraid they'll notice my anxiety. I just don't seem to be able to relax at any time. And what's even worse is that I feel less able to cope with stress now than I used to. Stress is getting the best of me, and I'm afraid that unless I can learn to recognize and deal with the situations I'm in, my anxiety will do me in.

Kathrina also tells you that she is experiencing many problems in leaving home and feeling that she can make it on her own. She says that she is not following the family ''program'' and lets you know that her parents are disappointed with some of the ways in which she is living. She does not want to cut herself off from her family, yet she has trouble in being everything her parents expect of her.

Assume that you and Kathrina agree to several counseling sessions to help her deal with her anxieties. Specifically, she wants guidance in learning coping skills that she can use on her own. Show how you would view her as a behaviorally oriented counselor and how you might proceed for several sessions.

Questions for Reflection

1. How do you view Kathrina's anxiety? Do you look at it as a problem in itself (and thus deal directly with behavior that seems to produce anxiety)? Or do you look at it as symbolic of underlying conflicts? How will your answer to this question have a direct bearing on the manner in which you work with her in your sessions?

2. What cultural themes would you pay attention to, if any? To what extent would you focus on her alienation from her family? Would you be inclined to focus more on her anxiety? her stress? her concerns over not living up to the expectations of her family?
3. What might you want to know from Kathrina about the ways in which her cultural experiences have affected her? If you are from a different background, would you expect any difficulties in understanding and working with her?
4. What specific behavioral procedures might you employ during your sessions? What suggestions would you make to Kathrina for work she can do by herself outside of the sessions?
5. What ways can you think of to teach her how to cope with stress? What self-help or self-management techniques could you suggest?
6. How might you deal with Kathrina's insomnia? What could you suggest to her concerning her ruminating over the events of the day when she is in bed? How might you design a program for her that would help her relax and sleep at night? What would you do during the sessions? What would you ask her to do outside of your sessions?
7. What cognitive factors might be affecting her behavior? How might her thinking patterns, beliefs, and self-statements be increasing her level of stress and leading to sleep disorders?
8. What other directions might you take in your work with Kathrina?

8. HAL AND PETE: A GAY COUPLE SEEK COUNSELING (RET)

Two homosexual men seek the services of a clinical social worker in private practice.

Some Background Data

Hal and Pete have been living together for several years. Much as heterosexual couples do, they experience conflicts in their relationship. Lately, the situation has taken a turn for the worse, and Hal wants to either resolve certain problems or break up the relationship. Pete is very anxious about being deserted, and he agrees to come for counseling as a couple. Neither of them is troubled with the fact that they are in a gay relationship, and from their perspective this is not the problem. They want you to know at the outset that they are not seeking counseling to "cure" them of their homosexuality. Rather, they seem to be having major problems that they are unable to work out by themselves and that lead them to wonder if they want to continue living together.

Pete feels unappreciated, and he does not feel that Hal cares for him in "the way I would like." He initially tells you the following:

I try so hard to do what I think Hal expects. It's really important that I please him, because I'm afraid that if I don't, he'll get fed up and simply leave. And if he left, I imagine all sorts of terrible things happening. First of all, I feel the constant threat of being left. I need someone to rely on—someone who will listen to me, who I know cares for me and accepts me the way I am, who wants to be with me, and who will approve of what I do. I feel I *must* have this in the person I live with. If I don't, this just proves that the other person doesn't love me. I need to be loved. My parents didn't love me, they never gave me the approval I needed to have, and I think that this alone is more than enough for me to have to bear. I feel that life often plays dirty tricks on me. For a long time I felt that I could *really* trust Hal and that he'd stay with me and approve of me and care about me, regardless of who I was. Now, after I trust him, he decides to tell me that I'm too demanding and that he's not able to handle all my demands. I don't think I'm demanding—I just want to be loved and accepted by some other significant person. If I can't find this in at least one person, then I can't see much value in living.

Hal responds with the following initial statement, in which he describes how it is for him to be in this relationship:

Frankly, I'm so tired of always feeling that I *must prove myself* and my constant love for Pete. No matter what I do or say, I typically end up feeling that I'm not enough and that regardless of what I do, it just won't measure up. I'm tired of hearing that I don't care. I'm sick of being made to feel that I'm insensitive, I hate being made to feel inadequate, and I don't want to constantly feel that I have to weigh everything I say for fear that I'll offend Pete and make him upset. I just can't stand having people be upset at me—it makes me feel lousy and guilty—as if I should somehow be more than I am, that I ought to be better than I am. If I can't get over being made to feel inadequate around Pete, I want out!

Questions for Reflection

Assume that Hal and Pete agree to attend six sessions as a couple. By the end of that time they would like to have decided whether they want to stay together. If they do decide to continue living together, they would be open to considering further counseling to continue working on their separate problems and finding ways of improving their relationship.

1. What are your initial reactions to Pete? to Hal? to them as a couple? How do you see them individually and as a couple? Would you want to work with them as a couple? Do you think that you could work with them effectively? Why or why not?
2. Are your feelings toward this gay couple different than they would be if the couple were heterosexual? What are your views toward homosexual relationships? How do you think they would influence your approach and the goals you had in mind? Would you tell them how you felt toward them—both as separate individuals and as a couple? Why or why not? What difference do you think it would make whether you shared your reactions with them?

3. Pete and Hal initially said that they did not consider the fact of their homosexual preferences to be a problem in itself and that they were not asking you to "cure" what they considered a nonexistent problem. Would you avoid attempting to change their sexual orientations? How might your answer to the above question determine the direction you would proceed in counseling this couple?
4. From the perspective of rational-emotive therapy, some of the following could be identified as *Pete's irrational beliefs.* Show how you would demonstrate to him that they are self-defeating attitudes that are the direct cause of his misery:
   - I *must* please Hal, and if I don't he'll leave, and the consequences will be horrible!
   - I *must* have someone to rely on, or else I can't make it on my own!
   - I *must* have someone to show me caring, love, approval, and if I don't get this, then life is hardly worth living!
   - If I don't get what I want from life, then life is damn unfair!
5. Again as an RET therapist, how might you work with *Hal's irrational beliefs*? How would you teach him to dispute them? How would you show him that these beliefs are at the root of his problems?
   - I *must* prove myself, I *must* be able to meet another's expectations of me—and if I don't, I'll feel inadequate, guilty, rotten, and deficient as a person!
   - If I don't meet Pete's needs, then I am *made* to feel inadequate.
6. Show how both Hal's and Pete's beliefs and assumptions are related to the problems they are having in their relationship. In what ways do you imagine that working on their irrational beliefs will affect their relationship?

9. JANET: A SUBSTANCE ABUSER (REALITY)

The client, a troubled woman of 33, is in your office at a community mental-health center because it is a requirement of her parole.

Some Background Data

Janet reports that she has always had difficulties handling her family and her personal life. She says that she had a relatively stable marriage until she found out her "old man was running around with other girls." Although she filed for a divorce from him, she never appeared in court, so she is uncertain about her marital status. She reports that after the separation he "disappeared" until quite recently, when he "reappeared out of nowhere" and took their son (now 15) to live with him. She also has two girls, ages 8 and 10, who still live with her. The client says that once her husband had left, she was forced to resort to stealing to support the family and her drug habit.

Janet has been addicted to cocaine for four years. During this period she has had behavioral problems with her two daughters, as well as the son. Eventually she moved in with her current boyfriend, and the behavioral problems with the children escalated. She reports that she is on parole for a theft charge and is afraid that she will have to go back to prison for parole violation because of her drug use.

Janet lets her parole officer know that she has seen you and that she wants to get some help "to get her life together." A few days later her parole officer calls and says that her urine test is "dirty," showing traces of several drugs. The parole officer asks about your treatment plan for therapy and requests that you write your opinion on whether the client should be back in prison.

Questions for Reflection

1. What ethical and legal implications does this case have?
2. What referrals might you need to make?
3. What type of information would you provide to the parole officer?
4. If Janet wanted to remain in therapy, what goals would you see as being important?
5. How would you apply the steps of reality therapy to this case?
6. What interventions would you make, and why?
7. How would you work with Janet if she avoided making an evaluation of her behavior?
8. Do you think you could work with her effectively given the fact that she has come to you as a stipulation of her parole? Why or why not? How could you tie this requirement into a reality-therapy perspective?
9. Besides reality therapy, what theoretical framework would be helpful to you in this case? Are there any theoretical approaches that you think would not be particularly helpful?
10. Show how your approach in working with Janet from a reality-therapy perspective would differ from your work with her from a person-centered framework.
11. How might you deal with possible manipulation by the client? What would you do if you suspected that she was using you simply to meet the requirement for parole and that she was not really involved in her therapy?
12. Do you see her as a candidate for hospitalization? In your opinion, is Janet a suitable candidate for conventional psychotherapy? Explain.

NOTE: Cases 10–20 are unidentified, so that you can practice selecting the theory (or theories) that you think would be most appropriate for them. I have several suggestions for handling these cases. First of all, you can try your hand at working with them without restricting yourself to any theory. You can also compare and contrast a theory, showing how you might work very differently with one theory than another or how you might blend two theories. For each of these 11 cases I suggest that you attempt to answer the following general questions, in addition to the questions that are raised after each case:

1. If you selected a particular theory, why did you do so?
2. As you approach each client, what basic assumptions are you making?
3. What is your initial assessment of each client? What are the major themes you would be likely to focus on in therapy with each person? Why?
4. What specific goals might you have in each case? How would you proceed with the client? How would you evaluate therapeutic progress?

10. SUSAN: GOING AGAINST FAMILY TRADITION

Susan has been struggling with a decision of hers that she is certain will result in tension within her extended family. After she was not able to resolve her problem by talking to her friends, she finally decided to seek professional help, but somewhat reluctantly.

Some Background Data

Susan, a 37-year-old Asian American, is planning to divorce her second husband. Roger has been a chronic alcoholic for years, and after trying to strengthen and save the marriage, she has faced the fact that he is incapable of making any commitment except to the bottle. She is resigned to ending the marriage but is frightened about "facing the world." In early sessions it becomes clear that "the world" really means her large extended family, a close-knit and powerful group. Her parents and aunts and uncles all emigrated from China following World War II. Although they have adjusted to American life, they still retain many Old World traditions and values. Susan is faced with the unpleasant task of telling them that she has decided to end her second marriage. They reacted violently to her first divorce. Their lack of understanding was exacerbated by the fact that her first husband was Chinese and that she was divorcing him to marry another man—Roger—who was Caucasian. Although she never openly told her family that she was obtaining a divorce because she was in love with another man, she is certain that they suspected the reason behind her actions. Now the second marriage is over, and she is frightened about facing their accusations and criticism.

Questions for Reflection

1. Consider how your values and reactions might be involved in this case. For instance, would you be inclined to support Susan's following her

inclination and marrying again? Would you be inclined to encourage her to think about the consequences of hurting her parents? What are your reactions to interracial marriages? What are your views on divorce and remarriage?

2. Assume that you discover that in Susan's culture women are supposed to remain married to the same man, even if he is an alcoholic and does not seem to want to change. Also assume that she tells you that she does not want to ruin her life by staying with a man who she thinks will not change. She is tired of trying to get him to be different and is now ready to work on changing herself in relation to her situation. How would you work with cultural themes such as these?
   - the notion that divorce brings shame to the family
   - the thought that she is being selfish and should consider the feelings of her parents
   - the belief that she has already made one serious mistake and should not be making another one
   - the role of shame and guilt in her decision-making process
3. Would you suggest that Susan ask Roger to come to one of her sessions with you? Would you suggest a session that involves her family so that she can work on the conflicts she is experiencing?
4. Do you think that you could help Susan if you were not familiar with her cultural background? If you did not have this knowledge, how might you acquire it? Or would you rather not have any generalized knowledge about her culture and simply treat her as a unique individual?
5. Considering Susan's cultural frame of reference, would you encourage her to confront her parents and deal directly and honestly with all the circumstances surrounding her divorce? Why or why not?

11. LUIS: STRUGGLING WITH A SEXUAL PROBLEM

The client, a computer technician at a large corporation who earns approximately $30,000 a year, appeared at a public-health clinic asking for help with sexual difficulties he was experiencing with his wife. When questioned why he was not seeking private help, he said that he had come to this particular clinic because it was noted for its treatment of sexual disorders. He said that except for the problems with his sex life he felt that his life was under control.

Some Background Data

Luis is 35 years old and has been married three years to a woman 12 years his junior. She does not work. He is of Hispanic background, and his wife is Caucasian. Although they are planning to have a family, he says that his wife does not willingly engage in sexual relations at any time. He if forced to initiate all sexual interaction, and they have intercourse approximately one or two times a month. In the past three months sexual activities have decreased even more. Luis says that his wife is unwilling to attend therapy and is completely closed to the idea of either or both of them seeking help. She is not aware that he has made an appointment at the public-health clinic. When questioned about other aspects of their relationship that might be problematic, the client insists that everything is fine and that he merely desires help with his sexual problem.

Questions for Reflection

1. Are there any key words that Luis uses that you would pay particular attention to?
2. Would you be inclined to provide Luis with a referral to a sex therapist? Why or why not?
3. What is your hunch about the validity of his assertion that besides this sex problem everything is fine with him?
4. Would you be inclined to refer him to a physician for a comprehensive physical? Why or why not?
5. If you did work with him, would you encourage him to persuade his wife to attend any of these sessions? Give your reasons.
6. Do you see it as important to explore the cultural backgrounds of this couple? What might you be looking for if you did?
7. What theoretical framework(s) would guide your interventions with Luis? In what direction would you proceed with him?

12. WILMA: A DEPRESSED ADOLESCENT

Wilma, a 17-year-old high school senior, was referred by her teacher for counseling because of severe bouts of depression. The counselor who did the intake interview gathered some of the following information about her.

Some Background Data

Wilma has never had a father. While her mother was pregnant with her, he decided to leave the family, saying he did not want to be burdened with any more children or responsibilities. Wilma's mother never remarried, and she attempted to keep a job and at the same time rear her children. During childhood Wilma was frequently left with different sitters, many of whom did not pay much attention to her.

Wilma recalls that as a child she suffered from frequent illnesses and was often absent from school. She developed extreme fears of school, and she was referred to the psychologist in her elementary school for therapy to deal with her "school phobia."

According to the school nurse, Wilma's mother was indulgent and overpermissive; the mother also talked about her guilt feelings over not being able to provide a "normal home" for her children. Wilma describes her home situation as having been far from a "closely knit family." Rather, she feels that her mother was permissive and did not care about the children. She remembers that her mother became extremely defensive whenever Wilma brought up the subject of her father. Her mother took many opportunities to describe what a miserable man he was and how they were much better off without him. Nevertheless, Wilma persisted in her interest in her father. But whenever she attempted to find out where he was, her mother reacted with anger and told her to "forget he ever existed."

Wilma's school adjustment during all of her school years left a lot to be desired. She had very few friends and reports that the children picked on her and teased her. She had a pattern of being somewhat withdrawn, sensitive, and timid. Her teachers reported on her cumulative record that she was a "good girl" who was conforming, conscientious, and hard working. It is clear that Wilma was handicapped by a weak ego development. Out of her basic insecurities, she attempted to please and win the approval of teachers, yet she typically felt inadequate and inferior to most of her peers.

The school psychologist who worked with Wilma when she was in the eighth grade gave her a battery of psychological tests with her mother's permission. Intellectually, she was functioning within the average range. She was also given several projective tests of personality that were designed to assess unconscious psychodynamics. The results indicated severe conflicts with her mother, with strong hostility directed toward her; feelings of rejection, inadequacy and inferiority; sexual conflicts—a desire for sex and a fear of the desire; deep feelings of depression, loneliness, emptiness, and isolation from others, severe difficulties with interpersonal relations; sibling rivalry; weak and unhealthy self-concept; and masochistic and self-punishing tendencies. To the question "Who am I," to which the school psychologist asked her to give 20 answers, some of her replies were "a bunch of molecules," "empty and vacant," "lost," "a person without a purpose for living," and "confused."

In her notes the school psychologist made a summary statement to the effect that Wilma appeared to very much want contact with others yet was both frightened of doing so and seemed severely lacking in interpersonal skills. Thus, she surrounded herself with high walls so that people could not hurt her.

Questions for Reflection

Assume that you would be Wilma's therapist for at least several months, and show how you would proceed with her, using these questions as a guide:

1. How do you see Wilma? How do you feel about working with her? To what degree do you think you could understand her and also help her understand herself?
2. In considering her history what hypotheses do you have concerning the causes of her present problems?
3. How much value do you place on knowing the data summarized above? Do you think that you can effectively work with a person like Wilma without such background data? How much might you rely on psychological tests to give you some information about her current state of functioning? How might you use these test results in your therapy sessions with her?
4. How might you deal with her resistance to therapy? For example, if she were withdrawn in the sessions and said little, how might you work therapeutically with her resistance?
5. In your estimation what impact did the absence of a father figure in her life have on her development and adjustment?
6. Is parental consent necessary? Explain.
7. Would you utilize any other sources of care, such as a psychiatrist or hospitalization? Explain. At what point might you turn to these sources?
8. Wilma indicates that she would like to be able to *accept affection,* although she finds this difficult to do. What is your hypothesis concerning the origins of her limited capacity to accept affection, when you consider her psychosexual development pattern? What guesses would you venture about the early experiences she had in both receiving and giving love?

13. ALAN: DEALING WITH SEXUAL ORIENTATION

Alan is experiencing a great deal of turmoil over his personal relationships. Although he is not certain that counseling will result in inner peace, he has decided to contact a psychologist in private practice for direction.

Some Background Data

Alan, 27, was reared in a relatively comfortable "White, Anglo-Saxon, Protestant" home. His upbringing was, according to him, "fairly typical." He describes a distant relationship with his father, who barely spoke with him. In turn, Alan depicts his mother and grandmother (who lived with the family) as close to the point of suffocation. "They were involved in my life, my affairs, everything." After serving a tour of duty in Vietnam, Alan returned home, went to college, and started studying dentistry. He also experimented sexually with different partners and gravitated toward relationships with other men, ultimately deciding that he was homosexual. Six months ago he fell in love with another man, and they are planning on buying a home together and marrying. Alan says he feels no responsibility toward his parents and has never told them about his personal life. "This was always the way things were, when I was in high school, when I dated. . . . My father never even asked me once what it was like when I was in Vietnam. My family's never known about my personal life, they've never even cared." His lover, however, has openly shared his lifestyle with his family and is now pressing Alan to do the same. Alan appears for therapy to deal with this issue. As he more precisely puts it: "I don't want to bring my parents into this, and I wish my lover would leave me alone on this matter. That's my past. I'm interested in our future. But he doesn't seem to understand that. I don't even know if you can help me. I think I should see a gay counselor. Unless you're gay?"

Questions for Reflection

1. Do you think that you could work effectively with Alan regardless of your sexual orientation? Might his sexual orientation present any problems for you as his counselor?
2. How would you go about helping Alan decide if he could work with you, especially since he wonders if you are able to help him?
3. Would you be inclined to encourage Alan to "come out" to his parents, even if this is not what he wants to do?
4. Would you be inclined to explore his background with his family as a possible factor in his choice of lifestyle? Why or why not?
5. Would you address his homosexuality if he said that this was not the issue that had brought him into counseling? What reasons do you have for either choosing to explore or not to explore his feelings and thoughts about his sexual orientation?
6. If you are not gay, do you think you have the ability to empathize with his situation? If you are not able to identify with him or if you have negative reactions toward homosexuals, what ethical issues are involved if you accept him as a client?

14. RAYMOND: AFRAID OF WOMEN

A friend of the client's suggested that he approach you for counseling. Raymond, who is 39, appears rather depressed and does not hold too much hope that therapy will help him feel better. He says that he does not have much purpose in life, that he is without direction, and that about all he feels is anger over the way his life is going.

Some Background Data

What follows is the essence of what Raymond tells you in the first session:

As I walk into the therapist's office, I ask myself "Why did I come here?" All I know is that I am feeling unhappy and empty in my life. I don't seem to be able to establish a meaningful relationship with a woman, and I feel angry and frustrated with myself. Every time I get with a woman, I feel very self-conscious and unsure of myself. I always go away feeling that I've been controlled by them and that I can't do or say what I want around them. Although I have relationships with women, they are generally unsatisfying and unhappy experiences for me. I also feel stifled in my personal life. My life seems sometimes to be nothing more than a set of routines and patterns. It seems that no matter what I do, I can always find something wrong with everything. I'm constantly getting down on myself and telling myself that what I do is not enough. It's very hard for me to just feel good about the things I do. It seems that I'm always feeling bad about something.

I also feel closed in around people. When I get into a group of people, I become very quiet and anxious and feel that I can't say or do anything. I find it hard to let go and have fun. I spend most of my time thinking about how self-conscious and closed in I feel.

I live with my father and find myself getting very angry with him almost constantly, and yet I'm always holding myself away from him for fear of controlling his life too much. My mother is dead, but when she was alive she was the dominant one in our family. I used to feel very controlled by her. No matter what I did, she would always tell me that I didn't love her, and I would always have to explain things to her. She always came to me to tell her problems.

Anyway, all I know is that I feel very unhappy, empty, and unfulfilled in my life. I've got to find something to help me make it, because sometimes I just feel as if it's not worth all this struggle. Sometimes I feel helpless to do anything.

Questions for Reflection

1. What possible cause do you see of Raymond's inability to "establish a meaningful relationship with a woman"?
2. How does the continuing influence of Raymond's mother control and dominate him? How might her domination be connected to his current state of being "self-conscious and unsure" of himself when he is with a woman?
3. Raymond constantly "gets down on" himself, and he feels that what he does is "not enough." How might you explain this feeling? What do you see as the underlying psychological factors associated with his self-critical attitude and his guilt over not being "enough"?
4. What do you think is the meaning of his feeling of being "closed in around people"?
5. If Raymond were your client, what else would you want to know about him? What aspects of his case would you choose to focus on, and what would be your therapeutic goals and procedures as you worked with him?

15. WAYNE: ANGRY OVER BEING IN A WHEELCHAIR

Wayne is concerned over feeling depressed much of the time, so he finally agrees to seek help at a community counseling center. He is struggling to find a sense of meaning in his life in spite of a physical handicap.

Some Background Data

Wayne at one time played on his university's basketball team. Then in his mid-20s he had a serious accident while riding his motorcycle in the desert. He has had both physical and psychological therapy, yet it is hard for him to get over his anger and his feeling of having been cheated. He tells you that he had everything going for him, and then life did him a dirty trick. He has bouts of depression and many periods of anger, especially when he thinks of all that he used to do that he can no longer do because of being in a wheelchair. Although he is still going to the university, he says that it is a real struggle. He has so much trouble in depending on others, and all too often they do not follow through, leaving him stuck alone.

Wayne is coming to you because he scares himself wondering if it is worth it to go on and also because his depression seems to be getting worse. He tells you that he is angry at those who let him down, angry at his friends who can walk and still play sports, angry about being cheated by life, and very angry at himself for being so stupid. He got involved in a support group at school through the Handicapped Center, and although this helped him feel less alone and more cared about, he realizes that he needs further work on dealing with his anger and depression and in finding a new meaning in life.

Questions for Reflection

1. What are the major issues involved in this case?
2. From what Wayne told you, would you be concerned about him as a suicide risk? What kind of questions might you ask of him to help you make this assessment? If you determined that he was a highly suicidal person, how would you proceed?
3. From which therapeutic approaches would you be inclined to draw in working with Wayne? How would your theory guide your practice? What kind of techniques would you probably use?
4. How might you deal with Wayne if he confronted you with a statement such as this: "You can't really understand my pain of loss. You're able to walk in this office, and I have to use my wheelchair. Unless you're sitting in my wheelchair, I don't think you can know what I face every day." Assuming that you are not physically disabled, do you think you'd be able to identify with his feelings of anger, depression, loss, and frustration?

16. CARL: AN ADOLESCENT IN SEARCH OF AN IDENTITY

Adolescence is a time when the identity issue is particularly critical, for there is the possibility of losing any sense of personal identity in the desperate search to be approved of by everyone and to belong. By submerging themselves in a group, young people can easily lose any sense of uniqueness. Thus, in counseling adolescents this issue will often have to be worked through in difficult sessions. Assume that Carl, a 16-year-old, is sent to you by his parents because of their concern that he is becoming more and more defiant.

Some Background Data

What you know about Carl is the following: He did not particularly want to come to counseling but very reluctantly agreed. He does not think it will do any good, and he thinks that his parents are the ones who should go to therapy, not him. They are the ones who are really messed up, according to Carl. He managed to get himself expelled from a private school for using drugs, and he did not finish school that year. Instead, he cut classes at a public high school, ran around with a gang of older adolescents, and generally did a lot to get attention.

Carl says that he has spent most of his time being everything his folks did not want him to be. He sees his father as a phony—a businessman who does not know how to live and who is searching for the top but will not know what to do when he finally gets there. Carl does not want to be like his father. He generally rebels against most of his parents' values.

What is important in Carl's world right now is to be liked by the gang he associates with, to fix up his car, to date lots of girls, and to have fun. He tells you that he is tired of hearing about the "responsibility trip" and that he does not want lectures from you on how he should live and what he should be.

Questions for Reflection

Think about ways in which you might begin and how you might work with Carl if both of you agreed that he would come in for three sessions.

1. What are your initial reactions to Carl? Which of these reactions would you share with him? keep to yourself?
2. Do you think that an "involuntary client" and counseling mix?
3. Where might you begin? What direction would you take, given that you may see Carl for only three sessions?
4. Carl did mention that he does not know who he is, that he is fighting the image of what his parents want for him, and that he is searching for approval. How would you work with him on the issue of his identity struggle?
5. In what ways would you use who you are in your work with Carl? Do you think he will respond to your confrontation? to your disclosures about yourself?

6. What struggles did you have in your own adolescence? Do you believe that the way you resolved (or failed to resolve) your own issues in those years is vitally related to your ability now to make a significant impact on Carl? Can you identify with any parts of Carl's experience? If so, what aspects? If you have a hard time identifying with Carl, do you think that you could effectively work with him for these limited sessions?

17. THE DAMIANS: "I RESPECT YOUR WISHES, AND YOU SHOULD RESPECT MINE"

The Damian family has been referred to you for family therapy through a mutual professional contact. John Damian is an accountant, and his wife, Eve, is an artist and an art teacher. Eve and John both decided it would be helpful to get the entire family involved in at least a few sessions.

Some Background Data

The Damians have two children. John Jr., the eldest, is in his first year of law school and is a good-natured, easygoing young man who is understandably preoccupied with his studies. Kara, their second child, is starting her sophomore year at a state university. She has always been a gregarious and popular girl and is successful in school although not as good a student as John Jr.

The placid upper-middle-class lifestyle of the family was disrupted at Christmas when Kara came home for winter break and announced: "I'm not going to participate in Christmas this year. I've decided to follow Sikh religion." The holidays passed with much crying and mutual recrimination. With the new year Kara has held onto her newfound religious convictions with increasing tenacity. She insists: "I'm not going to be a member of some cult or anything, but I like the ideas behind the Sikh religion much more than the hypocrisy of Christianity. This is what I believe. I'm not asking you guys to convert, I just want you to leave me alone. I respect your wishes, and you should respect mine."

John Sr. is outraged and appears at the first counseling session shouting "What have I done to deserve this?" Eve is crying and not saying much of anything. John Jr. looks as if he is uncomfortable and would prefer being home studying torts. Kara is calm and defiant.

Questions for Reflection

1. What do you see as being the important clinical issues in this case? How would you proceed during the initial session? What would you most want to accomplish at the first session?

2. What ethical issues are involved here?
3. Would you accept this family for therapy? Why or why not?
4. Who is the primary client here? Is it the parents, who are concerned about Kara? Is it Kara, who wants to be left alone with her choice of religion?

18. BRET: STRIVING TO OVERCOME A PHYSICAL DISABILITY

Bret is beginning to feel a sense of inspiration to succeed and not to allow his disability keep him from doing what he really wants to do. He is looking to you, his counselor, for emotional support.

Some Background Data

Bret, in his early 30s, has been a paraplegic since he survived a private plane crash five years ago. Although he had some psychotherapy before coming to see you, he largely quit on life because he thought that there were simply too many things he could not do anymore. Then he was watching the news and saw an account of 29-year-old Mark Wellman, who had become a paraplegic when he fell while rock climbing. Wellman captured the attention of the news media when he and a companion scaled the 3,000-foot sheer cliff of El Capitan in Yosemite National Park in California, using only his arms to inch up this massive rock. In doing so he became the first paraplegic to reach the top. Wellman, with the help of his companion, performed what seemed like an impossible feat and became an inspiration to disabled people.

Bret tells you that he felt very moved when he saw this news account and that he decided to turn his life around:

> I think I had just told myself that I couldn't meet the challenges of life anymore. But I was inspired by what I saw another disabled person accomplish. It made me feel that there is a lot more that I can do if I set my mind to it and work hard at getting what I want.

Questions for Reflection

1. What do you think your reactions would be to Bret if you met him for this first time and he asked for your support in getting on a new track? Where would you be inclined to go with him?
2. Would you want to encourage Bret to work on his feelings of discouragement and anger over his accident so that he could get on with new projects? Why or why not?
3. What theory might guide your interventions with Bret? Do you have any sense of some techniques that you might employ in working with him?

19. BRENDA: TIRED OF HIDING HER LESBIANISM

Brenda seeks counseling because she says that she is tired of feeling different and always having to hide her true identity as a lesbian. Although she was married and had two children, she eventually decided to divorce her husband. She then joined the army and has been doing well in her job ever since.

Some Background Data

Brenda wants to explore a number of themes in her life. She would finally like to confront her parents and tell them the truth about who she is, although she suspects that they know that she is a lesbian. Yet the subject is never discussed when they are together, and this is beginning to bother Brenda. She wonders if you would be willing to meet with her and her family so that she can open up a subject that she thinks has been kept closed for too many years. She would also like to feel freer in being who she is in her military career, but she finds herself in a real dilemma. She reminds you that the army is very dogmatic and intolerant when it comes to a homosexual lifestyle. If she were to openly disclose her identity and let her superiors know that she was in a long-term relationship with a woman, she feels sure that she would lose her position. She is hoping to get some clarity in talking with you.

Questions for Reflection

1. What do you see as the core issues in this case? What reactions do you have to accepting Brenda as a client?
2. Do you think that you could be supportive of Brenda in accomplishing the goals of "coming out" to her parents? Why or why not?
3. What are your values as they pertain to this case? Do you think your values would help or hinder you in establishing a working relationship with Brenda?
4. How would you help Brenda deal with her dilemma over wanting to be herself and still wanting to keep her job in the military?
5. What ethical issues would you want to consider in this situation?

20. ANGELICA: A DAUGHTER AT ODDS WITH HER FAMILY

Angelica is not following the script that her parents have written for her. Although she very much wants their approval, she is hurt that they will not support her wishes and decisions.

Some Background Data

Angelica is the eldest daughter of a close-knit but emotionally stifling Italian-American family. At 18 she lives with her parents, her paternal grandparents, and her four younger siblings. She has always been a bright and curious child and did extremely well in elementary school. In high school she continued her pattern of academic achievement, excelling particularly in mathematics. Her family did not pay much attention to her scholarly achievements, worrying much more about her lack of a social life. In reality, Angelica has many friends but no special boyfriend at this time. The family sees this as a failure, but she is more interested in math than social standing in high school cliques. With her senior year of high school under way, she has been planning on attending college. The family has agreed to let her attend a private university because she can drive there and still live at home and because several of her relatives attended school there. Her parents agreed to college attendance with this admonition: ''Try to meet a nice, rich Italian doctor or lawyer while you're there. You can get married when you finish school.'' To prepare for attending the university, Angelica took the Scholastic Aptitude Test and received an extremely high score on the math section. This attracted the interest of universities across the country.

In November of her senior year Angelica is approached by recruiters from MIT, Harvard, Yale, Stanford, and the University of California at Berkeley. She is shocked, then excited. But she is shocked again when her parents announce that they will not only disapprove of her attending any school other than the one they've picked for her, they will disown her if she does not follow their plan for her. You are Angelica's high school counselor. She presents you with this problem. She is relying on you for some sort of answer. When you try to direct her to seek outside counseling, she tells you that this is impossible and that she is relying on you to help her. In the meantime, Angelica's father contacts you and urges you to ''talk some sense into the girl.'' Finally, a recruiter from Harvard calls to talk to you about the school's plans to offer Angelica a full four-year scholarship.

Questions for Reflection

1. What are the issues in this case that interest you?
2. What advice, if any, would you give Angelica? What are some ways in which you might help her explore her options?
3. From the data presented, what cultural issues would you need to be aware of in working with both Angelica and her family?
4. What would you be inclined to do if you wanted to refer her and she would not accept a referral?
5. What would you say to her father when he requested that you ''talk some sense into that girl?'' Although Angelica is not concerned with having

a better social life or a boyfriend, her parents are. Would you want to intervene by meeting with her parents alone? Or would you want a session with her and her parents? Or would you want to meet only with Angelica? What are your reasons for your interventions?

POSTSCRIPT

The process of beginning to develop a counseling style that fits you is truly a challenge. It entails far more than picking bits and pieces from theories in a random and fragmented manner. As you take steps to develop an integrated perspective, you might ask: Which theories provide a basis for understanding the *cognitive* dimension? Which theories help you understand the *feeling* dimension? And what about the *behavioral* dimension? As you are aware, most of the nine therapies you have studied focus primarily on one of these dimensions of human experience. The task is to wisely and creatively select therapeutic procedures that you can employ in working with a diverse population. Knowing the unique needs of your clients, your own values and personality, and the theories themselves is a good basis for beginning to develop a theory that is an expression of yourself.

By now, I am sure, it is evident that it requires knowledge, skill, art, and experience to be able to determine what techniques work best with particular clients and with certain problems. It is also an art to know *when* and *how* to use a particular therapeutic intervention. Because building your personalized theory of counseling is a long-term venture, I do hope that you will be patient with yourself as you continue to grow through your reading, thinking, and experience in working with clients and through your own personal struggles and life experiences.

Provisional DSM-III-R Diagnosis of Ruth

Rather than identifying one specific major disorder, I will describe a number of possible provisional diagnoses that may be appropriate for Ruth's case. As you review the nine different theories, consider the following diagnostic classifications to see which category you think *best* fits the case of Ruth.

Panic disorder. In general, Ruth presents evidence of an anxiety disorder. Specifically, her pattern of symptoms meet the diagnostic criteria for *panic disorder.* Some of her symptoms are shortness of breath, dizziness, accelerated heart rate, trembling, sweating, hot flashes and cold sweats, fear of dying, and fear of going crazy. Panic attacks generally begin with the sudden onset of intense apprehension and terror. There is a feeling of impending doom. The typical symptoms associated with an attack are shortness of breath, dizziness, faintness, choking, palpitations of the heart, trembling or shaking, depersonalization, numbness or tingling sensations, hot flashes or chills, fear of dying, and fear of going crazy.

Dysthymic disorder. Ruth exhibits a chronic depression, or a long-term depressed mood that is part of her character but not severe enough to be considered a major depression. She also manifests self-defeating personality traits in that she consistently puts the needs of others ahead of herself and has low self-esteem. Ruth exhibits a number of physical complaints but does not indicate any serious physical disease necessitating surgery or serious medical intervention.

Identity disorder. Ruth's patterns fit the syndrome of identity disorder. The main features of this disorder include uncertainty about one's identity, including inability to accept oneself; inability to develop long-term goals; conflicts over career choice; confusion about developing friends; uncertainty about sexual orientation and behavior; and lack of clarity about religious identification and value systems. Such clients respond to their uncertainty with anxiety and depressed features and are preoccupied about their lack of self. These are the people who doubt themselves in everyday situations.

One of the most common questions asked by the person with an identity disorder is "Who am I?"

In looking over the provisional diagnoses described above, which ones do you tend to agree with most, and why? Do you think they are all equally applicable to Ruth? If yes, why? If no, why not? If you agree with none of these diagnoses, what diagnosis do you think best fits her, and why?

What are your legal and ethical responsibilities when diagnosing her? Under what circumstances, if any, would you be likely to share your diagnostic impressions with her?

TO THE OWNER OF THIS BOOK

I hope that you have found *Case Approach to Counseling and Psychotherapy* (Third Edition) useful. So that this book can be improved in a future edition, would you take the time to complete this sheet and return it? Thanks.

School and address: ______________________________

Department: ______________ Instructor's name: ______________

1. What I like *most* about this casebook is: ______________________________

____

____

____

2. What I like *least* about this casebook is: ______________________________

____

____

____

3. My general reactions to Ruth's case are: ______________________________

____

____

4. My general reactions to the experts who worked with Ruth are: ______________

____

____

5. Other specific cases in the book I found most helpful are: ______________

____

6. Specific cases I found least useful or would suggest deleting in future editions are: ________

____

7. The kinds of cases I would like to see added are: ______________________________

____

____

8. My general reaction to this book is: ______________________________

____

9. The name of the course in which I used this book is: ______________

10. On a separate sheet of paper, please write specific suggestions for improving this book and anything else you'd care to share about your experience in using the book.

Optional:

Your name: ______________________________ Date: ____________________

May Brooks/Cole quote you, either in promotion for *Case Approach to Counseling and Psychotherapy* or in future publishing ventures?

Yes ________ No ________

Sincerely,

Gerald Corey

FOLD HERE

FOLD HERE